T0198274

DEBUGGING AND PERFORMANCE TUNING FOR PARALLEL COMPUTING SYSTEMS

Ann H. Hayes
Margaret L. Simmons
Jeffrey S. Brown
Daniel A. Reed

IEEE Computer Society Press
Los Alamitos, California

Washington   •   Brussels   •   Tokyo

CONTRIBUTORS

Vikram S. Adve
David M. Beazley
Don Breazeal
Joan M. Francioni
Dennis Gannon
G. A. Geist
Rajan Gupta
Ming C. Hao
Don Heller
Marty Itzkowitz
Barton P. Miller
C. E. McDowell
Nick A. Nystrom
Cherri M. Pancake
Douglas M. Pase
Daniel A. Reed
Diane T. Rover
Karsten Schwan
Richard Title
Carl Winstead
Mary Zosel

Library of Congress Cataloging-in-Publication Data

Debugging and performance tuning for parallel computing systems /
Ann H. Hayes ... [et al.].
 p. cm.
Includes bibliographical references.
ISBN 0-8186-7412-1
 1. Parallel computers. 2. Debugging in computer science.
I. Hayes, Ann H.
QA76.58.D42 1996
005.2—dc20
 96-235
 CIP

IEEE Computer Society Press
10662 Los Vaqueros Circle
P.O. Box 3014
Los Alamitos, CA 90720-1264

IEEE Computer Society Press Order Number BP07412
Library of Congress Number 96-235
ISBN 0-8186-7412-1

Additional copies may be ordered from:

IEEE Computer Society Press	IEEE Service Center	IEEE Computer Society	IEEE Computer Society
Customer Service Center	445 Hoes Lane	13, Avenue de l'Aquilon	Ooshima Building
10662 Los Vaqueros Circle	P.O. Box 1331	B-1200 Brussels	2-19-1 Minami-Aoyama
P.O. Box 3014	Piscataway, NJ 08855-1331	BELGIUM	Minato-ku, Tokyo 107
Los Alamitos, CA 90720-1264	Tel: +1-908-981-1393	Tel: +32-2-770-2198	JAPAN
Tel: +1-714-821-8380	Fax: +1-908-981-9667	Fax: +32-2-770-8505	Tel: +81-3-3408-3118
Fax: +1-714-821-4641	mis.custserv@computer.org	euro.ofc@computer.org	Fax: +81-3-3408-3553
Email: cs.books@computer.org			tokyo.ofc@computer.org

Assistant Publisher: Matt Loeb
Acquisitions Assistant: Cheryl Smith
Advertising/Promotions: Tom Fink
Production Editor: Lisa O'Conner
Cover Design: Zizi Kolshorn
Printed in the United States of America by BookCrafters

The Institute of Electrical and Electronics Engineers, Inc

Foreword

Closing the gap between potential and measured perfomance of computing systems is a continuing problem of fundamental importance. The difficulty of the problem is exacerbated by the increasing complexity of systems as they become more parallel, more heterogeneous, and more distributed.

The problem domain contains many parameters which must be considered in any serious approach toward a solution. At the highest level hardware, systems software, and applications parameters must all be considered. At a level lower the number of processors, the nature of memory hierarchy, operating systems and resource management policies, languages and associated compilers, and compiled versus application source codes, for example, need consideration. At still a lower level the number and size of calls by applications programs to subroutines, libraries, and I/O magnify the number of parameters in the parameter space.

Any careful analysis of the problem requires data, both quantative and qualitative. Data collection calls for instrumemtation of the codes which in turn calls for libraries of intelligent tools. Data collection can lead to huge volumes of raw data which must be analyzed. Analysis of the data is aided by statistical, temporal, and spatial summaries. Extracting information from these data and various summaries is difficult and innovative visualization and human interfaces are needed. Any approach requires thoughtful attention to the integration of performance tools with systems software and user interfaces and the resulting interplay.

Workers in this important area of research recognized early on the difficulty of the problem and its increasing complexity with the advent of parallel processing systems. As part of their efforts to advance this area of research they organized over a period of years a series of workshops focused on software performance tools for parallel systems. The material reported herein comes from the fifth in this series of workshops.

In this fifth workshop a special emphasis was the bringing together performance tools developers, application tools developers, and vendors. In addition to reports on the status of "the current state of the tool development art," various lessons learned are reported, new research issues are identified, and technology transition issues are discussed and potential solutions are proposed.

Anyone interested in closing the gap between potential performance and measured performance of parallel computing systems should find this book of interest. A primary conclusion of the Workshop reported herein calling for "the creation of a national software tool evaluation and testing center" ideserves serious consideration.

Merrell Patrick
Arlington, Virginia

ACKNOWLEDGEMENTS

This book and the workshop from which it is derived (the fifth in the series), are the result of many persons' efforts. Without their help, neither would have materialized.

We especially thank Andy White and Hassan Dayem of Los Alamos and the administration of the University of Illinois for their continued support of our time to prepare both the workshop and the book. We are again indebted to Jan Hull for her organizational and interpersonal skills in handling the complex logistics for the meeting and the inevitable crises that arose. Jan was assisted in these efforts by Denise Dalmas. The preparation of the book was made immensely easier by the contributions and expertise of Yvonne Martinez and Tanmoy Bhattacharya, for which we are most grateful.

Realizing that tomorrow's resources must be developed and nurtured today, this workshop has always actively encouraged and supported student participation. This year we were fortunate to have a dozen graduate students attend the Workshop. These students served as scribes for the sessions, aiding considerably in the realization of this book.

Lastly, we are indebted for the support we have received from the National Science Foundation (NSF), the Advanced Research Projects Agency (ARPA), the Department of Energy (DOE), and from our corporate sponsors, Cray Research, Inc. and Sun Microsystems, Inc.

Contents

Chapter 1

Performance and Debugging Tools: A Research and Development Checkpoint

Daniel A. Reed[1]
University of Illinois
Urbana, Illinois 61801

Jeffrey S. Brown, Ann H. Hayes, and Margaret L. Simmons
Los Alamos National Laboratory
Los Alamos, New Mexico 87545

"Here they are, boys; get your tools ready." ... As they ran, they pulled weapons from under their coats, hatchets, knuckle-dusters, hammers, and bars of iron.

F. D. Sharpe (1938)

---

[1]Supported in part by the Advanced Research Projects Agency under ARPA contracts DAVT63-91-C-0029 and DABT63-93-C-0040, by the National Science Foundation under grants NSF IRI 92-12976, NSF ASC 92-12369, ASC 93-08242, NSF CDA94-01124, and by the National Aeronautics and Space Administration under NASA Contract Numbers NGT-51023, NAG-1-613, and USRA 5555-22.

1.1   Introduction

For several years, it has been economically and technically feasible to build parallel systems that scale from tens to hundreds of processors. Recognition of this feasibility has fueled the national High-Performance Computing and Communications (HPCC) program and the fierce competition among new and old high-performance computing companies for a share of the massively parallel market.

Though vendor competition has led to rapid architectural innovation and higher peak hardware performance, it has stretched academic, laboratory, and vendor software tool groups to the limit, forcing them to continually create tools for changing programming models and new hardware environments. By necessity tools embody knowledge of the execution environment, identifying performance bottlenecks or logical program errors in terms of application code constructs and their interaction with the execution environment.

Because the root causes of poor performance or unexpected program behavior may lie with run-time libraries, compilers, the operating system, or the hardware, tools must gather and correlate information from many sources. Not only does this correlation require interfaces for information access, the need for such information is most often gained only from experience. Experience comes with time, as tool developers understand the common programming idioms, the interactions of application code and the underlying hardware and software, and the user interfaces best suited for relating these interactions in intuitive ways. Simply put, developing good tools takes time, experience and substantial effort; small profit margins and short product life cycles, both leading to small installed product bases, have made it difficult for tool developers to create and support effective tools.

The goal of this workshop (and of its predecessors) was to bring together vendor tool developers, academic and government laboratory tool researchers, and application scientists to discuss the current situation and outline research issues and technology transition remedies. New architectures pose important unresolved research problems for tool developers. Moreover, transferring previous research results to products clearly requires new mechanisms if tool developers are ever to catch the speeding train of architectural change.

In this light, the remainder of this introductory chapter is organized as follows. In Sec. 1.2, we describe the motivations for the latest workshop and the broadening of its scope to include both performance and debugging tools. Based on this context, in Sec. 1.3, we describe the research issues raised by the participants and the implications of these issues for tool research. Finally, because tools lie at the nexus between system software and applications, tool developers must exploit the features of system software to support a user community. This necessitates investment of time and effort in many activities not normally associated with research and, as described in Sec. 1.4, poses a host of difficult problems. Finally, Sec. 1.5 concludes with a summary of recommendations for research and technology transition.

1.2 Workshop Motivations and Experiences

This book contains the papers and working group summaries from discussions during the fifth in a series of workshops on software tools for parallel computer systems. For the first time in the workshop series, developers of both debugging and performance analysis tools met together with application developers and vendors to discuss the technical and sociological problems facing the field. The goal of this combined workshop was the integration of both performance analysis and debugging tools, with the intent of maximizing the return from shared development.

As with the previous workshops in the series [30,33,31,32,40,41], sessions consisted of technical presentations, panels, and working group discussions. Each session of technical presentations included three different perspectives: academic software tool developer, application developer, and computer vendor. Our goal was a dialogue involving all three communities so that all might learn the others' needs and frustrations in building and using tools on parallel systems.

One lesson drawn from the workshop was that tool users and developers speak different languages, often failing to understand the needs or problems faced by the other group. As we will discuss in Sec. 1.4, the attendees concluded, as they did at the 1993 Performance Workshop [32], that a project combining vendors, academics, and users must be undertaken to develop techniques for testing and evaluating tools and encouraging the support and commercialization of effective tools.

A second lesson is that there are new and exciting problems to be solved. The World Wide Web (WWW), distributed metacomputing, and new programming models all pose unsolved problems for debugging and performance analysis tools. A subset of these issues is summarized in Sec. 1.3 below, and papers by the workshop participants elaborate on these issues in subsequent chapters.

1.3 Research Issues

As with all workshops, the attendees discussed a wide variety of topics, both during the formal sessions and during the extended working groups. Despite the diversity, three major research themes emerged:

- tools for task and data parallel languages,

- techniques for real-time adaptive system control, and

- optimization of heterogeneous metacomputing applications.

All three issues are united by the need for greater access to system internals and data and by the need for standard interfaces, both internally and for users.

Historically, performance and debugging tools have been developed independently of system software and compilers. This separation reflects both the integration of software from disparate sources (i.e., third party compilers and operating system kernels) and limited support provided by software systems for tool development. For example, operating systems typically provide debugger developers little more than a `ptrace` system call for controlling process execution and performance tool developers only a mechanism for accessing a coarse-resolution system clock. Similarly, compilers provide simple symbol table information in object files. For single processor systems, these features are sufficient to build breakpoint debuggers and profilers, though they are far from optimal. For parallel systems and workstation clusters, they are woefully inadequate.

At present, few compilers provide access to program transformation data, though debugging and tuning the performance of programs written in task and data parallel languages (e.g., like High-Performance Fortran (HPF) [20]) requires both compile-time and run-time data. Relating the dynamic behavior of compiler-synthesized code to the user's source code requires knowledge of the program transformations applied by the compiler and the code generation model. For example, if an HPF compiler generates message passing code for a distributed memory system, understanding how messages relate to array locality is a key to improving performance. Moving beyond tools for explicit parallelism (e.g., via message passing) will require far tighter integration of tools with compilers.

Likewise, few operating systems or run-time libraries provide mechanisms for selecting resource management policies or for configuring those policies based on knowledge of application resource demands or dynamic performance data. However, many experiments have shown that tuning policies to application behavior is key to improving performance for irregular applications with complex behavioral dynamics [17]. For example, Schwan et al. [8] have shown that allowing users to steer application load distribution and to automatically adjust thread locking policies based on expected synchronization delay can substantially improve performance for shared memory codes.

The explosion of WWW [3] use, together with rapidly expanding interests in distributed data mining and heterogeneous parallel computing, pose a different, though equally thorny, set of tool research problems. New types of debugging and performance tuning tools will be needed to create metacomputing applications that can exploit distributed computation resources (e.g., by distributing a computation across multiple, geographically dispersed parallel systems) and that can mine large data archives in response to complex queries. Measuring network latencies and bandwidths and adapting to changes in network loads will necessitate integration of "standard" tools for parallel systems with distributed network management mechanisms (e.g., like the Simple Network Management Protocol (SNMP) [34]).

Support for new programming models, tuning of resource management policies, and management of distributed metacomputations requires interfaces and access to data not readily available via present methods. Below, we briefly describe the data requirements for each of these three domains, with pointers to extended discussions by the workshop participants.

1.3.1 Task and Data Parallel Languages

High-level, data-parallel languages such as HPF [20] have attracted attention because they offer a simple and portable programming model for regular scientific computations. By allowing the programmer to construct a parallel application at a semantic higher level, without recourse to low-level message passing code, HPF is an effective specification language for regular, data parallel algorithms. Similarly, task parallel languages like Fortran M [9] allow application developers to decompose less regular computations into a group of cooperating tasks.

After investing substantial intellectual effort in developing a task or data parallel program, its execution may yield only a small fraction of peak system performance. And, even if the data parallel code is portable across multiple parallel architectures, it is highly unlikely that it will achieve high performance on all architectures. Even on a single parallel architecture, observed application performance may vary substantially as a function of input parameters. Thus, achieving high performance on a parallel system requires a cycle of experimentation and refinement in which one first identifies the key program components responsible for the bulk of the program's execution time and then modifies the program in the hope of improving its performance.

For this cycle of debugging and performance tuning to be effective and unobtrusive to practicing scientists, performance data must not only be accurate, it and program dynamics must be directly related to the source program. Failure to provide accurate data (or to relate it to the corresponding source code) makes the task of performance improvement and debugging both laborious and error-prone.

Data and task parallel compilers greatly heighten the distance between source language constructs and executable code, making it impossible to map dynamic program behavior to specific source code fragments without knowledge of the program transformations applied by the compiler and the run-time task management strategy. This problem is analogous to developing debuggers for use with code generated by optimizing compilers, though much more difficult.

To understand the causes for performance variability in data parallel codes, one needs high-level performance analysis tools and techniques. Unfortunately, most current performance tools are targeted at the collection and presentation of program performance data when the parallelism and interprocessor communication are explicit and the program execution model closely mimics that in the source code (i.e., as is the case for message-passing codes).

For data parallel languages like HPF, such tools can only capture and present dynamic performance data in terms of primitive operations (e.g., communication library calls) in the compiler-generated code; clearly, this falls far short of the ideal. At a minimum, to support source-level performance analysis of programs in data parallel languages, compilers and performance tools must cooperate to integrate information about the program's dynamic behavior with compiler knowledge of the mapping from the low-level, explicitly parallel code to the high-level source.

More generally, a new compact between compiler writers and debugger and performance tool developers is needed. Under this compact, the compiler and the tool are co-equals, each providing functions of use to the other — performance data can guide compile-time program optimization, and compilers can provide information needed to estimate program performance scalabilty. In short, it is the basis for developing a set of tools that can break the modify/compile/execute cycle inherent in current optimization and debugging models.

Three presentations at the workshop addressed techniques for supporting performance tuning of task and data parallel languages. Pase and Williams [29] describe techniques for performance analysis of data parallel and message-passing codes on the CRAY T3D, and Nystrom et al. [26] describe their experiences with performance tools on the CRAY T3D. Malony and Mohr [22] describe tools for use with object-oriented languages that leverage the capabilities provided by the Sage compiler toolkit. Finally, Adve et al. [1] describe techniques for supporting performance analysis of Fortran D and HPF programs by exploiting knowledge of compile-time program transformations.

1.3.2   Real-time Adaptive Control

It is increasingly clear that a large and important class of national challenge applications are irregular, with complex, data-dependent execution behavior, and dynamic, with time-varying resource demands. Because the interactions between application and system software change across applications and during a single application's execution, ideally, runtime libraries and resource management policies should automatically and unobtrusively adapt to rapidly changing application behavior. For example, recent studies of application input/output behavior [17,6] have shown that tuning file system policies to exploit knowledge of application access patterns can increase performance by more than an order of magnitude.

Distressingly, the space of possible performance optimizations is large and non-convex, and the best match of application and resource management technique is seldom obvious *a priori*. Current performance instrumentation and analysis tools provide the data necessary to understand the causes for poor performance *a posteriori*, but alone they are insufficient to adapt to temporally varying application resource demands and system responses.

As noted in Sec. 1.3.1, software developers currently must engage in a time-consuming cycle of program development, performance measurement, debugging and tuning to create non-portable code that adapts to parallel system idiosyncrasies.

One potential solution to the performance optimization conundrum is integration of dynamic performance instrumentation and on-the-fly performance data reduction with configurable, malleable resource management algorithms and a real-time adaptive control mechanism that automatically chooses and configures resource management algorithms based on application request patterns and observed system performance. In principle, an adaptive resource management infrastructure, driven by real-time performance data, would increase portability by allowing application and runtime libraries to adapt to disparate hardware and software platforms and would increase achieved performance by choosing and configuring those resource management algorithms best matched to temporally varying application behavior.

Several systems have been built that support application behavior steering (i.e., guiding a computation toward interesting phenomena) [19,28]. Typically, application behavioral steering is interactive, with an application scientist studying near real-time scientific visualizations and guiding the application code by changing key application variables. In contrast to application behavioral steering, there have been fewer efforts to interactively steer or adaptively control application performance. One notable exception is the Falcon system, by Schwan et al. [8], that allows application developers to insert software sensors in their source code to monitor application activity. Performance data from these sensors can activate actuators inserted in the code by the developer. These actuators can change program behavior based on current conditions and measured performance.

As with support for data parallel languages, developing an infrastructure for adaptive control of application and system performance will require new interfaces for information acquisition and control of resource management policies. Task management and input/output libraries must embody mechanisms for resource management policy selection and configuration to match application needs. For example, small sequential file read requests are well served by a input/output library caching and prefetching policy, but large and irregular requests are better served by a policy that directly streams data from storage devices to application code.

Two workshop presentations described experiences with performance steering of parallel systems. Eisenhauer et al. [7] describe the Falcon system for online performance monitoring and adaptive control of application behavior and resource management policies. Kunchithapadam and Miller [21] describe techniques for exploiting breakpoint debuggers and performance tools to build a steering environment.

1.3.3 Heterogeneous Metacomputing and the WWW

The widespread use of workstation clusters for parallel computing is based on their ubiquity, low incremental cost, stable software development environments, and interconnection via well-understood communication protocols (e.g., PVM [10] and [13]). These same communication mechanisms make possible heterogeneous metacomputing where groups of similar or disparate parallel systems are coupled to collectively solve large problems. And as the wide-area research computing network infrastructure evolves to higher bandwidth (e.g., the very high-speed Backbone Network Service (vBNS)), the granularity of feasible distributed computations will continue to decrease until they are limited largely by speed of light latencies due to geographic separation.

However, the truly important change will be the presence of large data archives accessible via the WWW. The WWW has become the standard mechanism for distributed data access and information exchange among large groups of scientists, and an increasingly large fraction of scientific data repositories accept queries via the WWW. Among the key technical challenges will be not only developing faster network access to service these archives, for instance, but regulating these resources as the demand for them skyrockets. The information mining issues inherent in such information availability will require changes in our economic, social, and technical models of computing and cost recovery. In short, parallel computing must be seamlessly integrated with the growing information fabric of the Internet, making parallel, heterogeneous, geographically distributed computing (i.e., metacomputing) the norm.

The hard technical problem will be managing access to distributed data repositories. Typically, one will wish to pose queries that require access to multiple, geographically distributed data bases. The key question becomes when to move the data to the computation and when to move the computation to the data. In short, exploiting the network, for access to the data archives and high-performance parallel systems for information mining will pose a plethora of difficult performance optimization problems. Because such distributed programs are likely to be based on autonomous agents [12] that cooperate to acquire and process information, distributed debugging and security verification are critical issues.

Two of the four workshop working groups considered the implications of metacomputing in considerable detail. One working group [38] considered tools needed to support development of NII-aware applications. A second group [39] considered tools needed to support workstation cluster computing. As a practical example of the problems debugging and performance tuning problems faced for workstation clusters, Geist et al. [11] and Hao et al. [15] describe their experiences building and supporting tools for PVM [10].

1.3.4 Tool Integration and Interfaces

The emerging debugging and performance tuning problems for task and data parallel languages, real-time adaptive control of irregular applications, and heterogeneous metacomputing are united by the need for new types of data and richer interfaces for acquiring that data. As noted in Sec. 1.3.1–Sec. 1.3.3, this includes access to compiler program analysis databases; runtime library scheduling and data management decisions; and network latencies, bandwidths, and remote system status for distributed applications.

Given the limited resources for tool construction, discussed in Sec. 1.4 below, collaboratively defining standard tool interfaces is key to developing portable tools that can operate on multiple hardware platforms. For example, building portable, compiler-independent HPF performance tools requires definition of access interfaces that export compiler information while hiding internal details. Yet with a few notable exceptions, it is impossible to obtain access to program transformation data without deep knowledge of a particular compiler's internal data structures and access to compiler source code.

Interface standardization must strike a delicate balance between technical needs and vendor competitive constraints. Unrestricted access to compiler transformations will reveal the structure and features of a particular compiler, something that may be viewed as a competitive advantage by a particular vendor. Similarly, access to SNMP network data [34] for distributed task management can reveal much about the structure, function, and capabilities of organizations transporting data on a wide area network. Simply put, access must be tempered by implementation complexity; portability mandates standards, and a widely implemented, though restricted standard, is preferable to a broad, though rarely adopted standard.

However, standard interfaces for access to compiler data structures and dynamic distributed data are necessary, but not sufficient, to construct a new generation of performance and debugging tools for emerging application domains. Standard, consistent, friendly user interfaces are equally important. Many performance analysis and debugging tools fail, not because they cannot acquire, correlate and present the appropriate data, but because they are difficult or unintuitive to use. There are countless examples of users eschewing more powerful, sophisticated tools in favor of simpler, inaccurate tools. The widespread use of print/write for debugging reflects this fact.

Several workshop presentations and one working group considered external and internal tool interfaces. Breazeal and Ries [4] describe a possible infrastructure for tool development at Intel, Itzkowitz et al. [18] discuss experiences with tool design at Silicon Graphics, and Heller [16] describes design principles for access to data on large production systems. Helmbold and McDowell present a taxonomy of race detection techniques for debuggers. Finally, one of the four workshop working groups [37] and a workshop panel explored the desirability of integrated toolkits.

From a user perspective, Beazley and Lomdahl [2] summarize their experience moving a large code from one parallel system to another and the difficulties they encountered in optimizing the code's performance; Winstead et al. [36] describe their experiences using the Pablo environment to optimize input/output performance on the Intel Paragon XP/S, and Gupta [14] summarizes application experiences with a variety of parallel systems. Finally, Pancake [27] summarizes the experiences of the Parallel Tools Consortium (Ptools) in bringing together users, tools developers, and vendors.

1.4   Technology Transition Issues

Despite major research advances in system software, libraries, and tools, the commercial software infrastructure for massively parallel systems has not kept pace with the rapid evolution of new parallel architectures. The critical importance of robust, flexible, and efficient software tools has been recognized at national HPCC meetings, including those in Pasadena [24,25] and Pittsburgh [35], though little has changed in the past five years. The workshop, like its predecessors, concluded that there are several fundamental reasons for the current dilemma, and they all relate to the lack of incentives for tool development and testing.

Massively parallel systems are a niche market, and the real cost of commercial software development for these platforms is high. The academic and laboratory research community is another potential source of software tools for parallel systems, but this community lacks the reward structure, the financial resources, and (often) the skills necessary to develop and support robust software tools. Moreover, because there is limited interaction between academic tool developers and potential tool users, many of the commercial and academic tools lack important features, are too difficult to use, or solve problems of little interest to application developers.

1.4.1 Software Tool Shortages

Is the dearth of effective software tools a new problem? No, the lack of good software development tools can be traced to the very origins of high-performance computing (e.g., early CDC Fortran compilers were very inefficient, and the CRAY 1 was delivered with essentially no software). However, as high-performance systems have become more widely available and accessible, the longstanding lack of tools has become more evident. More perniciously, the ferment in the HPCC market has led to short product life cycles, with vendors and application developers repeatedly moving to new architectures and programming models. Often, by the time system software has sufficiently stabilized and there is sufficient knowledge of common programming idioms to permit construction of robust and useful tools, the underlying hardware is no longer performance-competitive.

In short, the software infrastructure for massively parallel systems has been unable to keep pace with the rapid evolution of new parallel architectures. The paucity of basic software tools for application program development, debugging, and performance tuning has limited the use of massively parallel systems to a small cadre of hardy pioneers willing to brave a wilderness of experimental hardware, immature software, and frequently changing tools.

The critical importance of robust, flexible, easy-to-use, and efficient software tools has been emphasized repeatedly at national HPCC meetings, including those in Pasadena [24,25] and Pittsburgh [35]. Despite this recognition, little has changed in the past five years. Substantial research money is directed toward study and development of software tools, but as one speaker at the 1993 workshop on performance tools [32] asked, "Why don't users use the tools that tool developers develop?" The workshop attendees agreed that the fundamental reasons for this dilemma relate to the lack of incentives for tool development and testing.

First, the massively parallel systems market is small, and the real cost of commercial tool development is high. As vendors prioritize development of new systems, functioning hardware, operating systems and compilers receive the highest priority, for machines cannot be shipped without these. However, competitive pressures and development schedule slippage often lead vendors to ship their new systems prematurely, before other infrastructure such as software development tools can be created. Due to these pressures on vendors to ship, the temptation is very high for them to simply "repackage" internal development tools for external use, even when these tools are inappropriate for users.

From a financial perspective, developing robust software tools for a parallel system with projected sales of 500 units is nearly as costly as developing software for the burgeoning personal computer market, but without concomitant financial incentives. These same economics preclude creation of a viable third party software industry (i.e., the independent software vendors (ISVs)). One of the workshop working groups [23] addressed the implications of market size for tool development.

Second, another potential source of software tools, the academic and laboratory research community, lacks the reward structure, the financial resources, and (often) the skills to develop and support robust software tools. The academic computer science community is rewarded, both tangibly and intangibly, for development of software prototypes and publication of the ideas underlying these, but not for the additional development needed to make these prototypes really usable by the larger HPCC community. Moreover, because there is limited interaction between academic tool developers and potential tool users, prototype tools often lack important features or are simply not useful to application developers.

Although there are a plethora of reasons for this situation, most are subsumed under the rubric of limited collaboration and funding. Inappropriate tools often result because application developers, tool developers, and vendors are not intimate collaborators in the tool development process; current academic and commercial realities do not reward such collaboration. Moreover, vendors are reluctant to embrace, extend, and market academic software unless it is already robust, as evidenced by wide use within the application community. Finally, an undue emphasis on peak hardware performance, at the frequent expense of sustained, readily achievable performance, leads to rapid changes in hardware and system software.

1.4.2   Potential Technology Transition Solutions

Collaboratively developing robust, user-friendly performance tools for high-performance parallel systems is expensive and as intellectually challenging as national challenge science, yet it is often assumed to be "easy," despite the fact that tool developers on new systems face the same software problems as application developers, and their tools must interoperate with multiple applications. Moreover, effective tool development requires many mundane activities not normally associated with academic computer science research, namely testing early prototypes with friendly users who are application scientists, developing and testing intuitive user interfaces, and writing manuals and documentation. Most of the activities are not rewarded by the computer science research community. Activities such as supporting a user community, teaching training classes, and adapting software to new hardware and software releases will not bring tenure, peer adulation, better graduate students or (usually) larger research support; therefore, most academic computer scientists have little incentive to develop a tool beyond the prototype stage.

The workshop attendees concluded that a solution to this dilemma is the creation of a national software tool evaluation and testing center that would work with external academic researchers, local application scientists, and vendors to evaluate and test prototype software tools. One solution that is currently being explored is the Ptools Consortium [27], a loosely organized group of vendors and users primarily engaged in the development of software tools. However, as described below, the tools community believes a more rigorous, broad-based approach is also required that co-locates a formal testing and evaluation facility with one or more national groups of experienced computational scientists.

These views are not simply those of the editors. They mirror those expressed at the Pasadena [24,25] and Pittsburgh [35,40,41] meetings and at the eight performance and debugging tool workshops. The workshop attendees have repeatedly recommended a major project to understand the limitations of current tools, the requirements for future tools, and to exploit this knowledge to transfer useful software prototypes to the application community and to commercial vendors.

Clearly, however, one center cannot and should not supplant traditional mechanisms for technology transfer from academia to industry. We would envision a more synergistic relationship with these traditional mechanisms. Moreover, it is important to realize that there are many possible definitions of software tool "success" that do not include commercialization. Indeed, as argued earlier, commercialization is extraordinarily difficult, and many valuable tools have no commercial market. Pragmatically, success means that a software tool is useful, tested, documented, and widely used. Hence, the goal of a center would be to serve as a focal point for the software tool development, vendor, and computational science communities to increase the number and breadth of useful and necessary tools and to encourage commercialization. To realize this goal, the workshop attendees and organizers envision four foci.

1. *Early Prototype Evaluation*: Typically, academic tool researchers develop simple software prototypes to demonstrate a proof of concept prior to publication. Because most of these projects are small, there are few opportunities to test the ideas with appropriate external users and to learn what aspects of the approach have practical merit. By coupling academic tool researchers with a group of friendly users at supercomputing centers, where there is the infrastructure needed to support early prototypes, the tool researchers can gain early feedback on the practicality of their ideas. Those prototypes that show promise of potential usefulness to application developers could then be further developed with the center's assistance, and where appropriate, in cooperation with one or more vendors. An additional bonus from this stage would be also to gain new research ideas.

2. *Mature Prototype Testing and Extension*: A smaller number of prototypes are sufficiently mature to be used and useful to a user community not co-located with the tool developer. Major reasons for the importance of co-location include tool bugs, lack of documentation, missing features, and support for only a small number of parallel hardware platforms. Proximity to developers increases the likelihood of interaction to aid in overcoming these deficiencies. This class of tools, however, have passed an initial "usefulness test" — they are being used by at least a portion of the application community. Hence, the second focus

of a center would be to work with users to aggressively test these tools, identify bugs and inadequacies, work with the original tool developers to fix those bugs and add missing features, and (where appropriate) extend the tool to other hardware platforms.

3. *Vendor Cooperation and Involvement:* Both the promising early proto- types and the more useful, mature tool prototypes should have vendors involved in their evaluation and testing early in the cycle if commer- cialization is at all an option. Not every tool "vetted" by the center would be a candidate for adoption by one or more vendors; however, one would hope that many would be viewed as sufficiently useful to be of interest to vendors of high-performance parallel systems.

4. *Software Packaging and Support:* Finally, tools deemed useful and wor- thy of dissemination, but not adopted by one or more vendors, must be documented, packaged for installation at remote sites, and, when prob- lems arise, supported, patched, and upgraded. Although this work is mundane, some entity must assume this responsibility, else even good tools will not be used for long periods.

The need for "better" software performance analysis and debugging tools (where better means easier to use, more efficient, better integrated, and more informative) for high-performance parallel systems is a well-documented and widely recognized need. The Strategic Implementation Plan [5] of the *Committee on Information and Communications of the National Science and Technology Council* has noted that "Raising the productivity of the software industry through simplifying toolkits can yield significant dividends in the international marketplace and enable more rapid introduction of hardware advances into affordable production systems." Raising the productivity of ap- plications developers through appropriate, easy-to-use software performance and debugging tools creates a larger market for these affordable production systems. Providing a place where these tools can be effectively tested, evalu- ated and improved can ensure success in the entire high-performance parallel computing industry.

1.5   Conclusions

Building successful software tools requires a varied mix of technical expertise, marketing and evangelization, and software support. As systems become increasingly complex with shorter and shorter product cycles, the performance optimization and debugging problems become more intellectually challenging, and deploying effective tools based on anticipated user needs becomes increasingly difficult.

The goal of this workshop (and of its predecessors) was to bring together vendor tool developers, academic and government laboratory tool researchers, and application scientists to discuss the current situation and outline research issues and technology transition remedies. The remaining chapters of this book capture the current state of the tool development art.

References

[1] ADVE, V. S., MELLOR-CRUMMEY, J., ANDERSON, M., KENNEDY, K., WANG, J.-C., AND REED, D. A., "Integrating Compilation and Performance Analysis for Data Parallel Programs," in *Debugging and Performance Tuning for Parallel Computer Systems*, M. L. Simmons, A. H. Hayes, D. A. Reed, and J. Brown, Eds., IEEE Computer Society Press, Dec. 1995.

[2] BEAZLEY, D. M., AND LOMDAHL, P. S., "A Practical Approach to Portability and Performance Problems on Massively Parallel Supercomputers," in *Debugging and Performance Tuning for Parallel Computer Systems*, M. L. Simmons, A. H. Hayes, D. A. Reed, and J. Brown, Eds. IEEE Computer Society Press, Dec. 1995.

[3] BERNERS-LEE, T., CAILLIAU, R., GROFF, J., AND POLLERMANN, B., World-Wide Web: The Information Universe. *Electronic Networking: Research, Applications, and Policy 1*, **2** (1992), 52–58.

[4] BREAZEAL, D., AND RIES, B., "A Building Block Approach to Parallel Tool Construction," in *Debugging and Performance Tuning for Parallel Computer Systems*, M. L. Simmons, A. H. Hayes, D. A. Reed, and J. Brown, Eds., IEEE Computer Society Press, Dec. 1995.

[5] COMMITTEE ON INFORMATION AND COMMUNICATIONS, NATIONAL SCIENCE AND TECHNOLOGY COUNCIL. Strategic Implementation Plan: America in the Age of Information, Mar. 1995.

[6] CRANDALL, P. E., AYDT, R. A., CHIEN, A. A., AND REED, D. A., "Characterization of a Suite of Input/Output Intensive Applications," in *Proceedings of Supercomputing '95* (Dec. 1995).

[7] EISENHAUER, G., GU, W., KINDLER, T., SCHWAN, K., SILVA, D., AND VETTER, J., "Opportunities and Tools for Highly Interactive Distributed and Parallel Computing," in *Debugging and Performance Tuning for Parallel Computer Systems*, M. L. Simmons, A. H. Hayes, D. A. Reed, and J. Brown, Eds., IEEE Computer Society Press, Dec. 1995.

[8] EISENHAUER, G., GU, W., SCHWAN, K., AND MALLAVARUPU, N., "Falcon — Toward Interactive Parallel Programs: the Online Steering of a Molecular Dynamic Program," in *Proceedings of the Third International Symposium on High-Performance Distributed Computing* (Aug. 1994).

[9] FOSTER, I., AVALANI, B., CHOUDHARY, A., AND XU, M., "A Compilation System that Integrates High Performance Fortran and Fortran M," in *Proceedings of the 1994 Scalable High Performance Computing Conference* (1994).

[10] GEIST, A., BEGUELIN, A., DONGARRA, J., JAING, W., MANCHEK, R., AND SUNDERAM, V., *PVM: Parallel Virtual Machine: A User's Guide and Tutorial for Networked Parallel Computing*, MIT Press, 1994.

[11] GEIST, G. A., KOHL, J., AND PAPADOPOULOS, P., "Visualization, Debugging, and Performance in PVM," in *Debugging and Performance Tuning for Parallel Computer Systems*, M. L. Simmons, A. H. Hayes, D. A. Reed, and J. Brown, Eds., IEEE Computer Society Press, Dec. 1995.

[12] GOSLING, J., AND MCGILTON, H., "The Java Language Environment: A White Paper," Sun Microsystems, 1995.

[13] GROPP, W., LUSK, E., AND SKJELLUM, A., *Using MPI*, MIT Press, 1994.

[14] GUPTA, R. "Prospects of Solving Grand Challenge Problems," in *Debugging and Performance Tuning for Parallel Computer Systems*,

M. L. Simmons, A. H. Hayes, D. A. Reed, and J. Brown, Eds., IEEE Computer Society Press, Dec. 1995.

[15] HAO, M. C., WAHEED, A., KARP, A., AND JAZAYERI, M., "Multiple Views of Parallel Application Execution," in *Debugging and Performance Tuning for Parallel Computer Systems*, M. L. Simmons, A. H. Hayes, D. A. Reed, and J. Brown, Eds., IEEE Computer Society Press, Dec. 1995.

[16] HELLER, D., "Issues of Running Codes on Very Large Parallel Processing Systems," in *Debugging and Performance Tuning for Parallel Computer Systems*, M. L. Simmons, A. H. Hayes, D. A. Reed, and J. Brown, Eds., IEEE Computer Society Press, Dec. 1995.

[17] HUBER, J. V., ELFORD, C. L., REED, D. A., CHIEN, A. A., AND BLUMENTHAL, D. S., "PPFS: A High-Performance Portable Parallel File System," in *Proceedings of the 9th ACM International Conference on Supercomputing* (July 1995).

[18] ITZKOWITZ, M., YU, J., MCNAUGHTON, A., ORELUP, P., AND HANNA, C., "Visualizing Performance on Parallel Supercomputers," in *Debugging and Performance Tuning for Parallel Computer Systems*, M. L. Simmons, A. H. Hayes, D. A. Reed, and J. Brown, Eds., IEEE Computer Society Press, Dec. 1995.

[19] JABLONOWSKI, D., BRUNER, J., BLISS, B., AND HABER, R., "VASE: The Visualization and Application Steering Environment," in *Proceedings of Supercomputing '93* (Nov. 1993), 560–569.

[20] KOELBEL, C., LOVEMAN, D., SCHREIBER, R., STEELE, JR., G., AND ZOSEL, M., *The High Performance Fortran Handbook*, The MIT Press, Cambridge, MA, 1994.

[21] KUNCHITHAPADAM, K., AND MILLER, B. P., "Integrating a Debugger and a Performance Tool for Steering," in *Debugging and Performance Tuning for Parallel Computer Systems*, M. L. Simmons, A. H. Hayes, D. A. Reed, and J. Brown, Eds., IEEE Computer Society Press, Dec. 1995.

[22] MALONY, A., AND MOHR, B., "Program Analysis and Tuning Tools for a Parallel Object Oriented Language: An Experiment with the TAU

System," in *Debugging and Performance Tuning for Parallel Computer Systems*, M. L. Simmons, A. H. Hayes, D. A. Reed, and J. Brown, Eds., IEEE Computer Society Press, Dec. 1995.

[23] McGraw, J. M., "Leveraging software resources," in *Debugging and Performance Tuning for Parallel Computer Systems*, M. L. Simmons, A. H. Hayes, D. A. Reed, and J. Brown, Eds., IEEE Computer Society Press, Dec. 1995.

[24] Messina, P. and Sterling, T., Eds., *Pasadena Workshop on System Software and Tools for High-Performance Computing Environments*, SIAM, Jan. 1992.

[25] Messina, P. and Sterling, T., Eds., *Second Pasadena Workshop on System Software and Tools for HPC Environments*, Jan. 1995.

[26] Nystrom, N. A., Young, W. S., and Wimberly, F. C., "Methodologies for Developing Scientific Applications on the CRAY T3D," in *Debugging and Performance Tuning for Parallel Computer Systems*, M. L. Simmons, A. H. Hayes, D. A. Reed, and J. Brown, Eds., IEEE Computer Society Press, Dec. 1995.

[27] Pancake, C. M., "Collaborative Efforts to Develop User-Oriented Parallel Tools," in *Debugging and Performance Tuning for Parallel Computer Systems*, M. L. Simmons, A. H. Hayes, D. A. Reed, and J. Brown, Eds., IEEE Computer Society Press, Dec. 1995.

[28] Parris, M., Mueller, C., and Prins, J., "A Distributed Implementation of an N-body Virtual World Simulation," in *Proceedings of the Workshop on Parallel and Distributed Real-Time Systems* (Apr. 1993), 66–70.

[29] Pase, D. M. and Williams, W., "A Performance Tool for the Cray T3D," in *Debugging and Performance Tuning for Parallel Computer Systems*, M. L. Simmons, A. H. Hayes, D. A. Reed, and J. Brown, Eds., IEEE Computer Society Press, Dec. 1995.

[30] Simmons, M., Koskela, R., and Bucher, I., Eds., *Instrumentation for Future Parallel Computing Systems*. Addison-Wesley Publishing Company, 1989.

[31] SIMMONS, M. L., HAYES, A. H., AND REED, D. A., Santa Fe Workshop on Parallel Computer Systems, Oct. 1991, Santa Fe, NM.

[32] SIMMONS, M. L., HAYES, A. H., AND REED, D. A., Keystone Workshop on Software Tools for Parallel Computing Systems: A Dialogue Between Users and Developers, Apr. 1993, Keystone, CO.

[33] SIMMONS, M. L., AND KOSKELA, R., Eds., *Parallel Computing Systems: Performance Instrumentation and Visualization*, Addison-Wesley Publishing Company, 1990.

[34] STALLINGS, W., *SNMP, SNMPv2 and CMIP: The Practical Guide to Network Management Standards*, Addison-Wesley Publishing Company, 1993.

[35] STEVENS, R., Workshop and Conference on Grand Challenge Applications and Software Technology, May 1993, Pittsburgh, PA.

[36] WINSTEAD, C., PRITCHARD, H. P., AND McKOY, V., Tuning I/O Performance on the Paragon: Fun with Pablo and Norma. In *Debugging and Performance Tuning for Parallel Computer Systems*, M. L. Simmons, A. H. Hayes, D. A. Reed, and J. Brown, Eds., IEEE Computer Society Press, Dec. 1995.

[37] ROVER, D., MALONY, A., AND NUTT, G., "Integrated Environments Versus Toolkits," in *Debugging and Performance Tuning for Parallel Computer Systems*, M. L. Simmons, A. H. Hayes, D. A. Reed, and J. Brown, Eds., IEEE Computer Society Press, Dec. 1995.

[38] DILLY, R., "Tools and the NII," in *Debugging and Performance Tuning for Parallel Computer Systems*, M. L. Simmons, A. H. Hayes, D. A. Reed, and J. Brown, Eds., IEEE Computer Society Press, Dec. 1995.

[39] McGRAW, J., "Tools for Workstation Clusters," in *Debugging and Performance Tuning for Parallel Computer Systems*, M. L. Simmons, A. H. Hayes, D. A. Reed, and J. Brown, Eds., IEEE Computer Society Press, Dec. 1995.

[40] BROWN, JEFFREY S., Supercomputer Debugging Workshop '91, November 1991, Albuquerque, NM.

[41] BROWN, JEFFREY S., Supercomputing Debugging Workshop '92, October 1992, Dallas, TX.

Chapter 2

Tools: A Research Point of View

The future of high-performance computing is large-scale parallelism. Whether that scale is supported by massive numbers of loosely coupled computers, or by tightly-coupled highly parallel systems, there is no doubt that future parallel systems will encompass large numbers of processors working in concert to solve larger and more complex problems. Teraflop performance seems within our grasp due to recent rapid advances in hardware technology, both in processor design and communications infrastructure; however, software infrastructure for such systems has not kept pace. The capability to accurately and easily debug or to measure program performance is sadly lacking and this is particularly distressing since performance is the "raison d'etre" for parallelism.

Debugging and performance analysis tools have been the focus of many recent research efforts at academic institutions, government laboratories, and parallel computer manufacturing sites. In spite of these efforts, as several recent conferences have made quite clear, tool use is still appallingly low among the high-performance computing community. Three concerns have been cited as particularly critical:

- current tools do not meet the specific needs of scientific users, who must become overly expert in the implementation details to understand and use the tools;

- tools vary widely across current parallel platforms, so the steep learning curve must be repeated each time a user migrates to a new machine; and

- the lack of specialized support for heterogeneous or scalable applications deters users from investing the effort needed to make scientific libraries or applications parallel so that they could be used by others seeking to solve similar problems.

All of the three concerns listed above cannot begin to be satisfied until there is a viable user interface to the underlying software. Joan Francioni's paper, "Determining the Effectiveness of Interfaces for Debugging and Performance Analysis Tools," starts with this premise and she then develops a set of 25 effectiveness guidelines that are designed to assist tool developers in building effective interfaces to their tools.

In "Program Analysis and Tuning Tools for a Parallel Object-Oriented Language: An Experiment with the TAU System," Gannon, et al. point out that new users are now demanding that tools be robust, portable and easy-to-use because of the realization that software investment is so much more important than the money spent on hardware. They propose an experimental programming language and environment to deal with some of the issues that these demands raise. Another approach is put forward by Adve, et al. in "Integrating Compilation and Performance Analysis for Data-Parallel Programs" to solve these problems by integrating compilation and performance analysis to provide a bridge between source and compiled code for the user. A taxonomy categorizing methods of ordering events is used to detect race conditions in the paper by Helmbold and McDowell.

Integrating Performance and Debugging Tools as a way to detect and improve performance through a technique called steering is proposed by Kunchithapadam and Miller in "Integrating a Debugger and a Performance Tool for Steering." This approach allows dynamic alteration of an application based on performance criteria supplied by the programmer. G. A. Geist, et al. describe enhancements to Parallel Virtual Machine (PVM) through a graphical user interface XPVM to display real-time and post-mortem machine statistics.

Integrating Compilation and Performance Analysis for Data-Parallel Programs

Vikram S. Adve,[1] John Mellor-Crummey,
Mark Anderson, and Ken Kennedy
Center for Research on Parallel Computation
Rice University
Houston, Texas 77251-1892

Jhy-Chun Wang and Daniel A. Reed
Department of Computer Science
University of Illinois
Urbana, Illinois 61801

Abstract

The advantages of abstract, high-level programming languages like High Performance Fortran (HPF) will be fully realized only if programmers are able to understand and tune the performance of their applications without having to understand the details of the compiler-synthesized, explicitly parallel code. Providing such support will require extensive integration of compilation and performance analysis to overcome the deep semantic gap between source and compiled code. We describe the integration of the University of Illinois' Pablo performance environment and Rice

---

[1]Supported in part by ARPA contracts DAVT63-91-C-0029, DABT63-93-C-0040 and DABT63-92-C-0038, and by NSF gran ASC92-12369 and NSF Cooperative Agreement Number CCR-9120008.

University D compiler to form a prototype programming environment that supports performance analysis of regular, data parallel programs written in Fortran D. By this integration, the programming environment can help the programmer to understand the qualitative impact of code design choices on parallelism and communication, and understand dynamic performance characteristics in terms of the original source code.

1.1 Introduction

Message-passing programming models for distributed memory parallel systems provide efficient support for coarse-grain communication and parallelism, but are tedious to program and have typically resulted in non-portable software due to the plethora of machine-specific programming interfaces. Higher-level, data-parallel programming languages like Fortran D and HPF are designed to enhance the ease of programming as well as the portability of applications software for distributed-memory machines. These languages require the programmer to specify the fine-grain decomposition of the program and its mapping onto the physical machine, but shift to the compiler the responsibility of managing the numerous and complex details that arise in implementing the parallelism and communication.

The primary motivation for parallel processing, however, is to achieve high performance. In order to design and tune a program for high performance on a parallel system, the programmer must understand where the program spends most of its execution time, and then modify the program in an attempt to improve its performance. The advantages of a high-level, programming model will be fully realized only if the programming environment supports this process by explaining performance at the level of the abstract, high-level source program, *and* provides the functionality required to tune the performance characteristics of the computation.

Optimizing compilers for languages like Fortran D and HPF substantially transform the code in order to create an explicitly parallel program and in order to restructure the computation and communication to achieve high performance. Thus, the software developer's mental model of a program is quite different from the low-level, explicitly parallel program that actually executes on the parallel machine and most directly determines the performance characteristics. This semantic gap between source program and compiler-synthesized code creates at least three important obstacles to developing programs in these high-level languages. First, during code design and development, it is difficult for the programmer to reason about the impact of program design choices on performance. Second, when tuning the program based on performance feedback from runtime measurements, it is difficult both to understand the observed performance characteristics and to correlate these performance characteristics with their causes in the source code. Third, the communication patterns inserted by the compiler are difficult for the programmer to understand or control, and thus difficult to tune. For programmers to develop efficient parallel programs in such a high-level language, it is essential that the programming environment provide the support necessary to overcome these obstacles by bridging the semantic gap between source and compiled code.

Overcoming the obstacles described above requires extensive cooperation between the compiler and the performance measurement and visualization tools. The compiler must provide information about the mapping between the high-level source code and the compiled code, both in order to support code development and, in combination with runtime measurements of program performance, to explain the program's dynamic performance characteristics in terms of the developer's source code. The compiler can also use information from runtime measurements in subsequent recompilations to generate more efficient code.

The D System group at Rice University and the Pablo group at the University of Illinois are jointly developing a prototype integrated compilation and performance analysis system based on the Rice Fortran 77D compiler and the Illinois' Pablo performance environment. The project aims to demonstrate that, with extensive cooperation between the compiler and performance tools, the programming environment can provide the high-level performance support necessary for the development of efficient data parallel programs, as described above.

This paper describes our approach in developing an integrated environment and our preliminary experiences from the integration. The paper first motivates the need for integrated compilation and performance analysis and outlines the limitations of current data parallel compilers and performance analysis tools. We then describe the design and initial implementation of the integrated environment which uses Pablo's extensible performance data meta-format as a medium of information interchange between the Fortran D compiler and the Pablo performance analysis software. Finally, we describe preliminary experiments that illustrate the advantages of the integration, compare with related work, and conclude with a brief discussion and directions for future research.

1.2   Background and Motivation

The Fortran D compiler and the Pablo performance analysis environment individually provide sophisticated support for developing high-performance data-parallel programs, but each can benefit significantly from mutual integration. The following subsections describe the functionality of each subsystem, and then use an example to illustrate the need for integrated compilation and performance analysis.

1.2.1   Fortran D Compiler

A Fortran D program consists of a base Fortran 77 program annotated with data distribution directives describing how the principal arrays of the program are to be distributed across the processors in a parallel system. (The example below will illustrate the use of the data layout directives.) The Fortran 77D compiler uses this data-distribution to generate an explicitly parallel, *single-program multiple data* (SPMD) node program for a distributed-memory machine. The compiler first partitions the computation using the *owner-computes* rule [18], and then implements the necessary communication and synchronization by inserting calls to a message-passing library for the target machine.[2]

To generate and optimize the explicitly parallel program, the compiler transforms the code extensively. It converts the shared arrays (i.e., the global name space) to local arrays, perhaps introducing overlap areas to simplify the generated code. It reduces loop bounds and introduces guards as necessary to partition the computation among the processors. It computes what non-local array sections are referenced by each RHS reference to determine the communication required. It optimizes the communication by hoisting messages out of loops (message vectorization), combining messages between the same pair of processors (message aggregation), and moving message sends above

---

[2]While the Fortran D compiler includes support for irregular applications (those whose computational requirements and non-local data requirements cannot be determined at compile-time), the work described here focuses on programming environment support for regular applications alone.

preceding code blocks that do not modify the data being sent (vector message pipelining). It introduces collective communication such as broadcasts or reductions when required. In loop nests with loop-carried, cross-processor true dependences, it pipelines the computation to achieve partial parallelism, using strip-mining to amortize the overhead of message-passing by using fewer but larger messages (coarse-grain pipelining). Finally, it introduces explicit buffering for messages where necessary, and replaces the corresponding array references with buffer references to avoid unbuffering costs when possible.

1.2.2   Pablo Performance Environment

The Pablo environment consists of three primary components: an extensible data capture library [16], a data meta-format for describing the structure of performance data records without constraining their contents [4], and a graphical data analysis toolkit that allows users to quickly construct new performance data analyses [14,19].

The data capture library can trace, count, or time code fragments as well as capture entry to and exit from procedures, loops, and message-passing calls. A group of library extension interfaces allow instrumentation software developers to incrementally add new functionality to the library. For example, one extension computes histograms of input/output performance metrics, given an event trace of input/output events,[3] whereas another computes sliding window averages of performance data.

Perhaps the key source of the flexibility in all components of Pablo is a flexible performance data meta-format that separates data semantics from data structure. The Pablo Self-Defining Data Format (SDDF) is a data description language that specifies both the structure of data records and the data record instances, thus providing the ability to define and process new performance data records to suit the needs of a performance tool. Thus, SDDF provides a natural mechanism for information sharing between the Fortran D compiler and the Pablo performance analysis software.

---

[3]This input/output extension is the basis for input/output characterization in the national Scalable I/O Initiative and is used to tune the performance of input/output intensive scientific codes [22].

```
      parameter (n$proc = 8)

      real duz(64, 64, 64)
c     decomposition d(64,64,64)
c     align duz with d
c     distribute d(:,:,block)

c     <CODE ELIDED>

      do 50 j=1,64
        do 50 i=1,64
          do 50 k=64-2,1,-1
            duz(i,j,k) = duz(i,j,k)
     *                    - c(k) * duz(i,j,k+1)
     *                    - e(k) * duz(i,j,64)
 50   continue
```

Figure 1.1: Erlebacher source code fragment.

1.2.3   Performance Correlation Example

The need for integrated compilation systems and performance tools is best illustrated by considering the steps to analyze the performance of a simple Fortran D code using decoupled compilation and performance analysis tools. As an example, we use the Erlebacher code, an 800 line, ten procedure benchmark written by Thomas Eidson at ICASE. Erlebacher solves 3-D partial differential equations by performing tridiagonal solves using Alternating-Direction-Implicit (ADI) integration. The program operates in succession on each of the three dimensions, with each dimension consisting of a computation phase, followed by forward and backward substitution phases. Each substitution phase creates a computation wavefront across the array in the corresponding direction. Figure 1.1 shows a portion of the Fortran D data declarations and one loop nest of the source code. The decomposition, align and distribute statements instruct the compiler to replicate the first two dimensions of the array duz and to distribute the third dimension in contiguous blocks. The loop nest corresponds to the backward substitution phase in the third dimension.

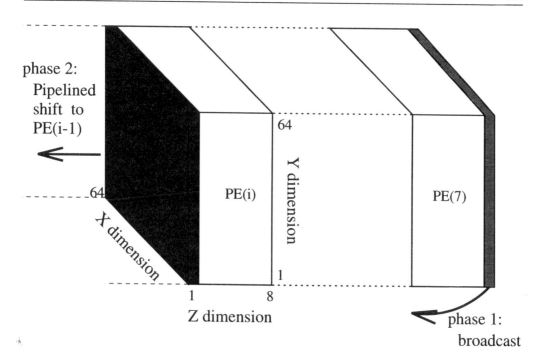

Figure 1.2: Array partitions and communication.

The Fortran D compiler translates the data declarations and the sequential loop of Figure 1.1 into the parallel, message-passing code for the Intel iPSC/860 shown in Figure 1.3. The compiler distributes the array across the processors as specified, but also adds overlap areas to hold off-processor values ($z = 0$ and $z = 9$) in order to simplify the generated code. It then distributes the iterations of the k loop across the processors, with iteration k being executed on the processor that owns the kth XY plane, as specified by the owner-computes rule. Communication is then required to satisfy references to non-local sections of the array. Merely inserting the communication inside the i loop, however, would result in frequent, extremely fine-grain messages (of one word each) and consequently too much communication overhead. Instead, the compiler strip-mines the i loop in blocks of 8 iterations and uses one message per block of 8 elements in order to amortize this overhead. It also inserts a broadcast to satisfy the source reference duz(i,j,64), and hoists the broadcast outside the i and j loops since this boundary XY plane is not modified within this loop.

Comparing Figure 1.1 with Figure 1.3 highlights the difficulty of the performance analysis task faced by a Fortran D application developer. There

```
      real duz(64, 64, 0:9)

C     --<< Fortran D initializations >>--
      lb$1 = max((my$p * 8) + 1, 2) - (my$p * 8)
      ub$1 = min((my$p + 1) * 8, 64 - 2) - (my$p * 8)
      ub$2 = min((my$p + 1) * 8, 64 - 1) - (my$p * 8)
      off$0 = my$p * 8

C     <CODE ELIDED>

      if (my$p .eq. 7) then
C         <CODE FROM PREVIOUS LOOP NEST ELIDED>
C       --<< Broadcast duz(1:64, 1:64, 8) >>--
          call buf3D$r(f, 1, 64, 1, 64, 0, 9, 1, 64, 1,
     *                 1, 64, 1, 8, 8, 1, r$buf1(1))
          call csend(113, r$buf1, 4096 * 4, -1, my$pid)
      else
C       --<< Recv duz(1:64, 1:64, 64) >>--
          call crecv(113, r$buf1, 4096 * 4)
      endif
C
      do j = 1, 64
       do i$ = 1, 64, 8
         i$up = i$ + 7
C        --<< Recv duz(i$:i$up, j, 9) >>--
         if (my$p .lt. 7) then
           call crecv(112, duz(i$,j,9), 8*4)
         endif
         do i = i$, i$up
          do k = ub$1, 1, -1
            k$glo = k + off$0
            duz(i, j, k) = duz(i,j,k)
     *                      - c(k$glo) * duz(i,j,k+1)
     *                      - e(k$glo) * r$buf1(j*64 + i - 64)
          enddo
         enddo
C        --<< Send duz(i$:i$up, j, 1) >>--
         if (my$p .gt. 0) then
           call csend(112, duz(i$,j,1), 8*4,
     *                log2phys(my$p-1), my$pid)
         endif
       enddo
      enddo
```

Figure 1.3:   Generated Fortran 77 fragment.

are significant structural and semantic differences between the two versions of the code:

- the single-threaded, global name-space, programming model is replaced by an explicitly parallel, local name-space, message-passing model;

- the use of overlap areas and explicit buffering complicates the relationship between global and local data layouts;

- the computation is substantially reordered to achieve partial parallelism, resulting in several, staggered wavefronts moving across the array;

- the loop indexing to handle boundary conditions is more complex;

- the pipelined communication requires careful tuning to appropriately trade off parallelism and communication, but this requires extensive understanding of the communication and computation performance characteristics of the underlying machine.

These deep differences between source and compiled code impose at least three kinds of obstacles to the development of efficient, data-parallel programs. First, during code development, it is difficult for a programmer to understand how the code being written will be parallelized, and thus difficult to understand the implications of algorithmic and code design choices on performance. Therefore, it is important that the programming environment provide at least a qualitative understanding of the parallelism and communication synthesized by the compiler and the impact of source code constructs on these.

Second, performance information obtained by measuring the executing program most directly relates to the characteristics of the explicitly parallel code, and is extremely difficult to interpret in relation to the source code written by the programmer. For example, for the code fragment above, current performance instrumentation and analysis tools [15,14,10,17] for distributed memory parallel systems would capture and present performance data from the generated Fortran 77 code of Figure 1.3. Thus, current Pablo performance displays for this program (shown in Figure 1.4) clearly show the performance characteristics of the message-passing program, including the volume of message traffic, processor utilizations, and the staircase communication pattern arising from nearest neighbor communication. While these

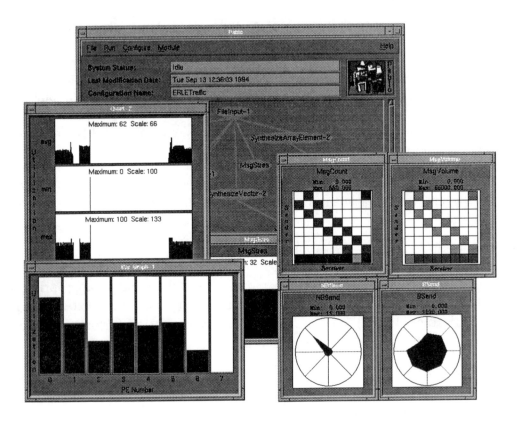

Figure 1.4: Erlebacher Dynamic Behavior (Pablo Performance Environment). See color plate I.

displays are useful, they fail to help the programmer understand where in the original source code the principal performance bottlenecks in the program originated, or the underlying causes of these bottlenecks. Without this understanding, the programmer will be unable to improve the program's performance. To support performance analysis and tuning without sacrificing the advantages of the abstract, data-parallel language, it is imperative that performance tools correlate performance information to the source code written by the programmer, and explain the impact of source code constructs on the performance.

Finally, complex compiler-synthesized communication patterns like the coarse-grained pipeline in Figure 1.3 are difficult for the programmer to manipulate for tuning. As Sec. 1.3.4 shows, tuning the pipeline requires a sophisticated and detailed understanding of the system performance characteristics. Instead, tuning such communication patterns more appropriately falls into the purview of the compiler, with the support of the programming environment.

To provide the various kinds of performance support recommended above, the performance environment needs detailed information about the relationship between the source program and the compiler-synthesized explicitly parallel code. This information could be obtained if the compiler made available the results of its analysis and relevant aspects of the code transformations it performs. Furthermore, the compiler can exploit dynamic performance data to tune communication patterns like the coarse-grained pipeline. Together, these requirements strongly motivate an integrated approach to compilation and performance analysis, with each component of the system making available analysis results to the other to raise the level of information provided by the programming environment. The following section describes our efforts to develop such an integrated programming environment, based on the Rice Fortran 77D compiler and the Pablo performance environment.

1.3 Compilation and Performance Analysis Integration

As suggested in Sec. 1.2.3, a careful integration of compilation and performance analysis will be essential for providing the necessary level of programming support for high-level, data-parallel languages. The integration of compilation and performance analysis can provide two categories of information not available to traditional performance tools or compilers alone: (1) mapping information describing how to assign measured performance costs to high-level source code objects such as data references, arrays, decompositions, loops and procedures; and (2) semantic information such as the data dependences causing remote communication and limiting parallelism, data access patterns describing the locations and frequencies of non-local references to array sections, explicit buffering costs introduced into the program, realignment or redistribution and the resulting communication. The first category is essential for presenting performance information to the programmer in terms of the source code, as is provided by standard performance tools for sequential and explicitly parallel languages. The second category of information can be used to provide more sophisticated, explanatory feedback to the programmer, describing the causes of performance bottlenecks in the program at a semantic level. Finally, in an integrated system, a data parallel compiler could exploit dynamic performance measurements to optimize future compilations.

The remainder of this section describes the integration of the Rice Fortran 77D compiler and the Pablo performance environment to form a prototype programming environment that supports performance analysis of regular, data parallel programs written in Fortran D. After an overview of the system organization, the following three subsections describe the three components of the performance support: static, qualitative feedback from compiler analysis; quantitative feedback from runtime measurements; and support for compiler self-tuning of pipelined communication. The description here focuses on the intended functionality of each of these components; more detailed descriptions of these components and their implementations to date are available elsewhere (in [7,9,2] respectively).

1.3.1   System Organization

Figure 1.5 provides an overview of the system being developed to integrate the Rice Fortran D compiler and the Illinois' Pablo performance environment. The system uses the Fortran D compiler to instrument the compiled code and also to emit data on compiler analysis and transformations; it uses the Pablo self-defining data format (SDDF) as a flexible medium of data interchange between the compiler and Pablo; it uses the Pablo instrumentation software's extension interfaces for capturing dynamic performance data; and it uses a new software toolkit to combine the static and dynamic performance data and relate it to the Fortran D source. Two types of user interfaces are under development. One, the D Editor, is a structured editor for Fortran that will provide users feedback about the parallelism and communication in a program. The other, an off-line performance browser, will also provide similar source-level performance feedback without an interactive editing capability, but with a language and compiler-independent interface. While the D Editor accesses compile-time analysis results via a direct interface to the compiler, the browser will obtain this information from the static data file emitted by a compiler. The infrastructure for obtaining and correlating runtime performance information with the source code will be shared by both environments.

To correlate and explain dynamic performance characteristics in terms of the source code, three types of information are used: static, symbolic, and dynamic. The *static data* summarizes compile-time information that is

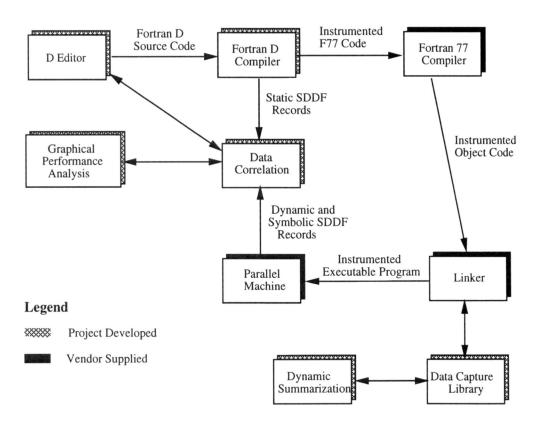

Figure 1.5: Fortran D compiler and Pablo performance environment integration.

relevant for performance analysis, and is written out by the compiler in a separate SDDF file. The *dynamic data* are known only during execution, and include such things as the duration of procedure invocation lifetimes and of message transmissions and receipts. Each dynamic record includes a reference to a static data record that is a starting point for associating the dynamic data with the original source code. Finally, the *symbolic data* may be known either at compile-time or runtime (depending on the source code) (e.g., array sections in a message, message sizes, or the distribution of an array in a phase of the program). If such a value is known at compile-time, it is preserved in the static SDDF file; otherwise it is emitted at runtime by instrumentation inserted for that purpose in the compiled code. A common interface provides uniform access to this information regardless of where individual symbolic records are stored.

Dynamic records and symbolic records that must be obtained at runtime are recorded by inserting calls to the Pablo data capture library [16]. The library has been augmented, via its extension interfaces, to support integration with the Fortran D compiler. Key changes made to the library are: (1) information that may be available statically or symbolically (e.g., message size) is no longer captured during execution, (2) each dynamic record includes the tag of a static record that provides information for data correlation, and (3) a new dynamic record type is introduced to record symbolic values. In addition to tracing individual message passing events, the Pablo instrumentation can also generate a statistical summary of message passing activity within a selected code fragment by analyzing the communication trace events as they are generated. Summarization is most commonly used to reduce instrumentation data volume when the compiler was unable to hoist message passing calls from a loop.

The results of compiler analysis are used to determine where instrumentation must be inserted in the synthesized message-passing code, and the calls to the appropriate library routines are inserted. This is done after all the other code generation so that the instrumentation does not interfere with the regular analysis and optimization functions of the compiler. Instrumentation currently supported by the compiler includes tracing entry/exit events for procedure calls, loop nests, and message library calls, and recording symbolic values not known at compile-time. Summary tracing for messages is not yet invoked by the compiler.

1.3.2   Static Feedback about Parallelism and Communication

Compile-time analysis can provide qualitative information about the major factors affecting program performance on distributed-memory machines, namely, parallelism and communication, and also on the impact of the source code on these factors. To illustrate the static feedback that can be provided, Figure 1.6 shows the D Editor, invoked on the source code of Erlebacher. (The two columns of bars in the top left of the figure provide dynamic information from runtime measurements and will be discussed in the following subsection.) The Overview pane at the top of the figure shows a "compressed" view of the Erlebacher source code, with only the subroutines and loop nests shown. The other panes are used to show the dependences, communication and array layouts for the selected loop (the same as the loop shown in Figure 1.1). Not shown is a second window that displays

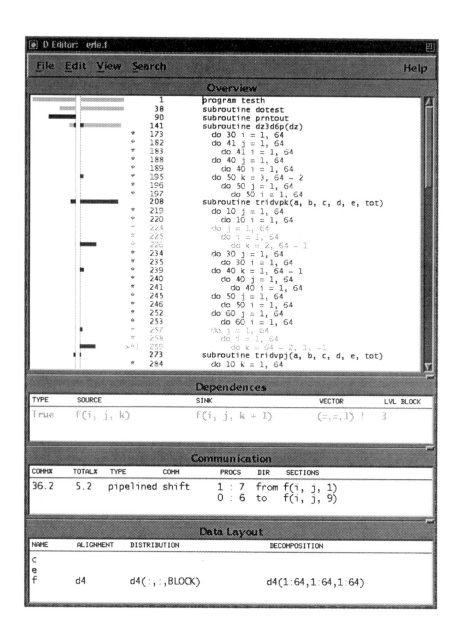

Figure 1.6: D Editor performance overview. See color plate II.

the source code, highlights non-local references, and uses arrows to display cross-processor, loop-carried data dependences (or optionally other types of dependences).

The information about parallelism and communication provided by the display includes:

- The degree of parallelism extracted by the compiler in each source loop: This is indicted by coloring the loop statement in the overview pane (red, yellow, and green respectively correspond to fully parallel, partially parallel or pipelined, and sequential or replicated loops). Thus, the loop marked by a > in the overview pane is colored yellow indicating that the loop (along with the enclosing loops) has been pipelined by the compiler, corresponding to the code in Figure 1.3.

- The placement, type and volume of communication inserted by the compiler: This is shown in the communication pane for each selected loop by indicating the location of messages relative to the loop (inside or outside), the nature of the communication (shift, pipelined shift, broadcast or reductions), the processors involved in the communication, and the specific local array sections that are communicated. The pipelined shift in our example is shown in the Figure 1.2. The broadcast that was hoisted out of the loop nest (see Figure 1.3) would be displayed when the outermost (j) loop is selected.

In addition, the editor displays the features of the source code that are most important in determining the parallelism and communication:

- The data distributions for the source arrays: For a selected loop, the lower-most pane shows all the array variables referenced in the loop along with the array alignment and distribution reaching that loop nest.

- The data dependences limiting parallelism or requiring communication: For a selected loop, the second (source) window shows the loop-carried, cross-processor data dependences for that loop, which would limit the loop to being sequential or partially parallel. Such dependences also show the need for loop-carried communication by indicating the cross-processor data-flow between iterations. Thus, referring to our pipelined loop nest in Figure 1.1, a dependence arrow would be shown from duz(i,j,k) to duz(i,j,k+1). Further technical information on each dependence is given in the dependence pane.

- The non-local source references requiring communication: These are indicated in the source window by coloring the references; the colors indicate the impact of the communication on the parallelism, using the same color metaphor as for the loops above. Thus, referring to Figure 1.1, the references duz(i,j,k+1) would be colored yellow (requiring pipelining) and duz(i,j,64) would be colored green (requiring loop-independent communication).

Thus, by accessing information from static compiler analysis, the programming environment can provide substantial information that is otherwise unavailable from the abstract programming model of these high-level languages. Overall, despite working from essentially a sequential, global-name-space, source program, the programmer can be given a fairly detailed qualitative understanding of the parallelism and communication characteristics of the code.

1.3.3 Quantitative Feedback via Data Correlation

While static feedback during code development helps the programmer understand where potential performance problems can arise, quantitative information is essential for comparing the relative impact of different performance bottlenecks and for focusing performance tuning efforts on the most important procedures, loops and arrays. The instrumentation support in the Fortran D compiler and Pablo provides the means to measure the execution times of procedure calls, loops and messages. In addition, static information from the compiler must be preserved and used to relate this dynamic performance data to the Fortran D source.

The Fortran D compiler preserves both mapping information and semantic information about the program in a static SDDF file. The mapping information provides the means to assign measured performance costs to source code objects. Such mapping information provided in the static SDDF file includes:

- The locations of procedure call sites in the source program, and the locations and nature (application, runtime or intrinsic) of the corresponding procedures. Using this information, measured procedure call lifetimes can be attributed to individual call sites, averaged across all the processors, and also aggregated for the individual procedures across all its call sites, as typically provided by profiling tools for sequential programs.

- The (set of) source loop nests that are translated into a particular loop nest in the SPMD program and vice-versa, and the nature of the transformations performed, if any.

- The data references or set of data references in the source program being satisfied by each message, and the reverse mapping as well.

- The data layout (decomposition, alignment and distribution) of each distributed array being communicated in each message.

- The messages generated for each redistribution or realignment executed at runtime.[4]

The semantic information in the static SDDF file provides most of the explanatory, static information described in the previous subsection and displayed in the D editor. It includes the loop-carried, processor-crossing dependences limiting parallelism and causing communication; the array sections (perhaps in symbolic form) being communicated in each message; the distribution and alignment that is "active" for each distributed array in each static section of SPMD code (the dynamic instrumentation may be needed to specify what is active in each interval of execution). In addition, the static file identifies the additional calls to runtime buffering and unbuffering routines synthesized by the compiler for each message send and receive, such as in Figure 1.3. This enables the performance tool to measure the overall overhead due to communication more completely.

The above static information provides a strong foundation for the integration of compilation and performance analysis. The details of how the above information is organized in the static SDDF file and how it is retrieved and used to correlate dynamic performance information with the data-parallel source are described in [2]. Of the major components of the static information described above, all but two have been implemented (i.e., are now

---

[4]The Fortran D compiler does not currently support dynamic redistribution or realignment, but is expected to do so in the future. Thus, provision for this pointer is included in the static message send record.

generated by the Fortran D compiler). The remaining two are the correlation of buffering calls with messages and the source-to-SPMD loop mapping information, and these will be implemented in the near future.

A performance correlation toolkit combines the above static information with dynamic performance measurement data to calculate many performance metrics for an execution of a Fortran D program. These metrics range from whole program metrics through metrics for individual procedures, procedure call sites, individual source code lines, and (sets of) array references. At each level, the metrics describe useful computation time as well as communication overhead, and, when applicable, are computed separately for inclusive and exclusive costs (i.e., including and excluding the corresponding cost incurred in descendent procedures). Finally, the metrics also include data on the relative frequency of remote array references to different sections of a distributed array.

Currently, our system supports visualization of only a small subset of the performance information computed. Our preliminary efforts have focused on integrating performance data with the Rice D editor. Below, we briefly illustrate our integration of performance information in the D editor; in Sec. 1.5 we describe integration plans for the Pablo performance environment.

The initial dynamic performance information in the D editor provides one of the simplest and most useful displays of dynamic performance data, namely profiling information showing the location of principal bottlenecks in the program. The overview pane of the editor (Figure 1.6) uses colored bars to present the computation and communication cost of the individual procedures and loops, relative to the full program. The blue bars (in the left column) show procedure invocation lifetimes, where the light bars represent the inclusive procedure lifetimes and dark bars represent the exclusive procedure lifetimes. The bars are normalized relative to the program's total computation time. The pink bars (in the right column) show similar metrics for the communication overhead due to compiler-synthesized message passing in loops as well as procedures. The system uses the mapping between messages and source references described in the static SDDF file to attribute the communication overhead to specific statements and (by aggregating these) to specific loops and procedures at the source level. Using the static information from the compiler, the editor also directly shows the specific loop-carried, cross-processor dependence that inhibited parallelism and required the pipelined communication. In addition, it also shows the pattern of communication associated with that loop (in this case, the pipelined shift described in Sec. 1.2.3), the array sections involved in the communication, and the fraction of total execution time and of total communication time spent in this communication. Thus, even with the limited correlation of static and dynamic data represented by the visualization primitives shown in the figure, the system is able to convey to the programmer the location, relative impact, and causes of communication overhead, all in terms of the source program most familiar to the programmer.

1.3.4 Compiler Self-Tuning of Pipelined Computation

In cases where low-level details of compiled code must be tuned to obtain an efficient program, it is important that the compiler carry out this tuning with as little user intervention as possible. Such compiler self-tuning typically requires computation and communication cost estimates that can be obtained using a combination of static and dynamic information.

Selecting the blocking granularity of pipelined computations (the parameter B in Figure 1.3) offers an important opportunity for self-tuning. Many researchers have developed simple as well as sophisticated models to compute the optimal block-size from parameters describing the computation and communication cost as functions of block size in each pipeline stage [5,6,12,13,18,11]. Any such model essentially chooses the granularity to balance the loss of parallelism in the initial and final phases of a pipeline when only a few processors are busy, against the communication overhead in the middle interval which is fully parallel (see the illustration on the right in Figure 1.7). The length of the initial and final phases is directly proportional to the pipeline granularity, whereas a component of the communication overhead in the middle interval is inversely proportional to the pipeline granularity. We derive a simple model to pick the block size under the simplifying assumption that the pipeline stages are perfectly balanced, i.e., every processor performs identical computations and communication time is identical between every pair of adjacent processors. In practice, imbalance or variability in computation time, communication overhead, or communication latency can cause pipeline delays. However, such delays are often data or timing dependent, so we choose to ignore their effects in our model.

Our model is as follows. Consider an $N_1 \times N_2$ matrix partitioned blockwise in the first dimension among P processors. The pipeline granularity B, $1 \leq B \leq N_2$, is the number of columns to compute in each pipeline stage. The total number of stages in the pipeline is N_2/B. The total number of

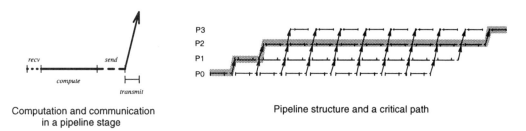

Computation and communication
in a pipeline stage

Pipeline structure and a critical path

Figure 1.7: Simplified view of a one-dimensional pipeline.

bytes of data transmitted per stage is $m_0 B$, where m_0 denotes the number of bytes per array element communicated. Using our model, we determine the optimal value of B, denoted B_{opt}, for which the total execution time of the pipeline is minimized. The total pipeline execution time can be computed as the length of any critical path through the pipeline. Under our assumption that the pipeline stages are perfectly balanced, many different critical paths exist, one of which is shown in Figure 1.7. The execution time along this critical path can be computed as follows (where processors are numbered $0 \ldots P-1$):

$$
\begin{aligned}
T_{pipe} \;=\; & \text{time until processor } P-2 \text{ starts computing } + \\
& \text{time for processor } P-2 \text{ to finish } N_2/B \text{ pipeline stages } + \\
& \text{time for processor } P-1 \text{ to receive its last message and complete} \\
& \text{its last stage}
\end{aligned}
$$

We express these quantities in terms of the send and receive overhead per pipeline stage and the computation time per pipeline stage, where each of these terms is written as a linear function of B. The linear and constant coefficients of these linear functions, along with N_1, N_2, and P, become the input parameters of the model. The resulting expression for T_{pipe} is in terms of these parameters, and differentiating this expression gives the value B_{opt} where $T_{pipe}(B)$ is minimized. The details are omitted and are available elsewhere [1].

To apply the model in practice, the input parameters mentioned above must be estimated or measured. In general, the coefficients for send and receive overhead can be treated as fixed for a particular system and measured once. The coefficients for computation time per pipeline stage may be more difficult to predict accurately. Initially, the compiler might use estimates of these parameters to compute a block size but could subsequently use measured values of these parameters to compute a "more optimal" block size and recompile the program.

We applied the above model (manually) to tune the forward and reverse pipelines in Erlebacher. The compiler currently chooses an arbitrary value of 8 for the block size. From a single execution of the program on 8 processors with an input matrix of $64 \times 64 \times 64$, we measured the requisite model parameters, except that we assumed that the loop has no fixed computation cost per pipeline stage. The model predicted the optimal block size to be $B_{opt} = 88.0$. We recompiled the program with an increased block size of $B = 64$. (We did not use the actual value of $B_{opt} = 88$ because any value other than a multiple or sub-multiple of 64 would have substantially complicated code generation.) On 8 processors, the measured execution time of each pipeline improved by an average of 34.9 percent while that of the overall program improved by 15 percent. Perhaps the key point, here, however is that the entire procedure used to apply the model is mechanical and can be applied automatically by the compiler with appropriate support from the performance environment to obtain the requisite parameters. Thus, substantial improvements in performance can be obtained after a subsequent compilation, with no intervention from the programmer. Such performance tuning support in the environment will be essential if the programmer is to be truly shielded from the low-level and architecture-specific details of parallelism and communication.

1.4   Related Work

Most tools for dynamic performance analysis of parallel programs focus on those with explicit parallelism and communication. A few performance tools for high-level languages include Prism [20] and NV [8] for CM-Fortran, the MPP-Apprentice performance tool for C, Fortran and Fortran 90 on the Cray T3D [21], and Forge90 [3] for Fortran 90 and HPF. These tools share the goal of presenting source-level performance information.

Prism provides statement-level performance annotations of CM-Fortran. The lack of aggressive optimization in the CM-Fortran compiler, however, makes it relatively easy to map communication costs back to the statement responsible. NV provides similar source-level feedback, but also uses the CM-Fortran compiler symbol table to aggregate communication costs per data object, which they demonstrate is useful for understanding the causes of performance bottlenecks.

Cray's MPP Apprentice is the most similar to ours in their approach to supporting source-level performance analysis in the presence of aggressive optimization. The tool relies on compiler support to track the effect of complex scalar optimizations and maintain a mapping of basic blocks in the source to basic blocks in the optimized code. They record this mapping in a compiler information file which is used by the performance tool to assign measured performance costs to the high level source. This mapping approach is very similar to ours, but the MPP Apprentice focuses on scalar optimizations.

Forge90 supports limited source-level performance feedback for HPF at the level of calls to communication primitives inserted by the compiler. In particular, they present performance costs to the programmer primarily in terms of the communication operations inserted just before each loop. (Their compiler only parallelizes loops with independent iterations, i.e., from which all communication operations can be hoisted out.) To our knowledge, they do not correlate these costs with the references, arrays, or distributions in the source code.

The static SDDF file generated by the Fortran 77D compiler includes explicit information relating source references, statements, and data objects to compiler-synthesized communication. The file also includes semantic information such as data dependences, buffering for individual messages, and identification of redistribution costs, that can be used to provide more comprehensive and intelligent dynamic performance feedback. To our knowledge, access to such information is not available in other dynamic performance analysis tools for parallel program.

Finally, as described in Sec. 1.3.4, a number of previous papers have described performance models for optimizing pipeline granularity. The only compiler implementation of such a model we are aware of is in the Paradigm compiler, which uses static estimates of the pipeline model parameters to apply the model [11]. Our integration of performance support and compilation enables us to use dynamic measurements of parameter values that are difficult to estimate (particularly, the computation time per pipeline stage), and we intend to investigate whether this yields higher performance through more accurate estimates of the optimal block size.

1.5 Summary and Future Directions

The advantages of abstract, high-level programming languages like High Performance Fortran will be fully realized only if programmers are able to understand and tune the performance of their applications without having to understand the details of the compiler-synthesized, explicitly parallel code. In such languages, however, the large semantic gap between the programmer's source code and the compiled code make it difficult to reason about performance during code development or to interpret measured performance data and relate it to the high-level source code. Alleviating these obstacles to the development of efficient, data-parallel programs requires extensive integration of compilation and performance analysis. In particular, compilers must provide information about the relationship between the source and compiled code, and the performance tools must use this information to provide performance feedback closely related to the user's source code. Furthermore, the compiler must assume the responsibility for tuning the synthesized low-level communication patterns.

In this paper we discussed the integration of the University of Illinois' Pablo performance environment and Rice University D compiler. The D compiler generates instrumented code and emits information on code transformations (mapping information) as well as other results of compiler analysis in the Pablo performance data meta-format. During code development, the results of static compiler analysis provide a qualitative understanding about parallelism and communication synthesized by the compiler, to aid algorithm and code design. During performance tuning, runtime measurements from an instrumented program are correlated with the original Fortran D code using the mapping information previously recorded at compile-time. In conjunction with other results of static compiler analysis, the performance tool is able to provide sophisticated, explanatory feedback on parallel program performance characteristics at the source-level.

Although the data correlation techniques described in Sec. 1.3.3 have been tested and their utility validated, some features are not yet implemented. One priority in our future work is to implement the remaining static SDDF records within the compiler. These include correlation of buffer copying calls with the corresponding message calls, and the static loop records for describing loop mapping information between source and SPMD loops. Some extensions to the correlation techniques described in Sec. 1.3.3 are also under consideration. Perhaps the most important is to add static records to describe the overall array sections communicated in a loop or loop nest so as to reduce the total volume of symbolic data.

The high-level performance display of Figure 1.6 exploits only a small fraction of the static and dynamic data correlations possible via our instrumentation infrastructure. In particular, we currently cannot display dynamic program behavior except via the Pablo environment's dynamic graphics. However, these displays do not tie performance data to specific Fortran D source code locations. Similarly, we lack displays of array reference patterns, although we have the requisite data to show the temporal and spatial pattern of array references due to specific Fortran D code fragments. To redress these limitations, we are developing a comprehensive performance data browser capable of displaying performance metrics and data reference patterns computed over user-specified code regions and execution intervals.

In addition, we believe an integrated performance tool must support performance queries. For example, a user might ask "show the non-local references to array A when function F is called from procedure G." To support this and other queries, the performance browser must be capable of extracting the relevant information from its data base of static, symbolic, and dynamic performance data and displaying that information in meaningful ways (e.g., with an array reference visualization).

From handling performance queries against a data base of existing data, a natural next step is handling queries about hypothetical program executions. By combining dynamic performance data with compilation information, an integrated system should be able to predict performance more accurately than is possible with dynamic data alone. For example, it should be possible to answer approximately a query such as "how would array reference locality change if array A is distributed by columns rather than rows?" by combining the Fortran D compiler's understanding of array dependences and loop bounds with dynamic data on past reference patterns.

References

[1] ADVE, V. S., KOELBEL, C., AND MELLOR-CRUMMEY, J. M., "Performance Analysis of Data-Parallel Programs," Tech. Rep. CRPC-TR94405, Center for Research on Parallel Computation, Rice University, May 1994.

[2] ADVE, V. S., WANG, J.-C., MELLOR-CRUMMEY, J. M., REED, D. A., ANDERSON, M., AND KENNEDY, K., "An Integrated Compilation and Performance Analysis Environment for Data-Parallel Programs," Tech. Rep., Center for Research on Parallel Computation, Rice University, May 1994.

[3] APPLIED PARALLEL RESEARCH. *Forge 90 Distributed Memory Parallelizer: User's Guide*, Version 8.0 Ed. Placerville, CA, 1992.

[4] AYDT, R. A., "SDDF: The Pablo Self-Describing Data Format," Tech. Rep., Department of Computer Science, University of Illinois, Apr. 1994.

[5] C.-T.KING, W.-H. AND NI, L. M., "Pipelined Data-Parallel Algorithms: Part II–Design," *IEEE Transactions on Parallel and Distributed Systems 1*, **4**, Oct. 1990.

[6] IRVIN, R. B. AND MILLER, B. P., "A Performance Tool for High-Level Parallel Programming Languages," in *Programming Environments for Massively Parallel Distributed Systems*, Basel, Switzerland, 1994, Birkhauser Verlag.

[7] MELLOR-CRUMMEY, J. M., ADVE, V. S., AND KOELBEL, C., "The Compiler's Role in Analysis and Tuning of Data-Parallel Programs," in *Proceedings of The Second Workshop on Environments and Tools for Parallel Scientific Computing*, Townsend, TN, May 1994, 211–220. Also available via anonymous ftp from softlib.cs.rice.edu in `pub/CRPC-TRs/reports/CRPC-TR94405.ps`.

[8] MILLER, B. P., CLARK, M., HOLLINGSWORTH, J., KIERSTEAD, S., LIM, S.-S., AND TORZEWSKI, T., "IPS-2: The Second Generation of a Parallel Program Measurement System," *IEEE Transactions on Computers 1*, **2**, Apr. 1990, 206–217.

[9] PALERMO, D. J., SU, E., CHANDY, J. A., AND BANNERJEE, P., "Communication Optmizations Used in the Paradigm Compiler for Distributed-Memory Machines," in *Proceedings of the 1994 International Conference on Parallel Processing*, St. Charles, IL, Aug. 1994, IEEE Computer Society Press, II:1–8.

[10] REED, D. A., "Performance Instrumentation Techniques for Parallel Systems," in *Models and Techniques for Performance Evaluation of Computer and Communications Systems*, L. Donatiello and R. Nelson, Eds., Springer-Verlag Lecture Notes in Computer Science, 1993.

[11] REED, D. A., "Experimental Performance Analysis of Parallel Systems: Techniques and Open Problems," in *Proceedings of the 7th Inter-*

national Conference on Modelling Techniques and Tools for Computer Performance Evaluation, May 1994.

[12] REED, D. A., AYDT, R. A., NOE, R. J., ROTH, P. C., SHIELDS, K. A., SCHWARTZ, B. W., AND TAVERA, L. F., "Scalable Performance Analysis: the Pablo Performance Analysis Environment," in *Proceedings of the Scalable Parallel Libraries Conference*, A. Skjellum, Ed., IEEE Computer Society, 1993.

[13] RIES, B., ANDERSON, R., AULD, W., BREAZEAL, D., CALLAGHAN, K., RICHARDS, E., AND SMITH, W., "The Paragon Performance Monitoring Environment," in *Proceedings of Supercomputing '93*, Nov. 1993, Association for Computing Machinery, 850–859.

[14] SHIELDS, K. A., TAVERA, L. F., SCULLIN, W. H., ELFORD, C. L., AND REED, D. A., "Virtual Reality for Parallel Computer Systems Performance Analysis," in *SIGGRAPH '94 Visual Proceedings*, July 1994, Association for Computing Machinery.

[15] TMC, *Prism User's Guide, V1.2*, Thinking Machines Corporation, Cambridge, Massachusetts, Mar. 1993.

[16] WILLIAMS, W., HOEL, T., AND PASE, D., "The MPP Apprentice Performance Tool: Delivering the Performance of the CRAY T3D," in *Programming Environments for Massively Parallel Distributed Systems*, Basel, Switzerland, 1994, Birkhauser Verlag.

[17] WINSTEAD, C., PRITCHARD, H. P., AND McKOY, V., "Tuning I/O Performance on the Paragon: Fun with Pablo and Norma," In *these proceedings*. IEEE Computer Society, 1995.

Integrating A Debugger and A Performance Tool for Steering

Krishna Kunchithapadam and Barton P. Miller
Computer Sciences Department
University of Wisconsin
Madison, Wisconsin 53706

Abstract

Steering is a performance optimization idiom applicable to many problem domains. It allows control and performance tuning to take place during program execution. Steering emphasizes the optimization and control of the performance of a program using mechanisms that are external to the program. Performance measurement tools and symbolic debuggers already independently provide some of the mechanisms needed to implement a steering tool. In this paper we describe a configuration that integrates a performance tool, Paradyn, and a debugger to build a steering environment.

The steering configuration allows fast prototyping of steering policies, and provides support for both interactive and automated steering.

1.1 Introduction

Performance optimization is a non-trivial activity that programmers perform. The canonical performance optimization cycle (Figure 1.1) can be divided into four steps:

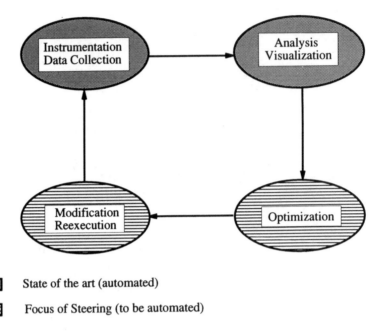

State of the art (automated)

Focus of Steering (to be automated)

Figure 1.1: The performance optimization cycle.

- *Instrumentation and Data Collection*: where programmers or tools instrument programs to collect performance data.

- *Analysis and Visualization*: where programmers use analysis and visualization tools to display and interpret the collected performance data.

- *Optimization*: where programmers choose ways to improve the performance of their programs.

- *Modification*: where programmers make optimizations either to the source code or to running programs.

Many performance tools have been built to assist programmers in automating the steps of Instrumentation and Data Collection, and Analysis and Visualization. However, programmers for the most part currently use ad-hoc and manual techniques during the steps of Optimization and Modification. *Steering* is an idiom for performance optimization that focuses on the Optimization and Modification steps of the performance optimization cycle.

Steering is different from adaptive algorithms in that it is an idiom that emphasizes the *external* optimization and control of programs. In adaptive algorithms, programmers write optimization code that is linked with their application. At runtime, the optimization code makes performance optimization decisions and modifies the execution of the application.

In a technique that uses external control, the application does not contain code that makes optimization decisions. External mechanisms are used to both make optimization decisions and to modify the application itself to effect any changes.

The primary advantage of external optimization and control is that it allows programmers to prototype their optimization policies without going through the potentially long compilation-reexecution cycle each time the optimization code needs to be changed. External control also does not preclude the future inclusion of a suitable optimization policy into the application for production use.

Even when steering is the performance optimization idiom used by programmers, the mechanisms and tools used for steering are often not generic. In this paper, we show how to combine the mechanisms of a performance tool that does external measurement of programs and a debugger that provides external modification of programs into a steering tool that can be used for external optimization and control. In addition to the steering configuration, we also identify a programming model based on the notion of tunable performance knobs that allows a programmer to separate the functionality of an application from its optimization. The use of tunable knobs in an application can simplify the specification and even the automation of performance steering.

1.1.1 Goals of Steering

Steering includes the set of activities that are performed at program execution time and that modify the subsequent behavior of the program. Support from compilers and performance tools can simplify the programmer's task of steering a program. For example, compilers may generate data dependence information into symbol tables that a tool like a debugger can use in modifying a program. Information about compiler optimizations allows programmers to choose appropriate steering modifications for their programs. Performance tools provide a steering tool with performance data about a program; the steering tool can then use this information to initiate steering actions when needed.

The steering tool also needs the support of programmers to effect steering changes to an application. Since steering emphasizes external control, the programmer needs to indicate to the steering tool what parts of the program should be modified (and in what manner) to steer a program. Programmers also need to structure their applications so that steering actions can be specified to a tool in a generic manner. We design a programming model based on the notion of tunable performance knobs that allows both external control of an application's performance via a steering tool and the simple specification of steering actions using a predicate-action idiom.

In this paper, we present the design of a generic steering tool by making use of mechanisms already present in some performance measurement tools and in symbolic breakpoint debuggers. The mechanisms for steering need to provide support for *when* a program should be steered, *what* should be modified to effect the steering, and *how* the change should be made to the executing program. Performance tools can help answer the when and what questions while a debugger can help answer the how question. A steering tool that is built by integrating a performance tool and a debugger can be used for both interactive and automated performance steering.

A performance measurement tool is used in the Instrumentation and Data Collection, and Analysis and Visualization steps of the performance optimization cycle. The programmer uses the results of the analysis to decide on an optimization. The steering tool then invokes a symbolic debugger that allows the programmer to make modifications to an application to effect the steering changes.

A program needs to be suitably structured for a programmer to be able to steer its performance. The design of programs for steering (for example, through the use of tunable performance knobs) is part of our current research, but is outside the scope of this paper.

1.1.2   Examples of Steering

There are many examples of performance steering. Some of the techniques developed for steering are ad-hoc or domain-specific, while others are of wider applicability. In this section, we will illustrate the technique of steering using a small set of examples.

Loop convergence control: A simple example of performance steering is in the domain of numerical computations. An iterative algorithm may use a loop convergence criteria to terminate. If the convergence threshold can be changed to improve performance without affecting the correctness of the algorithm, then the program may dynamically change the convergence criterion for better performance. More importantly, if a large number of iterative algorithms are combined in a multi-stage computation, a faster convergence at an earlier stage even at the cost of a somewhat poorer solution may be compensated for by a later stage.

Load balance, degree of parallelism: Load balance is an important determinant of performance in irregular applications [2]. It may also be possible to modify the performance of an algorithm by changing the amount of parallelism that is used. A tool that allows a programmer to dynamically create or destroy threads and to move tasks between different threads can be used to improve the performance of the application.

Performance knobs in databases: Some database servers are designed to have a set of tunable performance knobs that control the allocation of resources in the server [1]. The server periodically executes a tuning algorithm to choose a setting for the performance knobs (and hence resource allocations) that improves the performance of the server or satisfies some goal-requirements of the transactions that arrive at the server. This is an example where the application is structured to facilitate performance steering by the separation of the functional and performance code, and by the use of tunable knobs.

Array distributions: The performance of data-parallel programs is sensitive to the layout of array data across the nodes of a parallel machine [4]. Choosing good data layouts is non-trivial. A tool that measures array data related communication, presents such communication information to a programmer and accepts programmer hints for redistributing arrays into a more optimized layout performs steering. In this application domain, the steering tool needs support from the compiler and the runtime system. It is also possible for the steering tool to automate the process of choosing optimized data layouts using knowledge of the problem domain.

Changing algorithms: It is possible in suitably structured applications to change algorithms being used at runtime. For example, if a program invokes an algorithm via a function pointer, a steering tool can be used to change the function pointer to point to an function that is more suitable for the current performance context. Algorithms can also be changed by loading different dynamic libraries.

In the next section we describe the mechanisms present in the Paradyn performance tool that are relevant to performance steering. We then describe a steering configuration that uses the mechanisms of Paradyn and a symbolic debugger for performance steering.

1.2   Paradyn as a Performance Tool

Paradyn [5] is a performance tool based on a novel mechanism for automating the search for performance bottlenecks and low-overhead instrumentation techniques [3]. Paradyn is also extensible – any tool external to Paradyn may access the performance information that Paradyn collects via a well-defined *visualization* interface. The combination of the search mechanism, dynamic instrumentation, and the visualization interface allows us to use Paradyn as the performance measurement tool in a steering environment. This section provides a description of mechanisms of Paradyn that are relevant to performance steering.

1.2.1   The Metric-Focus Abstraction

Paradyn models an application as a collection of resources. Any program object for which performance data can be collected is a candidate resource. Examples of program resources include processes, machines, procedures, code blocks, variables, locks, barriers, message tags, memory, and caches. Resources are arranged in hierarchies by resource type. For example, a resource type of *Procedure* contains resources corresponding to the different procedures in a program, and each procedure contains resources corresponding to different code blocks that comprise the associated procedure. Similarly, a resource type of *SyncObject* contains resource types *MessageTag, Barrier,* and *Lock*, each of which contain resources corresponding to the individual instances of message tags, barriers, and locks respectively. A *focus* is a set of resources, one from each resource hierarchy. An example of a focus is *message tag* 9999 *used in procedure* foobar *of process* 2345 *on machine* host12.

Performance metrics correspond to numeric values (in suitable units) that characterize some aspect of the performance of a program. Metrics may be computed for any valid focus. Examples of metrics include *CPU time* and *message count*.

Paradyn collects and provides performance data in *metric-focus* combinations. An example of a metric-focus pair is *message count for message tag* 9999 *used in procedure* foobar *of process* 2345 *on machine* host12. Metric-focus combinations are used by Paradyn to guide the search for performance bottlenecks. External tools also obtain performance data from Paradyn's visualization interface in terms of metric-focus lists. The steering tool is organized as an external visualization process that communicates with Paradyn, using the metric-focus abstraction to present performance data to a user.

1.2.2 Dynamic Instrumentation

Along with the complexity of characterizing the behavior of a large application comes the problem of measuring performance data that is needed to perform the above characterization. As the size and execution-time of a program increases, so does the volume of performance data that can be collected. It is often not possible nor profitable to collect comprehensive performance data about a program; it is difficult to store large volumes of data and to present them to a user in a suitable form. Moreover, any software technique for collecting performance data from an application perturbs the application—the greater the amount of data collected, the larger the potential perturbation. Large instrumentation overhead may even result in performance data being collected in an environment that no longer matches that of the uninstrumented program, effectively rendering any performance measurement and analysis useless.

Paradyn uses *dynamic instrumentation* to reduce the volume of performance data that is collected, by postponing performance measurement till the demand for it arises. Dynamic instrumentation modifies the code and data segments of an executing program to collect performance metrics for foci. Since the instrumentation is made at execution time, programmers need not modify their source code, or use special compiler or linker options to build their binaries.

Paradyn uses dynamic instrumentation in conjunction with its automated search mechanism to focus instrumentation to restricted parts of a program. When a program starts to execute, dynamic instrumentation is used to collect very high-level performance information at a low volume and perturbation overhead. As the search along metric-focus pairs is refined, dynamic instrumentation is used to refine (by addition, deletion and modification) the instrumentation in the application to collect detailed performance data, but for a smaller program focus. The combination of a refined focus and detailed performance data keeps the instrumentation overhead and volume of performance information under control.

Finally, dynamic instrumentation can also measure its own overhead. This instrumentation overhead is presented as a performance metric to Paradyn's search mechanism. This allows the search process to control the amount of instrumentation added to a program (and the associated overheads) using a cost model.

A steering tool uses dynamic instrumentation to enable the collection of performance data needed to trigger steering activities, and to disable the collection of the data at the end of a steering session.

1.2.3 The Visualization Interface

Performance data that Paradyn (or any performance tool) collects can be used in many ways. Paradyn uses the data in conjunction with its search mechanism to search for performance bottlenecks. The same performance data can be visualized in different ways. Rather than provide a fixed set of visualizations, Paradyn provides access to the performance data it collects via the *visualization interface*. Any external process that wishes to consume performance data (not necessarily for visualization) can initiate the collection (via dynamic instrumentation) of performance data for valid metric-focus lists using this interface.

A steering tool can therefore use this interface to prototype steering policies without having to modify any code in Paradyn. Such an interface also imposes minimal restrictions on the structure of the steering tool.

1.3 The Steering Configuration

The steering configuration that we propose integrates the mechanisms of Paradyn and a debugger. Paradyn is used to collect performance data; optionally the steering tool can also use the performance search mechanisms of Paradyn during steering. The command interface of the debugger is used to make changes to a program and effect steering changes. During a steering session, there is a transfer of control between Paradyn and the debugger. The steering tool manages the control transfer, but the user of the steering tool needs to specify to the steering tool when to transfer control from Paradyn to the debugger. The user hints can be coded into the steering tool or be specified as a set of rules that are interpreted by the steering tool. The dynamic instrumentation interface of Paradyn requires a small modification to allow a debugger to attach to a program and perform steering changes.

Figure 1.2 describes the steering configuration.

1.3.1 Control of the Steering Tool

The steering configuration above does not include any policies for steering an application; it is a collection of mechanisms that can be used by the programmer. The simplest use of the steering tool is for interactive steering. However, the same configuration can also be used for automated steering.

In interactive steering, Paradyn measures the performance of an application and searches for types of bottlenecks specified by the programmer. When a performance bottleneck is detected, the steering tool alerts the programmer and transfers control to the debugger. The programmer can then make steering changes to the application and transfer control back to Paradyn. Alternatively, the programmer can bypass the search mechanisms of Paradyn and write performance search strategies into the steering tool using the performance data available via the visualization interface of Paradyn.

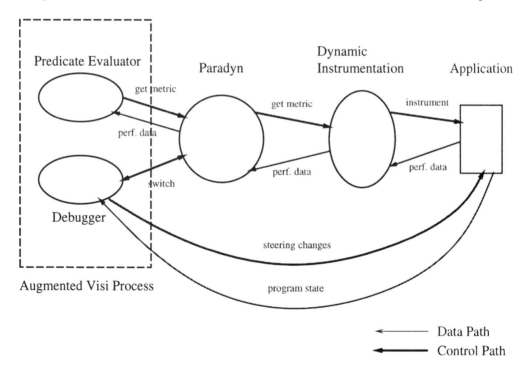

Figure 1.2: The steering configuration. See color plate III.

In automated steering, the programmer provides hints to the steering tool about what constitutes a performance problem, and how changes should be made to the application (i.e., what debugger commands should be invoked) to improve performance. The steering tool can use any algorithm to detect when the performance problems specified by the programmer occur and then automatically invoke the steering actions.

1.4   Conclusions

Performance steering is a runtime-based performance optimization idiom being used in many application domains that emphasize the external optimization and control of programs. A steering tool needs mechanisms to determine when a program should be steered, what needs to be changed, and how the steering should be effected. Performance measurement tools and debuggers already independently provide some of these mechanisms.

Performance measurement tools provide performance data and help answer the *when* question. Debuggers provide commands to modify the state of an executing program. Debugging commands can be used to answer the *how* question. Programmer hints specify what needs to be changed in a program to effect steering.

We show a steering configuration that combines the use of Paradyn as the performance measurement tool and any symbolic debugger as the modification tool. We also suggest a programming model based on tunable performance knobs that allows steering actions to be specified in a generic manner and simplifies the task of steering programs.

References

[1] BROWN, KURT P., MEHTA MANISH, CAREY, MICHAEL J., AND LIVNY, MIRON., "Towards Automated Performance Tuning for Complex Workloads," in *Proceedings of the 20th International VLDB Conference*, Santiago, Chile, September 1994.

[2] EISENHAUER, G., GU, WEIMING, SCHWAN, KARSTEN, AND MALLAVARUPU, NIRU., "Falcon-Toward Interactive Parallel Programs: The Online Steering of a Molecular Dynamics Application," in *Pro-*

ceedings of the 3rd International Symposium on High-Performance Distributed Computing, San Francisco, CA, August 1994.

[3] HOLLINGSWORTH, JEFFREY K., CARGILLE, JON, AND MILLER, BARTON P., "Dynamic Program Instrumentation for Scalable Performance Tools," in *Proceedings of the 1994 Scaleable Highe Performance Computing Conference*, Knoxville, TN, May 1994, 841–850.

[4] KUNCHITHAPADAM, KRISHNA AND MILLER, BARTON P., "Optimizing Array Distributions in Data-Parallel Programs," in A. Nicolau, D. Gelernter, D. Gross, and D. Padua, Eds., *Languages and Compilers for Parallel Computing, LNCS*. Springer-Verlag, 1994.

[5] MILLER, BARTON P., HOLLINGSWORTH, JEFFREY K., IRVIN, R. BRUCE, CARGILLE, JONATHAN, KUNCHITHAPADAM, KRISHNA, KARAVANIC, KAREN, NEWHALL, TIA, AND CALLAGHAN, MARK, "The Paradyn Performance Measurement Tools," in *Review for the IEEE special issue on Parallel and Distributed Systems*, October 1994.

Visualization, Debugging, and Performance in PVM

G. A. Geist,[1] James Kohl, and Philip Papadopoulos
Oak Ridge National Laboratory
Oak Ridge, Tennessee 37831-6367

Abstract

PVM has grown to become the de facto standard for distributed computing around the world. With the increasing numbers of users and applications utilizing the PVM environment, it becomes more important to have debugging and performance tuning tools that work with PVM. This paper describes our most recent developments in these two areas. For PVM debugging we have created a standard interface that allows existing parallel debuggers to attach to and debug PVM applications. For performance tuning we have created the XPVM graphical user interface which displays both real-time and post-mortem animations of message traffic and machine utilization by PVM applications. We also present our latest research into improving the performance of PVM.

1.1 Introduction

With thousands of users worldwide, PVM (Parallel Virtual Machine) [3] has become the de facto standard for distributed computing. The PVM software

---

[1]This work was supported in part by the Applied Mathematical Sciences subprogram of the Office of Energy Research, U.S. Department of Energy, under Contract DE-AC05-84OR21400, and in part by the the National Science Foundation Science and Technology Center Cooperative Agreement No. CCR-8809615.

package allows a collection of UNIX computers connected to a network to be used as a single, large, parallel distributed memory computer. PVM supplies functions to start tasks in parallel across this virtual machine, allows these tasks to send data between themselves, and coordinates their parallel execution. A wide variety of computers (including serial computers, vector computers, and even shared or distributed memory parallel computers) can make up a user's personal virtual machine.

The most popular use of PVM is the utilization of a small number of high performance workstations to achieve performance comparable to that of a supercomputer (at significantly less cost). The exponential growth in the use of PVM is due to its portability across many different computers, its robustness and ease of installation, and its perception as a standard parallel programming interface. PVM has already outlasted several parallel computer vendors.

Development of PVM at Oak Ridge National Laboratory (ORNL) began in 1989 and has now grown into a research project that includes researchers at ORNL, the University of Tennessee, Emory University, and Carnegie Mellon University. In addition to providing support for PVM, the PVM research team continues to explore and incorporate new features into PVM. The research directions are dictated by feedback from PVM users and by changing network and computing technology.

PVM has made parallel computing available to a much wider audience than the programming interfaces supplied by individual computer vendors. This means more people with little experience in parallel programming are writing their first "buggy" parallel codes.

When their programs do not execute as expected, they wonder, "What is going on?" They scratch their heads and wish for some way to see what is happening in their parallel programs. When their programs hang or get the wrong results, they wonder, "What went wrong?" They begin the tedious process of debugging the parallel code and wishing for an easy to use parallel debugger. When their programs finally run, they ask "How can I make the programs run faster?"

The research described in this paper focuses on visualization, debugging, and performance enhancements to PVM. In the next section we describe the performance monitoring program, XPVM. In Sec. 1.3 we describe several new internal interfaces built into PVM to allow third party debuggers to work with PVM applications. Sec. 1.4 presents some new and planned performance enhancements to PVM. Conclusions are presented in Sec. 1.5.

1.2 XPVM Visualization Package

XPVM is a graphical user interface for PVM. Even though the primary function of XPVM is to visualize what is going on inside a PVM application, the interface actually performs four separate functions. First, XPVM is a graphical console allowing a user to start PVM, add hosts, spawn tasks, reset the virtual machine, and stop PVM all by clicking buttons. Second, XPVM is a real-time performance monitor. While an application is running, XPVM displays a space-time diagram of the parallel tasks showing when they are computing, communicating, or idle. The display also animates the message traffic between tasks. Third, XPVM is a "call level" debugger. The user can see the last PVM call made by each task as the application is running. Fourth, XPVM is a post-mortem analysis tool. XPVM writes out a trace file that can be replayed, stopped, stepped, and rewound in order to study the behavior of a completed parallel run.

XPVM is built on TCL/TK [7], which is a library for developing X-Windows applications. TCL makes it easy to change, customize, and extend the XPVM interface. Figure 1.1 shows a snapshot of the XPVM interface during use.

The interface is divided into four parts. The top row of buttons performs the basic functions of the textual PVM console. Clicking on **Hosts** pulls down a menu of hosts that the user may add or delete by clicking on individual names. Clicking on **Tasks** pulls down a menu that lets the user spawn one or more tasks on the virtual machine. Pressing the **Reset** button pulls down a menu that allows the user to reset the views, tasks, or the entire virtual machine. The **Quit** button allows the user to get an application running and then quit XPVM, leaving the application and PVM running. The **Halt** button kills all running tasks, shuts down PVM, and then exits XPVM. The **Help** button provides a menu of help items ranging from general overview to specific button's functionality.

The second part is the network view. This scrolling window shows each of the hosts currently in the virtual machine and the network between them. Each host is represented by an icon that includes the PVM architecture name. The host name is listed underneath each icon. The icons are colored according to the state of the host. White indicates that there are no PVM tasks on the host. Green indicates that at least one PVM task is computing, and yellow indicates that all PVM tasks on the host are doing communication. The

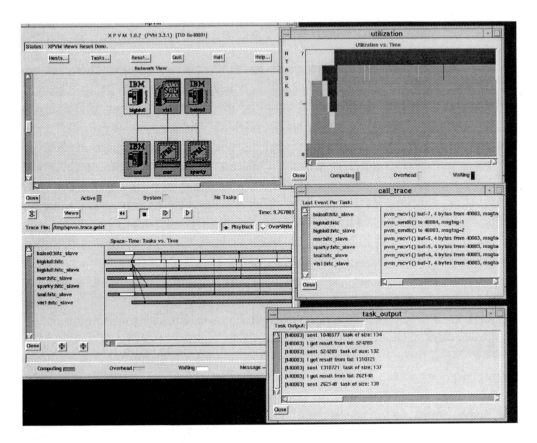

Figure 1.1: Snapshot of the XPVM interface being used for real-time monitoring of a distributed PVM application. See color plate IV.

network view gives the user a quick way to check if the hosts are efficiently utilized by observing how much of the time all the host icons are green.

The third part of XPVM is the view controls. This section of XPVM allows the user to specify a tracefile name, to pop up additional views, to control the post-mortem play of a tracefile using standard stereo tape player buttons, and to view the execution time as recorded in the tracefile.

The fourth part is the space-time view. This window lists all of the PVM tasks and on which host they are running. The list is sorted by host, to make it easy to see if one host is unduly loaded with a disproportionate number of tasks. The horizontal axis represents time. Beside each task a bar is drawn. The bar is green when the task is computing, yellow when it is sending or receiving messages, and white when it is idle waiting for a message. Messages between tasks are shown as red arrows between bars with end points reflecting the sending and receiving times. The view can be zoomed in or out to see details not visible at the current magnification. If the mouse pointer is brought into the window, a vertical blue line follows the pointer and the time display shows the relative position of the blue line. In addition, if any feature in the window is clicked on, for example, a red message arrow, then a description of this feature is displayed at the bottom of the window. For a message, this would include the sender, receiver, size of the message, and the message tag used.

There are several other views that are selectable from the **Views** menu in the view control panel. These include utilization, call-level debugger, and task output. By adding all additional views through this menu, XPVM's visualization capability can be expanded without affecting the primary interface. Sophisticated users could even add their own custom views to XPVM.

A utilization view is present in every performance monitoring package. It is a graph of the number of tasks versus time and shows the number of tasks computing, communicating, and idle at each moment. In XPVM the utilization view has three additional features. Because the number of tasks in PVM can be dynamic, the scale of the number of tasks changes dynamically during a run (growing but never shrinking). A vertical blue time line follows the mouse pointer in the utilization view exactly as in the space-time view. When this happens, the blue time line is simultaneously displayed in both views so that activities in one view can be correlated to the other. Lastly, when the space-time view is zoomed or scrolled, the utilization view automatically zooms or scrolls to display the same time range.

The call-level debugger is a window with the same list of tasks as in the space-time view. Beside each task is a line of text that displays the last PVM call made by this task with the arguments or return values to this call. This view is particularly useful when trying to determine why or if a parallel program has hung, because the last PVM operation performed by each task is clearly shown.

The task output view allows the PVM user to see the *stdout* output from all tasks spawned through XPVM. Optionally the user may also redirect the output to a file by typing a file name in the blank at the top of this window. This view is very useful for programmers who like to place diagnostic print statements in their programs.

Additional views are planned for future releases. In the future the following views will be added: message queues, network traffic/hot spots, and hierarchical host views for multiprocessor hosts. Figure 1.2 shows a sketch of what these views will look like.

The message queue view is a dynamic display of the number of bytes and messages building up in the queues for each task. Since communication in PVM is asynchronous, messages can be sent long before they are received. In addition messages can arrive from several sources faster than a single task can receive them. In both cases the messages are buffered in queues inside PVM. Understanding the behavior of these queues during an application's execution can help in performance tuning and debugging. There is also the potential for the size of a queue to grow so large that it consumes all available memory on a given host. This view is useful for detecting this catastrophic occurence.

The network traffic/hot spots is additional information displayed in the network view by animating the network drawn between the host icons. The instantaneous network volume and bandwidth are displayed on the links between hosts. Color is used to signify the volume of data flowing over a given link. Red means more data, blue means less, and black means no data. The idea is to make it obvious and intuitive where the network "hot spots" are for a given application. The thickness of the links is used to signify the bandwidth being obtained between two hosts. This information is calculated dynamically from the messages being sent in the application and implicitly takes into account the outside loads that may be on the same links. Thicker lines mean there is more bandwidth and thinner lines mean less. This is consistent with the phrase, "drinking through a fire hose."

A hierarchical host view appears when an MPP host icon is clicked. A window appears that mimics the network view in terms of network and host animations except that now the hosts become the individual nodes of the MPP and the network is replaced by an animation of the given MPP's communication network. Examples include grid, bus, crossbar, and tree networks.

Visualization tools such as ParaGraph [4] and Pablo [8] have more than 25 different views selectable by the user. These tools were developed to help parallel programmers do post-mortem analysis on codes run on massively parallel processors (MPP). Many of these views are not meaningful and in fact can be misleading in the heterogeneous distributed computing environment that XPVM is designed to work in. Other views presented by these tools can only be constructed after the code is finished and thus have no real-time equivalents. Presently, all XPVM views can be watched in real-

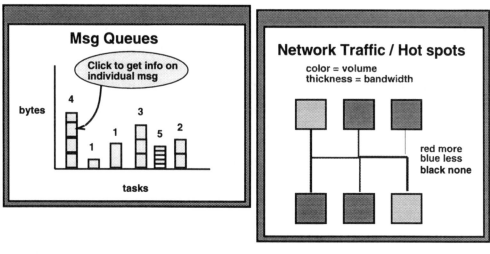

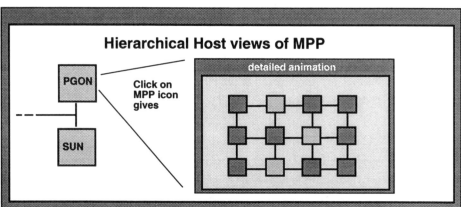

Figure 1.2: Sketch of future views being added to XPVM. Shown are message queue sizes and content, network traffic and hot spots, and hierarchical host views for multiprocessor hosts. See color plate V.

time as the code runs. The tracefile written by XPVM is in SDDF format as defined in Pablo. The Pablo tool has routines to convert to ParaGraph format. Therefore all the power of these analysis tools are available to the PVM user. For these reasons, the number of views available in XPVM has been kept small and focused on the most useful and important information in the PVM environment.

1.3   Debugger Interfaces

In a recent survey by the Ptools consortium it was revealed that 90% of parallel programmers use *PRINT* statements to discover what is happening in their codes. In the PVM environment the use of *PRINT* has been problematic. For example, where should a *PRINT* statement executed on some remote host be sent? The user's local screen? What if there is no local screen? To a log file? On what host? So many questions.

There are two recent additions to the PVM package that address the *PRINT* problem. First, the PVM console allows the user to specify *stdout* redirection to a file or to the console window. This redirection is inherited by all the tasks spawned through the console, and by all the children of these tasks. For situations where the console isn't or can't be used, a new PVM function *pvm_catchout()* has been added. The task that calls this function will receive the *stdout* of all the tasks it spawns. The calling task can then print these messages to a screen or to a file. The ability to see their diagnostic print statements appearing in a window on their local host is enough to satisfy most parallel programmers, as shown by the Ptools survey.

For programmers who wish to use a parallel debugger with PVM, third party debuggers such as TotalView [1] and ParaDyn [5] that work with PVM are now available. A PVM debugger interface was developed so that debugger developers could integrate their products into the PVM environment without having to modify the PVM source.

By calling the PVM function *pvm_reg_tasker*, the debugger can register with PVM as the official task starter on this host. The PVM daemon then defers all task spawning requests to this debugger. In most cases a debugger needs to actually start the tasks it has to debug. Task control can then be done through the third party debugger just like any non-PVM job, while PVM communication continues to go through PVM as usual.

Debuggers can now *attach* to running PVM tasks as well by asking PVM for a task's machine-dependent UNIX pid. This was another feature added to PVM at the request of third party parallel debugger writers.

PVM still maintains its own simple debugger scheme. If a task is spawned with the debug flag set, then PVM starts up a default debugger in a new X-window for each requested task. This scheme is not scalable, but it is effective in the initial stages of coding.

Two additional internal interfaces have been integrated into PVM. These interfaces allow third party resource managers such as Condor [2] and LSF to work with PVM applications. The function *pvm_reg_rm* registers the calling task as responsible for all new task placement into the virtual machine. Once registered, PVM defers all requests to this task. Similarly the function *pvm_reg_hoster* registers the calling task as responsible for managing the host pool, i.e., adding and deleting hosts. When no resource manager or hoster is registered, PVM performs these jobs as usual.

1.4   PVM Performance Enhancements

The PVM team continues to investigate schemes to enhance the performance of the PVM package. One advantage of this research is that any improvements in the performance of PVM automatically help the hundreds of applications written in PVM. This section describes performance features available in the latest version of PVM and experimental features not ready for release.

The communication routines *pvm_psend* and *pvm_precv* combine the initialize, pack, and send operations into a single call reducing the call overhead. The biggest performance gain is seen when using these routines on an MPP. Table 1.1 shows the performance of psend/precv compared to the native csend/crecv on the Intel Paragon. The table illustrates that psend/precv can be as fast as native communication routines on an MPP.

In order to reduce the number of data copies, an *InPlace* packing option was added. With this option the user's data is left in place in the user's memory and not copied into a send buffer. PVM keeps track of what data the user has packed and copies the different pieces directly from the user's memory to the network. This option not only improves the communication speed, but also reduces the buffer space required inside PVM.

Table 1.1 Comparison of PVM and Native Intel Paragon Communication Speeds		
Round trip time (microseconds)		
msg size (bytes)	csend/crecv	psend/precv
8	376	322
800	314	314
8000	670	676
80000	3978	4061

When a message is sent between two processors in an SGI, SUN, or DEC multiprocessor, PVM uses shared-memory to move the data up to ten times faster than PVM's TCP socket implementation (Table 1.2).

UNIX domain sockets are now used in PVM for all local host communication. These sockets were found to be twice as fast as TCP/IP.

Collective communication routines like those found in MPI [6] are now available in PVM. These include functions such as broadcast and global sum. These collective routines are being implemented to use native communication calls on MPP such as the Paragon and IBM SP2.

A number of other areas are under investigation to improve the performance of PVM applications in the future. These include exploiting high speed networks, using real network multicast, faster heterogeneous data encodings, buffered tracing, static groups, and context.

Standard PVM works with ATM networks by using TCP/IP. Experiments have shown that communication between two SPARC2 computers is up to five times faster on ATM than on ethernet. Other experiments have shown that an additional 30% improvement in possible by using an API below TCP. (FORE Systems supplies such an interface with their ATM cards.)

Network multicast is being incorporated into most new operating systems. Multicast sends one message onto a network that is received by a predetermined set of hosts. This is potentially much faster than the present method in PVM, which sends separately to each host. An experimental version of PVM which uses reliable multicast is being tested. Results are not yet available.

Currently, PVM uses XDR encoding to send messages in heterogeneous environments. XDR has the advantage of being very portable because the vendors supply the routines as part of the RPC library. XDR has the disadvantage of being rather slow both in its implementation and its execution. First, the sending task must convert the entire message into XDR format. After it is transmitted, the receiver must decode the message from XDR into

Table 1.2		
PVM Message Bandwidth Using Shared Memory		
vs. TCP Sockets on a SPARC10 Multiprocessor		
Bandwidth (MB/s) between two tasks		
msg size (bytes)	PVM shared memory	PvmDirectRoute
8	0.04	0.004
800	4.93	0.43
80000	19.04	6.46

this host's local format. Experiments have been done using a much faster encoding scheme called *Receiver makes Right* (RMR). In this scheme the sender always sends the message out as fast as it can, doing no encoding. The receiver has the responsibility of converting the message into the receiving host's format. The advantages are: The routines can be streamlined and thus much faster than XDR; the scheme requires the fewest possible conversions in a heterogeneous environment – at most one vs. always two for XDR; the RMR scheme fits nicely into other PVM extensions such as InPlace data packing; and the RMR scheme avoids the problem XDR has with 64 bit architectures, i.e., XDR is only defined for 32-bit words. The major disadvantage of RMR is that each receiver must be able to decode every other format, thus many decoding routines could be required. Given the number of machines that PVM supports this number could be as high as 580 routines, but by carefully reusing routines such as byte_swap, the actual number of routines that must be written and maintained is approximately 30. Another disadvantage is that RMR is not as portable as XDR because the vendors might not supply the decoders for new architectures they may build. One observation is that almost all new architectures use IEEE data format so this problem may be quite rare.

For XPVM to work PVM must send out trace events of what is happening in the virtual machine. These trace messages can be quite intrusive and cause a degradation in performance. (Tracing is turned off by default.) Experiments have shown that local buffering of even a modest number of trace events (20 events) can give a significant performance increase over no buffering for many (but not all) applications. Because buffered tracing is less intrusive, it also results in more accurate monitoring.

In order to implement faster collective communication operations and more efficient group operations on multiprocessors, investigations are underway to add the concept of static groups to PVM. Initially all groups are dynamic in PVM. Group members can join and leave asynchronously. What may be added is a way the user can specify that a group is now static – its membership will no longer change. Once this occurs, PVM can cache the group information on the tasks.

Finally, there are plans to incorporate the concept of *context* into PVM. Context as defined in the MPI documentation isolates a communication space and allows the creation of "safe" parallel libraries in PVM. Since math libraries simplify application development while also supplying fast, robust, parallel implementations, the addition of context into PVM will improve application performance. Unlike MPI, PVM will incorporate context as an option such that all existing code continues to run unchanged and users need not understand or use context calls unless they require them.

1.5   Conclusions

PVM's popularity around the world means that increasing numbers of programmers are being exposed to parallel computing. Because of the difficulties in writing and tuning parallel programs, it becomes important to have debugging and performance tuning tools that work with PVM. This paper has described the most recent developments in these two areas. For performance tuning we have created the XPVM graphical user interface which displays both real-time and post-mortem animations of message traffic and machine utilization of PVM applications. XPVM also functions as a PVM console allowing the user to start PVM and spawn tasks. There are also high level debugging capabilities in XPVM. For PVM debugging we have made it easier for users to see their diagnostic print statements (still the most popular method of debugging). For users who want to use a parallel debugger, PVM now contains a standard interface that allows third party parallel debuggers to attach to and debug PVM applications. We also presented recent performance enhancements added to PVM and show results where communication speed can be boosted by up to an order of magnitude. We described our latest research in improving the performance of PVM including exploiting ATM networks, multicast, faster encoding schemes, context, and buffered tracing.

References

[1] BBN CORPORATION, "TotalView," Product Literature.

[2] BRICKER, A., LITZKOW, M., LIVNY M., "Condor Technical Summary," University of Wisconsin-Madison, Computer Sciences Technical Report 1069, 1992.

[3] GEIST, A., BEGUELIN, A., DONGARRA, J., JIANG, W., MANCHEK, R., AND SUNDERAM, V., *PVM*, MIT Press, 1994.

[4] HEATH, M. T. AND ETHERIDGE, J. A., "Visualizing the Performance of Parallel Programs," IEEE Software, **8**, No. 5, September 1991, 29–40.

[5] MILLER B., HOLLINGSWORTH, J., CALLAGHAN, M., "The ParaDyn Parallel Performance Tools and PVM," University of Wisconsin-Madison, Computer Sciences Technical Report, 1994.

[6] MPI Forum, "MPI: A Message-Passing Interface Standard," *International Journal of Supercomputer Application* **8**, No. 3/4, 1994.

[7] OUSTERHOUT, J. K., "An X11 Toolkit Based on the Tcl Language," 1991 Winter USENIX Conference.

[8] REED, D., OLSON, R., AYDT, R., MADHYASTHA, T., BIRKETT, T., JENSEN, D., NAZIEF, B., AND TOTTY, B., "Scalable Performance Environments for Parallel Systems," *Proceedings of the Sixth Distributed Memory Computing Conference*, IEEE Computer Society Press, April 1991.

Program Analysis and Tuning Tools for a Parallel Object Oriented Language: An Experiment with the TAU System

Allen Malony[1] and Bernd Mohr
University of Oregon

Peter Beckman and Dennis Gannon
Indiana University

Abstract

Modern desktop program development environments have very sophisticated support tools that make the task of designing applications much easier. This tool support is most advanced for workstation and PC C++ compilers. However, these environments are also very often weak in the area of performance analysis. In this paper we describe a family of programming and performance analysis tools, the TAU system, that has been designed for use with the pC++ parallel object oriented language. By means of a simple example, we explore the tools and we describe how they interact with the pC++ compiler. Examples of performance analysis are given for two different parallel architectures.

[1]This research is supported by ARPA under Rome Labs contract AF 30602-92-C-0135 and Fort Huachuca contract ARMY DABT63-94-C-0029.

1.1 Introduction

Supercomputer programming environments have fallen far behind desktop and workstation systems in terms of the sophistication of the programming tools that are available to build new applications. Part of the reason for this is economic: the desktop market place is several orders of magnitude bigger than that of the supercomputing world. Another explanation is that the traditional supercomputer users are not accustomed to having good programming tools provided with high performance hardware. This is especially true of users of massively parallel processing (MPP) systems. Indeed, most users are delighted if there is a compiler that generates good code for a single processor.

However, the market for MPP supercomputer systems is undergoing a radical transformation from that of a captive of the international defense industry to a vital and energetic component of high-end computing in various commercial sectors. New users are demanding portable programming tools because they see their investment in software being far more important than the money they spend on hardware. Furthermore, because of their roots in desktop technology, they are demanding more than simple compiler environments and message passing libraries.

Unfortunately, there are major problems that must be overcome if we are to raise the level of parallel program software design to that of desktop and workstation tools. Specifically, we must learn more about the integration of programming environment technology and parallel algorithm design. There are several important issues here, including

- How do we integrate parallel computer performance tools with programming languages and systems so that one can design good algorithms without an over-emphasis on architectural detail?

- Can we build portable parallel program debuggers?

- How can the successful models of program development tools for software engineering tasks be extended to programming that incorporates explicit parallelism?

In this paper we examine and evaluate an experimental programming environment designed at the University of Oregon that addresses some of these issues. This system, called $\mathcal{T}$ (for $\underline{T}$uning and $\underline{A}$nalysis $\underline{U}$tilities), is part of the pC++ programming system being distributed by a consortium consisting of Indiana University, University of Oregon and the University of Colorado. pC++ is a programming language based upon a *concurrent aggregate* extension to C++ . The pC++ programming system has been ported to most of the major MPP platforms. It consists of a set of language preprocessors, runtime libraries, and tools for program execution, analysis and tuning. As an integrated program and performance analysis environment, $\mathcal{T}$ consists of six special graphical tools. The five below are discussed in this paper.

- *Cosy* is a tool that provides a point-and-click interface for controlling compilation, instrumentation, processor configuration, and program execution.

- *Classy* provides an interactive display of the class hierarchy graph of pC++ programs.

- *Cagey* is a program browser based on a static call graph display.

- *Fancy* provides a class browser and interactive text tool for exploring the application.

- *Racy* is a graphical tool for displaying the execution profiles generated by the pC++ performance analysis system.

We illustrate the use of these tools from the perspective of the design and evaluation of a single application in pC++ : a bitonic sort module that is used as part of a large N-Body simulation of cosmological evolution [3]. In the sections that follow we will demonstrate how the tools were used to analyze this module. Section 1.3 gives a brief description of the algorithm. Sections 1.4 and 1.5 show how the static analysis tools illustrate the structure of the program. In Sec. 1.6 we will describe how the dynamic analysis tools expose a potential performance bug.

1.2   The Bitonic Sort Module

To illustrate the programming tools in the $\mathcal{T}$ system we will focus on the task of analyzing and tuning a single application based on a classical parallel algorithm: Batcher's *bitonic sort*. Sequentially sub-optimal, but a very parallelizable sorting algorithm, bitonic sort is based on the *bitonic merge*, a natural application of divide-and-conquer. A bitonic sequence consists of two monotonic sequences that have been concatenated together where a wrap-around of one sequence is allowed. That is, it is a sequence

$$a_0, a_1, a_2, \ldots, a_m$$

where $m = 2^n - 1$ for some n, and for index positions i and j, with $i < j$, $a_i, a_{i+1}, \ldots, a_j$ is monotonic and the remaining sequence starting at $a_{(j+1)mod n}$, where a_0 follows a_n, is monotonic in the reverse direction. See Knuth [7] for details.

The bitonic merge can be stated in its most compact form as follows:

```
input: an array of items a[0:2**n-1] containing a bitonic sequence.
merge(a, n, direction){
    k = 2**(n-1)
    foreach i in 0 to k-1 do
        if(((direction == increasing) && (a[i] > a[i+k]) ||
           ((direction == decreasing) && (a[i] < a[i+k]))))
                    swap(a[i], a[i+k]);
    //now a[0:k-1] and a[k:2**n-1] are both bitonic and
    //for all i in [0:k-1] and j in [k:2**n-1]
    //          a(i) <= a(j) if direction = increasing and
    //          a(j) <= a(i) if direction = decreasing
    merge(a[0:k-1], n-1, direction); merge(a[k:2**n-1], n-1, direction);
    }
```

Merging a bitonic sequence of length k involves a sequence of data exchanges between elements that are $k/2$ apart, followed by data exchanges between elements that are $k/4$ apart, etc. The full sort is nothing more than a sequence of bitonic merges. We start by observing that a_i and a_{i+1} is a bitonic sequence of two items for each even i. If we merge these length two bitonic sequences into sorted sequences of length two and if we alternate the sort direction, we then have bitonic sequences of length four. Merging two of these bitonic sequences (of alternating direction) we have sorted sequences of length 8. This is illustrated in Figure 1.1 below where the vertical axis represents time steps going down the page.

A data parallel version of this algorithm is given by

```
sort(a, n){
    m = 2**n;                    // m = size of array
    for(i = 1; i < n; i++){  // merge(i) step
        k = 2**i;
        forall(s in 0:m-1) d[s] = (s/k) mod 2; // d is the direction
        for(j = k/2; j > 0; j = j/2){ // exchange(j) step
            forall(s in 0:m-1) d2[s] = (s/j) mod 2;
            forall(s in 0:m-1) where(d2[s]==1)  tmp[s] = a[s-j];
            forall(s in 0:m-1) where(d2[s]==0)  tmp[s] = a[s+j];
            forall(s in 0:m-1) where((d == d2) && (a > tmp)) a = tmp;
            forall(s in 0:m-1) where((d != d2) && (a <= tmp)) a = tmp;
        }
```

In an object parallel version of this algorithm we construct a set of objects e_i, $i = 0..n$ where each object contains a value from the sequence a_i and a temporary variable *temp*. The exchange step in the merge is replaced by communication where object i will *grab* a_{i+k} *from* e_{i+k} and store the value

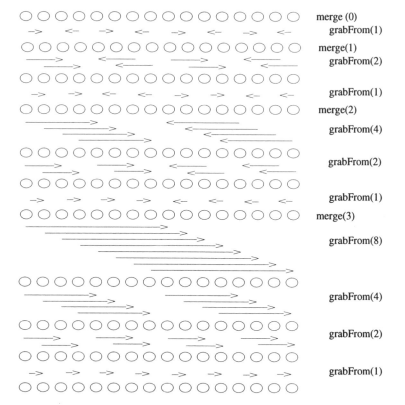

Figure 1.1: Data exchanges in the bitonic sort algorithm.

in its temp variable. In this operation, $k = 2^{n-1}$ if $i < 2^{n-1}$; $k = -2^{n-1}$ otherwise. Once the values have been accessed and stored in the temporary variable, we make a comparison and test. Object e_i will replace a_i with the *temp* value if the appropriate conditions are satisfied. The code for this can be derived from the data parallel version of the algorithm by rewriting it in terms of the action on a single array element as described above. As a C++ class this would appear as follows:

```
class ListItem{
  public:
      item a;           // the data item
      item temp;        // a temporary value for the data swap step.
      int direction;    // a flag that store the direction of the current merge
      int i;            // the position of this object in the aggregate
      ListItem *thisCollection;   // a pointer to the collection
      void merge(distance);       // the bitonic merge
      void sort(n);               // the bitonic sort
      void grabFrom(distance);    // access the data from another ListItem
      localMerge(dist);   // the test and swap step
  };

ListItem::sort(n){
    for(d = 1; d < n; d++)  merge(d);
    }
ListItem::merge(int level){
    direction = (i/(2**level)) % 2;
    for(int d = level-1; d >= 0; d--){
          int distance = 2**d;
          grabFrom(distance);
          localMerge(distance);
          barrier_sync(thisCollection);
        }
}
item::grabFrom(dist){
   if((i/dist) % 2) temp_data = thisAggregate[myPosition+dist].data;
   else             temp_data = thisAggregate[myPosition-dist].data;
}
ListItem::localMerge(int dist){
   int d2;
   d2 = (i/dist) % 2;
   if((direction == d2) && (a > temp)) a = temp;
   if((direction != d2) &&( a <= temp)) a = temp;
}
```

From the perspective of pC++ parallel programming, there is one very critical point in the code above. That is, there is a potential race condition in the merge step. To see this, observe that if each object in the collection is executing the merge function then, in the loop, one must make sure that the data read operation in `grabFrom` executes after the other object has completed the `localMerge` step of the previous iteration. To enforce this rule we have inserted a barrier synchronization step which causes all objects to wait at this position before advancing to the next iteration. The insertion of this operation has a serious impact on the asymptotic complexity of this algorithm. If there are 2^n processors, the standard algorithm has time complexity $O(n^2)$. By adding the barrier synchronization, we have increased the complexity to $O(n^3)$.

Another serious problem with the algorithm is that it is very inefficient if the number of processors available is less than 2^n. In the N-body application, we need to sort tens of millions of particles on machines ranging from 8 to 1024 processors. Consequently, we need a version of the algorithm that requires fewer processors. Fortunately, there is an easy way to increase the granularity of the computation so that each object holds a vector of particles. If we replace the `ListItem` class above with a class called

```
class Pvector{
    item a[K];    // K is the size of the local vector
    item temp[K];
    ...
};
```

and a standard quicksort function `qsort(direction)` to the class that sorts the local vector of item in the given direction, then the changes to the program are very small. We only need to make sure that the initial vectors are sorted and that they are resorted at the end of each merge step.

```
Pvector::merge(level){
    direction = (i/(2**level)) % 2;
    for(int d = level-1; d >= 0; d--){
        int distance = 2**d;
        grabFrom(distance);
        localMerge(distance);
        barrier_sync(thisCollection);
    }
    qsort(direction);
}
```

```
Pvector::sort(n){
    qsort(i%2);
    barrier_sync(thisCollection);
    for(d = 1; d < n; d++)  merge(d);
}
```

In addition to the changes above, the function `localMerge` must be modified to operate on a vector of data. If we assume that the quicksort computation runs with an average execution time of $DKlog(K)$ for some constant D and if we ignore the cost of the barrier synchronization, and assume that there are $P = 2^n$ processors available and the size of the list to sort is N, then the time to sort is roughly

$$T(N) = \frac{N}{P}log(P)(Clog(P) + Dlog(N))$$

where C is a constant that depends upon communication speed. Given a sequential complexity of $DNlog(N)$ we see that the parallel speed-up is of the form

$$Speedup(N, P) = \frac{\frac{P}{log(P)}}{1 + \frac{Clog(P)}{Dlog(N)}}$$

which, for large N, is of the form $\frac{P}{log(P)}$.

It is important to notice that at the end of each merge step, just before the quicksort is called, the local vector is a bitonic sequence due to its construction. Hence, it is possible to apply a sequential bitonic merge that runs in time $O(K)$ rather than the $O(Klog(K))$ quicksort. This changes the approximate execution time to be

$$T_{modified}(N) = \frac{N}{P}Clog^2(P) + D\frac{N}{P}log(\frac{N}{P}))$$

and the speed-up becomes

$$Speedup(N, P) = \frac{P}{1 + \frac{Clog(P)}{Dlog(N)}}$$

which, for large N, is of the form P.

Our focus for the remainder of this paper will be on using the $\mathcal{T}$ tools to explore several questions about this algorithm posed by the analysis above. In particular, we are interested in using the tools to consider the following.

1. Does barrier synchronization add a significant penalty to the complexity that is not accounted for in the analysis above? What percentage of the time is actually spent in barrier synchronization for problems of a size that is significant for the application?

2. Given that bitonic merge is communication intensive (in fact, the bisection bandwidth of the communication graph scales linearly with the problem size), what percentage of the time is spent in communication on different machines?

3. How significant is the improvement in the "modified" version of the algorithm which replaces the quicksort in each merge step by a local bitonic merge?

1.3   The pC++ Program Analysis Environment

In this section, we give a brief overview of $\mathcal{T}$, a first prototype for an integrated portable pC++ program and performance analysis environment.

Elements of the $\mathcal{T}$ graphical interface represent objects of the pC++ programming model: collections, classes, methods, and functions. These language-level objects appear in all $\mathcal{T}$ tools. By plan, $\mathcal{T}$ was designed and developed in concert with the pC++ language system. It leverages pC++ language technology, especially in its use of the Sage++ toolkit [2] as an interface to the pC++ compiler for instrumentation and for accessing properties of program objects. $\mathcal{T}$ is also integrated with the pC++ runtime system for profiling and tracing support. Because pC++ is intended to be portable, the tools are built to be portable as well. C++ and C are used to ensure portable and efficient implementation, and similar reasons led us to choose Tcl/Tk [11, 12] for the graphical interface.

The $\mathcal{T}$ tools are implemented as graphical *hypertools*. While the tools are distinct, providing unique capabilities, they can act in combination to provide enhanced functionality. If one tool needs a feature of another one, it sends a message to the other tool requesting it (e.g., display the source code for a specific function). With this design approach, the toolset can be easily extended. $\mathcal{T}$ can also be retargeted to other programming environments, for instance those based on Fortran, which the Sage++ toolkit supports.

One important goal in $\mathcal{T}$'s development was to make the toolset as user-friendly as possible. For this purpose, many elements of the graphical user interface are analogous to *links* in *hypertext* systems: clicking on them brings up windows which describe the element in more detail. This allows the user to explore properties of the application by simply interacting with elements of most interest. The $\mathcal{T}$ tools also support the concept of *global features*. If a global feature is invoked in any of the tools, it is automatically executed in all currently running tools. Examples of global features include `select-function`, `select-class`, and `switch-application`. For good measure, $\mathcal{T}$ comes with a full hypertext help system.

Figure 1.2 shows the pC++ programming environment and the associated $\mathcal{T}$ tools architecture. The pC++ compiler frontend takes a user program and pC++ class library definitions (which provide predefined collection types) and parses them into an *abstract syntax tree* (AST). All access to the AST is done via the Sage++ library. Through command line switches, the user can choose to compile a program for profiling, tracing, and breakpoint debugging. In these cases, the instrumentor is invoked to do the necessary instrumentation in the AST. The pC++ backend transforms the AST into plain C++ with calls into the pC++ runtime system which supports both shared and distributed memory platforms. This C++ source code is then compiled and linked by the C++ compiler on the target system. The compilation and execution of pC++ programs can be controlled by *cosy* (**CO**mpile manager **S**tatus display). This tool provides a high-level graphical interface for setting compilation and execution parameters and selecting the parallel machine where a program will run.

The program and performance analysis environment is shown on the right side of Figure 1.2. They include the integrated $\mathcal{T}$ tools, profiling and tracing support, and interfaces to stand-alone performance analysis tools developed partly by other groups [4, 6, 9, 13]. The $\mathcal{T}$ toolset provides support for accessing static information about the program and for querying and analyzing dynamic data obtained from program execution. A more detailed discussion of the $\mathcal{T}$ tools can be found in [8, 10, 1].

1.4   A Tour of the Sort Program: Static Analysis

The pC++ implementation of the Sort program is easily derived from the class object defined above. A pC++ *collection* of `Pvector` objects is created. The member functions of the `Pvector` class are divided into two categories: those functions that describe operations that are purely local to the object, and

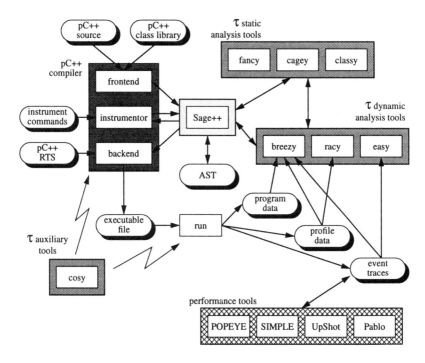

Figure 1.2: pC++ programming environment and $\mathcal{T}$ tools architecture.

those functions that involve global operations on the collection or interaction with other elements of the collection. The second category of functions are moved to the collection structure and are called *MethodOfElement* members. Our collection is derived from the library collection *DistributedArray*.

Currently, $\mathcal{T}$ provides three tools to enable the user to quickly get an overview of a large pC++ program and to navigate through it: the global function and method browser *fancy* (**F**ile **AN**d **C**lass displa**Y**), the static callgraph display *cagey* (**CA**ll **G**raph **E**xtended displa**Y**), and the class hierarchy display *classy* (**CLASS** hierarch**Y** browser). The tools are integrated with the dynamic analysis utilities through the global features of $\mathcal{T}$, allowing the user to easily find execution information about language objects. For instance, to locate the corresponding dynamic results (after a measurement has been made), the user only has to click on the object of interest (e.g., a function name in the callgraph display).

Figure 1.4 illustrates the view of our *SortedList* collection. From this *fancy* panel view, we can select any member function (with a mouse click) and get a text display of that function (e.g., `SortedList`). In addition to examining the code, the user can examine many other static properties of the program. For example, the inheritance graph for the classes and collections in the pC++ application are illustrated in Figure 1.3. Another display is the static call graph of our program. It is automatically generated and displayed with the *cagey* tool as illustrated in Figure 1.5. This view of the program is completely adjustable: the user can select the detail and depth of the displayed information by unfolding and folding selected function calls.

1.5   Compiling and Executing the Program: COSY

In our experiments, we need to run the pC++ program in a number of different configurations on different machines. These include several different levels of instrumentation (none, complete, and selective). In addition, we need to run the program with different numbers of processors on different machines. Keeping track of all the required compile and runtime flags necessary to accomplish our goal is a non-trivial task. The *cosy* tool provides a very simple set of menus for configuring and running a pC++ program. In our case, we restricted profiling to the quick-sort routine `Qsort`, the main bitonic sort `sort`, the bitonic merge `merge`, the routine that contains all the communications `grabFrom`, and the barrier synchronization code `pcxx_Barrier`. While there are many more small functions that are executed, we found that when we included them all, the size of the event trace file was too large and the execution time was severely distorted. However, when we used this restricted set of functions, the trace files were very compact and the impact of instrumentation on total execution time was less than 5 percent.

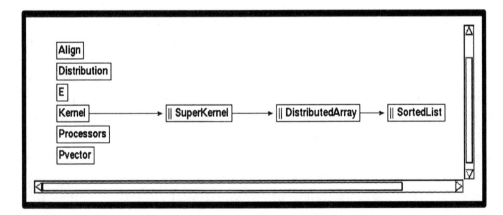

Figure 1.3: Class inheritance hierarchy graph display.

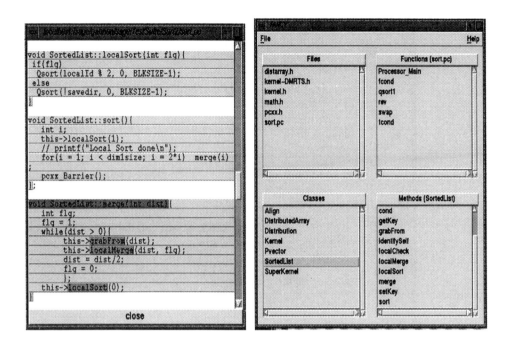

Figure 1.4: Class browser and code view tool. See color plate VI.

1.6 Sort Program Execution: Dynamic Analysis

Dynamic program analysis tools allow the user to explore and analyze program execution behavior. The most critical factor for the user during performance debugging is how the high-level program semantics are related to the measurement results. $\mathcal{T}$ helps in presenting the results in terms of pC++ language objects and in supporting global features that allow the user to quickly locate the corresponding routine in the call graph or source text by simply clicking on the related measurement result or state objects.

$\mathcal{T}$'s dynamic tools currently include an execution profile data browser called *racy* (**R**outine and data **AC**cess profile displa**Y**), an event trace browser called *easy* (**E**vent **A**nd **S**tate displa**Y**), and a breakpoint debugger called *breezy*. To generate the dynamic execution data for these tools, profiling and tracing instrumentation and measurement support has been implemented in pC++ . In this paper, we concentrate on the *racy* tool.

The $\mathcal{T}$ execution profile tool *racy* provides a very simple and portable means of understanding where a parallel program spends its time. The initial display is a set of bar graphs for each processor showing the percent of the

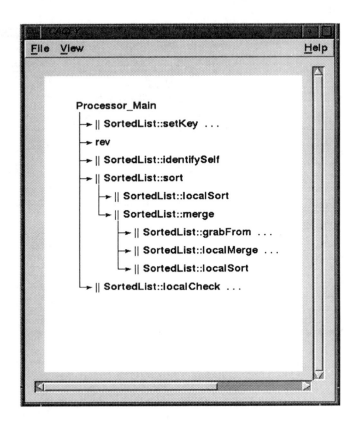

Figure 1.5: Static call graph window.

execution time spent in each of the profiled routines in the program. To study the questions posed at the end of Sec. 1.2, we have run the program on a data set of 1024 `Pvector` element objects each containing a list of 1024 items; a total of 2^{20} objects to sort. We ran this on 16 nodes of a Silicon Graphics Challenge machine, and on 16 and 64 nodes of an Intel Paragon. Recall that pC++ is completely portable, so all that was required to compile for these two environments was to use the *cosy* tool to select the appropriate system name; no source code needed to be modified.

The results for the 16 node SGI and the 64 node Paragon are illustrated in Figures 1.6 and 1.7. There are three displays in each figure. The processor profile bar graphs are shown in the lower right. By using the mouse we selected the bar graph that describes the *mean* profile shown at the top. The result is given in the upper right display. This version of the bar graph lists the names of each function and gives the numerical percentage values

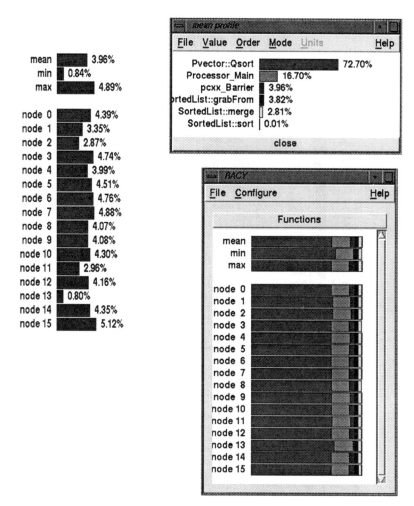

Figure 1.6: Performance profiles from racy on 16 node SGI challenge. See color plate VII.

of execution time. Because we are also interested in the time spent in the barrier synchronization we have asked *racy* to plot that for all processors. These data are shown by the chart on the left.

There are several interesting observations that we can make about our sorting program from these displays. First it is clear that the time spent in the barrier synchronization routine is not large. It is about 5 percent for the SGI and less that 2 percent for the Paragon. One interesting observation about the Paragon numbers is that high-numbered processors spend less

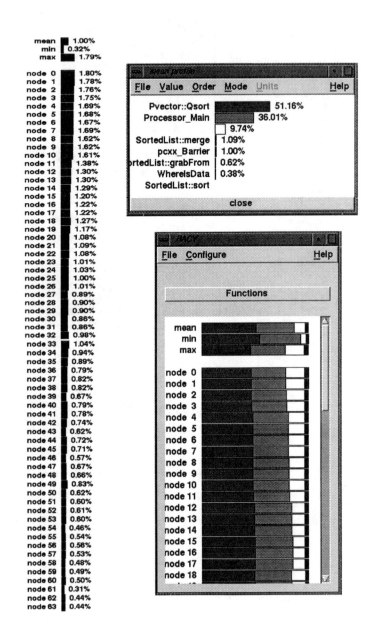

Figure 1.7: Performance profiles from racy on 64 node Paragon. See color plate VIII.

time in the barrier than do low-numbered processors. The reason for this is uncertain. Every aspect of the algorithm design is processor independent and the runtime system design is relatively symmetric with respect to processors (i.e., the barrier algorithm is based on a tree reduction). For the SGI, the time spent in the barrier is more random, relating to the fact that processors are occasionally interrupted to carry out other tasks as requested by the operating system.

The reader may notice that there is one difference between the SGI and the Paragon displays. In the Paragon version there is an extra function profiled that is represented by a white bar and is unlabeled in the upper right display. This function is the pC++ *poll loop* which supports the global name space on the distributed memory Paragon. This is the third largest consumer of time at 9.74%. In a distributed memory machine based on message passing, when a processor wishes to ask for data from another processor it must send a message. Because the Paragon does not support an active message interrupt, it is necessary to have each processor periodically poll for incoming requests and service them. In this case the profile information tells us that each processor spends more time polling for requests than it does in asking for data (in the `grabFrom` function). Hence, it may be possible to "fine tune" the runtime system so that it polls less often.

What have we learned about our algorithm? First, the barrier synchronization costs are relatively small, even though the asymptotic analysis suggests that they may be a problem. Second, we see that the largest cost is the time spent in the local quicksort (72% of the time on the SGI and 51% of the time on the Paragon). This observation leads us to consider the third question posed at the end of Sec. 1.2: How significantly can the algorithm be improved by replacing quicksort at each merge step with a local bitonic merge?

After making the experiments described above, we reprogrammed the algorithm so that the call to the quicksort at the end of each merge step is replaced by a call to a local bitonic merge operation. The difference in performance was impressive. The execution time of the original algorithm on 64 processors it was 30.13 seconds. After the change to the merge function, this time dropped to 3.56 seconds. On the SGI, the original version of the sort ran in time 47.4 seconds with 16 processors. After the algorithm change it ran in 5.1 seconds. Again, from using *racy* to plot the mean profiles shown in Figure 1.8 it is clear that the new algorithm is no more balanced than before and only improvements in interprocessor communications will make a significant difference in overall performance.

1.7 Conclusion

The evolving requirements for the use of high-performance parallel computing systems are presenting new challenges for programming environment technology. The $\mathcal{T}$ environment is representative of a new class of collaborative program and performance tools that, fundamentally, are integrated into a parallel programming system and support portable, high-level program observation, analysis, and interaction. In this paper, we demonstrated how the $\mathcal{T}$ tools can be used to explore the static program structure (class hierarchy, source code, and call graphs) and how the performance profiling tools can answer questions about dynamic system and algorithm behavior. In particular, we saw the importance of coupled program and performance analysis wherein serious bottlenecks in a code can be linked back to high-level algorithm design choices, as in the case of bitonic sort where a replacement of quicksort with bitonic merge at each merge step increased performance by nearly an order of magnitude.

Although the experience with $\mathcal{T}$ has been exceedingly positive, there are still several important directions we want to pursue. First, there is the obvious need for a parallel debugging system that provides high-level access to program objects. Hence, much of our current work focuses on

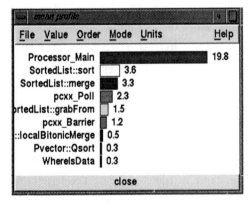
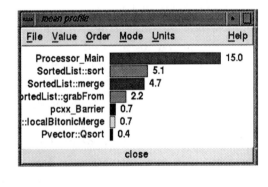

Figure 1.8: The modified algorithm. On the left, the mean profile showing total time spent in each function including the functions it calls for 64 nodes on the Intel Paragon. On the right, the same graph but for 16 nodes of the SGI Challenge. See color plate IX.

breezy, a parallel barrier breakpoint debugger that supports runtime access to pC++ program state. The *breezy* tool actually implements a robust infrastructure for program access upon which several external runtime tools can be built. A second direction is towards more expanded support for performance experimentation and diagnosis, particularly for scalability analysis. We are attempting to integrate a simulation-based performance extrapolation tool and a semi-automated performance diagnosis system [5] into the $\mathcal{T}$ toolset. In addition, we are working on better ways to maintain a database of program measurements that record the progress of a sequence of experiments and to display comparative performance behaviors across multiple executions for different numbers of processors. Finally, we are improving the design of the $\mathcal{T}$ tools to facilitate the transfer of the technology to other language environments, in particular HPF.

For more information ...

Documentation, additional papers, and source code for pC++, Sage++, and $\mathcal{T}$ are available via anonymous FTP from `cica.cica.indiana.edu` in the directory `~ftp/pub/sage`, or via World Wide Web at

$$\texttt{http://www.cica.indiana.edu/sage}$$

and

$$\texttt{http://www.cs.uoregon.edu/paracomp/tau}$$

References

[1] BROWN, D., HACKSTADT, S., MALONY, A., AND MOHR, B., "Program Analysis Environments for Parallel Language Systems: The TAU Environment," http://www.cs.uoregon.edu/ paracomp/papers/tenn/tenn.html, *Proc. of the Workshop on Environments and Tools For Parallel Scientific Computing*, Townsend, Tennessee, 162–171, May 1994.

[2] BODIN, F., BECKMAN, P., GANNON, D., GOTWALS, J., NARAYANA, S., SRINIVAS, S., AND WINNICKA, B., "Sage++: An Object Oriented Toolkit and Class Library for Building Fortran and C++ Restructuring Tools," *Proc. Oonski '94*, Oregon, 1994.

[3] FERRELL R. AND BERTSCHINGER, E., "Particle-Mesh Methods on the Connection Machine," *International Journal of Modern Physics*, **C**, 1993.

[4] HACKSTADT, S. AND MALONY, A., "Next-Generation Parallel Performance Visualization: A Prototyping Environment for Visualization Development," *Proc. Parallel Architectures and Languages Europe*, (PARLE), Athens, Greece, 1994.

[5] HELM, B. ROBERT, MALONY, ALLEN D., AND FICKAS, STEVE, "Capturing and Automating Performance Diagnosis: The Poirot Approach," to be published in *Proc. 9th Inter. Parallel Processing Symp. (IPPS '95)*, Santa Barbara, CA, April 1995.

[6] HERRARTE, V. AND LUSK, E., "Studying Parallel Program Behavior with Upshot," Technical Report ANL-91/15, Mathematics and Computer Science Division, Argonne National Laboratory, 1991.

[7] KNUTH, D., *The art of computer programming*, Vol. 3, Searching and Sorting, Reading, Mass., Addison-Wesley Publishing Company, 1968.

[8] MALONY, A., MOHR, B., BECKMAN, P., GANNON, D., YANG, S., BODIN, F., "Performance Analysis of pC++: A Portable Data-Parallel Programming System for Scalable Parallel Computers," http://www.cs.uoregon.edu/paracomp/papers/ipps94/ipps94.html, *Proc. 8th Int. Parallel Processing Symb. (IPPS)*, Cancún, Mexico, IEEE Computer Society Press, 75–85, Apr. 1994.

[9] MOHR, B., *Standardization of Event Traces Considered Harmful or Is an Implementation of Object-Independent Event Trace Monitoring and Analysis Systems Possible?* http://www.cs.uoregon.edu/ paracomp/papers/cnrs92/cnrs92.html, Proc. CNRS-NSF Workshop on Environments and Tools For Parallel Scientific Computing, St. Hilaire du Touvet, France, Elsevier, Advances in Parallel Computing, 1993, **6**, 103–124.

[10] MOHR, B., BROWN, D., AND MALONY, A., "TAU: A Portable Parallel Program Analysis Environment for pC++," http://www.cs.uoregon.edu/paracomp/papers/conpar94/conpar94.html,

Proc. of CONPAR 94 - VAPP VI, Linz, Austria, Springer Verlag, LNCS 854, 29–40, Sept. 1994.

[11] OUSTERHOUT, J., "Tcl: An Embeddable Command Language," *Proc. 1990 Winter USENIX Conf.*

[12] OUSTERHOUT, J., "An X11 Toolkit Based on the Tcl Language," *Proc. 1991 Winter USENIX Conf.*

[13] REED, D. A., OLSON, R. D., AYDT, R. A., MADHYASTA, T. M., BIRKETT, T., JENSEN, D. W., NAZIEF, B. A. A., TOTTY, B. K., "Scalable Performance Environments for Parallel Systems," *Proc. 6th Distributed Memory Computing Conference*, IEEE Computer Society Press, 562–569, 1991.

Race Detection – Ten Years Later

D. P. Helmbold and C. E. McDowell[1]
Computer and Information Sciences
University of California
Santa Cruz, California 95064

Abstract

This paper presents a taxonomy that categorizes methods for determining event orders in executions of parallel programs. These event orderings can then be used to detect race conditions in parallel programs. The paper also shows how race results from the past ten years fit into the event ordering taxonomy, and presents some new results as further evidence that in general the race detection problem is at best intractable.

1.1   Introduction

Parallel computers are an important part of high performance computing today and will continue to be so for many years. A significant number of these machines are programmed using a conventional language with extensions for some form of explicit parallelism and synchronization (e.g., *doall* or *fork* with message passing). Many of these programs are intended to be deterministic, but due to synchronization errors are nondeterministic. Other programs are intended to be nondeterministic, at least at some level. In both cases it may be desirable to identify the sources of nondeterminism. This is particularly

[1]This work was partially supported by a grant from the National Science Foundation (Grant # CCR-9102635).

useful for programs that were intended to be deterministic but might also be useful for intentionally nondeterministic programs provided the information about sources of nondeterminism is presented in a suitable manner.

Informally, a *race* exists between two program events if they conflict (e.g., one reads and the other writes the same memory location) and their execution order depends on how the threads[2] are scheduled. The formal definition of a race is given in the appendix. The appendix also contains a structural breakdown of races into four groups.

There are many questions that can be asked about the possible "races" in a parallel program.

- What ordering relationships *should* hold between statement instances (i.e., what statement instances conflict)?

- What ordering relationships *do* hold between statement instances?

- What are all of the races in this program?

- Are there any races in this program?

- What shared memory locations are accessed by a statement (instance)?

Current algorithms for detecting races in programs answer (or attempt to answer) one or more of the above questions.

In [8] we examine all possible ordering relationships that can hold between two program events and classify each possibility as either a non-race or belonging to one of four classes of races.[3] The remaining questions above are addressed by this paper. In Sec. 1.2 we present a taxonomy of event ordering approaches. Determining the possible order of events recorded or observed during the traced execution of a parallel program is important to most race detection algorithms. Sec. 1.3 places known results on event ordering into this taxonomy. This section also presents three new negative results. In Sec. 1.4 we summarize the current known algorithms that can correctly answer the question, "Are there *any* races in this program?" In Sec. 1.5 we briefly touch on the the issue of determining the conflicting accesses to shared data.

---

[2]For the purposes of this paper, the notions of *thread*, *task* and *process* are equivalent. We use the term "thread" throughout.

[3]Most of the definitions found in [8] are included in the appendix of this paper.

1.2   A Taxonomy of Event Ordering Approaches

Previously, results in race detection have been classified as static analysis, post-mortem trace-based, or on-the-fly. Static analysis techniques are generally applied at compile time, and do not require that the program be executed. The primary distinction between on-the-fly analysis and post mortem analysis is that in on-the-fly analysis the trace is analyzed as it is generated, thus the entire trace does not need to be stored. This permits more detailed tracing, often including all of the accesses to shared memory. On-the-fly race detection naturally focuses on those races involving the shared memory accesses reported during the execution. This is somewhat different from the problem generally addressed in post mortem trace analysis where an attempt is made to determine orderings between all blocks (without regard to exactly which shared memory locations were accessed, as space limitations generally prevent this information from being saved for post mortem analysis).

We were unable to come up with a formal characterization of race detection algorithms that corresponded directly to static, post-mortem and on-the-fly. For example many on-the-fly algorithms can be done post mortem with at most a constant amount of memory per traced item. Of course the number of events may make this prohibitive in practice for any constant. Likewise, any post-mortem approach could be done on-the-fly with a sufficiently large buffer. It might not be able to detect races as they occur, but the point is that there is no clear dividing line between the on-the-fly techniques and the post-mortem trace analysis methods. Finally, both on-the-fly and post-mortem algorithms might incorporate some information obtained by preprocessing the program (i.e., via static analysis).

Despite their apparent differences, we will unify the static analysis, post-mortem, and on-the-fly approaches by viewing each as a type of static analysis on an appropriately constrained programming model. We will constrain the programming model along two major axes. The first axis identifies the constraints on the control flow constructs used by the program. The second axis identifies the kinds of synchronization used by the program. The current known results on computing ordering relationships are described in Sec. 1.3 and summarized in Tables 1.1 and 1.2 at the end of this section. The following subsections detail the taxonomy.

1.2.1   Constraints on Control Flow

We consider three possible constraints on the control flow: no branching (i.e., all loops can be unrolled at compile time), no loops containing synchronization constructs, and unconstrained control flow. A loop that is always executed the same number of times does not present the same difficulties as a `while` loop iterating until a dynamic condition is satisfied. For the purposes of the above definition and the remainder of this section, the term "loop" applies only to those statements which cannot be unrolled at compile time.

Branch-free Programs

During a program's execution, each instance of a conditional statement takes a particular branch. When the program's execution is traced, a record is made of the events (or perhaps only the important events) executed by each thread and when they are executed. This record defines a branchless program since all of the branching has been "hard wired" when the trace was generated. The way the branches get "hard wired" depends on both the input supplied to the program and the outcome of control races in the traced execution.

Analyzing a trace is thus analogous to analyzing a branch free program. This leads to the questions "how hard is the ordering problem for branch free programs?" and "what can we infer about the original program that contained branches?"

One possible goal is to determine the races exhibited by the traced execution. Since only one execution is considered, each detected race will involve two unsynchronized events in the execution. Thus only concurrent races and some general races (see appendix) can be detected in this way.

A more powerful approach is to consider all possible executions of the branch-free program on a particular input. The key sub-goal of this approach is a partial order indicating which pairs of events are ordered or semi-ordered. From this partial order and the knowledge of which events conflict one can determine which pairs of events are races. Since the branch-free program has the same set of possible executions on every input, one can use the pairs of events that are races for any particular input to determine which statement pairs in the program form a race.

Note that some races can affect the evaluation of branch conditions. Thus, even an exact analysis of the branch-free program can lead to incorrect results for the original program generating the trace. Some races may be missed because the branches leading to them were not taken in the traced execution. Other races may be incorrectly included because some branch conditions would be evaluated differently in the executions responsible for them. See Figure 1.1 for an example of how races may be missed or incorrectly included.

Programs with Branches but No Loops

The problem becomes even more difficult when we consider analyzing programs with branching (but without loops). For each input, the program with branching can be viewed as a set of branch-free programs. Each legal combination of branch choices for that input leads to one branch-free program. A simplifying assumption [2] is that all branch combinations are possible, so that any set of branch choices is legal. Without this assumption it is $\mathcal{NP}$-hard to determine which branch choices are legal (see Theorem 2).

Each branch-free program associated with a branching program/input pair has its own set of races between events. What one would like to determine is a partial order over the events where there is an arc from event e_1 to event e_2 if and only if e_1 and e_2 are ordered (or semi-ordered) by every branch-free program represented by the program/input pair. As above, this partial order can be combined with conflict information to obtain those pairs of events forming races.

Now consider the possible inputs for the branching program. For each input there is a set of event pairs which are unordered (with respect to that input). Taking the union of these sets of event pairs gives us all pairs of events that are unordered on any possible input. Using information on which event pairs conflict, we can then list the pairs of events forming races in the program.

The set of pairs of unordered events must be computed separately for each possible input. As shown in Figure 1.2, two conflicting statements that are not ordered the same across all inputs do not necessarily constitute a race. The order in which S1 and S2 from Figure 1.2 are executed depends on the input, but is the same on each particular input. Although some might consider this a race, we feel that this behavior is neither nondeterministic nor particularly indicative of an error. By our definitions (see appendix), the code fragment in Figure 1.2 is race-free.

The assumption that all branch combinations are possible has the fundamental drawback that extra (spurious) races may be reported. Certain combinations of branches are often infeasible, and races in the branch-free program(s) using infeasible combinations of branches may result in infeasible

Thread A		Thread B	
A1:	j := 0;	B1:	i := 1;
A2:	i := 0;	B2:	if (i=0) then
A3:	if (i=1) then	B3:	j := 1;
A4:	k := 1;	B4:	k := 2;

Figure 1.1: This program fragment has conflicting updates to shared variables i, j, and k (as well as conflicting reads to i in the if conditions). Assume each labeled statement is an event. Consider the branch-free program that results when event A2 is executed after event B1 and before event B2. Event A4 does not appear in this branch free program as the condition "i=1" in event A3 is hard-wired to false. The general race (A4, B4) exists in the original program but not the branch-free program. Furthermore, the pair (A1, B3) is a race in the branch-free program but not in the original program. In the original program A1 is semi-ordered before B3.

Thread A	Thread B	ThreadC
if (input=1)	wait(x);	wait(y);
then post(x);	S1;	S2;
else post(y);	post(y);	post(x);

Figure 1.2: This program fragment contains two conflicting statements, S1 and S2. Although either S1 or S2 can happen first, for any given input either S1 happens before S2 or S2 happens before S1 but not both. By Definition 13, this program does not contain a race.

races being reported (as in Figure 1.2). A combination of branches may be
infeasible because two branch conditions may always compute the same value
or because statements in (or the absence of statements from) one branch may
determine the value of a later branch condition.

Unrestricted Programs

Programs containing loops (and/or recursion) present an additional difficulty.
If the number of loop iterations cannot be bounded at compile time, then
the number of events executed by the program (and the number of branch
conditions evaluated) is also unbounded. Thus a single program with loops
can represent an infinite number of branch-free programs.

For each choice of input, we obtain a version of the looping program.
Each version of the looping program represents a (possibly infinite) number
of branch-free programs. For each input, we can (at least conceptually) identify.[4] which pairs of events are ordered or semi-ordered, and (given conflict
information) which pairs of events form races for that input.

We can then proceed in the same way as the loop-free case. The union
over all possible inputs of these pairs of events forming races can then be
used to determine which pairs of statements in the program are races.

1.2.2   Type of Synchronization

The second axis identifies the type of synchronization used by the program.
At the top level we only distinguish two types of synchronization: monotonic
and non-monotonic. These terms were first applied to synchronization in
[7]. Intuitively, a synchronization construct is monotonic if once a blocking operation becomes unblocked, it remains unblocked for the duration of
the program (e.g., Post and Wait with no Clear - once an event is posted,
any Wait operations on that event become unblocked and the effect of the
Post cannot be undone). This intuitive description is only intended to give a
general idea of the classification and to motivate the choice of monotonic to
describe the class. The intuitive notion also accurately describes all "real"
monotonic synchronization constructs that we have examined but is not sufficient to precisely characterize the class. The formal definition is given below.

---

[4]Determining which pairs of events are ordered or semi-ordered is undecidable in general; see Theorem 3 However, the assumption that all combinations of branches are possible
alleviates this problem.

Definition 1 *A set of synchronization constructs is* **monotonic** *if every branch-free parallel program composed entirely of synchronization constructs from the set either always terminates normally (all threads complete) or always deadlocks in the same state.*

Monotonic synchronization operations include nested fork-join (e.g., nested parallel loops), ordered critical sections (i.e., properly paired and nested lock-unlock operations where whenever multiple locks are simultaneously held, they are always obtained in the same order), buffered send-receive where the sender names the receiver, and post and wait with no clear. Non-monotonic synchronization operations for which results have been published include post and wait with clear [2], and semaphores [13,19]

1.3 Details of Known Results in Our Taxonomy of Ordering Event Results

The taxonomy introduced in the previous section has six major categories {monotonically synchronized, non-monotonically synchronized}   × {no branches, no loops, unrestricted}. In this section we briefly describe the known results in the various categories and provide some new results. The categories are presented in order of increasing computational complexity. Since unrestricted programs create undecidability problems regardless of the synchronization primitives used, we have combined the two unrestricted program categories.

1.3.1 No Branches and Monotonically Synchronized

We proved in a previous paper [7] that computing the precise ordering relationships between events in branch-free monotonically synchronized programs can be done in polynomial time. (This generalizes a result of Netzer and Ghosh [18], see Sec. 1.3.1.) For completeness we include here several previous polynomial time results for determining the precise ordering relationships between events for programs using specific sets of monotonic synchronization constructs.

Table 1.1 What ordering relationships hold between statement (instances)?			
		Exact Solution	Approximations
Branch free	Mono-tonic	• restricted rendezvous w/o select [24], • fork/join is in $\mathcal{P}$ [14,4,21] • ordered critical sections are in $\mathcal{P}$ (Sec. 1.3.1), • post/wait no clear is in $\mathcal{P}$ [18], • all monotonic are in $\mathcal{P}$ [7]	
	Non-mono-tonic	• single semaphore is in $\mathcal{P}$ [13], • unrestricted rendezvous w/o select or restricted rendezvous with select, [24] • semaphores are co-$\mathcal{NP}$-hard, [19] • post/wait/clear is $\mathcal{NP}$-hard (Thm: 1)	semaphores [11]
No loops	Mono-tonic	• fork/join is $\mathcal{NP}$-hard (Thm: 2), • post/wait no clear is Co-$\mathcal{NP}$-hard[2] even if all paths are executable,	fork/join [14,4,21] post/wait no clear [1]
	Non-mono-tonic	• post/wait/clear is $\mathcal{NP}$-hard (Thm: 1 or [2]), • semaphores are $\mathcal{NP}$-hard	fork/join [14,4,21] post/wait no clear [1]
Unre-stricted	any	Undecidable (Thm: 3)	fork/join [14,4,21] ordered critical sections [22], semaphores [16], message passing [3], rendezvous [23,12]

Table 1.2		
Previous Results Grouped by Complexity		
Tractable - In $\mathcal{P}$		
Branch Free+rendezvous/noSelect/singleCaller		[24]
Branch Free+fork/join		[21]
Branch Free+ordered critical sections (bounded nesting)		[5]
Branch Free+Post/Wait/noClear		[18]
Branch Free+send/receive/1-wayNaming		[7]
Branch Free+semaphore/restricted-P-ops		[7]
Branch Free+single semaphore		[13]
Intractable - $\mathcal{NP}$-hard		
Branch Free+rendezvous		[24]
Branch Free+Semaphore		[19]
Branch Free+Post/Wait/Clear		Thm: 1
No Loops+Post/Wait/noClear		[2]
No Loops+fork/join (not all paths executable)		Thm: 2
Undecidable		
Branches+Loops+any synchronization		Thm: 3

Restricted Rendezvous

In 1983, Taylor [24] analyzed the complexity of determining the order in which events could occur for programs using Ada-style rendezvous synchronization. He considered various combinations of the following three restrictions on the programs:

1. no branches or loops,

2. no use of the select statment,

3. all entry calls for a particular entry occur in the same task.

In particular, when all three restrictions are applied he proved that the problem of determining which events could pair up to form a rendezvous could be answered in time linearly proportional to the number of operations in the program. This is equivalent to determining the order in which the events can occur.

He also proved that removing either the second or third restriction above resulted in a problem that was NP-complete.

Fork/Join

A number of methods have been developed in the context of on-the-fly race detection that could be used as polynomial time algorithms for determining event orders in branch free fork/join programs [14,4,21]. Some recent efforts have focused on reducing the number of events that must be traced [15] or recorded [17]. As these fork/join analysis algorithms read the trace only once and have limited storage requirements they can often be executed "on-the-fly," concurrently with the parallel program they are analyzing.

Critical Sections with Lock/Unlock

In programs that contain only fork/join synchronization, if there is a race between two events, then it must be a general race. With the addition of ordered critical sections, the races may be either general races (i.e., not protected by the same lock) or unordered races (i.e., protected by the same lock). These two kinds of races can be distinguished by comparing the locks held when the events were executed. For branch-free programs, this comparison can easily be done using $O(L^2)$ time and $O(L)$ space per event, where L is the maximum lock nesting depth. In practice the lock nesting depth is very small (i.e., 0 or 1) [5].

Post/Wait No Clear

Netzer and Ghosh [18] have an algorithm that precisely determines the event orderings for a trace of a program that uses Post/Wait synchronization with no Clears. The algorithm constructs a DAG where the nodes are the events in the trace and the edges represent the guaranteed orderings between events. That is, two events e_1 and e_2 are ordered (definition 6), if and only if there is a path from the node for e_1 to the node for e_2. The graph construction requires $O(np)$ time and $O(np)$ space where n is the number of events in the trace and p is the number of threads.

1.3.2   No Branches and Non-monotonically Synchronized

As can be seen in Table 1.1, most results in this section (and Secs. 1.3.3 and 1.3.4) indicate that exact solutions are not tractable. The only exception that we are aware of is a recent result by Lu et al. [13] showing that the exact solution for programs using only a single semaphore can be found in polynomial time. A brief description of Taylor's result applicable to this section can be found in Sec. 1.3.1.

Single Semaphore

Computing the exact ordering relationship between events for a loop-free program that synchronizes using only a single semaphore can be done in $O(n^{1.5}p)$ time [13] where n is the number of events and p is the number of threads. The algorithm presented by Lu, Klein, and Netzer determines if two events are ordered by solving a kind of scheduling problem. When P-operations are assigned a cost of $+1$ and V-operations are assigned a cost of -1, a branch-free program using a single semaphore can execute to completion if and only if it has a schedule whose cumulative cost is always ≤ 0. Thus one can tell if a program can complete by finding a schedule where the maximum cumulative cost is minimized. Although this kind of scheduling problem is $\mathcal{NP}$-complete in general, Lu, Klein, and Netzer show how a solution for series-parallel graphs can be modified to determine if two events in a branch-free program are ordered.

As presented in their paper, the algorithm of Lu et al. determines some events to be ordered that should not be (according to our definitions). This derives from their claim that if you artificially order two events and then fail to find a complete schedule, the events cannot occur in that order (and hence are always ordered in the reverse direction). It could be that two events can occur in the artificially added order, but then the program deadlocks later in its execution. Only a small change to their algorithm is needed to get the preferred result. Instead of insisting on a schedule for the entire program it is only necessary to find a prefix of a schedule that includes the two artificially ordered events. Their algorithm provides the necessary information to determine if such a prefix exists.

Post/Wait/Clear

With the addition of the Clear operation, determining precisely the ordering relationships for branch-free programs becomes $\mathcal{NP}$-hard.

Theorem 1 *Deciding if there exists a race between two conflicting statements in an arbitrary shared memory parallel program, containing explicit thread creation and Post/Wait/Clear synchronization but no loops or branches, is $\mathcal{NP}$-hard.*

Proof: The proof is by reduction from 3-SAT. We construct the following program which encodes an instance of the 3 CNF satisfiability problem. This program will contain a race if and only if there is a satisfying assignment to the 3 CNF formula.

- Define signal START.

- For each variable X define 4 signals, Xt (X is true), Xf (X is false), and XisT XisF (X has a value).

- For each clause C define a signal Ct (C is true).

- For each variable X create two threads, TXt and TXf as follows:

TXt:	**TXf:**
wait START	wait START
clear Xf	clear Xt
post XisT	post XisF
wait Xt	wait Xf
for each C containing X	for each C containing not X
post Ct	post Ct
end for	end for

- Create two other threads - main and racer as follows:

main:	**racer:**
for each variable X	for each variable X
post Xt	wait XisT
post Xf	wait XisF
end for	end for
post START	*race statement*
for each clause C	for each variable X
wait Ct	post Xt
end for	post Xf
race statement	end for

- **Claim:** The race statements can execute concurrently if there is a truth assignment satisfying all of the clauses.

1. Run main until just after "post START."

2. Run to completion each TXt if X true in truth assignment or TXf if X false in truth assignment.

3. Run to completion remaining TXt's and TXf's.

4. Observe that all Ct, XisT and XisF are now posted.

5. **Claim:** If there is no truth assignment satisfying all of the clauses then the race statement in racer must execute before the race statement in main.

1. All Ct must be posted before main executes the race statement.

2. For some X, both TXt and TXf must have posted signals for all Ct to be posted (otherwise the clauses are all satisfiable).

3. Either Xt or Xf must have been posted twice, and thus the race statement in racer must have already been executed.

NOTE: The operations on the XisT and XisF events are not necessary for the theorem. However, if these operations are removed then the program will have many executions which end in deadlock.

Semaphores

Determining precisely the ordering relationships for even branch-free programs containing semaphore synchronization is co-$\mathcal{NP}$-hard [19].

The results in this area are therefore restricted to approximations. Helmbold et al. [10] and Netzer and Miller [20] have pursued two complimentary approaches. The first group has been attempting to find as many races (unordered blocks) as possible, while the other has been trying to reduce the number of reported races that cannot actually occur.

1.3.3 No Loops and Monotonically Synchronized

Excluding arbitrary loops is necessary to avoid termination problems and the undecidability shown in Sec. 1.3.5. Loops executing a fixed number of times can be unrolled. This clearly affects the complexity of any analysis algorithm, but is essentially what happens in any trace based approach to race detection. Loops that do not contain synchronization operations and which are guaranteed to terminate are allowed because they do not affect the order analysis between events.

Theorem 2 *Deciding if there exists a race between two conflicting statements in an arbitrary shared memory parallel program (containing explicit thread creation but no loops) is $\mathcal{NP}$-hard.*

Proof: By reduction from 3SAT. Create a parallel program that forks executing the statements `x:=1; print(x);` in one branch and `if(3SAT formula over input) then x:=0;` in the other branch. There is a race between the `print(x)` and the assignment `x:=0`, if and only if the formula is satisfiable for some input.

The key difference between this result and the Post/Wait no Clear result of Callahan and Subhlok (see Sec. 1.3.3) is they assume all paths are executable and this trivial proof hinges on whether or not one path is executable. The set of programs where all paths are executable is clearly a subset of all programs and hence they have shown that with the addition of Post and Wait the problem is still $\mathcal{NP}$-hard even for the smaller set of programs.

Post/Wait No Clear

Callahan et al. [1] have studied simple programs containing only if-then-else conditionals and Post/Wait synchronization without Clear (i.e., no loops). The Post/Wait operations are permitted to specify events within an array. They claim that as generally used, the index expressions for these events are amenable to standard dependence analysis for computing a dependence distance (i.e., the difference between the parallel loop index and the array index used by the Post or Wait). In an earlier paper [2] they prove that the problem of determining if a program is race free is Co-$\mathcal{NP}$-hard for even these relatively simple programs under the further assumption that all program paths are feasible.

In [1], they have gone on to develop a dataflow formulation of the problem for which they can compute an approximate solution in polynomial time (the paper does not give the actual complexity). This approximation only applies to programs that are "serializable." By that they mean that if all parallel loops and parallel case statements (the only types of forking they support) are executed in sequential order (the cases from the parallel case are executed in the order they appear textually) then the program will complete without blocking. i.e., no Wait will be encountered until after a Post for the same event has been executed.

They give an algebraic formulation of the problem when the program is further restricted to contain only one Post for each event variable. The algebraic formulation provides an exact solution that appears faster in practice than the previous method. However, it involves a transformation to a system of linear equations and determining if there exists a non-negative integral solution to the system of equations. Although such integer linear programming problems are $\mathcal{NP}$-hard, the systems generated in practice are claimed to be generally small enough so that this is not a problem.

1.3.4   No Loops and Non-Monotonically Synchronized

As already indicated, all results in this area show that exact solutions are not tractable. Some approximation algorithms can be found in [14,4,21,1].

Post/Wait/Clear

The Co-$\mathcal{NP}$-Hard result from [2] also applies here. In fact, with the addition of Clear, even detecting races in branch-free (i.e., no conditionals or loops) programs is $\mathcal{NP}$-Hard (see Theorem 1).

Semaphores

Determining precisely the ordering relationships for branch-free programs containing semaphore synchronization is co-$\mathcal{NP}$-hard [19]. Therefore the problem is also co-$\mathcal{NP}$-hard when branches are permitted.

1.3.5   Unrestricted Programs

If programs are allowed to have branches and unbounded loops, determining the ordering relationships between statement instances is undecidable, regardless of the type of synchronization used.

Theorem 3 *Deciding if there exists a race between two conflicting statements in an arbitrary shared memory parallel program is as hard as the halting problem.*

Proof: Given an arbitrary (sequential) program P and input $\mathcal{I}$, we create a new parallel program containing a new shared variable x initialized to 0. The parallel program forks, executing "print(x);" in one branch. The other branch first checks that the parallel program's input equals $\mathcal{I}$. If the input matches $\mathcal{I}$ then program P is simulated and when (if) the original program halts, the statement "x := 1;" is executed. If the input does not match $\mathcal{I}$ then the second branch terminates without accessing variable x. There is a race between the "print(x);" statement and the "x := 1;" assignment if and only if program P halts on input $\mathcal{I}$.

Nevertheless, programmers must still uncover data races in their parallel programs. Therefore approaches that compute approximate answers to the problem have been studied and continue to be investigated [23,12,6].

1.4 Are There *Any* Races in This Program?

Because the problem of detecting races in parallel programs is in general intractable, approximations must suffice. There are two ways to err: report races that do not really exist (*infeasible races*) or fail to report some of the races.[5] The problem with the former is that the user may be inundated with infeasible races and miss the real race. The problem with the latter is that a program may be reported to be race free when in fact it is not. A compromise that has been achieved in some situations is to guarantee to report a *non-empty* subset of the actual races. While some races may still be missed, if a program (or execution) is reported to be race free, then the report is accurate.

1.4.1 Fork/Join

Mellor-Crummey [14] describes a method for analyzing programs containing only properly nested fork/join parallelism. This approach requires $O(VN)$ space where V is the number of shared variables and N is the maximum nesting depth of the forks. Also each monitoring operation requires $O(N)$ time. The method is called Offset-Span labeling and is similar to *English-Hebrew* labeling [21]. In particular the label for each thread that is created

---

[5]A related problem has been observed by Netzer and Miller [20]. Even reporting only races that can actually occur (feasible races) can be too much. There may be a small number of important "first" races towards which the programmer should be directed and then a possibly large number of other "artifact" races.

during the execution of the program is computed based only on the labels of its immediate predecessors (the thread executing the fork or the threads resulting in a successful join). The length of each label is proportional to the current nesting depth and at most three labels must be stored on-the-fly for each shared variable. The most significant contribution of Offset-Span labeling is that a single execution is sufficient to identify a non-empty subset of the races that could occur for a given input.

1.4.2   Critical Sections

Dinning and Schonberg [5] describe an approach to detecting access anomalies in programs that contain critical sections (i.e., properly nested binary semaphores). This approach can use any existing method for determining when two blocks are ordered (e.g., Offset-Span labeling) ignoring the orderings imposed by the unlock-lock operations. As one would expect, ignoring the unlock-lock orderings results in many false anomalies. This is solved by adding lock covers to the labels for blocks in critical sections. A lock cover indicates what locks are held when a block executes. If there is no nondeterminism "propagated" by the critical sections then the access anomalies reported will include at least one anomaly (if there are any) from the set of access anomalies that could occur given the input supplied during the analyzed execution. Nondeterminism is propagated by a critical section if the occurrence of some event depends on the ordering of some critical section. This property can be conservatively checked statically in polynomial time.

In addition to needing the lock covers, this approach requires a larger history for each shared variable than the approaches described in Section 1.3.1. For each shared variable the history may contain as many as $T \times R$ labels and lock covers representing the latest writes and similarly for the reads. T is the maximum degree of concurrency and R is the number of lock covers which is bounded by 2^K where K is the number of locks.[6] Dinning and Schonberg claim that the use of nested critical sections is rare resulting in very few lock covers in practice.

---

[6]Simply checking the intersection of the locks held when accessing a variable is not sufficient. One access may be protected by locks a and b, another by locks b and c, and a third by locks a and c. Although the intersection of the locks held is empty, there is no concurrent race between the three accesses.

1.4.3   Semaphores

We have developed an algorithm for analyzing traces of programs that contain semaphore synchronization. In [11] we proved that our algorithm will find at least one race from the set of possible races that can occur for a given input if any exist.

1.5   What Shared Memory Addresses are Accessed by a Statement (Instance)?

Operationally, race detection systems can be divided into three groups, compile time systems, post-mortem trace based systems and on-the-fly systems. A distinguishing characteristic is the degree to which the aliasing problem is solved/avoided. Compile time approaches must attempt to solve the problem (e.g., conventional vectorizing compiler analysis). Space limitations generally prohibit post-mortem systems from storing all shared memory accesses during data collection. Instead some type of summary information is recorded and then the actual addresses are estimated or re-generated when needed. On-the-fly systems have no such space limitation and can use the actual memory addresses in the analysis, thereby eliminating any aliasing problems.

Any monitoring/trace based approach can therefore easily answer the question: "Given shared memory location X, what statements access X?" By "easily" we mean that the cost of answering this question is dominated by the cost of determining the ordering relationships. In general it will add a constant time cost to the processing of each statement (event).

For compile time systems there has been a large body of work performed on this problem restricted to statements within the same loop nest. This work answers a variation of the previous question, the new question being:

> Given two statements, S1 and S2, can they access the same location?

For two statements outside of a common loop nest there has been no published work that we are aware of.

1.6   Conclusion

We have presented a taxonomy of approaches for determining event orders in executions of parallel programs (which can then be used for race detection). The purpose of this taxonomy is to organize the previous results and determine just how much we actually know today about the "race detection" problem. We then summarized previous results and placed them into the taxonomy (Table A.1). Finally we have presented some new results that provide further evidence that analyzing all but the most restrictive programming models is at best intractable.

References

[1] CALLAHAN, D., KENNEDY, K., AND SUBHLOK, J., "Analysis of Event Synchronization in a Parallel Programming Tool," in *Proceedings of Second ACM SIGPLAN Symposium on Principles and Practice of Parallel Programming (PPOPP)*, *SIGPLAN Notices*, 21–30, March 1990.

[2] CALLAHAN, D. AND SUBHLOK, J., "Static Analysis of Low-Level Synchronization," in *Proc. Workshop on Parallel and Distributed Debugging*, 100–111, May 1988.

[3] DAMODARAN-KAMAL, S. K., AND FRANCIONI, J. M., "Nondeterminacy: Testing and Debugging in Message Passing Parallel Programs," in *Proc. ACM/ONR Workshop on Parallel and Distributed Debugging*, 118–128, 1993.

[4] DINNING, A. AND SCHONBERG, E., "An Empirical Comparison of Monitoring Algorithms for Access Anomaly Detection," in *Proceedings of Second ACM SIGPLAN Symposium on Principles and Practice of Parallel Programming (PPOPP)*, 1990.

[5] DINNING, A. AND SCHONBERG, E., "Detecting Access Anomalies in Programs with Critical Sections," in *Proc. Workshop on Parallel and Distributed Debugging*, 79–90, May 1991.

[6] HELMBOLD, D. P. AND McDOWELL, C. E., "Computing Reachable States of Parallel Programs" (extended abstract), *SIGPLAN Notices: Proceedings of the ACM/ONR Workshop on Parallel and Distributed Debugging*, 26(12):76–84, December 1991.

[7] HELMBOLD, D. P. AND McDOWELL, C. E., "A Class of Synchronization Operations that Permit Efficient Race Detection," Technical report, U. of Calif. Santa Cruz, UCSC-CRL-93-29, 1993.

[8] HELMBOLD, D. P. AND MCDOWELL, C. E., "What is a Race in a Program and When Can We Detect it?" Technical report, U. of Calif. Santa Cruz, UCSC-CRL-93-30, 1993.

[9] HELMBOLD, D. P. AND MCDOWELL, C. E., "A Taxonomy of Race Conditions," Technical report, UCSC-CRL-94-34, 1994.

[10] HELMBOLD, D. P. AND MCDOWELL, C. E. AND WANG, J. Z., "Detecting Data Races from Sequential Traces," in *Proc. of Hawaii International Conference on System Sciences*, 408–417, 1991.

[11] HELMBOLD, D. P. AND MCDOWELL, C. E. AND WANG, J. Z., "Determining Possible Event Orders by Analyzing Sequential Traces," *IEEE Transactions on Parallel and Distributed Systems*, 1993. Also UCSC Tech. Rep. UCSC-CRL-91-36.

[12] LONG, D. L. AND CLARKE, L. A., "Task Interaction Graphs for Concurrency Analysis," in *Proc. 11th Int. Conf. on Software Engineering*, 1989.

[13] LU, H-I., KLEIN, P. N., AND NETZER, R. H. B., "Detecting Race Conditions in Parallel Programs that Use One Semaphore," Technical report, Brown Univ., 1993.

[14] MELLOR-CRUMMEY, J., "On-the-fly Detection of Data Races for Programs with Nested Fork-Join Parallelism," in *Supercomputing '91*, 24–33, November 1991. Albuquerque, NM.

[15] MELLOR-CRUMMEY, J., "Compile-Time Support for Efficient Data Race Detection in Shared-Memory Parallel Programs," in *Proc. ACM/ONR Workshop on Parallel and Distributed Debugging*, 129–139, 1993.

[16] MCDOWELL, C. E., "A Practical Algorithm for Static Analysis of Parallel Programs," *Journal of Parallel and Distributed Computing*, June 1989.

[17] NETZER, R. H. B., "Optimal Tracing and Replay for Debugging Shared-Memory Parallel Programs," in *Proc. ACM/ONR Workshop on Parallel and Distributed Debugging*, 1993.

[18] NETZER, R. H. B. AND GHOSH, S., "Efficient Race Condition Detection for Shared-Memory Programs with Post/Wait Synchronization," in *Proc. International Conf. on Parallel Processing*, 1992.

[19] NETZER, R. H. B. AND MILLER, B. P., "On the Complexity of Event Ordering for Shared-Memory Parallel Program Executions," in *Proc. International Conf. on Parallel Processing*, volume II, 93–97, 1990.

[20] NETZER, R. H. B. AND MILLER, B. P., "Improving the Accuracy of Data Race Detection," *SIGPLAN Notices (Proc. PPOPP)*, 26(7):133–144, 1991.

[21] NUDLER, I. AND RUDOLPH, L., "Tools for Efficient Development of Efficient Parallel Programs," in *First Israeli Conference on Computer Systems Engineering*, 1988.

[22] STERLING, N., "WARLOCK - A Static Data Race Analysis Tool," in *Proc. Winter Usenix*, 97–106, 1993.

[23] TAYLOR, R. N., "A General-Purpose Algorithm for Analyzing Concurrent Programs," *CACM*, 26(5):362–376, May 1983.

[24] TAYLOR, RICHARD N., "Complexity of Analyzing the Synchronization Structure of Concurrent Programs," *Acta Informatica*, 19(1):57–84, 1983.

APPENDIX A

In this appendix we present our terminology for races and the ordering relationships between events. A complete discussion of this terminology can be found in [9]. In [9] we also define four additional orthogonal attributes of races: the affect on control flow (control/data race), the severity (benign/critical race), the affect on other races (depends on), and the feasibility (feasible/infeasible).

Definition 2 *An* **event** *is a contiguous sequence of one or more atomic operations executed by a single thread.*

Definition 3 *A* **simple statement** *is a syntactic structure from a program such that if any instruction in the machine level translation of the statement is executed every instruction from the machine level translation of the statement will be executed.*

A **compound statement** *is any syntactically contiguous sequence of simple statements.*

Definition 4 *Two events from different executions of the same program are* **equal** *(i.e., can be considered to be the same event) if*

- *they occur in the same thread,*

- *their constituent atomic operations are derived from the same simple source program statements, and*

- *both events are the nth occurrence of their constituent atomic action sequences by the thread.*

Definition 5 *Let events e_1 and e_2 be two events occurring in an execution of a program. If e_1 completes before e_2 begins then we say e_1* **happened before**[7] *e_2, written $e_1 \rightarrow e_2$. If e_1 begins before e_2 ends and e_2 begins before e_1 ends then the two events* **overlap**. *If either e_1 and e_2 overlap or $e_1 \rightarrow e_2$, then we write $e_2 \not\rightarrow e_1$.*

---

[7]This is a strictly *temporal* relation and should not be confused with Lamport's *causal* "happened before" relation.

Definition 6 *Fix an input to the program. Event e_1 is* **ordered before** *event e_2 if in every execution of the program on the input in which either event occurs, $e_1 \rightarrow e_2$.*
Two events, e_1 and e_2, are **ordered** *if e_1 is ordered before e_2 or e_2 is ordered before e_1.*

Definition 7 *Fix an input to the program. Event e_1 is* **semi-ordered before** *event e_2 if for that input*
- *every execution where both e_1 and e_2 occur, $e_1 \rightarrow e_2$,*
- *there exists an execution containing e_1 but not e_2 and*
- *every execution that contains e_2 also e_1.*

Two events, e_1 and e_2, are **semi-ordered** *if e_1 is semi-ordered before e_2 or e_2 is semi-ordered before e_1.*

Definition 8 *Two events are* **unordered** *if they are neither ordered nor semi-ordered.*

Definition 9 *Two simple statements* **conflict** *if they both access the same shared resource and one (or both) of the accesses modifies the resource. The accesses can be explicit as in access to a shared variable or implicit as in a communication port used for message passing.*

Definition 10 *Two different events* **conflict** *if they represent the execution of conflicting simple statements.*

Definition 11 *Fix an input to the program. If two conflicting events are unordered (with respect to the input) then there is a* **race** *between the two events on the input.*

Given two events that occur in some execution[8] of a program for a fixed input, in any particular execution on that same input:

- the two events will overlap or

- one will happen before the other or

- only one of the two events will occur or

- neither of the two events will occur.

---

[8]This need not be the same execution for both events.

The possible combinations (except neither event occurring) are shown in Table A.1.

Definition 12 (Kinds of Races.) *The following four kinds of races are disjoint.*

concurrent race: *In every execution of the program on the fixed input where both e_1 and e_2 occur, they overlap.*

general race: *There exist executions of the program on the fixed input in which e_1 and e_2 overlap and executions where either $e_1 \rightarrow e_2$ or $e_2 \rightarrow e_1$.*

unordered race: *There exist executions of the program on the fixed input in which $e_1 \rightarrow e_2$ and executions in which $e_2 \rightarrow e_1$ but no execution in which e_1 and e_2 overlap.*

omission race: *There exist executions of the program on the fixed input where e_2 occurs but e_1 does not and there exist executions where either $e_1 \rightarrow e_2$ or e_1 occurs but e_2 does not, but there are no executions on the fixed input where either e_1 and e_2 are concurrent or $e_2 \rightarrow e_1$.*

Table A.1
Summary of Possible Ordering Relationships

		There exists executions where			
$e_1 \rightarrow e_2$	$e_2 \rightarrow e_1$	overlap	e_1 only	e_2 only	
yes	yes	yes	y/n	y/n	general race
yes	yes	no	y/n	y/n	unordered race
yes	no	yes	y/n	y/n	general race
yes	no	no	y/n	yes	omission race
yes	no	no	y/n	no	not a race
no	yes	yes	y/n	y/n	general race
no	yes	no	yes	y/n	omission race
no	yes	no	no	y/n	not a race
no	no	yes	y/n	y/n	concurrent
no	no	no	yes	yes	omission race

Definition 13 *A program contains a race between statements s_1 and s_2 if there is an input $\mathcal{I}$ and events e_1 and e_2 such that:*

1. *e_1 represents the execution of an instance of s_1,*

2. *e_2 represents the execution of an instance of s_2,*

3. *s_1 and s_2 contain (or are) conflicting simple statements, and*

4. *there is a race between e_1 and e_2 on input $\mathcal{I}$.*

Determining the Effectiveness of Interfaces for Debugging and Performance Analysis Tools

Joan M. Francioni
Computer Science Department
University of Southwestern Louisiana
Lafayette, Louisiana 70504

Abstract

The general objectives for debugging tools and performance analysis tools are well known: identify program bugs; identify performance bottlenecks. The criteria for determining the effectiveness of a tool in achieving these objectives, however, is not well defined. In addition, there are no adequate mechanisms for measuring the effectiveness of the interface of debugging and performance analysis tools. These problems are manifested in two main situations. In one, tool developers have trouble sometimes knowing whether or not their own strategies are effective in dealing with issues relevant to "real" parallel programs. In the second, researchers who develop new tools/strategies/methodologies for debugging or performance analysis must convince the users as well as the research community of the tool's worth. In this paper, we discuss the issues relevant to the interface of performance and debugging tools for parallel programs and present a set of criteria for evaluating tool effectiveness in this regard. In addition, we propose a benchmarking-type system for measuring relevant characteristics of such tools.

1.1   Introduction

We have learned much in the past decade about designing and building tools
for debugging and analyzing the performance of parallel programs. Some
tools and techniques that have been developed are more effective at this
than others. Some tools and techniques that were effective for early parallel
systems are no longer effective and some tools and techniques are less effective
than they could be, due, to a large extent, to the tool's interface with the
user. What is it that makes an interface effective? For the most part, we have
only folklore to answer this. In the absence of well defined criteria, authors
of parallel debugging and performance analysis papers are forced to present
their own set of traits about parallel programs or about what programmers
notice about parallel programs in order to motivate their solutions to the
problem (see, for example, [1,2,3,4,7]). As the field matures, however, it is
worthwhile to step back and try to define more specifically what is necessary
for a tool to be effective. That is one intent of this paper.

Simply put, a tool is effective when the programmer can ascertain useful information for debugging and performance tuning. This requires two
things, one of which is that the tool can accurately collect and/or compute
the necessary information. The other is that the tool can communicate this
information to the user via the interface. In this paper, we take a more detailed look at what kind of information is relevant in testing, debugging, and
analyzing the performance of parallel programs. Based on these observations,
we offer a set of 25 effectiveness guidelines designed to assist tool developers
in building effective interfaces.

The second intent of this paper is to introduce SWAMP as a test platform
for measuring the characteristics of parallel debugging and performance analysis tools. When fully implemented, SWAMP will provide tool developers
with a set of realistic parallel programs that can be used for testing the effectiveness of debugging and performance analysis tools and their interfaces.

1.2   Basic Information Necessary

To know whether a tool is good at doing what it is supposed to do, we must
first understand what the tool is supposed to do. As defined in the report
of the 1991 workshop on Parallel Computer Systems: Software Performance
Tools, a programmer wants to know three things about a parallel program:

(1) is the program running correctly?; (2) how well is the program running?; and (3) can the program's performance be improved? [12]. For testing and debugging a program, the programmer wants a tool that will help in identifying if a bug exists and where the source of the bug is located. For analyzing the performance of a parallel program, the programmer wants a tool that will help in describing the program's performance; will show if the performance is less than optimal; will describe where key performance code is located; will offer guidance on how performance problems can be resolved; and will estimate how much effort is required to resolve them. This section discusses the "what" in further detail.

1.2.1 Testing versus Debugging

It is only necessary to fix what is broken. Therefore, the first step to any debugging and performance analysis of a program is the testing of the program. Although testing is usually integrated into the other activities, it is a separate and distinct phase of programming, with the separate goal of detecting existence of a problem versus source of a problem. As such, different information is needed about a program for testing than is needed for strictly debugging or analyzing the performance of the program. We consider three forms of testing here.

The first form of testing is to ascertain program correctness for the particular system configuration being used. Program correctness is determined primarily by investigating the program's results. Two problems arise with this form of testing for parallel programs. First, a particular set of results for a particular set of inputs can only be judged to be correct if it is also known that this set of results is the only possible output for this set of inputs, i.e., there are no race conditions in the program that affect the program's final output values. (See [6] for a discussion of harmful and safe races.) Another problem is that the correctness of output can not always be completely determined due to the nature of the algorithm. In these cases, programmers must test their programs by examining the program's behavior rather than its output to determine if the code is consistent with the intended algorithm. Again, race conditions in a parallel program come into play.

The second form of testing is to test whether the performance of a parallel program is optimal for the particular system configuration being used. "Optimal" is frequently an unreachable goal, of course. But programmers want to be able to determine if work to improve the performance of the system is warranted.

Both above forms of testing are hard for parallel programs in the same way that they are hard for sequential programs: it is difficult to choose the right test data to adequately test the program. As far as this paper goes, however, we accept that as a fact of programming.

The third form of testing, which is unique to parallel systems, can be described as prediction testing, and it is applicable to both the other forms of testing. The idea of prediction testing is that both the correctness and the performance of the program are considered for system configurations that are different from the one on which the program is run. Different system configurations would include a data structure reorganization, a different algorithm, more or fewer processors, larger or smaller problem size, and different network topology, bandwidth, or latency. Notice that the program or underlying system is not actually changed to reflect the different configuration. Rather a prediction of how the program will behave in the other configuration is made. This is useful in that the resources for the different system configurations do not have to be dedicated to this program unless there is evidence that assigning those resources to the program will be productive. Unfortunately, this is also hard to do. The kind of information needed for prediction testing is the same as in the other two forms of testing.

Table 1.1 outlines the kind of information that is needed by a programmer to support the testing described here. (These entries are quite general, but are further clarified in the subsequent tables.)

1.2.2   Correctness Errors

Debugging a parallel program may cause different headaches than debugging a sequential program, but the basic reason why both tasks can be extremely difficult is that the relationship between the external manifestation of an error and the internal cause of the error may be quite obscure. It is also believed that the very idea of a program having an error in the first place is troublesome to the programmer.

Debugging has elements of problem solving or brain teasers, coupled with the annoying recognition that you have made a mistake. Heightened anxiety and the unwillingness to accept the possibility of errors increases the task difficulty [10].

Nonetheless, it must be done.

We provide a framework for categorizing correctness errors of parallel programs based on correctness errors in sequential programs. Basically, se-

Table 1.1   **Information to Support Testing**
Existence of races   Flow of control   Optimal performance   Performance as is

quential correctness errors can be grouped into one of three categories: logical errors, coding errors, and language errors. Logical errors include problems such as erroneous control flow and incorrect boundary conditions. They are the errors that correspond to a programmer's incorrect understanding of what the program is supposed to be doing. Alternatively, programmers frequently make coding errors, such as infinite loops, parameters out of order, or loop structures that are off by one. In these cases, the overall logic of the program is understood, but the code does not match what the programmer is thinking. The third category, language errors, includes errors stemming from an incorrect usage of the programming language. Examples of this type of error would be using global variables where local variables should be used or passing variable rather than value parameters to a function.

Parallel programs can, of course, have all these same errors. But they can also have errors specifically related to the parallel nature of the program. This is what we mean when we say "parallel program errors" and we con sider them in the same groups as described above. Thus logical parallel program errors include errors in code dependencies (when the necessary order of computations is not enforced), communication topology, and data distribution. Such errors result from a misunderstanding by the programmer of exactly what can and cannot be done in parallel. Coding parallel program errors, on the other hand, might include such errors as memory overwrites and communication misspecifications. As in sequential errors, these kinds of errors are of the "typo" variety. Within the language error category for parallel programs are errors such as those caused by erroneous send/receive syntax and semantics, incorrect object definitions and classifications, and inappropriate data distribution maps.

Errors from different categories can, and often do, result in the same program behavior. For example, misspecifying the values in a receive statement or misunderstanding the semantics of the type field of a receive statement can both cause multiple messages to be accepted at a receive where only one should be acceptable. The result in both cases could be a race condition or a deadlock situation. We can not expect a debugging tool to be designed to find errors in only one category. The point of presenting the errors in these categories is to consider all relevant errors, since it is difficult to ensure that every kind of error is listed. Given these kinds of correctness errors, we are interested in identifying the kind of information that will be useful to a programmer in trying to detect the errors.

Items relevant to debugging correctness bugs are shown in Table 1.2. The first item, data values, includes values of variables at the end of program execution as well as during. The data distribution map depicts how the data is distributed among the processors or different memory banks. Data accesses and message communications can reflect the ordering of events that occurs during a program's execution. The other main way of depicting event order is via the control flow of program functions. At some point during the debugging phase, it is usually necessary to get down to event specifics such as the sender/receiver of a message, the process that last accessed a data item, and the relative time of an event. In general, it is most useful to be able to examine the program state at various times during the execution of the process. To be able to do this during execution, as opposed to looking at a trace after execution, requires that a parallel breakpoint can be enforced. In addition to the values of variables, the program state would also be defined by information on pending messages and blocked processes. To be able to relate program behavior back to the source code statement(s) that caused it, it is also necessary for the program state to include some form of the program counter.

1.2.3 Performance Errors

The performance errors that are relevant to parallel programming can also be grouped into categories. We consider five categories here, starting with the most general: system efficiency. System efficiency errors are those that cause suboptimal performance of a program because resources are used inefficiently. Errors of this sort include distributing work to some but not all of the processors, unnecessary synchronization barriers, or changing the data distribution in an untimely fashion. The second category is redundancy either in accessing data or in computation. Example redundancy errors are

Table 1.2
Information to Support Debugging
Data values
Data distribution map
Data access timing profile
Communication events
Control flow
Program state
pending messages
blocked processes
program counter

overlapping data distributions so that the same data appear in more than one partition, broadcasting a message rather than doing point-to-point communication, and having more than one process compute the same thing. As in the next category, redundant situations are not always erroneous. In fact, sometimes redundancy increases the performance of a program. For instance, overlapping data distributions may result in unnecessary redundant computations on that data in one situation but may prevent costly nonlocal data accesses in another. It depends on the specific system and program. The category of data locality errors represents errors in data access where the overhead associated with a nonlocal access either dominates or interferes with the program's computation. It includes such programming errors as making multiple nonlocal accesses to a data item rather than copying it to a local variable, poor initial data distribution, or not changing the data distribution midstream when the cost of the redistribution is outweighed by the benefits of local accesses. A fourth category of performance errors is coding efficiency.

Although in a perfect world programmers should not have to worry about hardware and system software level performance, we still do. Errors that can adversely affect the system's performance include poor code organization and inappropriate communication topology. The last category, and the one traditionally least dealt with is I/O. All programs have I/O and many are inefficient at it. Two examples of I/O errors are printing out results "immediately" rather than accumulating them to be printed later in a group, and having processes read data individually rather than having one process read the data and distribute it to the others or vice versa. Again, which strategy ends up taking longer depends on the specific system and program.

Table 1.3 gives a list of information that is useful in detecting the kinds of performance errors discussed above. (In the table, "data access" refers to either a read/write in a shared memory system or a send/receive in a distributed memory system.) Some of the information can be simply logged, but most of it must be computed. Again, we are not concerned in this paper with how the tool gets the information about the program, only in what kinds of information are relevant to the problem at hand. So, for example, how a tool can get accurate timing of tasks without the probe effect disrupting the timing is recognized as a hard problem, but is also beyond the scope of this paper.

1.3   Effectiveness in Presentations

The full execution of a parallel program frequently involves a very large state space. In addition, multiple threads of control exist, each potentially affecting the flow of control of all the others. This combination results in what has been termed a maze effect for the programmer who is trying to keep track of all that is going on, and when, in a parallel program [5]. Keep in mind also that many programmers of parallel programs do not always write perfectly well structured code [9]. The major objective of the debugging and performance analysis tool interface is to reduce the maze effect and present as clear a picture as possible of the program's runtime behavior to the programmer.

We have identified information that is relevant to testing, debugging, and performance analysis of parallel programs. Although we are not discussing how in this paper, we assume this information can be captured from programs either by measurement, simulation, modeling, or some combination thereof. When it comes to depicting the information, however, there are many options from which to choose. For example, a presentation could be textual, graphical, aural, or even something else entirely. Which is the best choice? The interface itself will likely include different modes of presentation. For any particular mode, there are many factors that affect the cognitive effectiveness of a presentation. (See for example [11].) But there is still the question of what makes any one kind of presentation specifically effective for debugging and analyzing performance. In this section, we present a set of

Table 1.3.
Information to Support Performance Analysis
Speedup
Processor utilization
Load balance
System overhead
Data access distribution by location
Data access timing profile
Duration of computation phases
Duration of nonlocal accesses
Timing of tasks
Communication/computation rate
Cache hits
Network communication packets
Page replacement choices
System queues
Routing protocol
I/O event profile
Program counter

guidelines for determining the effectiveness of a presentation in helping programmers (1) to identify that correctness or performance errors exist; and (2) to understand the cause of the problem.

In a special issue of the Journal of Parallel and Distributed Computing on visualization of parallel programs, Bart Miller presented a set of criteria for a useful visualization [8]. We can easily generalize these criteria to be for any kind of presentation, not just visualizations. We use a generalized version of these criteria as a framework for presenting 25 effectiveness guidelines. (Other than the first criterion, all italicized criteria are from [8].) The guidelines are presented as questions such that a positive answer indicates effectiveness. The extent of the effectiveness could then be determined by the followup question: "How well?" The criteria and guidelines are as follows.

Overall tool interfaces should assist in testing, debugging, and analyzing the performance of parallel programs. The overall interface of a tool may consist of many different forms of presentation. Desirable characteristics of those presentations are dealt with in the remaining criteria. Broadly speaking, the tool must provide the information relevant to the task at hand.

1. Does the interface provide the information listed in Tables 1.1, 1.2, and 1.3?

Presentations should guide, not rationalize. Presentations should depict information that can lead a programmer to discover things about a program that are not already known versus simply illustrating what is obvious or easily computed. For example, displaying information about process id's rather than process names is easier but less relevant to the program's structure. Specific guidelines in this category are as follows:

1. Does the presentation exhibit relevant program structure and behavior?

2. Does the presentation facilitate negotiation of the program maze?

3. Can the "area of notice" be mapped to source code?

4. Is irrelevant program behavior hidden?

5. Does the presentation facilitate comparisons among different runs?

Presentations should be appropriate to the programming model. Ideally, it would be best if programmers could have all feedback in terms of the intuitive model used in designing their program. We are a long way from this ideal. On the other hand, it is reasonable to expect that if a program is written in a shared memory model, the feedback should also be in these terms rather than in terms of message communication profiles. Other appropriate aspects of a programming model include levels of abstraction and application-specific information. Instrumentation level information, however, is inappropriate. Specific guidelines in this category include:

1. Does the presentation match the user's conceptual model of the program?

2. Are different levels of abstraction presented?

3. Is application specific information presented?

4. Is the presentation independent of instrumentation techniques used?

Scalability is crucial. Programmers who write parallel programs must be able to study the behavior of their programs under varying system and problem sizes. They also need feedback about which parts of the code are scalable. Three specific guidelines for this category are as follows:

1. Can data of a subset of processes as well as of the entire system be presented?

2. Are scalable parts of a program distinguished from nonscalable parts?

3. Are areas of high potential speedup identified?

Avoid the "Watchmaker's Fascination." Subcriteria: Extras should inform, not entertain. It is possible to generate pretty pictures that are not very informative. It is also possible to overload a user with too much information at one time. Guarding against both of these cases is important in an interface. Relevant guidelines in this area include:

1. Do all parts of the presentation contribute to the objective of the presentation?

2. Is emphasis in the presentation via accent features intentional?

Presentations should be interactive. Users need to be able to study different aspects of their programs. They should also be able to direct the interface to give more appropriate information as they find out more about what they are looking for. Guidelines specific to this category are as follows:

1. Is a mechanism for manipulating and searching data provided?

2. Are complementary displays presented?

3. Are different perspective displays presented?

Default presentations should provide useful information. According to the first group of guidelines, all displays should have useful information. In particular, however, interfaces should provide a set of default presentations that can be used, with little effort, to understand the basic behavior of a program. Not all displays should be restricted to the property of "little effort required for use." More specifically, the three guidelines below address this criteria.

1. Are novice-level displays included that are easy to initiate?

2. Do presentations support varying degrees of expertise effectively?

3. Are relationships among different components available?

Presentations should provide meaningful labels. In general, it should not be assumed that parts of a presentation are obvious. Labeling should be considered necessary. Care must be taken, however, to make sure that it adds to the overall presentation rather than gets in the way. There are two guidelines for this criteria, as follows:

1. Are major components of the presentation labeled as part of the presentation?

2. Is detailed labeling information accessible but not intrusive?

Presentation controls should be simple: User-friendly, user-friendly, user-friendly. It is not just for PCs anymore. Users want simplicity and understandable functionality in their tools. If they do not feel like they can get this from the tool, they will go back to the tried and true "printf" statement.

1. Are navigation controls between different parts of the system provided?

2. Are controls easy and straightforward to use?

1.4   Validating Interface Effectiveness

Acceptance of a debugging or performance analysis tool by the parallel programming community will certainly be quicker when the tool is portable, efficient, and easy to use and install. Unfortunately, these traits alone do not ensure effectiveness of a tool. It has been said at many meetings and in the literature [8,12] that testing new tools out on users is the best way to determine a tool's effectiveness. Getting users to try a new tool, however, is a less than trivial task. The tool developer not only has to find willing users, but must also convince them to go through the effort of setting up their programs to work with a new tool and to take the time to learn how to use the tool. Part of the reason why users are unwilling to try out new tools is that tool developers themselves are not always able to say whether or not their own strategies are effective in dealing with issues relevant to "real" parallel programs.

In the hardware world, the use of benchmarks for validating a certain level of performance is well known. They provide a means for measuring a performance characteristic that can be used on multiple platforms. Benchmark programs have their limitations and disadvantages as well. In particular, benchmark results are used to imply system performance above and beyond what the benchmark is capable of measuring. Also, when a benchmark becomes widely used, systems can be designed that perform well on the benchmark to the detriment of other performance characteristics. Nonetheless, benchmarks do provide a means for understanding the effectiveness of systems in certain contexts and also a means for comparing the performance of different systems within those contexts.

One solution to the problem of providing adequate test platforms for measuring the characteristics of parallel debugging or performance analysis tools is to set up a test suite of programs that can be used for software systems in the same way as benchmark programs are used for hardware systems. Such a test suite, called Suite of Wrong Answer Multiprocessor Programs (SWAMP) is currently being created. The intent is to maintain this test suite and make it easily available to tool developers and users. The objectives of SWAMP are

1. to represent error conditions of realistic parallel programs; and

2. to be a dynamic collection, such that new programs can be added as neces sary.

Making SWAMP into a dynamic collection of programs will keep it current and discourage tools that work well only on a static set of programs. Each test program will be stored in the form of a test session which includes trace files of actual executions along with a script describing how and in what order the trace files should be considered. The full set of SWAMP files will eventually be made available for general accessibility via modes such as anonymous ftp and the world wide web.

1.5 Concluding Remarks

The effectiveness of any tool is dependent on its interface to the user. No matter how powerful a tool is, if someone does not know how to use it properly, the power is wasted at best and even harmful at worst. In this paper, we have provided a set of guidelines designed to assist tool developers in judging the effectiveness of the interface to their debugging and performance analysis tools. For the most part, the guidelines indicate what should be included as part of an interface presentation. But tool developers often succumb to the temptation to do everything at once. Hence, there are also guidelines that attempt to control overload situations.

Ultimately, a tool is effective for any one user if that user can use the tool to debug and/or tune the performance of a parallel program. In general, however, tool developers are interested in designing tools that are effective for many users. Additionally, users are only interested in working to learn new tools which they think will be effective. The paper introduces SWAMP as a test suite that can be used to facilitate determining a tool's effectiveness for both these purposes.

Acknowledgements

The author thanks Diane Rover and Bart Miller for their helpful comments and suggestions on this paper.

References

[1] 1994 Scalable High Performance Computing Conference, Proceedings, papers in five "Tools" sessions, Knoxville, TN, May 1994.

[2] ACM/ONR Workshop on Parallel and Distributed Debugging, Proceedings, in *ACM SIGPLAN Notices*, **24**, No. 1, Jan. 1989.

[3] 2rd ACM/ONR Workshop on Parallel and Distributed Debugging, Proceedings, in *ACM SIGPLAN Notices*, **26**, No. 12, Dec. 1991.

[4] 3rd ACM/ONR Workshop on Parallel and Distributed Debugging, Proceedings, in *ACM SIGPLAN Notices*, **28**, No. 12, Dec. 1993.

[5] DAMODARANKAMAL, S. K., "Testing and Debugging Nondeterministic Message Passing Parallel Programs," Ph.D. Thesis, University of Southwestern Louisiana, Spring 1994.

[6] DAMODARANKAMAL, S. K. AND FRANCIONI, JOAN M., "Nondeterminacy: Testing and Debugging in Message Passing Parallel Programs," in *Proceedings of the 3rd ACM/ONR Workshop on Parallel and Distributed Debugging*, published as ACM SIGPLAN Notices, **28**, No. 12, Dec. 1993.

[7] *Journal of Parallel and Distributed Computing*, special issue on "Tools and Methods for Visualization of Parallel Systems and Computations," **18**, No. 2, June 1993.

[8] MILLER, BARTON P., "What to Draw? When to Draw? An Essay on Parallel Program Visualization," *Journal of Parallel and Distributed Computing*, **18**, No. 2, June 1993, 265–269.

[9] PANCAKE, CHERRI M. AND COOK, CURTIS, "What Users Need in Parallel Tool Support: Survey Results and Analysis," in *Proceedings of 1994 Scalable High Performance Computing Conference*, Knoxville, TN, May 1994, 40–47.

[10] SHNEIDERMAN, B., *Software Psychology*, Winthrop Publishers, 1980, 28.

[11] TUFTE, E. R., *The Visual Display of Quantitative Information*, Graphics Press, Cheshire, CT, 1983.

[12] Workshop Summary on Parallel Computer Systems: Software Performance Tools, Santa Fe, NM, Oct. 24, 1991.

Chapter 3

Tools: A Vendor Point of View

In order to provide increasingly higher levels of performance, high-performance computing hardware vendors have moved rapidly from relatively simple serial machines to parallel distributed and shared memory architectures. As these new architectures gain acceptance and move into the mainstream of production computing, users demand a development environment that makes code development as easy as it was on the serial machines. The challenge to tool developers is to achieve this in the presence of a much more complex underlying architecture and programming model. The vendor presentations at this workshop were focused on work in the areas of parallel debugging and performance analysis, with an eye to integrated environments. Five vendors presented current research and development in this area: Thinking Machines Corp., Intel Corp., Silicon Graphics, Inc., Hewlett Packard, and Cray Research, Inc.

Rich Title presented work done at Thinking Machines Corporation on the MIMD version of the Prism debugger, called Node Prism. The paper discusses several extensions to Prism to support a message-passing paradigm: a rich language to select process node sets (pnsets) over which subsequent debugger commands are executed, debugger output filtering mechanisms, the implementation of a parallel call stack or "where tree," design extensions for scalable performance, and enhanced distributed data visualization.

Don Breazeal of Intel Scalable Systems Division presented a building block approach to parallel tools construction. The paper advocates the development of a tool infrastructure to expedite the transfer of scalable tools technology from the research to the commercial community, and one that will react more quickly to changing architectures and user requirements. A description is given of the problems associated with traditional tool development, followed by a proposed tool infrastructure that will allow for more efficient and responsive tool development.

Marty Itzkowitz of Silicon Graphics presented recent work on visualizing performance on parallel supercomputers. The paper describes recording mechanisms, visualization techniques for single and multi-threaded performance data, communication between the compiler and performance tools, and possibilities for future work.

Ming Hao presented work done at Hewlett Packard Laboratories on multiple views of parallel application execution. The paper describes the design of a prototype synchronized visualization and debugging environment called VIZIR. VIZIR synchronizes and controls the activities of a user's favorite debugging and visualization tools providing an integrated environment for process control and interrogation of message passing parallel programs running in a potentially heterogeneous computing space.

Doug Pase of Cray Research presented work on the Apprentice performance tool for the CRAY T3D. The paper discusses related work, an overview of the T3D computational environment, design tradeoffs, an overview of Apprectice features, a case study, and concludes with possibilities for future work.

A Scalable Debugger for Massively Parallel Message-Passing Programs

Steve Sistare, Don Allen, Rich Bowker
Karen Jourdenais, Josh Simons, and Rich Title
Thinking Machines Corporation
Cambridge, Massachusettes 02142

Abstract

Developers of message-passing codes on massively parallel systems have to contend with difficulties that data-parallel programmers do not face, not the least of which is debuggers that do not scale with the degree of parallelism. In this paper, we present new scalable interaction paradigms and their embodiment in a time– and space–efficient debugger with scalable performance. The debugger offers scalable expression, execution, and interpretation of all debugging operations, making it easier to debug and understand message-passing programs.

1.1 Introduction

Our motivation in doing this work is to provide developers of message-passing applications with the same level of scalable debugging support currently enjoyed by data-parallel programmers. In a data-parallel program, there is one logical thread of control, and thus it is no more difficult to debug this thread when it is running on 1024 processors than when it is running on one. On our target machine, the CM-5, we have previously developed a programming environment called Prism that supports debugging, data visualization, and performance analysis of data-parallel programs [6, 7]. In our latest work, we have enhanced Prism to extend these capabilities into the message-passing realm in a scalable fashion. The new Prism is called Node Prism, and it looks and feels very much like the data-parallel version. The architecture of Node Prism is designed to run efficiently and in parallel using the command set described in the next few sections.

1.2   Scalable Command Set

Node Prism gives the user the ability to pick any set of processor nodes, using a broad range of selection criteria, to be the target of debugging operations. Once such a set is defined, it may be established as the current processor-node set, or *pnset*. Any subsequent debugging commands, whether they are initiated by clicking on a pushbutton in the graphical user interface or by typing a command, are broadcast to all the nodes in the current set. The debugging commands are then executed in parallel.

The pnset feature in Node Prism allows the user to create semantically meaningful sets of processors that are performing similar tasks, with more flexibility than is offered by other debuggers. The user can then treat each logical group as a unit during debugging, regardless of the size of the group. This approach to debugging is as scalable as the application itself.

The flexibility and scalability of the pnset approach may be contrasted with the lack of such qualities in several other debuggers for message-passing programs. In pndbx [8], TotalView [1], CXdb [3], and UDB [9] the user may choose to talk to either one or all nodes, but nothing in between. They are thus painful to use when the user wants to perform an operation on a subset of the nodes, because it requires that the target node be changed repeatedly and the command re-issued. IPD [4] goes a step further by allowing lists and ranges of processors, identified by node ids, to be specified. XIPD [5] allows nodes to be chosen graphically, but the selection is still ultimately based on node ids.

Prism provides a rich language for the definition of named sets of processor nodes (PNs). As in IPD, lists and ranges of nodes may be specified. In addition, set membership may be based on expressions involving program data, and any legal source-language expression whose result type is boolean may be used in this context. The expression is evaluated on each node, and the node becomes a member of the set if the result is true. Access to such program data is critical in enabling the user to create semantically meaningful sets of nodes. A number of predefined sets are also available, including *stopped, running, interrupted, break, done,* and *error,* which reflect the execution status of the nodes, and *all,* which includes all nodes. Lastly, standard set operators such as set intersection, difference, and union are provided for combining sets. An example of a set definition that takes advantage of all these features is the following:

$$\text{stopped} * \{i + j < 30 \text{ \&\& sum}(a) > 0\}$$

In the parsing process, the characters { and } are used to delimit source-language expressions; thus, i, j, and a are interpreted as program variables, and the "+" in $i + j$ is interpreted as addition. Therefore, $i + j < 30$ && sum$(a) > 0$ is evaluated on each node, and the collection of nodes on which it is true forms a set that replaces the delimited expression in the evaluation process. Identifiers and operators appearing outside of the braces are interpreted as set names and set operators; thus *stopped* refers to the predefined set of nodes whose execution is stopped, and the "*" represents set intersection. The intersection is then evaluated, completing the definition. For convenient reference, names may be associated with set definitions using the *define pnset* command:

define pnset *name definition*

The given name may then be used in any context that requires a set-valued operand.

A special display called the pnsets window graphically shows the membership of all defined sets (see Figure 1.1). It has two primary functions: to facilitate selection of the current pnset, and to allow the user to see the state of a large number of boolean conditions on all of the nodes at a glance. Referring to Figure 1.1, we see that each pnset is displayed as a two-dimensional grid containing one cell per node. The 2D layout is arbitrary, though in the future we expect to allow the user to specify its geometry. A cell in the grid is filled in if its corresponding node is a member of the set. On a color monitor, cells of the predefined sets known to Prism are color-coded for additional visual cues; green is used for the running set, red for the error set, etc. Graphical gestures for zooming and panning are provided. Zooming grows (or shrinks) each grid, allowing visual acuity to be traded off against

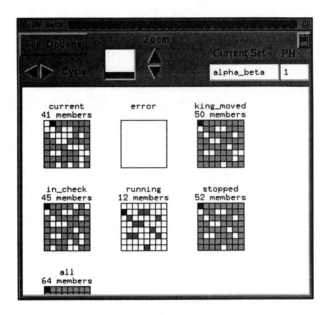

Figure 1.1: The pnsets window.

the number of sets that will fit in the window. Panning allows off-screen sets to be seen, and may be accomplished by clicking and dragging on either the data surface itself or the data-navigator box, found in the upper left of the window. These gestures for panning are standard in all Prism windows with a large data surface, such as the array-visualizer window, discussed in Sec. 1.3. The user may also hide infrequently used sets, causing them to be removed from the display, so that a select few may fit on screen without the need for panning.

The current pnset may be established in a number of ways. The simplest is to double-click on a grid in the *pnsets* window. One can also use the keyboard to enter a *pnset* command, giving it a set name or expression as an argument. In addition, the current set may be temporarily overridden on any given keyboard command by appending a *pnset* clause to the end of the command.

The ability to define and name sets of nodes using flexible selection criteria that includes access to program state is a powerful and important feature of Prism. It provides a level of abstraction in the debugging process that has been missing thus far.

1.3   Scalable Output

Having a scalable command set solves only half of the user-debugger interaction problem. The other half involves controlling the amount of information that the commands generate and concisely representing debugger state for large numbers of nodes.

Debugger responses to commands originate in the debug servers on the nodes (discussed in more detail in Sec. 1.4), and may take the form of confirmational messages that an action was performed, informational messages about the state of the process after an action is performed, or error messages indicating an action could not be performed. Indeed, each node could respond with a different message, or multiple messages, with different numbers of messages coming from different nodes. In Node Prism, we take the approach of finding a minimal set of unique messages from all those returned and then printing each message, along with a concise label indicating the processor nodes which returned that message. We implement this by hashing all messages on the control processor (CP) to find duplicates. After a request is sent to the nodes, each message reply from each node is hashed; if a match is found, the node id is added to the set of nodes associated with that message. When all messages have been received, the hash table is traversed, and the messages printed. This simple scheme works surprisingly well, and makes the amount of information presented to the user essentially independent of the number of processors. An example is the output from the following *step* command, issued when the processors were stopped at one of three breakpoints:

```
(prism all) step
PNs 0:7,32:63: stepped to procedure
  "pawn_moves" at "chess.c":50
PNs 8:15: stepped to procedure
  "rook_moves" at "chess.c":533
PNs 16:31: stepped to procedure
  "bishop_moves" at "chess.c":436
```

At first glance, the use of the CP to hash messages may seem like a limiting approach, but in practical terms this is not the case. Analysis of the inner loops for the string-hashing code shows a per-character cost of 15 control-processor cycles. At a clock speed of 32 MHz, this yields a rate of 2.1 million characters per second. Assuming 80 characters per message, and

1024 processors, we may thus hash and reduce 26 messages per node per second. This is more than adequate, and makes a CP-based implementation the preferred method, due to its simplicity, when compared with a parallel node-based implementation that has better theoretical scaling properties.

Certain types of debugger output and information are not amenable to the unique message treatment used above and are handled differently. One example is the stack back trace, which is problematic because it involves a huge amount of data when taken across all processors. Dumping the trace from each successive processor is fruitless, because the user cannot keep track of it all, and is wasteful, because it ignores the similarities between many of the back traces. Node Prism provides a new abstraction called the *where tree* that overcomes these problems. The where tree is a multiprocessor generalization of the back trace, and each *function node* of the tree represents a function call made on one or more processors. Traces from two processors are grouped into the same function node if both processors made a call to the same function at the same call site. Figure 1.2 shows a sample where tree in which all processors made the same function calls from main through generate_moves but start to diverge thereafter. Some processors then call bishop_moves, some call king_moves, and still others call pawn_moves. This tree was generated by a SPMD program; a MIMD program with multiple executables would generate multiple, independent where trees. Prism currently handles the SPMD case only.

Construction of the where tree is accomplished by successively merging the back trace from each processor node into the existing tree, which is initially empty. The algorithm simultaneously descends through the tree and the back trace, attempting to find a match for the stack frame at each level. If a matching function node is found at a given level, then the frame's processor is added to the set of processors for that node. The criteria for a match between a function node and a frame is threefold: first, that the function of the tree node and the frame is the same; second, that the function is called by the same parent function in each case; and third, that the call is made at the same place in the parent function, where place may be identified either by source-line number or program counter. After finding a match, the children of the node are then inspected to find a match for the next frame. If a match is found, the algorithm descends into both the child and the next frame. If a match is not found among the children, then a new child is created, and the remainder of the frames are added to the tree in a chain rooted at the new child.

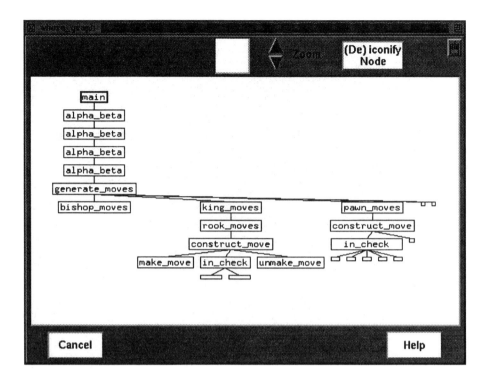

Figure 1.2: The where tree.

When a processor continues execution, its frames must be removed from the tree, and this is done in a similar manner. A descent is made through the tree, visiting each function node containing the processor. The processor is removed from the node's set, and if the set becomes nil, the node is removed from the tree.

In our implementation, construction of the tree is done on the control processor, and thus takes time $O(n)$, where n is the total number of stack frames to be added. This serial method has not proven to be a bottleneck, as the per-frame cost is quite low. If it were, however, it would be easy to derive a parallel algorithm that combines back traces pairwise, then combines trees pairwise, and so on until a single tree per distinct executable remains.

Despite the sharing of function nodes in the where tree, it is often still the case that the entire tree cannot be seen at once at the maximum level of detail. Therefore, various methods for filtering its contents are provided. The zoom buttons allow the amount of detail shown in each function node to be varied. We provide six zooming levels, which incrementally add more information to each function node, ranging from a box and sticks skeleton through the maximally zoomed level shown in Figure 1.3. At this level, each function node contains (from top to bottom): the function name, function arguments, a bitmap grid showing the processors involved, and the line numbers where functions are called. Identical function arguments are combined for separate processors, and the bitmap grid automatically scales up or down to fit the number of processors to the available screen space. Figure 1.4 shows the appearance of these features in successive levels of the zooming progression. At coarser zoom levels, such as in Figure 1.2, the user may click on any function node to get a pop-up dialog showing the complete information available at that node. The user may also pan through the tree using the mouse or traverse it using the arrow keys. Lastly, portions of the tree that the user does not wish to focus on may be iconified, leaving the rest of the tree at the current zoom level (see Figure 1.5). Iconified nodes remain iconified across changes of zooming level and stepping operations, provided of course that the nodes are not deleted as a result of the step.

The where tree proves to be a compact representation of the combined back traces because at any given time many processors are performing similar computations with similar function-call histories. It thus gives a concise snapshot of the execution history of all processes, which allows the user to understand relationships between computations on different processors. The where tree also provides a convenient means of organizing debugging operations, for the user may double-click on any function node to make the current pnset be the processors at that node. It would then be possible to issue a *print* command to print local variables for all processors in that function, for example.

The printing of data is another area where simple aggregation of textual output is an insufficient mechanism for reducing complexity and data volume. The ability to apply graphical representations to the data is essential in this regard. Prism provides a fixed set of graphical representations called *visualizers* that may be applied to arrays of data, or array-valued expressions, and allows the user to navigate through the data as necessary. The arrays may exist entirely on one node or may be distributed across nodes. In a data-parallel program, the data distribution is known by the compilers, and this information can be used by Prism to automatically reconstruct the distributed array. In a message-passing program, the distribution is known only to the programmer, so some means of specifying this distribution is

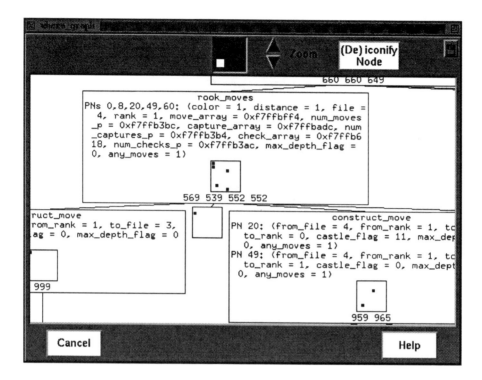

Figure 1.3: A maximally zoomed where tree.

necessary. Currently, Prism reconstructs arrays by simply adding an extra axis indexed by node; this sometimes matches the programmer's intent and sometimes does not. In the future, we will allow the programmer to specify and name different types of distributions that can then be associated with program variables. Thereafter, requests to print these variables will refer to the distribution and reconstruct the data automatically.

A typical Prism visualizer is shown in Figure 1.6; here, a Julia set is being computed by the underlying program. For more details on visualization in Prism, see [6].

1.4   Scalable Performance

Node Prism is itself a message-passing program that runs under timesharing along with its debugee and any other unrelated applications. It has a component that runs on the control processor, containing the user interface, as

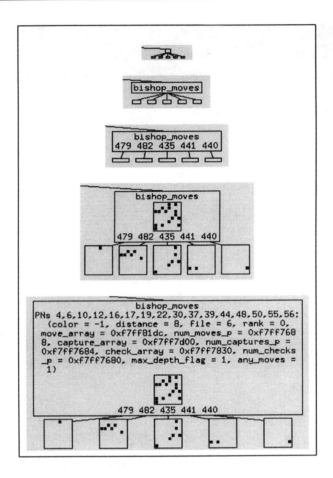

Figure 1.4: Zooming a node in the where tree.

well as a node component which acts as a stripped-down debug server. This is similar to the approach taken in TAM [2]. The node component is capable of examining and controlling any debugee process on that node via the UNIX ptrace mechanism. The parallelism inherent in this implementation is essential for the efficient execution of Prism's debugging paradigms.

Commands are decomposed into requests that are broadcast to all processing nodes, and each node independently decides if it is in the current processor set and performs the requests accordingly. Debugger performance thus scales with machine size. Requests are defined at a fairly high level, and perform actions such as stepping by one source line, evaluating a program expression, or returning a stack back trace (see Table 1.1). One could imagine

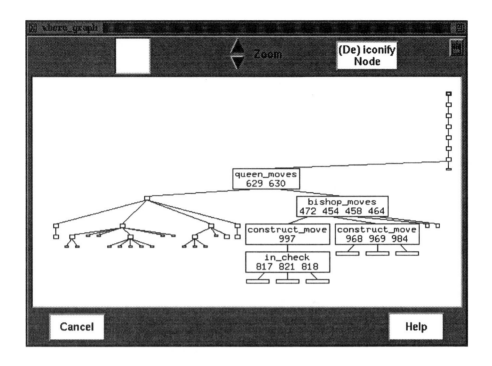

Figure 1.5: The use of iconification in the where tree.

implementing requests at the ptrace level, but it is *not* the case that identical sequences of ptraces get executed on every node to perform debugging operations, so any parallelism would be difficult to achieve. For example, to step over a branch instruction, a trap must be inserted (using ptrace) at the branch target as well as at the instruction following the branch, whereas to step over straight-line code, only one trap need be inserted. Thus, the exact ptrace sequence to execute a step on many nodes depends on the current program counter on each node, and ptrace is thus an inappropriately low-level interface to the node portion of the debugger. A higher degree of functionality is required in each request to ensure that the debugger's work can be done in parallel.

High request functionality comes at the price of storing some symbol table information on each node, however, and there is a tradeoff between performance and the amount of node memory taken by the symbol table. At one extreme, the entire table could be stored on each node, allowing arbitrary debugging operations to be performed in parallel. This is impractical and wasteful, as symbol tables can reach tens of megabytes in size.

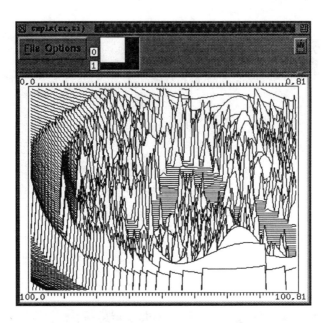

Figure 1.6: A data visualizer in Prism.

We have taken an intermediate approach, which is to store on each node just enough symbol-table information as is necessary to allow debugging operations to be performed in parallel, while not requiring an excessive amount of information to be downloaded on each request. The line-number table, the function table, and the file table are all replicated on each node. The line-number table, which maps program addresses to line numbers, allows stepping operations to be done in parallel. The function table, which maps addresses to function symbols, allows partial stack back traces to be generated in parallel. The file table maps addresses to symbols that identify source-files, and is needed to generate more detailed back-trace information. The rest of the symbol table is kept on the CP. Other symbols needed to execute a request are broadcast on a per-request basis and are freed when the request terminates. For example, the partial back trace returns a unique list of all functions encountered on all nodes. The CP then broadcasts parameter symbols and types for these functions to the nodes, allowing them to symbolize the function arguments and complete the back trace.

Table 1.1	
The Most Common Prism Requests	
request	description
load	load symbol table
run	run program
attach	attach to an existing process
detach	detach process from debugger
set-event	create a new event (breakpoint)
delete	delete an event
status	show currently defined events
call	call function in debugee
continue	continue execution
step	step one instruction or source line
interrupt	interrupt debugee execution
where-start	return partial back trace
where-finish	return completed back trace
assign	assign new value to variable
eval-data	evaluate program expression
examine	formatted memory examine
whatis	return type of variable
pnset-define	define new pnset
pnset-current	set current pnset
pnset-query	return current value of pnset
pnset-delete	delete pnset
quit	terminate debugging session

Symbols are copied to the nodes as a side effect of being part of a request. Each request is a data structure containing all the information needed to carry out the request. Fields of the request data structure may themselves be complex structures such as parse trees for expressions, so a means of transmitting arbitrary, linked structures to the nodes is required. We provide this by performing a depth-first traversal of the request data structure, flattening the structure into a buffer that is broadcast to the nodes. To avoid infinite recursion on circular structures, each pointer that is traversed is first tested in a hash table and added if not present. The traversal is facilitated by a routine that takes the address of a structure and its type, and returns a list of pointers contained within the structure and their types. With such a routine, we can write a generic data structure traverser that separates the mechanics of the traversal from the actions performed on each structure. This makes it easier to implement the series of traversals that are necessary to handle each request.

On the nodes, the flattened bytes are received and reconstructed into the linked data structure. Symbols are treated specially during the reconstruction. When a pointer to a symbol is encountered, the pointer's value (as found in the flattened buffer, and hence equal to the address of the symbol on the CP) is tested in a node-specific hash table. If there is no match, then a local copy of the symbol is created, and an association between the symbol's CP address and its local address is added to the table. If there *is* a match, then the local address of the symbol is retrieved from the table, the bytes of the symbol in the flattened buffer are discarded, and the parent structure of the symbol is made to point to the existing local symbol. In addition, the local reference count of the symbol is incremented. The process of testing and translating symbol addresses ensures that requests become properly integrated with symbols that reside permanently on the nodes. This is important for the correct execution of code that tests symbols for equality using their addresses, and also saves memory by not needlessly duplicating symbols.

At this point, the request has been reconstructed on each node and can be performed. After this is done, the request structure is once again traversed, and all symbols encountered have their reference count decremented. Those whose count goes to 0 have their address translation removed from the hash table and are deleted. (This is somewhat of a simplification; reference counting of data structures with indirect self-reference is tricky, and the details are left to the reader.)

The symbol management techniques described herein have been quite successful at reducing the per-node memory requirements to modest levels, with little or no impact on performance. The response to user commands appears instantaneous and is independent of both the size of the current pnset and the size of the machine.

1.5   Conclusion

We have implemented a debugger for message-passing programs that incorporates scalability in all aspects of its operation, including command processing, presentation of information, command execution, and performance. We have also presented new debugger-interaction paradigms that promote greater understanding of parallel programs. The ability to define named sets of processor nodes based on program state is new, and allows the user to organize debugging activities around semantically meaningful sets of nodes in a scalable fashion. Output from commands is aggregated and attributed to *pnsets*, reinforcing the illusion of a single debugging thread of control per pnset. The where tree provides a compact representation of the execution state of all processes, as well as the relationships between them, and further supports the pnset abstraction by allowing nodes of the where tree to be selected as the current set. Taken together, these improvements allow users to debug their message-passing programs more quickly and efficiently.

References

[1] BBN CORPORATION, *Using the Xtra Programming Environment*, BBN Advanced Computers, Inc., Cambridge, MA.

[2] BREAZEAL, D., ANDERSON, R., SMITH, W., AULD, W., AND CALLAGHAN, K., "A Parallel Software Monitor for Debugging and Performance Tools on Distributed Memory Multicomputers," *Proceedings of the Supercomputer Debugging Workshop '92*, October 1992.

[3] CONVEX COMPUTER CORPORATION, *Convex CXdb User's Guide*, Convex Press, Richardson, TX.

[4] INTEL SUPERCOMPUTER SYSTEMS, *iPSC/2 and iPSC/860 Interactive Parallel Debugger Manual*, Intel Corporation, Santa Clara, CA.

[5] PANCAKE, CHERRI M., "Direct Manipulation Techniques for Parallel Debuggers," *Proceedings of the Supercomputer Debugging Workshop '92*, October 1992.

[6] SISTARE, S., ALLEN, D., BOWKER, R., JOURDENAIS, K., SIMONS, J., AND TITLE, R., "Data Visualization and Performance Analysis in the Prism Programming Environment," *Proceedings of the IFIP TC10/WG10.3 Working Conference on Programming Environments for Parallel Computers*, April 1992, edited by N. P. Topham, R. N. Ibbett, and T. Bemmerl.

[7] THINKING MACHINES CORPORATION, *Prism User's Guide*, Cambridge, MA.

[8] THINKING MACHINES CORPORATION, *CMMD User's Guide*, Chapter 6, Cambridge, MA.

[9] ZIMMERMAN, S., "UDB: A Parallel Debugger for the KSR1," *Proceedings of the Supercomputer Debugging Workshop '92*, October 1992.

A Building Block Approach to Parallel Tool Construction

Don Breazeal[1]
Intel Corporation, Scalable Systems Division

Bernhard Ries
Intel Corporation
European Supercomputer Development Center

Abstract

Research into parallel programming tools has focused primarily on technical issues dealing with methods for monitoring, analyzing, and visualizing parallel program behavior. For the most part, the results of this research have not been incorporated into commercial tool products, and user acceptance of commercial tool products remains low. We examine the obstacles facing the developer of commercial parallel tools and how the parallel computing environment affects what is brought to market. We present a framework, or *tool infrastructure*, as a vehicle to enable development and transfer of scalable tools technology.

[1]Supported in part by: Advanced Research Projects Agency; Information Science and Technology Office; Research in Concurrent Computing Systems; ARPA Order No. 6402, 6402-1; Program Code No. 8E20 and 9E20. Issued by ARPA/CMO under contract #MDA972-89-C-0034

1.1   Introduction

The acceptance and success of parallel programming tools has been much lower than the tool community's expectations [8,6]. Many hypotheses have been presented as to the cause of the users' reticence. Most of these have to do with tool technology such as presentation, monitoring, and analysis techniques. We propose that some of the major obstacles are the ways in which tools are constructed and the environments in which tool builders work. Solving the technical barriers to effective monitoring, analysis, and presentation will not be sufficient to provide users with the commercial tools they require.

The numerous and conflicting demands made of programming tools quickly consume the tool development resources available to most organizations, causing delivered tool technology to lag behind other parallel technology such as compilers, operating systems, and hardware. Essentially, the problem is that the environment in which tools and tool builders must operate changes rapidly, and in unexpected ways. Since the amount of change cannot be controlled, tools must be developed so that they can adapt as the environment changes. We propose a tool infrastructure consisting of basic components that can be used as building blocks for tool construction. Such an infrastructure allows the tool builder to adapt programming tools to advances and changes in other system components, as well as to integrate components from external sources. In addition, external tool builders can use components to more easily integrate their tools with a system supporting the infrastructure.

The rest of this paper is organized as follows: Sec. 1.2 describes the tool builder's environment, Sec. 1.3 describes what is needed to deal with this environment, Sec. 1.4 proposes a specific method for meeting these needs, Sec. 1.5 contains some examples of how tools could be implemented using the tool infrastructure, Sec. 1.6 examines some related work, Sec. 1.7 describes current status of the work and future plans, and Sec. 1.8 provides a summary of the work.

1.2   The World of the Tool Builder

In this section we explore the various changing aspects of the tool builder's environment by breaking it into its various components. We then describe the effect on the tool builder caused by each of these components.

1.2.1 Environment

The tool builder's environment can be described in terms of the external factors affecting it. These factors are:

1. There are (too) many ways to program parallel systems

   An active area of research is development of new ways to program parallel systems, in order to improve usability. This has resulted in an explosion of the number of programming paradigms available on any given vendor's system. For example, a typical distributed memory parallel system in 1995 will probably support C, Fortran, C++, pthreads, MPI, PVM, some proprietary message-passing protocol (e.g., NX [11]), some lightweight message-passing protocol (e.g., active messages), and possibly one or two data parallel languages (e.g., HPF). A few years beyond 1995 will undoubtedly see new languages and paradigms.

2. Parallel system technology is evolving rapidly

   Rapid proliferation of parallel processing technology hampers tool development efforts. Because the high-performance computing community is always attempting to reach new levels of performance and usability, new architectures, processors, interconnect networks, memory subsystems, and so on, are continually produced. Vendors tend to deliver a new system architecture every two to three years. If tools are developed assuming a particular combination of architectural features, they cannot be easily retargeted to accommodate changes or advances in technology.

3. Parallel tools technology is still primitive

   It is not clear what is required from tools for parallel and distributed systems. The technology is still evolving, and this is an active research area at many institutions around the world. As advances in tool technology are made, the tool developer often finds it difficult or impossible to incorporate new technology into an existing tool. The result is general dissatisfaction in the user and research communities with the tools that are produced.

4. The tool builder must solve the serial problems as well as the parallel problems

Parallel and distributed systems present all of the same problems that serial systems do, plus the added complexity of whatever programming paradigms are used to achieve parallel execution. The serial problems have in many cases been solved, but the technology is not available to the parallel tool builder in a form that can be readily adapted or extended to support a parallel system.

5. Although small, the parallel tool user community is diverse

   The technical high-performance computing community is a relatively small one compared to the commercial marketplace. The number of users is small, so the number of users of any given tool will be small compared to the number of users of programming tools developed for the commercial market. However, these users are much more diverse than those found in other markets, since they are from backgrounds as varied as oil exploration, defense, or financial trading. From such differing backgrounds, a range of requirements for programming environments is generated.

6. The tool builder develops tools as part of a business

   The commercial parallel tool builder is usually employed by a system vendor. (Some are employed by software companies, but most of these issues apply to them as well.) The goal of the vendor is to sell hardware systems. It is the employee's responsibility to make that the highest priority. System vendors also employ people working on compilers and operating systems, and advancements in those areas must usually be reflected by modifications to the tools. In addition, such advancements are often prototyped without tools support, and the tool builder's time is required to specify, design, and evaluate the tool support hooks. Lastly, as noted above, most system vendors develop a new system approximately every two to three years. New systems often have radically different architectures, interconnect networks, processors, operating systems, compilers, programming models, and so on. Full toolsets are required on these new systems.

1.2.2 Requirements

Given this environment, the tool builder is pulled in several directions at once. The tools must support multiple programming paradigms, and if possible they should support all the models supported on the system. The tools should operate in a way that makes sense to a diverse community of users whose primary expertise is not in computing. The tools should incorporate advanced technology developed in the research community. And finally, the tools should make the vendor's system more marketable, both by impressing prospective customers and by being useful to existing customers.

To satisfy these requirements, the tool builder's priorities are:

Priority 1: port existing tools to new platform

Priority 2: add support for new paradigms provided by OS or compiler

Priority 3: any other improvements (usability, technology, etc.)

1.2.3 Reality

Most vendor organizations lack the time and resources needed to accomplish everything listed above. One obvious way to manage the situation is for the tool builder to try to constrain the problem. However, care must be taken, because any assumptions made in the process are likely to turn out to be wrong. For example, Intel plans release of a High-Performance Fortran (HPF) compiler in early 1995. However, at the time of the release of the compiler there will be no explicit debugging or performance tuning support for HPF in the Intel tools, because resources were needed for other tasks.

Another example, ironically almost the opposite of the Intel experience, is the development of the MIMD version of the Prism debugger [14] by Thinking Machines Corporation. TMC's Prism environment fully supported their data parallel programming model (much like HPF), but full support for message-passing lagged the release of the CMMD [5] message-passing system on the CM-5 by well over a year.

From these examples, we conclude that the tools in question were not constructed so that they could be easily adapted to support a new programming model. Thus, the tool builder cannot make *any* assumptions about the target system (at least not without considerable risk).

1.3 Breaking the Cycle

So far we have painted a fairly bleak picture for the future of tools on scalable systems. If tools can help users be more productive, then what can be done to improve the situation?

1. Demand for tools must be demonstrated through funding.

   Although surveys show that users will employ parallel tools when they are available and of sufficient quality, tools are frequently unused because they do not meet user requirements [10]. "To date, insufficient monies and impetus have existed for parallel system vendors to provide adequate staffing for software tool development" [7]. We do not address this issue any further in this paper, other than to propose a method for reducing the long-term cost of software tool development.

2. Tool Builders need to construct their tools to be able to adapt to the environment they are operating in.

3. Researchers need to package the results of their research in a way that eases integration into a vendor tool.

In the remainder of this paper we propose a method of tool development that addresses issues (2) and (3).

1.3.1   Back to Basics

In order to produce tools that can be adapted to a variety of environments and uses, tool builders must spend effort on basic software engineering. Whether the tool builder is a developer working for a system vendor, or a researcher at a lab or university, tools should be constructed to meet the following requirements:

- software re-use
- data abstraction
- system independence
- open interfaces
- standards compliance
- consistency

In addition, parallel tools should support requirements specific to parallel systems:

- scalability
- heterogeneity

Very often these fundamentals are overlooked in tool construction due to schedule and resource constraints, or lack of foresight in how the tool might be useful. Outside the industry community, the focus is frequently on prototyping tool technology, rather than building a piece of software that will have long-lived usefulness. Such prototypes are built with monolithic designs.

The rush to implement a prototype dooms any attempt to transfer the technology to industry, since monolithic tools with seamless, vertical architectures cannot be easily separated into components that can be re-used, adapted to new models, ported to new systems, or integrated with new interfaces. Anyone wishing to integrate technology from a monolithic tool must either re-invent or re-implement the technology, or spend time and resources extracting it from the monolithic tool.

Note that this is not meant to diminish the contributions of tool researchers, nor their tools. It is merely an observation of a difference in focus.

At Intel Supercomputers we have observed that users, especially users from large sites (large in number of users), have their own tools that have been developed at the local site. They prefer these tools because they can use them on several different systems, and if the developer of the tool is local it is easier to get quick attention when there is a problem. Whatever the reasons, we get a number of requests for user access to the internal interfaces of our parallel programming tools.

1.4 A Tool Infrastructure

We propose an infrastructure for tool construction using simple, general tool components with public interfaces as tool building blocks. These components export public interfaces in much the same object-oriented way that widgets do in X Window toolkits. We have defined a prototype infrastructure, PROTEIN (for PROgramming Tool Environment INfrastructure), which attempts to satisfy the criteria listed above.

In PROTEIN, each component encapsulates a single piece of tool functionality, in an attempt to make each component serve a single purpose. There are some components that are more complex. These are exceptions required by the parallel nature of the target system.

The PROTEIN tool infrastructure definition is intended to address these problems. By providing a modular framework supporting serial and parallel tool functionality and defining levels of support needed from operating systems, compilers, and hardware to support that functionality, PROTEIN provides the basis of a portable and re-targetable toolset as well as a platform for research and development.

To build tools from PROTEIN components, the tool builder writes a wrapper program which simply glues PROTEIN components together to achieve the desired functions. To re-target or port the tool to a different system or programming paradigm, it should be a simple matter of replacing some components. To add new functionality, simply add a component or two. To enhance a tool using some functionality from a research tool, simply plug a component from the research tool into the first tool.

This plug-and-play approach to tool components allows:

- rapid adaptation to new paradigms

- easy integration of new technology

- a high degree of portability

- multiple interfaces on the same tool

- multiple back-ends on the same interface

- researchers and external tool builders do not have to re-invent basic tool support

The infrastructure consists of a collection of components that assist the tool builder in the implementation of programming tools. The main focus is on monitoring tools such as debuggers, profilers, or system performance analysis tools, although all aspects of program development are addressed. PROTEIN components can be categorized according to function as shown in Figure 1.1. Monitoring components used to inspect and control the state of parallel applications and of the parallel target system form the core of the infrastructure. A second important category consists of components that support the analysis and transformation of application programs in the form of source code, executable code, or application data gathered through monitoring. These components depend on support that is provided by components external to the tool infrastructure. PROTEIN accesses these external components through a well-defined set of support interfaces that encapsulate and hide the specifics of the target system. The monitoring and program analysis

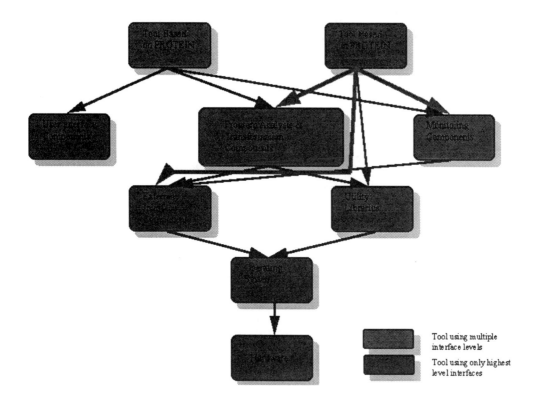

Figure 1.1: Categories of tool infrastructure components, showing dependency hierarchy. See color plate X.

components also depend on support implemented by PROTEIN in the form of a number of utility libraries. Tools built using PROTEIN may also directly access the external support interfaces and utility libraries. Finally, the infrastructure includes mechanisms that simplify the task of implementing consistent user-interfaces for parallel programming tools.

Infrastructure components are organized in a hierarchical fashion, so that tool builders do not need to learn how to use too many interfaces at one time. Low-level interfaces present specific aspects of the hardware or operating system, while higher level interfaces provide parallel monitoring, and even higher-level interfaces provide facilities for doing the bookkeeping of process management and control for, say, a parallel debugger.

Proof-of-concept for the utility of exporting internal tool interfaces has been shown by providing some tool developers with access to the Intel Paragon Tools Application Monitor (TAM) [3, 13], which acts as the back end of the Interactive Parallel Debugger (IPD) [4]. A third-party software vendor was able to port a parallel debugger that targeted a network of workstations to the Paragon by using the TAM interface. The format of Paragon performance data, the Self-Defining Data Format (SDDF) [2] developed by the University of Illinois' Pablo Project [12], was also exported and put to use by external developers and researchers.

1.5 An Example Infrastructure

In this section we propose an infrastructure that provides components adequate for supporting a parallel debugger and a parallel performance tool. We first describe the individual components of the infrastructure, then describe how they can be combined to produce a debugger and a performance tool. In order to keep this discussion to a reasonable size, the example infrastructure is only a subset of the full infrastructure we have defined.

External Support Interfaces   These interfaces provide a system-independent way of accessing information provided by the OS and compiler.

- Operating System Interface

  This interface provides access to debugging and performance monitoring facilities provided by operating system software. It uses a common interface for different operating systems.

- Compiler Interface

  This interface supports automatic instrumentation of program code and generation of traditional debug information.

Monitoring Components   These components provide monitoring facilities to support debugging and performance monitoring.

- Parallel Software Monitor

  The Parallel Software Monitor provides debugging support for parallel applications. It is capable of performing debug operations in parallel and communicating with the debugger in an optimal way.

- Performance Monitoring Library

  The Performance Monitoring Library provides base functionality for collecting and storing data on the run-time behavior of applications and the target system.

- Debug Engine

  The debug engine does bookkeeping to keep track of the state of the target application, and coordinates debugging activities including process control, data access, expression evaluation, and access to message-passing or shared-memory synchronization.

Program Analysis and Transformation Components These components provide facilities for analyzing and transforming data that describe the program and its behavior.

- Symbol Table Navigator

  The Symbol Table Navigator provides an abstract interface to symbolic mapping of program data. It allows tools to describe program state (such as addresses) in terms of symbolic names used in program source (functions, variables, line numbers, etc.).

- Data Analysis Modules

  These modules can be used to analyze and transform quantitative data, mostly for use by performance tools. This includes statistical analysis, sorting, scaling, and so on.

User Interface Components These components provide building blocks for both graphical and command line user interfaces.

- Command Parsers

  Command parsers are constructed from a shell interpreter such as Tcl (Tool Command Language).

- GUI Library

  This library provides basic user interface functionality commonly required by most graphical programming tools, as well as visualization functionality needed for graphical display of data such as event traces or array contents.

Utility Libraries These libraries provide common facilities for mechanisms that tie various components together.

- Scalable Data Transport Mechanism

  The Scalable Data Transport Mechanism implements efficient communication mechanisms for use in parallel servers, applications, or tools. This includes support for distributed command execution in the form of remote procedure calls as well as support for the efficient movement of large amounts of data to a single destination.

1.5.1 Parallel Debugger

To build a parallel debugger from infrastructure components, we first divide the debugger's functionality into three parts: the user interface, which presents the tool and its functions to the user; the front end, which coordinates the activities of the back end, does bookkeeping to keep track of the state of the target application, and relates the state of the application to the user's source code; and the back end, which controls and accesses the individual processes of the target application.

The user interface is built from either Graphical or Command Line Interface components. The front end is built from the Debug Engine and the Symbol Table Navigator. The back end is built around the Parallel Software Monitor, which in turn is built from the Operating System Interface and the Scalable Data Transport utility. Figure 1.2 shows how the various components fit together to make a parallel debugger.

1.5.2 Parallel Performance Tool

The parallel performance tool is not as straightforward as the parallel debugger, since the tool itself is composed of several separate pieces. First, there is a Performance Monitoring Library, which is called by the application to collect performance data. Second, there is a Compiler Interface which inserts calls to the the Performance Monitoring Library into the target application. Finally, there is a Performance Tool which analyzes and displays performance information.

The Performance Monitoring Library is a monitoring component built from the Operating System Interface and the Scalable Data Transport Utility.

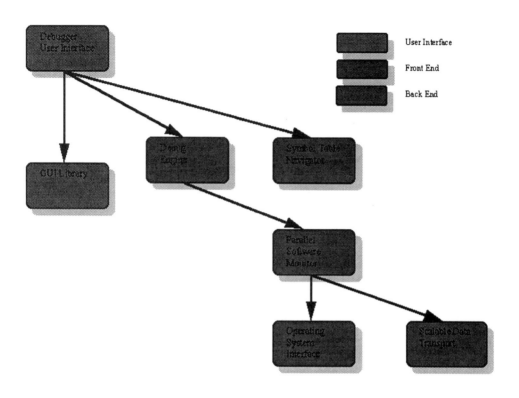

Figure 1.2: A parallel debugger built from infrastructure components. See color plate XI.

The Compiler Interface is self-contained. The Performance Tool is built using Graphical or Command Line Interface components, Data Analysis Modules, and the Symbol Table Navigator (to map performance problems into the target source code). Figure 1.3 shows a block diagram of the Parallel Performance Tool.

1.5.3   Advantages of Using the Infrastructure

The advantages of using the building block approach include code re-use, retargetability, portability, extensibility, and the implementation of an open system.

Code Re-Use

Code re-use improves reliability and reduces development cost. Several components in the example infrastructure are re-used by the two example tools.

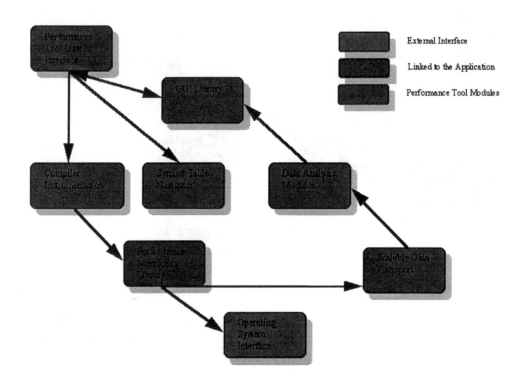

Figure 1.3: A parallel performance tool built from infrastructure components. See color plate XII.

The Operating System Interface is used by both tools. The Performance Tool uses it for access to performance counters, while the Debugger uses it for access and control of target processes.

The Compiler Interface is used by the debugger to generate traditional mappings of symbols and line numbers to addresses, while the performance tool uses it to generate calls to performance monitoring routines.

Command Parsers for any tool can be built using a shell interpreter such as Tcl (Tool Command Language).

The GUI Library is used by both tools for such interface components as a source browser, a system topology display, and general dialogs, alerts, and so on.

Retargetability

Suppose the parallel debugger supports a message-passing programming model, and must be extended to support a data parallel language such as HPF. This requires the debugger to be able to transform user requests from the syntax of the data parallel language into nodes, processes and messages, as well as to transform program state back into the data parallel model.

To do this, the compiler must generate some mapping data through a compiler interface. A new module for accessing the data and making the appropriate tranformations must be implemented. A new user interface would probably be required as well. The new HPF transformation module could be placed between the user interface and the debug engine, as shown in Figure 1.4, to retarget the debugger to a new programming model with minimal changes.

Portability

Moving a parallel tool to a new system is a complex task. It would be unrealistic to assert that use of the building block approach makes porting a tool to a new system easy or painless. However, it helps to isolate system dependencies so that changes need only be made in selected parts of the infrastructure. How extensive these changes might be depends on how different the original system is from the new system.

Extensibility

To integrate new technology from an external source, the tool builder only needs to capture the external technology in a new infrastructure component, then plug the component into an existing tool. The difficulty of this depends, of course, on the complexity of the new technology.

Open System

Finally, allowing external tool builders to access the internal interfaces of the infrastructure is something that the high-performance computing community demands. HPC tool builders want to be able to implement their local tools on a new system without having to reinvent all of the wheels that they know the vendor uses inside the system tools. By enabling these external tool

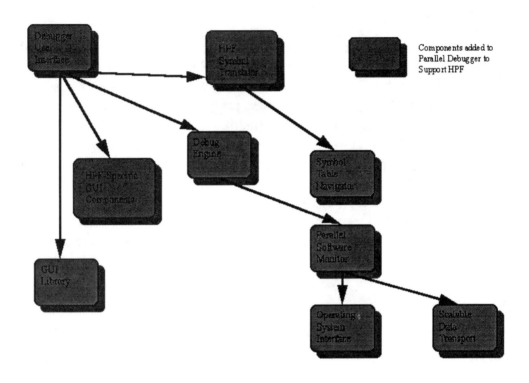

Figure 1.4: An HPF debugger built from infrastructure components. See color plate XIII.

builders, more tools are moved onto the system, presumably making it easier to use, which after all is the purpose of the tools.

1.6 Related Work

There has been little work on tool construction methods in the parallel tools community. A more general case of the problem has been addressed in the object-oriented frameworks such as those proposed by Taligent [16] and others. The reality is that these solutions are overkill for a parallel tools community with limited resources and an incomplete understanding of the technology needed to make parallel programming easy.

Some tool communication mechanisms, such as those provided by Tcl and

Tk [9] or SunSoft ToolTalk [15], have been used to access tool component functionality, but these facilities send character-string messages that must be parsed and interpreted, so they are not useful at the fine granularity needed for a component-based approach. The need to execute an entire tool to access a small piece of its functionality is also problematic.

The bdb debugger [17], developed at Cray Computer Corporation, was built using an approach similar to the building block method, with functionality divided into libraries, and communication between components using Tcl and Tk. The division between components was at a much coarser granularity than proposed for PROTEIN, and there was no stated goal of opening the internal interfaces to the public.

The Pablo Performance Analysis Environment [12] uses a component based approach for the analysis and visualization of event trace data. Pablo is modeled after the component-based graphics visualization environment AVS [1]. Both of these systems focus on the visualization of data, rather than providing a general environment for parallel tool construction.

1.7 Status and Plans

The PROTEIN infrastructure is work-in-progress. Versions of the parallel software monitor, the symbol table navigator, and an expression evaluator all exist, as well as components of the GUI library. Other interfaces are in the definition phase. An operating system interface is being prototyped.

We view the move to the use of tool building blocks as an incremental one, where pieces of the tools become building blocks, rather than one in which everything is reorganized at once. We will continue this conversion over the next year or so.

1.8 Conclusions

In the rapidly changing world of high performance computing, the debugging and performance tuning tools produced by industrial developers must be highly adaptable. The building block approach to parallel tool construction, as exemplified by the PROTEIN tool infrastructure, is one way to provide this adapability. By utilizing such an approach, tool builders will be able to integrate new technology more easily, target new systems more rapidly, support a variety of programming paradigms, and provide an environment for tools research and development.

Parallel tool developers who embrace an approach such as this will spend less time working on adapting tools to the changing environment and more time on improving tool technology, which will ultimately make parallel systems easier to use.

References

[1] ADVANCED VISUAL SYSTEMS, INC. *AVS User's Guide*, release 4 edition, May 1992.

[2] AYDT, R. A. "The Pablo Self-Defining Data Format," University of Illinois, Urbana-Champaign, March 1992.

[3] BREAZEAL DON, ANDERSON, RAY, SMITH, WAYNE D., AULD, WILL, AND CALLAGHAN, KARLA, "A Parallel Software Monitor for Debugging and Performance Tools on Distributed Memory Multipcomputers," in *Proceedings of Supercomputer Debugging Workshop '92*, Dallas, TX, Oct. 1992, 221–230.

[4] BREAZEAL, DON, CALLAGHAN, KARLA, AND SMITH, WAYNE D., "IPD: A Debugger for Parallel Heterogeneous Systems," in *Proceedings of the ACM/ONR Workshop on Parallel and Distributed Debugging*, Santa Cruz, CA, May 1991, 216–218. [Extended abstract].

[5] *CMMD User's Guide*, version 3.0 edition, May 1993.

[6] COOK, C., PANCAKE, C., AND WALPOLE, R., "Supercomputing '93 Parallel User Survey: Response Summary," Technical Report 94-80-2 (1994), Dept. of Computer Science, Oregon State University, Feb. 1994.

[7] HAYES, ANN H., SIMMONS, MARGARET L., AND REED, DANIEL A., "Workshop Recommendations," in *Workshop Report: Instrumentation for Parallel Computer Systems: A Dialogue Between Users and Developers*, Keystone, CO, April 1993, 9–13.

[8] KUEHN, JEFF, "A User Perspective of Debugging on Supercomputers," in *Proceedings of Supercomputer Debugging Workshop '92*, Dallas, TX, Oct. 1992, 35–50.

[9] OUSTERHOUT, JOHN K., *Tcl and the Tk Toolkit*, Addison-Wesley Publishing Company, 1994.

[10] PANCAKE, C. M., AND COOK, C., "What Users Need in Parallel Tool Support: Survey Results and Analysis," in *Proceedings of the Scalable High Performance Computing Conference*, Knoxville, TN, May 1994, 40–47.

[11] PIERCE, PAUL AND REGNIER, GREG, "The Paragon Implementation of the nx Message Passing Interface," in *Proceedings of the Scalable High Performance Computing Conference*, Knoxville, TN, May 1994.

[12] REED, D. A., AYDT, R. A., MADHYASTHA, T. M., NOE, R. J., SHIELDS, K. A., AND SCHWARTZ, B. W., "The Pablo Performance Analysis Environment," University of Illinois, Urbana-Champaign, 1992.

[13] RIES, BERNHARD, ANDERSON, RAY, AULD, WILL, BREAZEAL, DON, CALLAGHAN, KARLA, AND SMITH, WAYNE D., "The Paragon Performance Monitoring Environment," in *Proceedings of Supercomputing '93*, Portland, OR, Nov. 1993, 850–859.

[14] SISTARE, S., ALLEN, D., BOWKER, R., JOURDENAIS, K., SIMONS, J., AND TITLE, R., "A Scalable Debugger for Massively Parallel Message-Passing Programs," *IEEE Parallel and Distributed Technology*, Summer 1994, 50–56.

[15] SUNSOFT, "The Tooltalk Service," White paper, SunSoft, Inc., June 1991.

[16] TALIGENT, "Building Object-Oriented Frameworks," White paper, Taligent, Inc., http://www.taligent.com/building-oofw.html, 1994.

[17] YOUNG, BENJAMIN, "bdb: A Library Approach to Writing a New Debugger," in *Proceedings of Supercomputer Debugging Workshop '91*, Nov. 1991, 1–9.

Visualizing Performance on Parallel Supercomputers

Marty Itzkowitz, Jun Yu, Allan McNaughton,
Pete Orelup, and Chris Hanna
CASE Performance Tools, Visual Magic Division
Silicon Graphics, Inc.

Abstract

Understanding the behavior of programs run on modern parallel supercomputers requires the capture, processing, and visualization of a great deal of performance information. This paper describes the techniques used in Silicon Graphics[TM] CASEVision[TM]/ WorkShop and CASEVision[TM] WorkShopProMPF products.[1] First we describe the recording of performance experiments, and the notion of execution phases and sampling. Then we describe the various visualization techniques that are used for single-process programs. We then describe techniques for understanding multi-threaded programs, and go on to discuss the communications between performance tools and the compilers. Finally, we present our conclusions.

1.1 Introduction

Modern parallel supercomputers can capture an astounding volume of performance information. In order to make these systems useful, it is essential to be able to visualize the recorded performance information and present it

---

[1]Silicon Graphics, is a registered trademark and CASEVision is a trademark of Silicon Graphics, Inc.

so that the user can really understand the behavior of the programs being measured. In this paper, we describe the visualization techniques used to display performance data in Silicon Graphics^{TM} CASEVision^{TM}/WorkShop and CASEVision^{TM}/WorkShopProMPF products, and show how they address this need.

The remainder of this introduction describes the recording of performance experiments and the sampling paradigm. The second section describes visualization techniques for single-process performance data. The third section describes visualization techniques for multi-threaded programs, and the fourth section discusses the communications between the compiler and the performance tools for parallel programs. The final section presents our conclusions.

1.1.1 Recording Experiments

The CASEVision/WorkShop Performance Analyzer is designed to record experiments on single- or multi-threaded applications and provide an interactive browser for examining the recorded information. To record an experiment, the user first selects which of the various types of experiments to run and then uses the debugger interface to set up and run the experiment. There are various types of predefined experiments available from an experiment menu in the debugger's Performance Panel, as well as a 'Custom Task' option to allow the user to select individual instrumentation and data collection options. Several types of experiments are designed to examine the behavior of the process's instruction stream. Other experiments can be used for tracing I/O and/or system calls, heap allocation and deallocation, page faults, and/or floating-point exceptions.

Experiments looking at the process's instruction stream provide several alternative metrics of both inclusive and exclusive time. Exclusive time is time spent in the function itself, while inclusive time counts the time in the function and in all descendant functions that are called. Total-time experiments use callstack sampling to determine inclusive time (function appears anywhere in the callstack) and exclusive time (function appears at the bottom of the callstack). Personal computer (PC) sampling experiments determine exclusive time only, based on statistical PC sampling of the running executable. CPU-time experiments determine exclusive time based on PC sampling of an instrumented executable, and use entry and arc counts from the dynamic callgraph to distribute inclusive time to callers. Ideal-time experiments use basic-block count data obtained by instrumenting the executable to compute an exact execution count of each instruction in the program. From the exact counts, we derive aggregate instruction counts, call counts, loads and stores, floating-point operation counts, and an estimate of the exclusive time of execution based on simulation of the pipeline in the CPU. Inclusive time is propagated to callers based on entry and arc counts from the dynamic callgraph.

1.1.2   The Sampling Paradigm

An important aspect of performance experiment recording is the notion of 'sample points.' Typical programs do not execute uniformly over an entire run, but rather execute in phases with differing performance characteristics. By setting sample points, which tell the debugger to capture all performance data up to that point in the program, the user can demarcate the various phases of execution, and examine their performance independently. By default, sample traps are set at the entry to the system call 'exit' and whenever the process execs or opens or closes a dynamic shared object. Users may also set any number of additional sample traps; they may be set as breakpoints that fire whenever the process reaches a particular function, line or instruction in the program, or as watchpoints that fire whenever a data variable is read or written or when the process makes a system call, or whenever a periodic (timer-based) interval elapses. The interface also allows a user to take a manual sample, simply by clicking on a button at any point during the run. The performance analyzer can examine the data between any two sample points, as will be described below in Sec. 1.2.1

Whenever the target process forks or sprocs, an additional thread is established; performance recording is initiated on the new thread and, of course, continued on all existing threads. The experiment will contain the data for all threads, and the Performance Analyzer can be used to browse the data for each thread independently.

1.2   Supercomputer Performance Visualization

The previous section described the recording of performance experiments; this section describes the visualization techniques for examining the data for a single thread.

1.2.1   Performance Analyzer Overview

After an experiment is recorded, the Performance Analyzer is used to look at the data. The initial display of the Performance Analyzer is shown in Figure 1.1. The display is divided into three principal sections.

The upper third of the display shows a list of the functions in the program, annotated with whatever performance data is appropriate to the particular type of experiment. The middle third of the display shows usage information as a function of time, and the lower third of the display shows a timeline for the experiment.

The Function List

The experiment shown in Figure 1.1 is an ideal-time experiment on the performance analyzer itself. By default, this kind of experiment shows inclusive and exclusive idealized time, and call counts for each function. A menu can be used to add or delete annotations, and to sort by any of the data values. Other types of experiments will cause the function list to be annotated with other data; a bottleneck or total time experiment will show total time, inclusive and exclusive; a CPU time experiment will show inclusive and exclusive CPU time; an I/O tracing experiment will show read and write calls, and bytes read and written, etc.

The Usage Graph

The middle part of the display in Figure 1.1 is a stripchart of time, showing the amount of time spent in each of a number of states. The kernel is responsible for maintaining the timers for each state, and the data is captured through the same process interface used for debugging. An expanded view of the stripchart is shown in Figure 1.2.

The states measured are user-CPU time, system-CPU time, time spent waiting for I/O, for paging, waiting for the CPU, as well as time in various sleep states. They are shown as percentages on a stacked bar graph.

The Timeline and Calipers

The lower third of the display is called the timeline, and contains markers for any sample points recorded in the experiment, and a pair of calipers that can be used to mark off an interval of the total time of the experiment. By

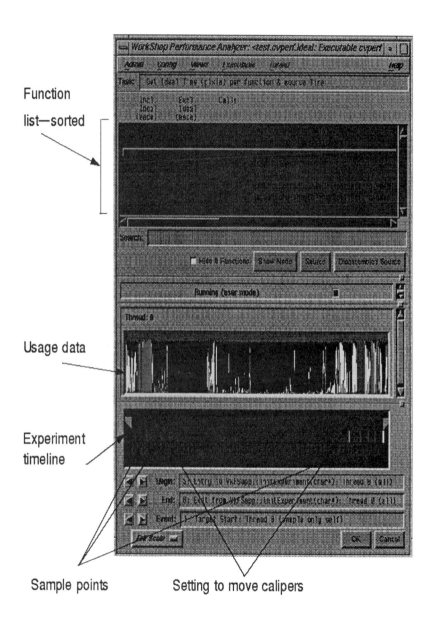

Figure 1.1: Performance Analyzer Main Window Display See color plate XIV.

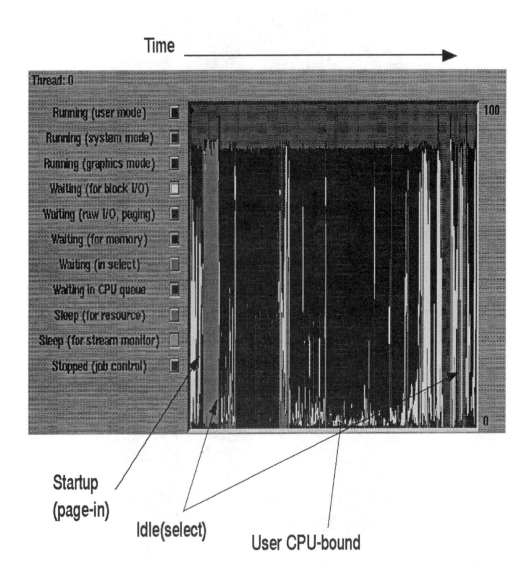

Figure 1.2: Usage Stripchart for a single thread. See color plate XV.

default, it comes up showing data for the entire run, that is, between the time the process started and the time the default trap on entry to the 'exit' system call fired. Any additional sample points will show up as tick marks on the time line, and the calipers can be set between any two of these. The function list display and all other displays only show the data for the portion of the run demarcated by the calipers.

Below the timeline are three fields which define the left and right caliper points, and a selected sample event. A callstack view is available that will show the callstack at whichever sample event is selected. The default experiment takes samples every second, and the user can step through the callstacks to see which main functions mark off the phases of execution of the program.

1.2.2 Program Structure Navigation

The function list can be very useful in understanding where the program is spending its time; however, it is often insufficient to help the user understand how the program is structured. To help the user navigate through the program's structure, a call graph view is provided that will show the interconnects between functions. The call graph view is shown in Figure 1.3.

The call graph shows one or more interconnected functions. Each function is shown as a box, with the function name and various values of performance data for that function given in the box. Calls between functions are shown as arcs in the graph, and each arc is annotated with the count of times it was traversed. Both statically-determined arcs and dynamic arcs, generated by calls through function pointers, are shown.

There are two main modes of usage of the graph: butterfly mode and chain mode. In butterfly mode, a selected function is shown with all of its callers and callees. In chain mode, two nodes are selected, a source node and a target node, and all paths (chains) between them are shown. In chain mode, the graph may be pruned by deleting all paths through a particular node, or all paths not through a particular node. In addition, the graph may be expanded and contracted by selecting any node and asking to expand all of its children or its parents, or by hiding the node or a subtree.

Despite these interface features, navigation of complex program graphs remains a challenging problem. For some programs, the current interface is precisely what is needed to understand them. For others, however, the graph is simply too complex to be easily visualized, and we are exploring other techniques to allow the user to understand his or her program.

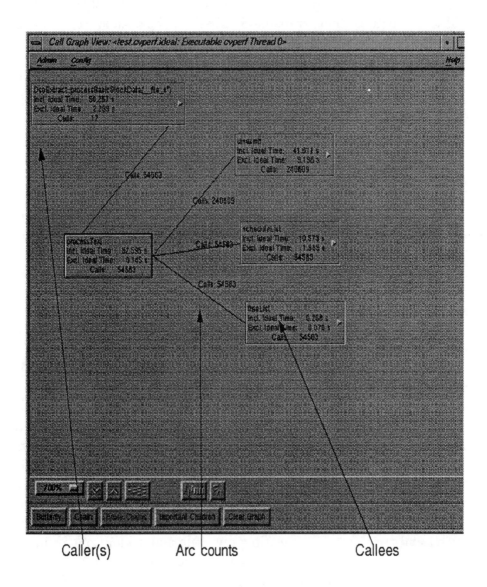

Caller(s)   Arc counts   Callees

Figure 1.3: Call graph view.

1.2.3 Instruction-level Data

While function-level data can show the user where time is being spent, improving the performance often requires a more detailed way of looking at the data. The Performance Analyzer can show performance data at the machine instruction level in the Disassembly View, as shown in Figure 1.4.

For ideal-time experiments, the disassembly data can show each instruction and how many times it was executed, as well as the detailed interaction between the program's instruction stream and the machine pipeline. The disassembly view is annotated with instruction counts, cycle counts, branches-taken counts for conditional branch instructions, and pipeline notations (referred to as 'pixstats' data). The pixstats data are shown as the last three columns of the annotations on the right. This shows the boundaries of each basic block (yellow lines above some of the annotations) and, for each instruction in the basic block, the clock period relative to the start of the block the instruction issued in, how many clock periods the instruction stalled, if any, and the reason for any stall. Reasons shown include delays for function unit availability, delays for operand availability, and branch delays. Superscalar issue is shown as ditto marks replacing the clock period for instruction issue, indicating that the instruction issued in the same clock as the previous instruction.

Where the original source is available, the disassembly view shows it intermixed with the generated machine instructions.

1.2.4 Source-level Data

Although disassembly data can be quite valuable, users are more often interested in source-level data, as shown in the Source View in Figure 1.5. It is invoked by double clicking on a function in the function list, or on a node or arc in the graph.

Like the function list and disassembly display, the source display can be annotated with whatever performance data is appropriate to the experiment being examined. The source for the file containing the selected function is shown, annotated with performance data. To help the user find the important lines of source, those lines whose performance notation represents more than 80% of the maximum value in the file will be shown with a yellow square next to the annotations. Furthermore, the scrollbar for the source will have yellow tick marks indicating the locations of the heavy-hitter lines.

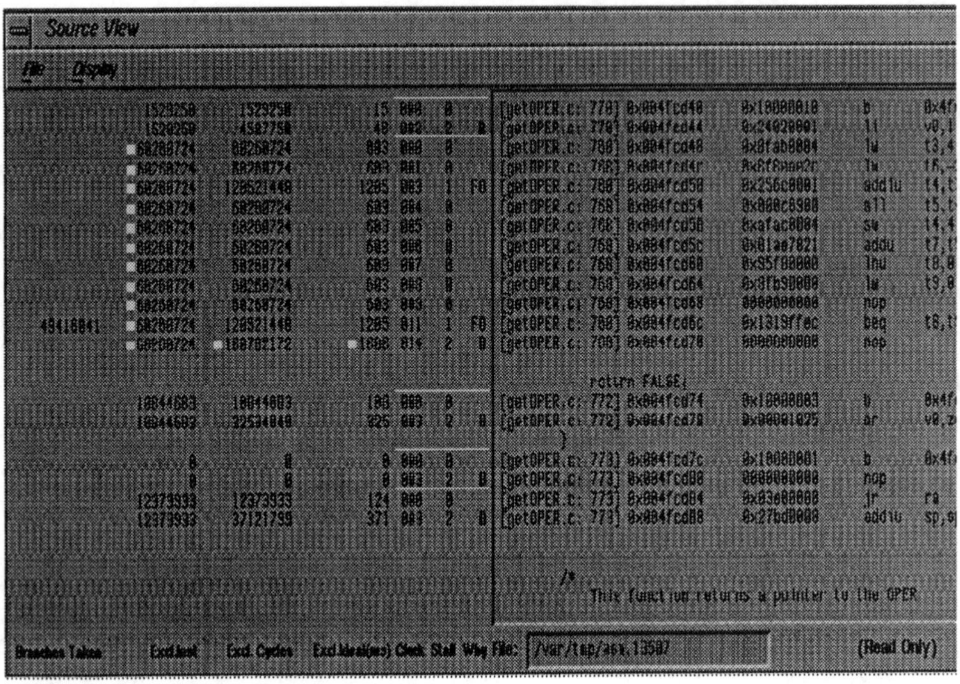

Figure 1.4: Annotated disassembly view. See color plate XVI.

1.2.5 Working Set Data

The current version of the tools does not directly capture working-set data for an application. For an ideal-time experiment, however, the basic-block counts can be used to determine which instructions on each instruction page were actually executed, and can show the utilization of these pages in the Working Set View, Figure 1.6.

Pages are shown for the selected dynamic shared object (DSO). In this context, a DSO is either the main portion of the executable, or one of the dynamic shared libraries with which it is linked. Each page is shown as a block, with the colored segments showing the proportion of instructions on that page actually executed (dark blue), not executed but coming from functions that were executed (yellow), or belonging to functions that were not executed (red). A page that was not touched at all is shown as green. Words in the instruction space that are not actual instructions, but which

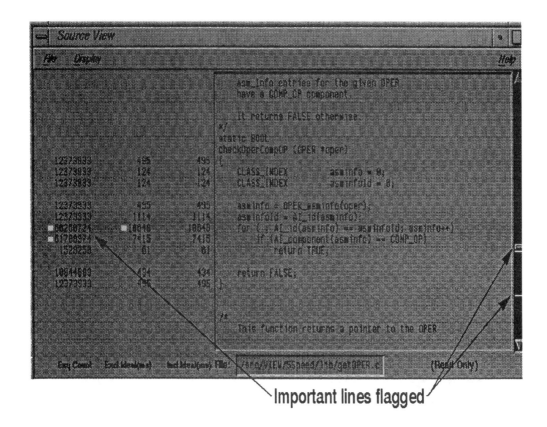

Important lines flagged

Figure 1.5: Annotated source view. See color plate XVII.

represent tables used to resolve references into dynamic shared objects, are shown as light blue.

The Working Set View has controls that allow the user to save a map of all the functions in a dynamic shared object, and to save the list of all functions in the working-set of the program for whatever operations are included in the current caliper setting. Another tool, the Cord Analyzer, can be used to examine the layout of multiple working sets for a particular shared object, as used for various operations in one or more programs; it can also compute a function ordering which will minimize the working-sets for various operations, and minimize the paging at the transitions between operations. A function list in the Cord Analyzer allows the user to see which functions are used in which operations.

List of DSOs

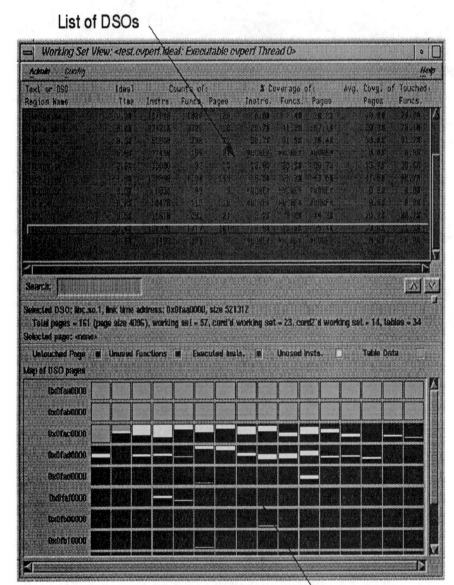

Figure 1.6: Working Set View. See color plate XVIII.

1.3   Parallel Performance Visualization

So far, we have discussed various ways to visualize performance data for each thread of a parallel program. Each of the views described above is for a single thread. When the data are displayed from an experiment run on a parallel application, a thread menu can be used to switch between threads. This next section will discuss other ways of looking at the data to show the performance characteristics of all of the threads in a parallel application.

1.3.1   Parallelization Obstacles

The most important characterization of any parallel program is one that delineates those regions of the code that are serial from those that are parallel. For serial regions, it is important to show whether they are serial because they perform better in serial, or if they are serial because they can not safely be run in parallel. For FORTRAN programs, the CASEVision/WorkShopProMPF Parallel Analyzer View can show the structure of the program, as shown in Figure 1.7.

The Parallel Analyzer View shows a list of the loops in the program, with an icon next to each showing its parallelization state. (The current version shows only loops, but future versions will show other parallel constructs, such as those described by the Parallel Computing Foundation (PCF) directives.) The state is normally determined by our automatically parallelizing compiler, but users may write explicitly parallel code as well. Loops are shown as parallel, serial (for any of several reasons), or unparallelizable. An unparallelizable loop is one for which the compiler has determined that it would prefer to run the loop in parallel, but there were one or more obstacles that made parallelization unsafe.

When a loop is selected, all of the obstacles to parallelization, as well as any messages or questions that the compiler has about the loop, are shown. Next to each obstacle is a highlight button that will cause the relevant lines of source and any relevant tokens (variable or function names) to be highlighted. Where questions are asked, the user interface presents a menu of answers which the compiler can use in subsequent compilations to get improved parallelization and optimization. Compiler communications are discussed further in Sec. 1.4 below.

The Parallel Analyzer interoperates with the Performance Analyzer. If they are both looking at the same program, the Parallel Analyzer will ask

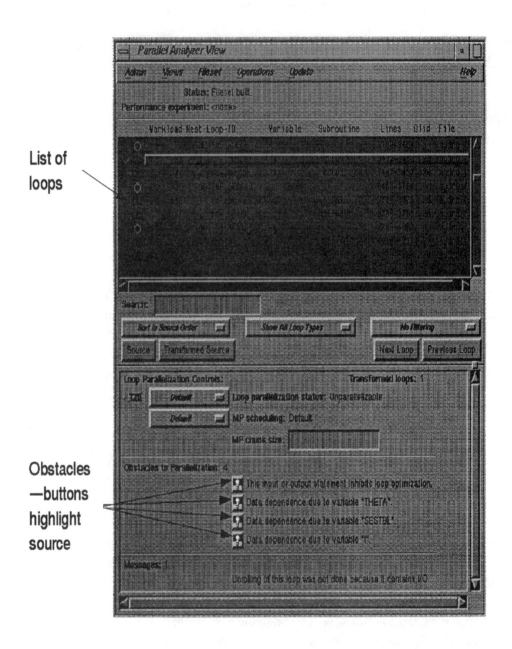

Figure 1.7: Parallel Analyzer view. See color plate XIX.

the Performance Analyzer for the performance data for each loop in the program, and will annotate its list of loops with that data, thus allowing the user to concentrate on those loops that are both unparallelizable and responsible for significant execution time of the program. When the two programs interoperate, they will share a common source view, which will show both loop annotations from the Parallel Analyzer, and performance data from the Performance Analyzer. The loop annotations are in the form of colored brackets marking the boundaries of each loop, with the color coded to reflect the loop's parallelization state.

1.3.2   Load Balance Data

One of the most interesting characteristics of parallel applications is the balance of load across the threads. The current performance analyzer does not show these data directly, but requires the user to look at each thread in turn.

A future version of the tools will address this issue. We intend to add a new view, the Function View, that will show detailed information for a single function across multiple threads. Although a tabular display seems quite straightforward, it does not scale very well to programs with many threads. One possibility is to use a graphical display of the relative CPU time across threads.

1.3.3   Synchronization Performance Data

Another important characteristic of parallel applications is the time spent in synchronizing the threads. It would be nice to see how long it takes each thread to dispatch, to wait for a lock, and/or to send or receive a message. Future work will be directed towards visualization of these data.

1.4   Compiler Communications

Although the Performance Analyzer can show measured data for an application, there is other information available from the compiler that describes what the compiler has determined about the application. Some of that information is visualized in the Parallel Analyzer, while other information is not yet made visible. The remainder of this section describes future work that will be done to further integrate all of the data about an application to help the user understand and tune his or her program.

1.4.1 'Love Letters' from the Compiler

In our current compilers, some information about parallelization is externalized into a file that the parallel analyzer uses to show the user obstacles to parallelization. For some compilation options, additional 'Love Letters' are written by the software pipeliner to show exactly how the instructions were sequenced to make the best use of the machine pipeline. Currently, these appear as comments that can be correlated with the disassembled source of the compiled program. Future work will go towards extracting this information, and other information about optimization, and displaying all of this information both in a hierarchical display of program structure and as annotations to the user source and/or disassembly.

1.4.2 'Mash Notes' to the Compiler

Another technique being developed will allow the performance analyzer to send 'mash notes' to the compiler. Currently, the Parallel Analyzer can ask some questions of the user and convey the answers to the compiler by means of inserted directives and/or assertions in the code; only a few questions are asked now, all concerning the ability of the compiler to automatically parallelize the code.

The compiler can actually use a great deal of additional information in order to optimize the code. For example, how a particular loop nest is best optimized will depend on the relative execution frequencies of the inner and outer loops. With no help from the user, the compiler must simply guess as to the relative frequencies of each loops; if the user knows, he or she could insert a directive, passing this information to the compiler which can then generate superior code. For example, a user might very well know that the inner loop spans three spatial dimensions, while the outer loop spans thousands of interacting particles.

1.5 Conclusions

We have described various techniques used to visualize the performance of parallel programs, both on a per-thread basis, and for the program as a whole. Experiments can be recorded for total time, CPU time, ideal time, as well as I/O and system calls, heap allocation and deallocation, page faults and floating-point exceptions. By setting sample points during the recording of experiments, the user may look at data for part of a run, rather than only for the entire run.

For an individual thread, the user may examine the measured data on the function, source-line, or instruction level. Measured data includes exclusive and inclusive time, loads, stores, and floating point operations, and interactions between the instruction stream and the machine pipeline. Each thread of a multiprocess application can be examined separately.

For Fortran programs, the user can also look at the structure of program loops, and determine which can be parallelized, and which can not. For those that can not, all obstacles to parallelization will be shown.

Future work will be directed towards better display of load balance across threads, display of the performance of synchronization primitives, and improving the communications among the parallelizing compiler, the visualization tools, and the user.

Multiple Views of Parallel Application Execution

Ming C. Hao, Abdul Waheed, Alan Karp, Mehdi Jazayeri
Hewlett Packard Laboratories
Palo Alto, California 94304

Abstract

VIZIR is a visualization and debugging environment that has been prototyped at Hewlett Packard Laboratories for analyzing and synchronizing the concurrent behavior of parallel programs. VIZIR key features include: (1) Interactive Program Execution Status Lights: Color indicates various states of the process, such as busy, idle, sending or blocked for messages, and program error states. These lights have proved very useful in debugging message-passing deadlock; (2) Consistent Time Stamps; (3) On-line Multiple Synchronized Views using multiple tools: VIZIR synchronizes visualizes and animates views using ParaGraph and Matlab. Debugging, performance, and analysis are synchronized. Processes in the parallel application can be halted by the debugger at the same point that performance and data visualization is being done.

1.1 Introduction

Problems involved in developing message-passing application programs for any parallel architecture are non-trivial. Visualizing the program behavior has proved to be a useful technique for debugging and analyzing the concurrent behavior of parallel programs but the asynchronous nature of distributed systems makes the task even more challenging. VIZIR is a synchronized visualization and debugging environment that has been prototyped at Hewlett Packard Laboratories to meet these challenges of tool development and to facilitate the task of distributed programming. Its main objective is to use the strengths of network-based computing for sequential programs and to apply the existing technologies and tools to solve the problems of distributed program development. VIZIR enables users to add multiple visualization tools of their choice to this environment in order to understand the dynamic execution behavior of their applications.

Tool development for programming parallel and distributed systems has been an active area of research but has largely fallen short of user expectations [10]. In many cases users are not satisfied by the way a particular tool works and by the learning curve associated with using it to accomplish a specific task. VIZIR allows a user to use a favorite tool by making it a part of the programming environment. In order to realize this environment, the following issues are involved:

- Enabling a programmer's favorite existing debugging and visualization tools to become a part of this program development environment. This has become an important issue in view of increasing indifference of the users toward "novel" parallel program development tools.

- Synchronizing and controlling the activities of the debuggers and visualizers to provide a consistent view of program execution to the user.

- Integrating heterogeneous types of visualization tools, such as general-purpose and conventional performance visualization tools across different platforms. This is necessary to address a wide range of requirements of various types of program behavior visualizations, such as application performance, system performance, and program data visualizations.

We have addressed these issues in the design of VIZIR to assist users in developing parallel programs using PVM [4] message-passing libraries for a cluster of workstations. We have enabled several commonly used debugging tools, such as Softbench's softdebug, Hewlett Packard's DDE, and IBM's XDE. Similarly, we have integrated popularly used parallel program visualization tools such as ParaGraph into our system, in addition to commercially available visualization tools, such as Matlab and AVS for customized program performance and data visualizations.

In a distributed programming environment, an application consists of multiple processes running on one or more physical nodes that are distributed in a network. VIZIR executes each of these application processes under the control of an available (and perhaps a user's favorite) debugger. One debugger executing a single process presents the same scenario as debugging a single sequential application. The only difference is the message-passing among these otherwise independent processes. Visualization has been recognized as an appropriate technique to represent message-passing and program execution behavior [8]. Several tools have been developed and used to represent various aspects of concurrent program and system behavior [9]. VIZIR enables the use of these visualization tools by providing three major functionalities:

- multicasting message-passing events among the application processes;

- integrating visualization tools to represent multiple perspectives of application behavior; and

- controlling and synchronizing the execution of application processes and visualization tools.

Figure 1.1 depicts the overall architecture of VIZIR and its functionality. Despite the distributed processes, the environment allows the user to control the configuration and actions of all the distributed application processes and tools. It is important to note that VIZIR is running locally, whereas the other application processes, debuggers, and visualization tools might be running locally or remotely. Therefore, VIZIR acts as a controller for the whole environment which is the key to resolving the problems involved in visualizing distributed application programs. We present the major functions of VIZIR related with distributed program visualization in the following.

Parallel program visualization tools have to rely on some mechanism for multicasting events among the concurrent processes, in order to represent this activity graphically. Program code is instrumented and linked with the available communication library to multicast these communication events. However, most of the instrumentation systems for parallel programs in general and distributed programs in particular perturb the application behavior mainly due to additional message-passing required for generating and communicating the trace data. VIZIR does not need explicit message-passing to obtain information about program execution events which might double the

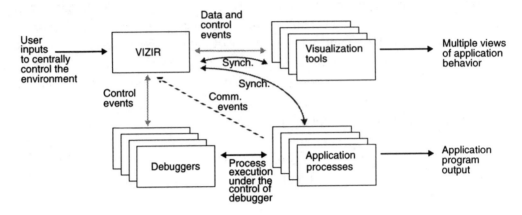

Figure 1.1: Views of a parallel application.

actual communication cost of an application. Instead, it relies on a Event Sense Protocol (ESP [6]) to multicast message-passing and program execution events among the application processes. Multi-Events Protocol (MEP [7]) uses light-weight inter-client communication primitives to make receiving these events faster. Additionally, there is no explicit binding between applications and VIZIR's multiple event processing and synchronization activities. Whenever an application process executes a particular message-passing function, it sends that event to the event queue of the underlying system which can be triggered by VIZIR. Once VIZIR receives the event, it assigns the event a time-stamp and generates a corresponding trace record. This trace record can be further processed and passed on to the visualization tools for dynamically visualizing the application behavior.

1.2   Features of VIZIR

The design features of VIZIR have been used to provide several distributed program visualization features. Efficacy of the presently available visualization tools for distributed programs is limited due to the unavailability of these features. This section briefly presents some of these features.

- *Interactive Program Execution Status Lights:* VIZIR indicates the states of all the processes at all times during program execution using status lights. Color indicates various states of the process, such as busy, idle, sending or blocked for messages, and program error states. These lights have proved very useful to debug message-passing bugs, such as message deadlocks. There are four sets of these lights: application execution status, message communication status, command execution status, and user-defined lights to locate the hot spots.

- *Consistent Time Stamps:* Generation of consistent time stamps has been a non-trivial constraint for existing distributed program visualization tools [1]. VIZIR overcomes this problem because its architecture relies on MEP and makes it a centralized controller for the whole environment. When the applications are running on different workstations, it is not possible to have a notion of consistent global time. VIZIR does not have the application processes generate the time-stamps with the events. Instead, it only collects and orders the information about event occurrences through MEP and tags the time-stamps. Since VIZIR orders all incoming events before generating time-stamps, therefore, they are consistent. Also, there is negligible delay between a communication call and triggering that event using MEP, therefore the time-stamps are reliable for all practical purposes.

- *On-line Multiple Views using Multiple Tools:* Visualizing the behavior and performance of a parallel or distributed program is always a multidimensional assessment. Not only does it take multiple tools but also multiple views and multiple domains [11,12] are needed to represent a complete picture of program behavior to the user. VIZIR provides on-line, typical performance visualization and animation views that are implemented in ParaGraph. It can also allow the use of general-purpose data analysis tools such as AVS, Matlab, Gnuplot, and Mathematica to represent multiple perspectives on application performance and behavior. Figure 1.2 represents some of these views.

1.3 Summary and Conclusions

VIZIR is an on-going experiment in Hewlett-Packard Research Labs. VIZIR provides standard window inter faces to existing visualizers/debuggers with on-the-fly control and synchronization. Processes in the parallel application can be halted by the debugger at the same point that performance and data

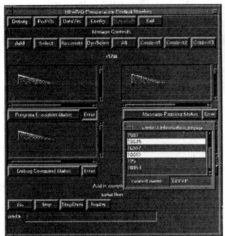

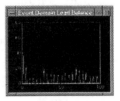

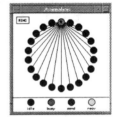

Event domain views using Matlab as an analytic and
visualization engine, integrated with VIZIR.

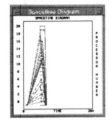

VIZIR provides control and
synchronization of the environment.

Typical application visualization displays from
ParaGraph, synchronized and integrated with VIZIR.

Figure 1.2: Multiple views from multiple domains and tools to visualize
and analyze on-the-fly execution behavior of a distributed program. See
color plate XX.

visualization is being done. In addition, For example, performance and data
errors detected by performance and data analyzers may automatically trigger
the debugger to halt the process. Although we have applied our mechanisms
to prototype debugging environment for parallel programs, they have much
wider applicability. This approach can be used any time we want to do
the same thing on more than one machine. Examples include administering
cluster, sharing large volume of data such as video.

Acknowledgments

Thanks to Dr. Chris Hsiung for his encouragement and suggestions. Vineet
Singh and Milon Mackey also provided useful technical discussion.

References

1. BEGUELIN, A. L., "Xab: A Tool for Monitoring PVM Programs," *Proc. of the Twenty-Sixth Hawaii Int. Conf. on System Sciences*, Wailea, Hawaii, Jan. 1993, 102–3.

2. CHEN, MINDER AND NORMAN, RONALD J., "A Framework for Integrated CASE," *IEEE Software*, March 1992, 18–22.

3. GEIST, G., et al., "A Machine-Independent Communication Library," *Proc. of the Fourth Conf. on Hypercubes, Concurrent Computers, and Applications*, Los Altos, 1990.

4. GEIST, G., et al., "PVM 3.0 User's Guide and Reference Manual," ORNL/TM-12187, Feb. 1993.

5. HAO, MING C., KARP, ALAN, SINGH, VINEET, et al. "On-the-Fly Visualization and Debugging of Parallel Programs," *Proc. of International Workshop on Modeling, Analysis and Simulation of Computer and Telecommunication Systems (MASCOTS '94)*, Durham, NC, Jan. 31-Feb. 2, 1994.

6. HAO, MING C. KARP, ALAN, SINGH, VINEET, "Concurrent Application Control in Collaborative Computing," HPL-94-37, Hewlett-Packard Laboratories, Palo Alto, April 1994.

7. HAO, MING C., et al., "Multi-Event Based Protocols for Distributed Program Interactions," HPL, Hewlett-Packard Laboratories, Palo Alto, July 1994.

8. HEATH, MICHAEL T. AND ETHERIDGE, JENNIFER A., "Visualizing the Performance of Parallel Programs," *IEEE Software*, **8** (5), Sept. 1991, 29–39.

9. KRAEMER, EILEEN AND STASKO, JOHN T., "The Visualization of Parallel Systems: An Overview," *Journal of Parallel and Distributed Computing*, **18** (2), June 1993, 105–117.

10. PANCAKE, CHERRI M., "Supercomputing '93 Parallel User Survey: Response Summary," 94-80-2, Oregon State University, Feb. 1994.

11. ROVER, DIANE T. AND WAHEED, ABDUL, "Multiple Domain Analysis Methods," *Proc. of the 3rd ACM/ONR Workshop on Parallel and Distributed Debugging*, May 1993, 53–63.

12. WAHEED, A. AND ROVER, D. T., "Performance Visualization of Parallel Programs," Visualization '93, San Jose, CA, Oct. 25–29, 1993.

A Performance Tool for The CRAY T3D

Douglas M. Pase, Winifred Williams
Cray Research, Inc.
Eagan, Minnesota 55121

Abstract

The MPP Apprentice performance tools help application developers tune the performance of CRAY T3D applications. The instrumentation and displays of the tool are designed to handle long-running programs and large numbers of processors. The method of instrumentation, data collection, and presentation perspective are significantly different from many popular performance tools today. Run-time pass counts and elapsed times are combined with compile-time information files containing information from both the front and back ends of the compiler. Performance characteristics are displayed from the perspective of the user's original source code. An analysis engine derives secondary statistics, identifies performance problems and the speedups possible by correcting such problems, and offers suggestions where possible. This paper will demonstrate that the approach taken in the MPP Apprentice performance tool scales well and accurately identifies performance problems from a variety of programming models using a real customer example.

1.1   Introduction

The CRAY T3D is a massively parallel processor (MPP) which connects 32 to 2048 high performance scalar commodity microprocessors together in a high-speed three-dimensional torus network. Applications for the T3D may be developed in C or Fortran using message-passing or a shared memory paradigm. Additionally, Fortran applications can be developed using the CRAFT worksharing or data parallel features, which provide array and loop distribution mechanisms [13].

The MPP Apprentice performance tool helps application developers tune the performance of their CRAY T3D applications by illuminating performance bottlenecks where they occur [7]. The instrumentation and displays are designed to handle long-running codes on large numbers of processors. When possible the MPP Apprentice performance tool provides suggestions about what might be causing bottlenecks and how they might be corrected. It also provides explanations of system functions the user might not realize are being called and pointers to the most profitable places to improve the code. The remainder of this paper is organized as follows: Sec. 1.2 surveys related work in performance tools; Sec. 1.3 gives a brief description of the CRAY T3D computational environment and types of problems of concern to application developers; Sec. 1.4 talks about technology tradeoffs and analyzes the intrusiveness and accuracy of the MPP Apprentice instrumentation. Section 1.4 also gives a brief functional description of the Apprentice. Section 1.5 shows how the tool was used so speed up a customer code by a factor of 20, from 24.5 MFlop/s to 494 MFlop/s. Section 1.6 provides some concluding remarks about the strengths and weaknesses of this approach, and how the current tool might be improved.

1.2   Related Work

Much work has been done in the area of performance tools for parallel systems, with entire issues of journals being devoted to them. (Two issues that are worthy of note are volume 8, number 5 (September 1991) of IEEE Software, and volume 18, number 2 (June 1993) of Journal of Parallel and Distributed Computing.) Researchers in parallel tools have expended considerable effort in the area of event trace visualization and data gathering. Indeed, the vast majority of work in performance tools for massively parallel systems has been to develop event trace technology.

Tools that record traces of the execution of parallel threads within a program include SCHEDULE [3], SHMAP [2], ParaGraph [4], Traceview [10], IPS-2 [12], and AIMS [18]. Many others can be found in the literature as well. An excellent survey article on visualizing the behavior of parallel systems can be found in Kraemer and Stasko [8]. Trace tools typically record task-oriented events, e.g. the creation or destruction of tasks, entry and exit of subroutines, message sends and receives, and display events as they occur within the machine. Many tools provide a display which gives progression in time along one axis and processors along another axis. Individual events are marked off in time at the processor on which they occurred. When the tool has semantic knowledge about two or more events, as occurs in message send/receive pairs, links may be drawn tying such events together visually. The focus is on what is happening within the hardware at some level. To assist the programmer, some tools, such as AIMS, provide a link back to the source so that a programmer can easily see what piece of code generated the event. Of the trace tools mentioned, SHMAP is unique in that it records references to memory as its events. This permits the user to see an animation of array reference patterns, displaying how arrays are accessed over time.

Event trace tools are particularly appealing because they allow a user to see what is going on within the machine. Trace tools can do this without having extensive semantic knowledge of the application or system, which significantly eases the burden on the tool builder. By showing the user a global schedule of their program, every problem (down to the level of detail for which events were recorded) becomes visible. Persons initially working in the field of parallel computing were required to know characteristics of the hardware in order to develop new algorithms and software systems on top of the parallel hardware. For those who understand details of the architecture, the perspective provided by trace tools can be very intuitive. However, a difficulty arises in that event trace visualization tools can present so much data, much of which is collected from correctly functioning code, that the user can get lost in irrelevant details.

A major concern with tools that are based on event trace visualization technology is the scalability and intrusiveness of instrumentation. The volume of data to collect, store, interpret, and display is proportional to the product of the frequency of collection, the number of processors, and the execution time during which events are recorded. Also, if the sampling method is in software, the act of recognizing and recording the events can severely perturb the behavior of the program. A program that records events frequently (e.g., once every thousand clock periods) for a modest number of processors (e.g., 256) over a typical run (e.g., an hour of wall clock time) can collect more data than many systems have space to store (e.g., on the order of 1 terabyte), and disturb the program behavior to the point where the data collected are meaningless. Dynamic instrumentation [6] begins to address the volume aspect of this problem by adjusting at run-time what is measured. The AIMS tool [18] addresses the issue of distorted measurements by reverse engineering the costs of instrumentation and removing them from the measurements to compensate for its intrusion.

The scalability of the display system is also a concern for event trace tools. A large volume of data will overwhelm a user, unless that information can be displayed in such a way that anomalies can clearly be recognized and their sources can be identified [14, 15]. Tools needed to construct scalable displays, such as Kiviat diagrams for showing the behavior of many processors, are available in the Pablo tool [16]. Pablo is a meta-tool, that is, it is a tool for constructing performance visualization tools, that is extremely flexible and adaptable.

1.3 CRAY T3D Programming Environment

The CRAY T3D is a massively parallel processor (MPP) built from high performance commodity microprocessors connected together by a high bandwidth 3-dimensional torus. The processing elements (PEs) are Digital Equipment Corporation Alpha EV4 microprocessors running at 150 MHz. The CRAY T3D architecture is scalable from 32 up to 2048 PEs. This wide range of scalability is possible because the CRAY T3D uses a non-uniform memory access (NUMA) design. Each PE has 8K bytes of on-chip data and instruction caches, local memory, and the ability to reference the local memory of any other PE. Only values in a processor's local memory can be cached. The relative cost of accessing data stored at each level in the memory hierarchy is approximately one order of magnitude cheaper than the next more distant level. Thus, attention to locality of reference is extremely important. In terms of network bandwidth global loads cost twice as much as global stores, because loads require round-trip communication whereas stores are uni-directional.

Because the T3D is a parallel machine with all the potential for data races, a rich set of synchronization, communication, and work-sharing mechanisms are provided. The CRAY T3D programming environment includes the CRAFT programming model [13], PVM message passing system [1], a shared memory access library, and data-parallel execution of a Fortran 90 subset. All of these features can be mixed or matched within the same program or even within the same subroutine, as needed. The CRAFT programming model provides facilities for distributing arrays and work across the available PEs. It is similar in some respects to High Performance Fortran (HPF) [5], but offers simpler data distribution mechanisms and more extensive control over work distribution. Standard shared memory synchronization mechanisms, such as locks, events, and barriers, are also provided. The shared memory access library permits the programmer to directly access non-local memory through a subroutine interface. The CRAY T3D programming environment is a feature-rich programming environment. Ineffective use of these features can cause problems with the performance of a code. The MPP Apprentice must seamlessly support the wide variety of programming styles possible from this diversity of features.

Performance problems one encounters on the CRAY T3D are generally not very different from performance problems encountered on any other MPP. Timing thresholds which determine a performance problem may be different, because the relative speeds of hardware functions are different. But the general types of problems are the same. Performance problems to which we have paid special attention in this tool's design are: load imbalance, excessive serialization, excessive communication, network contention, poor use of the memory hierarchy, inappropriate work distribution, and inappropriate array distribution. We will examine each of these in the section below.

1.3.1   Load Imbalance

Load imbalance refers to an uneven distribution of work across processors, which causes some processors to be starved for work when others have excess work. Processors that are starved for useful work cannot help the computation progress, and represent the inefficient use of an important resource. Generally speaking, a program that distributes the work load fairly evenly across all processors will run more quickly and less expensively than a program which does not. Exceptions to this rule can occur when the cost of distributing the work, or distributing (communicating) the data needed to make the work possible, is more expensive than the cost of the idle processors.

A load imbalance can occur in many ways, and all result in PEs being blocked on some form of synchronization. Generally, the type of synchronization which causes the problem is one that blocks multiple PEs, then allows them to proceed together. Examples of this are explicit barriers and events, and implicit barriers within constructs such as shared loops and master regions. Load imbalances can also occur when multiple PEs are blocked waiting on the receipt of a message, all for what is logically the same reason. For example, a load imbalance can occur when PEs block waiting for the transmission of a broadcast from a host processor or another PE. It is not important how the broadcast was generated. What is important is that all PEs are waiting for the completion of what is logically the same operation before they can proceed with the computation.

Compute efficiency can be lost by any type of synchronization when access to the mechanism forces many PEs to become idle while waiting for the synchronization criterion to become satisfied. But for the purposes of this paper load imbalance will refer to the problem of PEs being forced into an idle state by a synchronization or communication mechanism which, when satisfied, releases all PEs to return to a non-idle state. Such mechanisms include explicit and implicit barriers, events, broadcasts, binary cascaded reductions, and similar operations.

1.3.2 Excessive Serialization

Compute efficiency can also be lost by synchronization on locks and critical regions when many processors block because of contention for a critical resource. This type of loss is called serialization. Serialization is a condition in which processors are blocked because only one processor is allowed access to a critical resource at a time. Other mechanisms which may be responsible for serialization are master regions and atomic update operations. (Conceptually, atomic update operations permit statements such as X(IX(I))=X(IX(I))+V(I) to complete without race conditions. For a description of atomic update operations see Sec. 5.5 in Pase, MacDonald, and Meltzer [13].)

Program serialization occurs when only one PE is allowed to execute at a time. Execution can be serialized by any type of synchronization mechanism that protects some critical resource. Examples of these are locks, critical regions, master regions, and atomic updates. Locks and atomic updates are generally used to protect access to data, while critical regions and master regions are used to protect access to code. Locks, critical regions, and atomic updates permit other PEs to work on unrelated tasks or data. They cause a PE to block only when it attempts to access the protected data or code. Master regions require that all PEs participate, and all but one are idle until its completion. Any of these synchronization mechanisms can be a cause of excessive serialization.

Locks, atomic updates, and critical regions do not inherently cause PEs to become idle, because PEs are free to do other work. They only become idle when they attempt to access a protected resource. Master regions, on the other hand, require all PEs to participate, and do force PEs to become idle. In a master region all PEs join at a barrier, after which exactly one PE (the master PE) is allowed to proceed. When the master PE has completed the code within the region, all PEs are then permitted to proceed. Because all PEs are forced to participate but only one is allowed to do any work, it is very important that there be as little work as possible within a master region. It is also important to execute master regions infrequently and when the processors are fairly well synchronized, in order to minimize the idle time accumulated waiting for the last PE to enter the region.

1.3.3 Excessive Communication

A program may use explicit message passing (PVM) routines to communicate data and/or synchronization information on the CRAY T3D system. In message passing, one processing element explicitly sends a message to another PE, which explicitly receives it. When the sending PE has more work to do than the receiving PE, the receiving PE may become idle until the message arrives. This idle time appears in one or more of the PVM library subroutines. When the communication time is greater than expected, it can be an indication of any of the following conditions: load imbalance, excessive serialization of tasks, poor distribution of data, or network contention.

Large transfers, many small transfers, network contention, or any combination of these can cause a long wait time at a receive call. Unfortunately, point-to-point communication can be used in so many different ways that it is difficult for a tool to analyze how it is being used. Without semantic knowledge of the application a tool is left merely to report how its use impacts performance. As discussed above, broadcasts, multicasts and reductions offer greater structure and more can be said about them.

1.3.4 Network Contention

Network contention occurs when multiple messages compete for network resources. Network messages can be generated from shared memory references, synchronization constructs, or calls to explicit message passing routines. Network contention is a second order effect; that is, it indirectly affects performance by slowing down communication across the machine. Network contention can affect any operation that requires network resources, including global shared memory references and the use of locks, events, or critical regions. When problems occur with synchronization constructs, message routines, or other features that use the network, it is usually best to consider the first order effects, such as load imbalances, before pursuing network contention as a cause of poor performance.

1.4 Memory Hierarchy

The way a program makes use of the memory hierarchy can have a tremendous impact on its performance. The memory hierarchy includes processing element registers, data cache, private memory, local shared memory, and global memory. The instruction and data caches are 8K bytes each, and both are direct-mapped caches with 32 byte cache lines. Clearly, the closer data are to the PE that will use it, the less time it takes to bring the data from memory into that PE. It is approximately ten times slower to fetch a value from memory local to a PE than from data cache to a PE, and approximately ten times slower to fetch a value from the memory of a remote PE than from memory local to a PE.

1.4.1 Shared Work and Array Distribution

Shared loops distribute the loop iterations across all processing elements within a partition. The choice of loop distribution mechanism affects the cost of starting a loop, distributing a block of iterations, terminating or shutting a loop down, and executing the individual iterations. To gain the greatest benefit from shared loops, these costs must be balanced against each other.

Array distribution can affect performance across the whole program; the overall effect of a change can be undesirable even when it improves performance locally. Inappropriate shared array distribution is much more subtle than other problems because changing the distribution of one or more arrays can affect performance in non-linear ways. Problems caused by inappropriate array distributions can include any combination of the following: excessive communication, network contention, or load imbalance from poor distribution of loops.

1.5   Design Considerations and Apprentice Technology

The major goal of our work has been to develop a tool which would aid application developers and scientists in recognizing and removing performance bottlenecks from production codes running on a massively parallel processor. Such a tool should display the available information in a way that a user can clearly and easily recognize problems when they exist. The tool itself should also be able to recognize common problems, point them out to the user, and when possible, provide an explanation of the problem and suggestions for correcting it. The issues we consider to be of primary importance in meeting this goal are: accuracy of the measured values, space consumed for recording and storing measured values, granularity of the measured values, and the usability and scalability of the performance debugging system. The importance of these issues should be quite evident, although their interrelationship might not be.

The accuracy of data when it is recorded by totally independent hardware systems can be quite high, but most systems do not have the luxury of such expensive data gathering machinery.[1] Instead, data on a program's behavior are usually gathered in software, and the very act of measuring the behavior can affect the observed behavior. For example, data from the measurements must be stored in user data space. Storing or updating these values can perturb instruction and data cache, which can cause cache misses–hence delays–in code where there may have been none in an uninstrumented version. Memory access times are also sensitive to layout with respect to cache line boundaries, DRAM page boundaries and other hardware or operating system defined mechanisms. The inclusion of instrumentation can alter the layout, which alters program behavior. Furthermore, if the instrumentation space is too large, many codes which fit into memory during production runs will not fit into memory when instrumented.

A related problem concerns the granularity at which events can be ac-

---

[1]Cray vector processor hardware performance monitors (HPM) [17] count user events such as user memory references and instructions executed exactly, and vary only slightly from one run to the next because operating system context switches contribute to the counts. HPM data collection does not interfere with program execution in any way.

curately obtained. The act of recording an event in software perturbs the behavior of a parallel program by some amount. We call this the Heisenberg Principle for Software, because the act of observing the behavior of software causes the behavior of that software to change. Since MIMD systems have multiple processors which execute independent instruction streams, the cost of instrumentation is often different for each processor. When processors synchronize or share messages, the delays recorded by the performance monitoring instrumentation will differ by some amount, generally the amount that the instrumentation cost differs between processors. In some parallel codes, delays in events can cause work to be executed on a different processor, or in a different order on the same processor than it would have been executed had the delays not occurred. This is especially true of codes that use some form of adaptive load balancing for distributing work. Since the relative cost of instrumentation may vary from task to task, the impact of a given task can be different between instrumented and uninstrumented runs. For these reasons, instrumentation that takes many cycles to execute can only be used infrequently if the data it collects are to be believed, even if the timer itself is very accurate.

The technology used to place instrumentation in the executable program can affect the useful granularity of that instrumentation. It also affects the ease with which the system can be used, the type of information that can accurately be gathered, and other important characteristics. For example, instrumentation can be placed in source code, perhaps by a filter as occurs in ATExpert [9] and SHMAP [13], or by an interactive editor such as in AIMS [18]. This has the advantage of making portability easier, because it isolates the instrumentation from other parts of the system, such as the compiling and linking environment. It may also be restricted to coarser granularity instrumentation because the compiling system does not distinguish instrumentation from other user code. The most information is available when the instrumentation is inserted by the compiler because the compiler has more information about, and more influence over, the execution than any other part of the system. It has the drawback, along with source-level instrumentation, of requiring the user to recompile the code for instrumented runs. Compiler instrumentation can also be implemented with low impact on the execution, by recognizing and making use of unused registers and other resources. It can also avoid perturbing any optimizations the compiler may use. Instrumentation systems may also begin with object (*.o) or executable (a.out) files, or even running programs. Doing so increases convenience for the user by requiring fewer steps to obtain performance data, however, at the cost of losing some information.

The Apprentice is a post-execution performance analysis tool. The work reported in this paper differs from previous work in parallel tools in several ways. The volume of performance data collected by the instrumentation system is proportional to the size of the instrumented code and is not proportional to program execution time nor number of processors on which the program is executed. The Apprentice combines data collected during compilation with run-time data to identify undesirable performance. Our method of instrumentation does not interfere with compiler optimizations, and easily ties back to source. Figure 1.1 gives a block diagram of how the Apprentice is used. The application to be analyzed is first compiled with a special switch to activate Apprentice instrumentation. This causes the compiler to insert additional instructions into the code stream and to generate a compiler information file (CIF) which contains a map of the code structure as the user sees the program, and a map of the executable as the machine sees the program. The user next executes the code, which emits a run-time information file (RIF). The Apprentice takes the RIF and interprets it according to the maps in the CIF to tell the user how the code behaves. The mapping from run-time information to source code is illustrated in Figure 1.2.

The most important difference is that our tool does not rely on event traces to record program behavior. In this regard it is more like Paradyn [11] and ATExpert [9] than "traditional" MPP performance tools. The Apprentice instead records pass counts and the total time spent within different sections of the user's program without regard for when the time was spent there. Apprentice instrumentation is inserted by the compiler after all phases of optimization are complete. The compiler places timers and counters within each basic block to be emitted into the object file. Timers and counters accumulate the number of passes through, and the total time spent within, each basic block. These values are then accumulated across all processors, as illustrated in Figure 1.3, and stored in the run-time information file. The amount of information collected is proportional to the size of the instrumented code and is not proportional to the number of processors nor running time used. Our data files are typically under one megabyte in size, even for applications with tens of thousands of lines of source code.

In theory this has the disadvantage that information on the global schedule is lost, something which event trace-based instrumentation attempts to retain. A global schedule indicates what each processor is doing across the

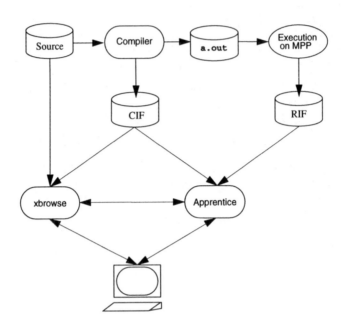

Figure 1.1: Block diagram of apprentice usage.

progression of time, which can show not only that a problem occurs, but also
what role each processor has in creating the problem. In some cases this can
mean that the MPP Apprentice will recognize that a problem has occurred
and what part of the code is most affected by it, but not know what caused
it. In practice it has the advantage of scaling well to large programs, large
numbers of processor elements, and long-running times. In comparison, event
trace visualization tools do not scale well to thousands, or even hundreds of
processors, nor do they work well post-processing long-running programs.

A key to accurate fine granularity data is low-cost instrumentation. To
keep the instrumentation cost low, we accumulate pass counts through and
time spent within each section of code down to the basic block level. We
make extensive use of the Alpha read-process-CPU clock (rpcc) instruction
for our lightweight timer. When a code is compiled, additional information,
such as the number and type of instructions within each code block being
measured, is emitted into the CIF. The Apprentice then combines the information gathered from the code execution (contained in the RIF) with
information in the CIF to determine many details about the execution that

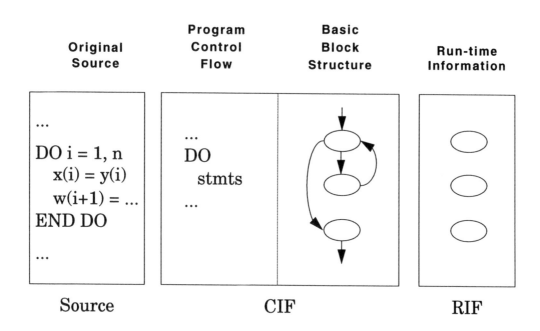

Figure 1.2: Mapping between source and run-time information.

would be far too expensive to collect using run-time instrumentation alone. Apprentice instrumentation records data at a granularity of only a few tens to a few hundreds of clock periods separating instrumentation points. Event trace technology must separate instrumentation points by thousands of clock periods.

When a user initially invokes the MPP Apprentice on an application's RIF file, a sorted summary of statistics is provided for the program and each routine. The summary is sorted based on total time in order to bring the most critical routines to the user's attention first. The summary includes the total time for each instrumented and uninstrumented routine, which assists the user in identifying performance problems in math and scientific library routines or in routines the user has chosen not to instrument. For uninstrumented routines, only the total time is available. For instrumented routines the summary includes the time spent in parallel work, I/O, and overhead. Overhead is defined as anything that would not occur in a sequential version of the program and includes time spent in overheads related to the implicit shared memory programming model, such as the time spent in synchronization routines or waiting on global memory, time spent in explicit shared

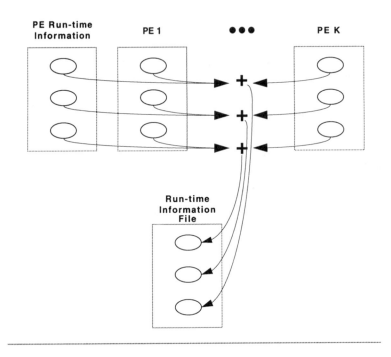

Figure 1.3: Accumulation across PEs of performance data.

memory constructs, such as gets and puts, and time spent in message routines, such as Parallel Virtual Machine (PVM) calls. A breakdown of each type of overhead and the total amount of time in it is also available for the entire program and all routines.

From the summary the user is able to navigate to finer-grained performance data or to other types of performance information. Any of the performance information available for routines, e.g. the overhead breakdown, is also available for all the code blocks nested inside the routine. We will use the term "code object" to refer to a program, routine, or nested code block throughout the rest of this paper. There are also a number of other types of performance information available within the Apprentice. One of the most powerful is an analysis and observations engine that derives secondary statistics from the measured values and looks for patterns specific to known performance problems. It draws the most critical problems to the user's attention, provides information on the impact of potential improvements, and makes suggestions for improvements where possible and appropriate.

As mentioned earlier, accuracy of the data gathered is of primary concern. It is not sufficient to have accurate timers and counters; the values measured must also reflect the behavior of the program when the instrumentation is not present. Instrumentation systems which give detailed behavior information cost too much in performance to leave active during production runs, so executing a code with instrumentation in place is executing the code in an artificial environment. Whatever numbers one obtains from such executions are only useful to the extent that they reflect execution without the instrumentation. For this reason we have arranged our timing code so that whenever possible it does not time our instrumentation. Sometimes this is unavoidable, but in those cases we remove the cost of instrumentation at the time the program is visualized. It is worth emphasizing that while time spent in instrumentation can be removed, it is much more difficult to compensate for behavioral changes caused by including instrumentation at all.

Preliminary results indicate that our method of instrumentation is sufficiently fast and accurate to be useful in this environment. To determine this we measured the space dilation, accuracy, and execution time dilation for three medium sized codes. Space dilation is the increase in space required for instrumentation, both code and data, relative to the total program space. Execution time dilation is the increase in execution wall clock time for a version which has been fully instrumented relative to the wall clock time of the same code with no instrumentation. The accuracy of the reported time is the difference between the total CPU time reported by MPP Apprentice, which is the wall clock time multiplied by the number of PEs used to execute the program, and the total CPU time of an uninstrumented version of the same code executed with the same input data, relative to the uninstrumented execution time. The results are shown in Table 1.1. These numbers represent the greatest impact the instrumentation will have on these codes, because the entire code was instrumented. Programmers can selectively instrument individual routines, which will have a smaller impact on time and space dilation. It may also reduce the impact on loss of accuracy.

We have also obtained encouraging partial results for more challenging codes. For one 16,000 line application the space dilation was 10.5%, which is still quite reasonable. We expect larger codes to have greater space dilation because the proportion of user code, which is what we instrument, is greater relative to the system code and libraries which are included in any executable file. We also expect that small codes, particularly codes with very small basic blocks, will cause greater challenges for accuracy, because of the greater relative cost of instrumentation. For one very small code, well under

	Lines of			Accuracy	
Type of application	code, without comments	Space dilation	Uninstrumented wall clock time	of reported time	Execution time dilation
Table 1.1 — Accuracy of MPP Apprentice Instrumentation					
CFD	3,489	8.5%	22 sec on 64 PEs	25% high	136%
Chemistry	2,060	0.8%	85 sec on 32 PEs	6% low	181%
2D Particle-In-Cell	3,967	2.2%	52 sec on 32 PEs	8% low	63%

1,000 lines, the MPP Apprentice reported a total execution time that was 37% higher than was measured for the uninstrumented execution wall clock time. Neither execution was measured in system dedicated time so there are important variables which have to be eliminated as the cause of this inaccuracy, but the magnitude of this number is large enough that it bears careful investigation.

1.6   Usability

A great deal of time and effort was spent working with users, beginning very early in the design phase, to ensure the Apprentice would be easy to use and understand. Coupled with the power and variety of information available through the RIF and CIFs, this makes the MPP Apprentice tool a powerful performance tool for analyzing long-running codes on large numbers of processors. The experience of our users supports this hypothesis. The example that follows is a particle code taken from one of the first T3D customers. In the course of a few days the customer was able to take this code from 24.5 MFlop/s to 494 MFlop/s on a 64-node T3D (note that this was without the assistance of any of the tool developers). We will use this customer's example to demonstrate the ease of identifying and resolving different types of performance problems within the MPP Apprentice performance tool.

1.6.1   Original Version

The original version of the user's code ran at 24.5 MFlop/s and took 4.66 seconds to execute.

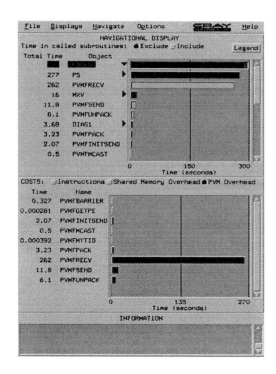

Figure 1.4: Main window of Version 1. See color plate XXI.

Figure 1.4 shows the main window of the MPP Apprentice tool with the original version of the code. The upper display within the main window is the Navigational Display that is used to drive all other displays within the MPP Apprentice tool. It shows statistics for the program and for each routine called within it. Arrows facing right indicate that information is available for nested levels. Arrows facing down indicate that the code object has been expanded to show nested levels. The name of code objects at each nested level are indented slightly for visual clarity, e.g., the routine names are indented slightly from the program.

Using the legend window (Figure 1.5) to identify the different colors of the bars, one can quickly see that over 90% of the total program time is attributable to parallel overhead. The most time-consuming routine is PS, and all of the time within it is also attributed to overhead. With the program code object selected in the Navigational Display and the Costs Display in the middle of the main window toggled to PVM Overhead, most of the time is spent in PVMFRECV and smaller amounts in eight other PVM routines. PVMFRECV also shows up as an uninstrumented function in the

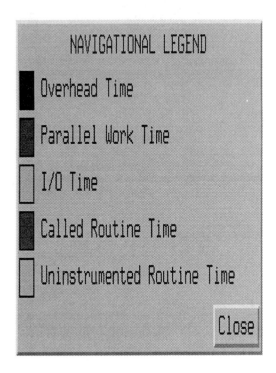

Figure 1.5: Apprentice legend. See color plate XXII.

Navigational Display, and one can see by the length of its bar, when compared with the bar for the whole program, that it accounts for most of the time in the program. As a source of overhead, time spent in a call to PVMFRECV is also added into any code objects that call it. Thus routine PS and routine PVMRECV can both account for almost all of the total program time if PS calls PVMFRECV.

Since such a large percentage of the total program time was being spent in PVM routines, the first code modification made was to replace calls to PVMFBARRIER with CRAFT barrier routines, and to replace all other PVM calls with the explicit shared memory constructs, get and put.

1.6.2   Version 2

The first set of modifications improved the performance to 211 MFlop/s, and reduced the program time to 0.54 seconds. This is a speedup of 8.6 times the previous version of the code. In Figure 1.6 we can see that roughly 70% of the total program time is still attributable to overhead. We can see

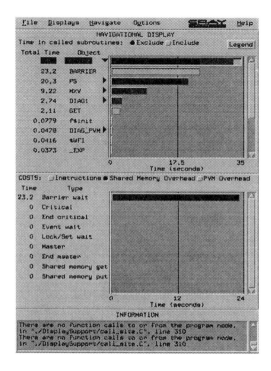

Figure 1.6: Main window of Version 2. See color plate XXIII.

that the CRAFT barrier routine is now the most time-consuming routine, with routine PS following closely behind it with roughly 90% of its total time in overhead. The Costs Display is now toggled to show Shared Memory Overheads and the CRAFT barrier shows up there also.

One of the ways to approach this problem is to identify the locations where the CRAFT barrier routine is called, and see how much time is spent at each call site location. Figure 1.7 is the call sites display for the barrier routine. It shows all the locations from which the barrier routine was called. The location is identified by the routine name and line number in the original source file. The total time spent in the barrier routine when called from each location is given numerically to the left of the location and graphically to the right of the location. One can quickly see the problem is at the location where the barrier routine is called from routine PS at line 455 in the original source code. This also explains all of the overhead time we saw for routine PS in the Navigational Display. While this call site dominates the others, there are other significant call sites as well that would be worth examining.

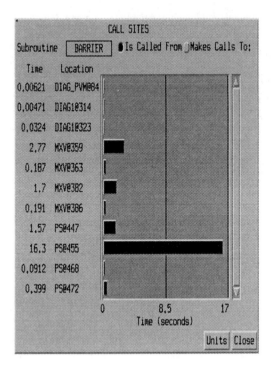

Figure 1.7: Call sites display for the barrier routine in Version 2.

1.6.3   Version 3

By handling the most significant barrier problem and a few others as well, version 3 of the code increases the performance to 494 MFlop/s and reduces the program execution time to 0.23 seconds. This is a speedup of 2.3 times the previous version of code, and 20 times the original version of the source code. (See Figure 1.8.) While this is a significant speedup, the MPP Apprentice can continue to guide the user through performance improvements. Figure 1.9 shows the program- level observations for this version of the source code. There are various types of performance numbers, including information on time spent loading instruction and data caches. Note particularly the last item in the window, labeled "Navigation Information." It tells the user specifically what performance problem to attack next and the performance improvement that could be expected by its resolution. The astute reader will notice that the MFlop/s numbers are reported as being slightly higher by the observations than what we report here. This is because there is time spent in uninstrumented routines which is not used in the observations' calculations

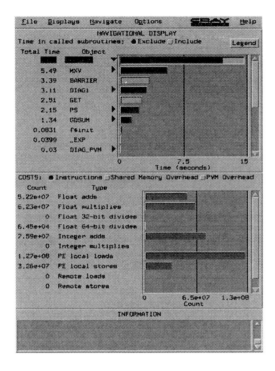

Figure 1.8: Main window of Version 3. See color plate XXIV.

of computation rate.

1.7   Conclusions

We have demonstrated that the Apprentice is a useful tool for debugging certain types of performance problems with applications running on the CRAY T3D. The fact that a user was able to speed up a code by a factor of 20 with relative ease is an indication of this. The intrusiveness of the instrumentation is sufficiently small to make the tool useful for even large codes running for long periods of time on many processors. This new style of tool promises greater range of usefulness than trace tools that are prevalent now.

A deficiency that will have to be improved is that the MPP Apprentice cannot always show what is causing certain types of load imbalances, even though it can indicate that they do occur, and where in the code they occur. Simple information that is available, such as the statistics gathered on each PE for various pieces of code, can help considerably, and we are currently investigating how to exploit such information. However, some problems of this type will remain beyond our grasp because we do not retain global schedule

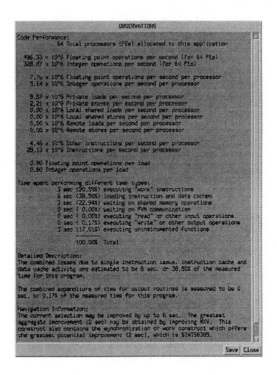

Figure 1.9: Program-level observations for Version 3.

information.

References

[1] BEGUELIN, ADAM, DONGARRA, JACK, GEIST, AL, MANCHECK, ROBERT, AND SUNDERAM, VAIDY, "A User's Guide to PVM–Parallel Virtual Machine," Oak Ridge National Laboratory, ORNL/TM-11826, July 1991.

[2] DONGARRA, J., BREWER, O., KOHL, J. A., AND FINEBERG, S., "A Tool to Aid in the Design, Implementation, and Understanding of Matrix Algorithms for Parallel Processors," *Journal of Parallel and Distributed Computing*, **9**, No. 2, June 1990, 185–202.

[3] DONGARRA, JACK J. AND SORENSEN, DANNY C., "SCHEDULE: Tools for Developing and Analyzing Parallel Fortran Programs," in *The Characteristics of Parallel Algorithms*, Leah H. Jamieson, Dennis B.

Gannon, and Robert J. Douglass, Eds., MIT Press, Cambridge, MA, 1987, 363–394.

[4] HEATH, MICHAEL T. AND ETHERIDGE, JENNIFER A., "Visualizing the Performance of Parallel Programs," *IEEE Software*, **8**, No. 5, Sept. 1991, 29–39.

[5] "High Performance Fortran Language Specification," Version 1.0 High Performance Fortran Forum, Rice University, Houston, TX, May 1993.

[6] HOLLINGSWORTH, JEFFREY K., MILLER, BARTON P., AND CARGILLE JON, "Dynamic Program Instrumentation fo Scalable Performance Tools," Scalable High Performance Computing Conference, Knoxville, May 1994.

[7] "Introducing Apprentice," an on-line help file for the Cray MPP Apprentice, Cray Research, 1993.

[8] KRAEMER, EILEEN AND STASKO, JOHN T., "The Visualization of Parallel Systems: An Overview," *Journal of Parallel and Distributed Computing*, **18**, No. 2, June 1993, 105–117.

[9] KOHN, JAMES AND WILLIAMS, WINIFRED, "ATExpert," *Journal of Parallel and Distributed Computing*, **18**, No. 2, June 1993, 205–222.

[10] MALONY, ALLEN D., HAMMERSLAG, DAVID H., AND JABLONOWSKI, DAVID J., "Traceview: A Trace Visualization Tool," *IEEE Software*, **8**, No. 5, Sept. 1991, 19–28.

[11] MILLER, BARTON P., CALLAGHAN, MARK D., CARGILLE, JONATHAN M., HOLLINGSWORTH, JEFFREY K., IRVIN, R. BRUCE, KARAVANIC, KAREN L., KUNCHITHAPADAM, KRISHNA, AND NEWHALL, TIA, "The Paradyn Parallel Performance Measurement Tools," University of Wisconsin - Madison Computer Sciences Department Technical Report #1256, Nov. 1994.

[12] MILLER, BARTON P., CLARK, MORGAN, HOLLINGSWORTH, JEFF, KIERSTEAD, STEVEN, LIM, SEK-SEE, AND TORZEWSKI, TIMOTHY, "IPS- 2: The Second Generation of a Parallel Program Measurement System," *IEEE Transactions on Parallel and Distributed Systems*, **1**, No. 2, April 1990, 206–217.

[13] PASE, DOUGLAS M., MACDONALD, TOM, AND MELTZER, ANDREW, "The CRAFT Fortran Programming Model," *Scientific Programming*, **3**, No. 3, John Wiley & Sons, Fall 1994.

[14] TUFTE, EDWARD R., *Envisioning Information*, Graphics Press, 1990.

[15] TUFTE, EDWARD R., *The Visual Display of Quantitative Information*, Graphics Press, 1983.

[16] REED, D. A., OLSON, R. D., AYDT, R. A., MADHYASTHA, T. M., BIRKETT, T., JENSEN, D. W., NAZIEF, B. A., AND TOTTY, B. K., "Scalable Performance Environments for Parallel Systems," *Proceedings of the Sixth Distributed Memory Computing Conference*, April 1991, 562–569.

[17] *UNICOS Performance Utilities Reference Manual*, SR-2040 7.0, Cray Research, Eagan, MN 1992.

[18] YAN, J. C., "Performance Tuning with AIMS–An Automated Instrumentation and Monitoring System for Multicomputers," *Proceedings of the 27th Hawaii International Conference on System Sciences*, Wailea, Hawaii, January 4–7, 1994, **II**, 625–633.

Chapter 4

Tools: An Applications Point of View

Parallel architectures have presented the computing community with both opportunities and challenges. With the emergence of potentially scalable machines on the marketplace comes the chance to solve problems that until now have been intractable. At the same time, issues of performance, load balancing, program correctness, and efficiency, have surfaced and kept the technology from being widely accepted by the general community. What sort of debugging aids are the most helpful to the user in attempting to gain the maximum performance from these machines, while at the same time ensuring that the results obtained are actually correct? How does one guarantee that data movement and program flow are efficient and maintain integrity throughout the execution of the program?

In this workshop, speakers outlined some successes and some causes for concern with respect to several large applications. In "A Practical Approach to Portability and Performance Problems on Massively Parallel Supercomputers," David Beazley discusses various schemes to run a molecular dynamics code on the CM-5 and obtain optimal performance. Don Heller discusses, from a user's perspective, the pitfalls and management strategy for parallel codes in the paper "Issues of Running Codes on Very Large Parallel Processing Systems."

In his talk on NEED, Karsten Schwan presents data obtained from running large molecular dynamics and atmospheric modeling simulations. These codes are characterized by very high I/O requirements. The paper by Rajan Gupta offers several proposals for future massively parallel processing computers, based on his group's extensive experiences with running large, complex quantum chromodynamics applications.

Carl Winstead presents results of using the Pablo tool to analyze I/O performance on the Intel Paragon MPP computer. Lessons learned in successful code porting to the CRAY T3D are discussed in Nicholas Nystrom's paper.

Issues of Running Codes on Very Large Parallel Processing Systems

Don Heller
Scalable Computing Laboratory
Ames Laboratory, US Dept. of Energy
Iowa State University
Ames, Iowa 50011

Abstract

Production jobs occupy all of a system's memory, I/O capacity and computing cycles for an extended period of time. They are expected to run efficiently and reliably, and will make similar demands on the system and network. When reliability is suspect, as in the first generations of parallel computing, programmers and system managers can take measures to improve their ability to resolve problems. When efficiency is suspect, the same strategies can be adapted for performance monitoring. However, the techniques appropriate for development systems, such as interactive debugging, are often not available in production mode. Advance planning and a few simple but effective tools are required to capture useful information during execution and at termination.

1.1 General Issues

Our main premise is simple:

> Production mode limits one's ability to analyze behavior and determine system state.

Consequently, one must plan ahead and design programs and systems to yield useful information before termination. There are several levels of software support that are needed:

- between jobs, fast system verification;

- by operator request, system and application status reports;

- on normal exit, system and application performance data;

- on error, process or system dump.

Throughout, we want detailed logs and succinct summaries. In general, the programs and operating system must cooperate to define useful information to be provided in a compact and easily accessible format. This information must be available at all times during execution and must be valid at a point of failure. An agent of the program and OS must accompany the program to help obtain the data; the agent must not fail even if the program does. It would be best if the agent could easily be integrated into other tools. Performance displays that relate to the application itself are enormously useful in the transition from "early adopter" programming staff to "satisfied customer" users and management because they help find behavioral or methodological bugs as well as coding or performance bugs.

We start with some disclaimers and announce our prejudices. These are opinions based on personal experience, occasionally on reason and insight. Other opinions exist, and might even have merit, and this is certainly not an exhaustive treatment. We have some definite prejudices:

- Large systems should be dedicated to computing and moving useful data.

- No resource should be quietly squandered.

- No resource should be squandered without understanding why.

- Non-performance analysis is crucial.

- Simple tools are sufficient.

Much of this is due to our "early adopter" mindset, left over from the 1980's, when hardware, system software and application software could be expected to fail with equal (and too high) probability, and such tools as existed were written by users. For some additional discussion see [1].

Debugging could be as easy as: think, insert print statements, filter the output. It probably is not, but one should always try the simple tools first. Performance analysis of a parallel program could be as easy as: run multiple instances of the usual workstation tools, look for anomalies. It probably is not, but one should always try the simple tools first. In any event, system and application programs intended for production use should be augmented with tools that can be run by a system operator, whom we view as a knowledgeable person but not a programmer.

The "early adopter" mindset has some problems and consequences. First is the view that local memory is inadequate. This motivates a small microkernel, distributed OS services, distributed application codes, and the strong belief that the SPMD model may not be adequate. Consequently, debugging must involve several cooperating application programs and I/O drivers, written in at least two different languages, and not all compiled with the right options. Secondly, the I/O subsystem is inadequate, and even if it were not, the system resides as one element of a large network. The network is the source of data, of course, but there are at least two major obstacles to confront: the network causes half the problems, and the network is under someone else's control. Debugging network software written by someone else is not easy, and in any event should not be done by application programmers. Lesser problems involve job management and accounting; in principle not hard to implement, but still under someone else's control.

On a message-passing system, everyone complains that the communication is slow, but ultimately it is too slow with regard to program development costs, and not with regard to run-time. Since careful attention must be paid to the ratios of communication to computation and overhead to bandwidth, the machine characteristics intrude on the application very early in the development cycle. Performance debugging often reduces to changing some fundamental assumptions after the program is "finished." So, isolating communication into better libraries and using tools such as program generators or HPF to avoid writing communication code altogether is a big help. Single-processor analyses, such as from `g/prof` or multiple instances of a debugger session, tell one very little about the nature of cooperating programs.

There is one additional point to cover: locally modified OS source code. Assuming one is on good terms with the system vendor, one could have access to some very seductive possibilities. On the plus side, bugs can be fixed sooner, new support tools written with new features with which to experiment, and the system tuned to fit local conditions. On the other side, this will void the warranty, create new bugs, and be always one release behind if this application depends on the new features. *Read-only source code is very useful, writable source code is dangerous.*

At some point, there is a transition from "early adopter" to "satisfied customer." System verification is an essential tool to demonstrate stability and to analyze instability quickly. The stability tests are not simply a matter of fulfilling a purchase contract, but are necessary to win over the users and their managers. Performance displays must relate to the application, not just to the program in the transition from programmers to users.

Now we consider development mode vs. production mode. There are a number of distinguishing points, but the one that matters to this discussion is programmer vs. operator. When there is a problem at 3:00 a.m., who gets the call? Who is on the spot, and what skill levels are there? How much time is available before the errant job must be removed from the system? If you know in advance that the job will be killed quickly by a non-expert if something is wrong, then you must plan ahead or the bug will never be found. Interactive debuggers can only be run on development systems by developers, and therefore have limited benefit on a production system.

There are some simple but effective defensive measures that should be installed in all application programs subject to an operator's whim. If something looks wrong, an inquiry program will be run. We might call these *oblivious* inquiries if they tell you nothing about the internal details of the program. For example, an oblivious system inquiry about component utilization would give CPU and communication link ratings, as does Intel's SPV (SPV = system performance visualization, a fancy front panel). An oblivious process inquiry about component utilization would give a breakdown of system and user time, as does the Unix `ps` command. If several ratings are near 0, the operator could easily be persuaded that the program is broken. In a multi-system configuration, finding the culprit system is already a challenge. Even if everything is functioning normally, the operator should run the inquiry on a regular basis, for reassurance and to develop a notion of normal behavior; this will make it more likely that abnormal behavior will be correctly diagnosed. This is where a *non-oblivious* process inquiry may be more useful. It is easily determined which application program is running. The programmer should provide to the operator a specific inquiry program for the application. In normal cases, this would give some application-based performance measures or progress reports, and is a good sales technique as well as diagnostic tool.

The usual performance and debugging tools are either count-driven (such as `prof, gprof`), or trace-driven (such as `paragraph`). An application-derived agent could be as simple as a debugger script with post-processing. Log files of some type are also useful. Since most count-driven tools depend on normal completion of the program, they have little value as inquiry tools during execution.

Non-performance analysis is related to debugging, but does not go quite as far. It is simply a matter of gathering enough information from the system and program to support another run under debugger control. The first level is a system test to check the hardware; vendor-supplied system tests usually are at such a low and detailed level that they require a system restart. This clearly is not appropriate when there is a half-dead application running. After all, maybe the system is working correctly. The second level is an oblivious system inquiry, including a component inventory, differential node dumps, and quiescence detection. The third level is a set of oblivious process inquiries, including information about memory allocation and requests, differential process dumps, and a record of the last messages sent, received and requested. The final level is a non-oblivious process inquiry, which may run the debugger (scripted or interactive), examine trace-driven data, or run an application-derived agent.

Differential dumps are a simple but useful tool. Consider as analogy two executions of the Unix command `od` (octal dump) on separate corefiles from the same program, followed by `diff` (text comparison). Anything reported is interesting, the more so when tied to the source code by a more sophisticated method. Some program variables would be expected to be constant across the processors, some might vary according to the processor number, and others may be drawn at random from a known set. Identifying inconsistencies, or failure to obey calculable relations, such as numerical formulae or set unions, will narrow the set of nodes to be examined in more detail.

Local examination of the nodes should concentrate on *resource insanity* (linked lists that are not, application memory leaks or system memory leaks) and *resource starvation* (buffer space, local memory bus bandwidth, interprocessor channel bandwidth).

A global examination of the nodes should look for *cross-node inconsistencies*, and *message-passing algorithm faults* (clogged pipeline, deadly embrace, misplaced messages).

On a large system, it is likely that only a few nodes need to be examined in detail, and the first problem is to quickly and accurately identify a small set of nodes containing the culprits. The next most likely case is that all nodes are involved in the problem, but the situation is symmetric in some way, and thus it is still sufficient to look at a few nodes.

Here are some examples. If there are processes waiting on a resource, the process state may indicate this condition. If there is no free memory or free buffer space, then one should compute the free space on each node and show the outlyers. If the program uses explicit message-passing, it may happen that A waits for a message from B. Denote this waiting as $A < B$; as it is a partial order, do a topological sort, and look at the first and last nodes and the equivalence sets (Unix `tsort` finds these).

Now, some of these conditions and measurements are transient; it is more or less a judgment call for the operator to decide how often to repeat the inquiry, and whether to kill the program or restart a server.

Elaboration. If the system includes some diagnostic hardware, such as a power-on self-test or a secondary diagnostic network and console, it would be useful to maintain state information in a user-accessible location via non-root library functions or inquiry commands.

Concerning resource starvation, if a local resource such as buffer space needs to increase with the number of nodes, then it will be difficult to diagnose large production-mode problems on a small development-mode system. Probably a series of instrumented runs on increasingly larger systems will suggest where the problem occurs.

Concerning clogged pipelines, message-passing algorithms can fail if an intermediate node acts on only part of its messages. Either the recipient node (where unconsumed messages reside) should be sped up, or the source node should be throttled. A tool that lists all messages currently in the system is a great help in identifying particular nodes for detailed study, and tracking stray messages.

Concerning deadly embraces, if $A < B$, and $B < A$, and C waits as a consequence, we want to know that C is not part of the problem. A and B will show up as an equivalence set.

Launching messages into the void is a nasty problem, if the OS deletes them. The library send routine probably returned an appropriate error code that was ignored. Nevertheless, it would help if the OS or communication library kept a count of such disasters, for access by an inquiry program.

1.2 Self-protection

Here we consider ways for the application programmer to make it easier to diagnose problems. Most of these require a conscious decision at the time of program development, namely that the program will not function properly. This is just common sense. Some information must be gathered during execution and made available for extraction. The information could be maintained in a log file, or could be dumped to a file on termination, and, depending on the programming language, a signal handler may be required. Log files have the disadvantage that they are usually not up-to-date on abnormal termination. The system-defined process status is usually inadequate, as we require counters for activities and errors, timers for activities, and a record of recent activity. The call stack from a debugger (current routine and args, its caller, etc.) is helpful but again incomplete.

Every program calls a system-defined exit routine, explicitly or not, which cleans up memory and actually exits. It would be better to first list the messages found in the communication buffer, including unsatisfied message requests, and give some system-maintained performance measurements. An additional feature would allow the programmer to determine some interesting memory locations, say from application performance measurements, a history or logging mechanism, or from interactive debugger experience. These could be enrolled in a standardized data structure, perhaps with separate rosters for *abnormal* exit, via a configuration file or calls to library routines. The program could use this roster to produce a time-stamped sequence of process states. An external agent could obtain the configuration file, then the data from enrolled locations, and produce a current status report. On exit from the application, the program could list data from the appropriate roster, and call the system exit routine.

Not all applications would require such a collection of services but we shall assert that *All I/O subsystems should be equipped with a library routine and an external agent for device controller / driver / server status*, including current status, most-recent activity report, historical log files, and cumulative traffic and error statistics, such as counts, historical averages and ranges, and rates, **especially error and retry rates**. Complications can easily occur with multinode I/O subsystems, where one must correlate log files from different programs, and with coupled multivendor subsystems.

1.3   Application Source Code Management

Consider a program that originated on an ordinary system and has since been ported to two parallel machines:

serial code	programmer A
parallel code 1	programmer B
parallel code 2	programmer B or C

Which is the "official" version? Where are new features installed first? How far apart are the versions? Is the distance increasing? Usually, A is busy with new features while B and C are improving performance, so the distance is increasing. This is a real problem that can be addressed via language features as in HPF or via careful source code management and a preprocessor. However, when it comes time to debug the program, relating problems back to unprocessed source code will be difficult.

There are some problems specific to explicit message-passing codes. When there is a library function interface to the message-passing hardware, one is likely to lose the ability to enforce type checking on both ends of the message. In any event, matching send and receive source code at compile time is generally impossible. Most errors in message-passing systems could have been caught at compile time, though we have no firm evidence for this claim.

A simple technique is to establish message type management. The message type is an integer tag sent as part of the message header to help identify the message contents. Most vendors define ranges of types for user and system messages. One especially terrible idea is for the vendor library code to use message types in the user range. The MPI context field, adapted from Zipcode, solves this problem and others. Another bad idea is to use one message type for multiple purposes. Indeed, we prefer to have each message type pointing to a few lines of code, with certain message types being captured by the OS. The reasoning is that the debugger or exit routine will yield message type information, and if the types indicate more than one usage then not enough information about the program has been revealed.

Message header information in general helps to resolve errors observed that are away from the source of the error, such as message transmission problems, that are observed by the recipient, or even worse, observed by some node neither the source nor recipient. We might even want to time-stamp messages on a send and a receive, and not have anomalies or misrepresentations of performance, but this is difficult on systems where the local clocks are not coordinated.

1.4   nscan

We now describe a program `nscan` for nCUBE systems, developed by the author while at Shell Development Company. The motivation for development was primarily to check the system state between production jobs, and secondly as a diagnostic tool during job execution. No information about the application program is used. The nCUBE/2 nodes are organized as a hypercube with additional I/O subsystems, themselves 16-node hypercubes. `nscan` can select all or part of the system, and can report at several levels of detail on the operating system, processes, and memory. The OS microkernel is in assembler, and once one is over that considerable hurdle, is not too hard to understand (OK, maybe I *am* nuts). We use the same OS feature as required by a debugger, a special message type captured by the OS and responding with data from a given address or register. There is no impact on the application processes beyond the OS handling of these queries. If there is no response, the OS is judged to have failed, and an operator reboot is suggested. The output of `nscan` is text that is easily searched for summaries and warnings.

The following list indicates the information available from `nscan`.

```
hardware and OS
  version numbers
  physical node number, local memory size
  last allocation: logical node number, start time
  current state, processor special registers
  timers: cpu active, idle
  message counts: sent, received, transmission errors
  most recent message received on each channel: size, src, dest, type
```

```
     error counts: invalid interrupts, hard and soft memory errors
     "interesting" local variables
process
     identifier, program name, parent process
     current state, working directory
     timers: cpu active, waiting for message
     message counts: sent, received
     messages in queue: size, source, type, type interpretation
     free space in communication buffer
     alarm, sleep wakeup times
     memory regions
     open file table, controlling I/O node
     much more low-level data that is seldom useful

local memory
     byte counts: total available, occupied, free
     allocated and free blocks, queue pointers

sanity checks:
     expected values and ranges
     consistency (relations among local OS variables)
     linked lists and queues
```

A hard memory error (uncorrected ECC) would motivate replacement of the node, as would soft errors (corrected ECC) above a certain threshold. One good feature of the OS, not present initially, is that the ECC counters are preserved across a system reboot that does not cycle electrical power.

One important failing is that the OS does not maintain the source and type of the process's last requested message; this is available only on the runtime stack of a blocked process, and the offset depends on the particular library routine that was invoked. We had previously modified the OS on the nCUBE/1 to account for this and other missing information, but chose not to do so on the nCUBE/2.

1.5   Conclusion

Too often, performance measurements are bolted onto a program only after it has been completed, and debugging information is obtained only after the occurrence of a problem. Our primary recommendation is that some judicious choice of state and historical information be maintained and accessible as part of the program design from the beginning. For better or worse (it is getting better), one can expect a parallel program to encounter bugs or performance problems, and it would be prudent to plan ahead. Even without problems, the program and system complexity warrants continuous monitoring.

Acknowledgements

Thanks go to the workshop organizers for their invitation to speak on this topic, and to my former colleagues at Shell Development Co. and Shell Oil Co., where we installed nCUBE systems for seismic data processing, and experimented with many of the ideas described here.

References

[1] HELLER, D., "Ten Steps for Managing Parallel Computing Projects," *IEEE Parallel & Distributed Technology*, Spring 1994, 6–8.

Opportunities and Tools for Highly Interactive Distributed and Parallel Computing

Greg Eisenhauer, Weiming Gu, Thomas Kindler
Karsten Schwan, Dilma Silva, and Jeffrey Vetter
Georgia Institute of Technology
Atlanta, Georgia 30332

Abstract

Advances in networking, visualization and parallel computing signal the end of the days of batch-mode processing for computationally-intensive applications. The ability to control and interact with these applications in real-time offers both opportunities and challenges. This paper examines two computationally-intensive scientific applications and discusses the ways in which more interactivity in their computations presents opportunities for gain. It briefly examines the requirements for systems trying to exploit these opportunities and discusses Falcon, a system that attempts to fulfill these requirements.

1.1 Introduction

The world of computationally-intensive computing is moving away from the batch-oriented style of processing. Users accustomed to spreadsheets and WYSIWYG word processing are not satisfied with the traditional hands-off, get-your-data-when-the-batch-queue-empties mode of running parallel programs. At the same time, high-speed network interfaces and the proliferation of high-end graphics workstations offer an opportunity to open new windows into application behavior. Falcon, a system developed at Georgia Tech, provides tools and techniques for exploiting these developments, and it uses them to create new opportunities for application understanding, debugging and tuning.

Traditional debuggers rely on halting the system in order to examine and modify the program state. While such debuggers are useful, they are often inadequate to detect the race conditions, synchronization errors or other problems endemic to parallel and distributed programs. Similarly, traditional uniprocessor code profilers and analyzers have a role in tuning parallel programs, but they are ineffectual for analyzing synchronization overheads, bursty computational demands, or other problems more unique to non-sequential applications. Neither type of tool provides the insight into dynamic program behavior that is often necessary to debug and tune parallel and distributed programs. Perhaps more importantly in the long term, neither type of tool encompasses mechanisms for dynamically manipulating running programs.

To address these deficiencies one needs mechanisms for "observing" a running application and "adjusting" its state or behavior. Collectively, these mechanisms are a *monitoring and steering* system [10]. The on-line manipulation or steering of parallel and distributed programs has been shown to result in performance improvement in many domains. Examples of such improvement include the automatic configuration of small program fragments for maintaining real-time response in uniprocessor systems [18], the on-line adaptation of functional program components for realizing reliability versus performance tradeoffs in parallel and real-time applications [2, 8, 9], and the load balancing or program configuration for enhanced reliability in distributed systems [26, 23, 1].

Further benefits are gained if monitoring and steering mechanisms are not limited to system-level constructs but are instead made available in a reasonable way at the application level. In addition to supporting standard program tuning practices, application-level monitoring and steering have the potential to produce real gains in application productivity by allowing users to accomplish more useful work with the same number of compute cycles. How is this possible? Truly interactive parallel programs, created with application-level monitoring and steering, will give users significant insight into the *progress* of the computation. If users have access to the computation and the ability to guide or direct the computations at runtime, they have an unparalleled power to evaluate and experiment with the program.

Consider the case of scientific computing, where many applications are trying to model or simulate the real world. A truly interactive program would let users interact with that world as it evolves. Rather than planning a dozen batch-style simulation runs with a dozen different parameter values, the user can adjust the application dynamically and examine the response. Rather than discovering at the end of a twenty hour simulation run that the system wandered into an unreasonable state early on, it can be monitored for reasonableness as it progresses. These *process tuning* situations are often neglected because they do not fall into the traditional realm of program tuning or debugging. However, the advantages of additional high-level insight into the application in these cases are an important benefit of interactive parallel computing.

This paper first examines two computationally-intensive scientific applications and discusses the ways in which more interactivity in their computations presents opportunities for gain. It then briefly discusses the requirements and techniques for exploiting these opportunities and examines the aspects of Falcon which fulfill these requirements. The paper also presents our conclusions and plans for future work.

1.2   Interaction Opportunities in Selected Applications

Parallel and distributed programming models and applications vary widely, as do the situations in which one might wish to employ a monitoring and steering system. The utility of a general, low-perturbation monitoring system in both debugging and performance tuning is widely accepted. Unfortunately, most such systems do not make their facilities easily accessible at the application level. If we are to realize the application-level process gains discussed in the introduction we must consider the demands of application-level monitoring and determine how steering might be used. This section examines two large parallel applications and discusses ways in which a monitoring and steering system might benefit each.

1.2.1   MD

MD is an interactive molecular dynamics simulation developed at Georgia Tech in cooperation with a group of physicists exploring the statistical mechanics of complex liquids [34, 5]. The specific molecular dynamics systems being simulated are n-hexadecane (C_{16}-H_{34}) films on a crystalline substrate $Au(001)$. In the simulation, the alkane system is described via intramolecular and intermolecular interactions between pseudoatoms (CH_2 and terminal CH_3 segments) and the substrate atoms. The calculational cell is a square cylinder which is periodically repeated in the x-y directions. Temperature is controlled via infrequent scaling of the particles' velocities. The alkanes remain associated in a chain with very predictable bond lengths throughout the simulation. A typical small simulation contains 4800 particles in the alkane film and 2700 particles in the crystalline base. A visual representation of this physical system appears as Figure 1.1.

For each particle in the **MD** system, the basic simulation process takes the following steps: (1) obtain location information from its neighboring particles, (2) calculate forces asserted by particles in the same molecule (*intramolecular forces*), (3) compute forces due to particles in other molecules (*inter-molecular forces*), (4) apply the calculated forces to yield a new particle position, and (5) publish the particle's new position. The dominant computational requirement is calculating the long-range forces between particles, but other required computations with different characteristics also affect the application's structure and behavior. These computations include finding the bond forces within the hydrocarbon chains, determining system-wide characteristics such as atomic temperature, and performing analysis and on-line visualization.

The implementation of the **MD** application attains parallelism by domain decomposition. The simulation system is divided into regions, and the responsibility for computing forces on the particles in each region is assigned to a specific processor. In the case of **MD**, we can assume that the decomposition changes only slowly over time and that computations in different sub-domains are independent outside some cutoff radius. Inside this radius information must be exchanged between neighboring particles, so that different processors must communicate and synchronize between simulation steps. The resulting overheads are moderate for fairly coarse decompositions (e.g., 100-1000 particles per process) but unacceptable for finer grain decompositions (e.g., 10 particles per process).

The **MD** simulation offers many opportunities to improve the performance through both on-line interactions with the end user and program steering by algorithms, including:

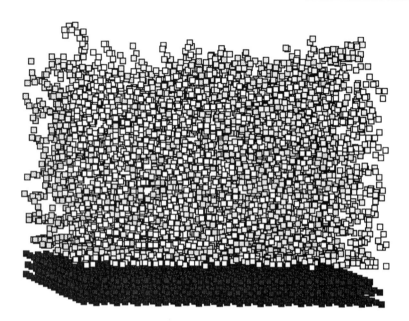

Figure 1.1: A visual representation of a sample system for the molecular dynamics simulation. The white-yellow particles are the pseudoatoms of the alkane chains. The red particles represent the gold substrate. See color plate XXV.

- Decomposition geometries could be changed to respond to changes in physical systems. For example, a slab-based decomposition may be useful for an initial system, but a pyramidal decomposition might be a better choice if a probe is lowered into the simulated physical system.

- The interactive modification of the cutoff radius could improve solution speed by computing uninteresting time steps with some loss of fidelity, if this is desired by the end user.

- The boundaries of spatial decompositions could be shifted for dynamic load balancing among multiple processes operating on different sub-domains. This can be performed by an algorithm or by end users.

- Global temperature calculations, which are expensive operations requiring a globally consistent state, could be replaced by less accurate local temperature control. On-line analysis could determine how often global computations must be performed based on the temperature stability of the system.

From our experience with **MD**, we believe that these are important opportunities to exploit in order to increase the usability and efficiency of the application. For example, we have seen that the performance of the application is extremely sensitive to load balance shifts that can dramatically limit efficiency with even moderate numbers of processors. The ability to dynamically rebalance and perhaps even reconfigure the decomposition to match the evolving physical system is essential to performance for a long-running system.

1.2.2   Atmospheric Modeling

The simulation of complex global natural phenomena is one of the biggest challenges facing computational science because of its extreme computational and data handling requirements. The ultimate goal in climate modeling, the simultaneous simulation on a global scale of physical and chemical interactions in ocean and atmosphere, is still far from our reach. It is difficult to run and test a model with typical runtimes of hours for each simulation day. One simple reason for this is that changes to a model often do not have the desired effect upon the model results. This occurrence is particularly common when parameters must be chosen to simulate processes that are not well understood or whose influence can only be approximated at the scale of the current model. The result in these cases is a set of sometimes arbitrarily chosen parameters that must be adjusted individually. On-line visualization, interaction and program steering have the potential to simplify and significantly shorten model development time and improve model results as well as to help improve traditional measures of simulation performance.

Earth and atmospheric scientists at Georgia Tech have developed a global chemical transport model (GCTM) [16] which uses assimilated windfields [32] for the transport calculations. These types of models are important tools to answer scientific questions concerning the stratospheric-tropospheric exchange mechanism or the distribution of species such as chlorofluorocarbons (CFC's), hydrochlorofluorocarbons (HCFC's) and ozone. This model uses a spectral approach to solve the transport equation for each species. In a spectral model, all variables are expanded into a set of orthogonal spherical basis functions, called spherical harmonics. Derivatives with respect to the latitude or the longitude are more easily and accurately calculated in this spectral domain, though the variables must be transformed back into a grid domain for the chemistry calculations. Details of this solution approach, which is quite common in global models, can be found in [11], [27], [14], [33] or [6]. Our model contains 37 layers, which represent segments of the earth's atmosphere from the surface to approximately 50 km, with a horizontal resolution of 42 waves or 946 spectral values. In a grid system, this corresponds to a resolution of about 2.8 degrees by 2.8 degrees. Thus in each layer 8192 gridpoints have to be updated every time step. A typical time step increment is 15 simulated minutes. Figure 1.2 represents a visual sample from this application.

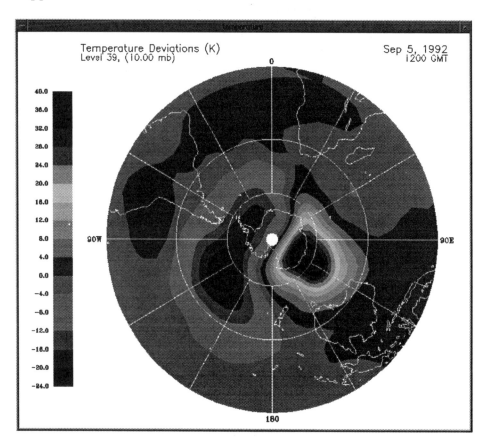

Figure 1.2: A sample plot of southern hemisphere temperature distribution as used by the global climate transport model. See color plate XXVI.

There are many ways in which more interactivity in this parallel application could significantly benefit end users. For example, a typical problem in model development is that there are dramatic differences in scale between some global phenomena and the many physical processes that comprise it. Gross measures such as vertical windfields have small values on a global scale, yet on a smaller scale phenomena such as thunderstorms cause large vertical air displacements and play important roles in vertical mixing in the atmosphere. Computing the entire globe on a scale where all such phenomena could be accurately represented is far too computationally expensive to consider. One way of approaching this problem is to use parameterizations inside models which bear an indirect relationship to the small-scale phenomenon and that attempt to match observed phenomenon on the global scale. Unfortunately, the construction of these parameterized models is an exploratory and error-prone process. Section 1.3.1 describes ways in which basic interactive monitoring and steering can aid in this model construction process.

Other more ambitious approaches to the same problem might involve allowing the user to interactively identify interesting subareas for simulation at a higher resolution in time and/or space. This differential focus approach would allow those regions to be modeled with better fidelity without invoking the huge computational cost of using a higher resolution uniformly over the entire model. In some cases these areas might be selected algorithmically, but in other cases what constitutes an interesting situation or area could depend upon a subjective judgment by a human observer.

One can certainly imagine writing a program with a user interface that allows this level of interaction, but our goal is to achieve this without turning scientists into graphical user interface (GUI) programmers. The next section presents some tools and techniques that we have developed to further this goal.

1.3　Requirements and Tools for Interactive Computing

This section examines the general techniques and tools required to support program tuning in general and specifically to support the user/program interactions presented above. We first examine examples of some displays that support the interaction goals discussed previously. Then we discuss the monitoring and steering systems required to create and support these displays.

1.3.1 Displays

Displays which are useful for understanding application behavior vary as widely as do applications and programming models. It is not possible, within the bounds of this paper, to survey all possible displays or even all useful approaches to display construction. Instead we present sample displays and interactions so that we can explain the monitoring and steering infrastructure required to support them. This section presents two types of displays targeted to different levels of abstraction in a parallel program. The first example is an application-specific display of the type required to achieve some of the process-oriented gains in application development discussed above. The second example is a programming-model specific display useful for program debugging and tuning.

Application-Specific Displays

The previous section has indicated that user interactive steering has the potential to improve an application's performance and functionality. However, many uses of steering are application-specific and so are graphical displays that are used to present the run-time program and performance information to the end user and to accept the user's steering commands. By examining a sample display used for steering the atmospheric modeling code, we can explore how these displays are used to understand and control the application and how they are interfaced to other parts of the monitoring and steering system.

The graphical display discussed in this section is specifically built for interactive steering of an atmospheric modeling code that simulates the distribution of atmospheric species such as Carbon 14 (C^{14}) and CFC. Figure 1.3 shows a screen display of the distribution of C^{14} at a latitude of 70° N. The display has two logical parts: one for showing both the computed and the observed concentration values of C^{14} atoms in air to the end user, and the other for accepting steering requests from the user. The computed results of the C^{14} distribution is represented by a plotted curve from atmospheric layer 0 to 37, and it is updated for every model time step. The observed C^{14} concentration at a number of atmospheric layers is represented by discrete

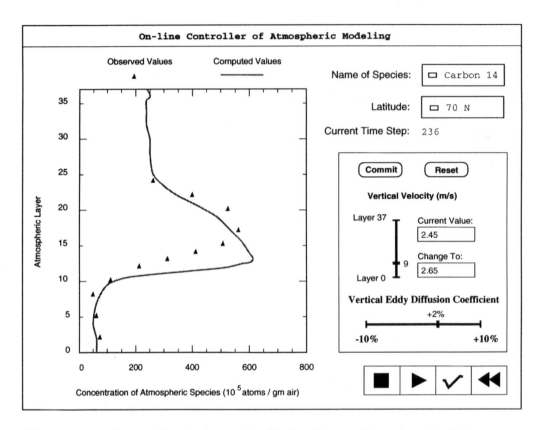

Figure 1.3: An application specific display for on-line control of the atmospheric modeling code. See color plate XXVII.

triangular points, and is used to judge whether the current computation is "correct" or "wrong." When noticeable discrepancies between the calculated values and the observed values are detected, the user can dynamically modify the application execution to "correct" the computations. For example, the curve shown in Figure 1.3 demonstrates that the computed concentration of C^{14} is consistently higher than the observed values from layer 10 to 15, but it is lower from layer 16 to about 23. The simulation may be adjusted to remove this discrepancy; the end user can alter the vertical wind velocity at these atmospheric layers. After typing in new vertical wind velocity values, the user needs to click the **commit** button on the display to send the steering command to the application. The program will use these new parameters for computations from the next model time step. The user can also stop the application's execution (by clicking the □ or **stop** button), change parameters, and restart the execution (by clicking the ▷ or play button). Before restart, the user can roll back the computation to a previously checkpointed time step (by clicking the ◁◁ or rewind button). At any point the user can checkpoint the application execution (by pressing the checkpoint button). The user can also use the application's default checkpointing policy which automatically saves execution history after a predefined number of time steps.

The above application specific display has a two-way communication link with the application code. In one direction, it receives computed and observed concentration values of atmospheric species from the application, and displays these values to the user. In the other direction, the display accepts steering commands and sends them to the application. A clean interface between the display and the application code is needed. Our Falcon system provides a flexible mechanism for dynamically connecting and disconnecting displays to the application. This mechanism will be addressed in Secs. 1.3.2 and 1.3.3.

Programming Model-Specific Displays

Both of the application programs described in Sec. 1.2 have been implemented on shared-memory multiprocessors using a threads-based programming model. In this model, independent threads of computation are created on the various processors, and they control access to shared data by using mutex locks and conditions [4]. The amount of time a thread spends waiting to be granted a lock or for a particular condition to occur directly impacts the amount of useful work it can perform in a given time. Therefore, understanding the interactions of threads over time is one of the most important aspects in understanding the behavior of these programs.

This section examines one display that we have found useful in diagnosing performance problems in threads-based programs. The threads lifetime view depicted in Figure 1.4 shows thread behavior over time. In particular, it represents each thread as a horizontal bar which assumes different colors and patterns when the thread is in different states, such as running, waiting for a mutex, or waiting for a condition. A vertical line is drawn from the parent thread to the child thread at the time of thread fork event. When a thread joins another thread after it exits or when a detached thread calls thread_exit, the narrow bar representing the thread terminates. In the case of thread_join, another vertical line is drawn from the caller thread to the thread to which it joins. The space after a joined thread can be reused by

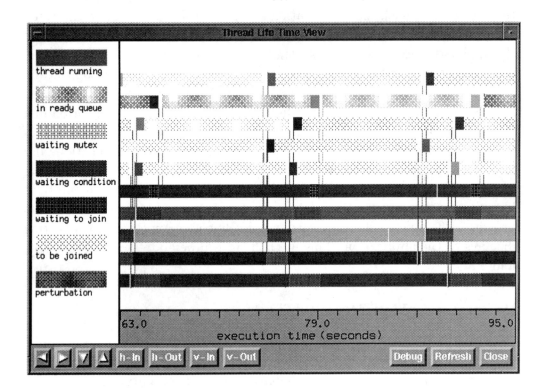

Figure 1.4: A thread life-time display derived from traces of MD program behavior. See color plate XXVIII.

threads forked later. The display contains buttons with which one can move around and zoom in on different threads and regions of time. In addition to this lifetime display, there is another simultaneous display that relates thread colors to their names. We have excluded this name mapping view for space considerations.

The particular set of threads shown in Figure 1.4 represents a snapshot of the MD application's execution with the molecules partitioned into five domains. The bottom five threads are threads responsible for calculating the inter-molecular forces for each domain. These threads live for the duration of the calculation. The top five positions are held by threads that calculate intra-molecular forces. These threads are forked by the inter-molecular thread only for a single timestep in the simulation. At the end of their calculations for that timestep, they perform a join operation and exit when both they and the thread that forked them complete the calculations for that timestep. When the next iteration begins, a different thread (with a different color) is forked and the process repeats.

Figure 1.4 is interesting for **MD** because it makes clear some aspects of thread synchronization that are difficult to determine without such a display. Each domain must acquire updated particle location information from its neighboring domains before it can proceed with the next iteration. This waiting time appears as the grey "waiting for condition" state in the display. Rather than requiring *all* threads to finish before *any* thread begins the next iteration, **MD** domains only synchronize with their immediate neighboring domains. This allows individual domains to begin the next iteration even before other threads have completed the current iteration. This flexibility helps **MD** compensate for the effects of minor variances in load balance between domains. In the figure one can see that blocks of solid compute time, which occur when a domain starts a new iteration, occur first in the second thread from the bottom and later in threads of more distant domains.

To produce displays of this type, the important constructs in the programming model must be instrumented. In this case, we have instrumented the Cthreads parallel programming library [22] so that every operation that can affect the state of a thread produces a record in an event stream. In order to produce a reasonable display, these events must contain accurate timestamps and they should not excessively disturb normal execution of the program. The next section will discuss the system requirements and tools in Falcon that support the sample displays presented above.

1.3.2 On-line Monitoring

The first step to interactivity is gaining easy access to the applications' runtime information. This information ranges from records of the utilization of processors to detailed execution and waiting times spent by each processor and from values of certain variables (e.g., "temperature" of a simulated molecular system, "concentration" of an atmospheric species) to complete current program states of the application. Therefore, the capture, collection, and analysis of on-line program and performance information should be an integral component of any system that supports interactivity. Instead of focusing on supporting on-line interactivity, however, past work in program monitoring has focused on helping programmers understand the performance of their parallel codes, minimizing or correcting program perturbation due to monitoring, reducing the amounts of monitoring or trace information captured for parallel or distributed program debugging [24, 13], and the effective replay [17] or long-term storage of monitoring information. In comparison, interactivity, in the form of on-line program steering, specifically requires its *on-line* monitoring system to be able to: (1) capture *application-specific* information, (2) impose *controlled overheads* on the execution of monitored applications, (3) deliver monitoring information with *low latency*, and (4) provide incremental analysis of monitoring information vital for on-line steering.

The monitoring system is required to handle application-specific data because much of program steering is inherently application-specific. With MD, for example, steering can be used to improve load balance based on the molecule partitions and boundaries of these partitions. The boundaries can be adjusted by the user during program execution to obtain a better load balance. In steering the atmospheric modeling code, parameters concerning certain atmospheric species can be dynamically changed to effect different results on these atmospheric species. In addition, application-specific monitoring permits non-computer science end users to view, analyze, and steer their programs in terms of their specific attributes (e.g., "time step size" or "current energy").

Controlled monitoring overheads are useful for several reasons. First, since one purpose of application steering is to improve program performance, excessive monitoring overheads can easily offset the performance gains obtained by steering. Second, steering decisions based on inaccurate information may produce unexpected results. In the case of MD steering based on the work load information of each processor, perturbed information can cause inaccurate, sometimes unnecessary, adjustments of partition boundaries. In the worst case, thrashing of boundaries can occur and application execution will actually be slowed.

Steering latency is the period of time between the occurrence of a program activity or state and the time when it is acted upon by a steering agent; monitoring latency is the period of time between the capture of an activity by the on-line monitor and the passage of that activity to the steering mechanism. Excessive monitoring and steering latencies can cause steering decisions to be made based on obsolete program and performance information, which can result in unpredictable and often negative effects on an application's execution. In the atmospheric modeling code, if the visualized windfield and values of atmospheric species are presented to end users several time steps behind the actual application execution, users may adjust parameters based on "old" information.

Falcon – an integrated system for on-line monitoring and steering of large-scale parallel and distributed applications – is designed to incorporate the attributes necessary for effective on-line monitoring and steering. An overview of the Falcon monitoring system is presented next, followed by discussions of its mechanisms for code instrumentation, event collection, and on-line trace data analysis.[1] Falcons program steering system will be described in Sec. 1.3.3.

System Overview of Falcon

Falcon is a set of tools that collectively support on-line program monitoring and steering of parallel and distributed applications. There are three major conceptual components of the on-line monitoring component of Falcon: (1) a monitoring specification and instrumentation mechanism, which consists of a low-level *sensor specification language*, a high-level *view specification language*, and an instrumentation tool, (2) mechanisms for on-line information capture, collection, filtering, and analysis, and (3) a graphical user interface and some graphical displays for interfacing with the end user. These components are shown in Figure 1.5.

The following steps are taken when using Falcon. First, the application code is instrumented with sensors and probes generated from sensor and view specifications. Such monitoring specifications allow users to express specific program attributes to be monitored and based on which steering may be performed. During program execution, program and performance information of interest to the user and to steering algorithms is captured by the inserted sensors and probes, and the information collected is partially analyzed. Falcon's runtime facilities consist of monitoring data output queues attaching the monitored user program to a variable number of additional components performing low-level processing of monitoring output. Partially processed monitoring information is then fed to the central monitor and graphical displays for further analysis and for display to end users. Trace information can also be stored in a trace data base for postmortem analysis.

The monitoring and user interaction 'controllers' in the Falcon runtime system activate and deactivate sensors, execute probes or collect information generated by sampling sensors, and also react to commands received from the

---

[1]A more detailed description of the complete Falcon system and its performance can be found in [7].

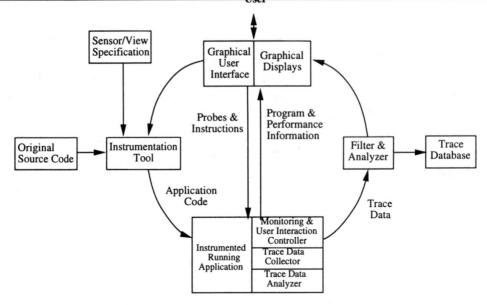

Figure 1.5: Conceptual components of Falcon.

monitor's user interface. For performance, these controllers are divided into several *local monitors* residing on the monitored program's machine so that they are able to rapidly interact with the running program. In contrast, the *central monitoring controller* is typically located on a front end workstation or on a processor providing user interface functionality.

Instrumentation and Monitoring Specification

Instrumentation of a target application and its run-time system is the first step toward application steering. Hardware monitoring and data collection require instrumentation of the hardware platform on which the target application is running. Software monitoring and data collection require instrumentation of the program's source code, the system libraries, the compiler, or any combination of the above. We do not rely on hardware monitoring due to its cost, inherent inflexibility and inability to provide high-level application-specific monitoring information.

Software instrumentation points are called *sensors* in Falcon. Falcon offers three types of sensors: sampling sensors, tracing sensors, and extended sensors. A *sampling sensor* is associated with a counter or an accumulator. When a sampling sensor is activated, the associated counter value is updated.

A *tracing sensor* generates timestamped event records that may be used immediately for program steering or stored for postmortem analysis. In either case, trace records are stored in *trace queues* from which they are removed by local monitors. An *extended sensor* is similar to a tracing sensor except that it also performs simple data filtering or processing required for steering before producing output data. Sampling sensors inflict less overhead on the target application's execution than tracing and extended sensors. However, the more detailed information collected by tracing sensors may be required for diagnosis of certain performance problems in parallel codes. Furthermore, the combined use of all three sensor types enables users to balance low monitoring latency against accuracy requirements concerning the program information required for program steering.

In order to control monitoring overheads, sensors can be controlled dynamically and *selectively* to monitor only the information currently being used by the end user or the steering algorithms. First, sensors may be turned off if events captured by those sensors are not currently used by the end user or the steering algorithm.[2] Second, sampling and tracing rates can be dynamically reduced or increased depending on monitoring load and tolerance of inaccuracies in monitored information. For example, a tracing sensor that monitors a frequently accessed mutex lock can reduce its tracing rate to every five mutex lock accesses, thereby improving monitoring perturbation at the cost of reducing trace accuracy. A selective monitoring example can be found in the MD code, where a large amount of execution time is spent in a three-level nested loop computing forces between particles. At each loop level, distances between closest points of particles and bounding boxes of molecules are calculated and compared with the cutoff radius to eliminate unnecessary computations at the next loop level where specific particles are considered. To evaluate the efficiency of this scheme, at each loop level we use a "cheap" sampling sensor to monitor the hit ratio of distance checks and a more "expensive" tracing sensor to monitor the correlations between the calculated distance and hit ratio at the next loop level. To reduce the perturbation, the "expensive" tracing sensor is not turned on until ineffective distance checks are detected.

Using Falcon's monitoring specification language [30], programmers may define application-specific sensors for capturing both the program and performance behavior to be monitored and the program attributes based on which

---

[2]Related work by Hollingsworth and Miller [13] removes instrumentation points completely to reduce the overheads of these turned-off instrumentation points to zero.

steering may be performed. The specification of a sample tracing sensor is
shown below:

```
sensor work_load {
        attributes {
                int     domain_num;
                double  work_load;
        }
};
```

The sensor **work_load** is used to monitor the work load of each molecule
domain partition in **MD**. It simply describes the structure of the application
data to be contained in the trace record generated by this sensor. This
declaration generates the following sensor subroutine.

```
int
user_sensor_work_load(int process_num, double work_load)
{
    if (sensor_switch_flag(SENSOR_NUMBER_WORK_LOAD) == ON) {
        sensor_type_work_load  data;
        data.type = SENSOR_NUMBER_WORK_LOAD;
        data.perturbation = 0;
        data.timestamp = cthread_timestamp();
        data.thread = cthread_self();
        data.process_num = process_num;
        data.work_load = work_load;

        while (write_buffer(get_buffer(cthread_self()), &data,
                    sizeof(sensor_type_work_load)) == FAILED) {
            data.perturbation = cthread_timestamp() - data.timestamp;
        }
    }
}
```

Note that there are four *implicit fields* for any event record that describe
the event's sensor type, timestamp, thread id, and perturbation. The body
of this subroutine generates entries for an event data structure, then writes
that structure into a trace buffer. A local monitor later retrieves this structure from the buffer. Each sensor's code body is also surrounded by an `if`
statement, so that it can be turned on or off during program execution.

Event Collection and On-line Trace Analysis

In many monitoring systems, all monitoring activities, including trace data capture, collection, and analysis, are performed by code inline with the thread of user computation. One problem with this approach is that the target application's execution is interrupted whenever a monitoring event is generated and processed. The lengths of such interruptions are arbitrary and unpredictable if complicated on-line trace analysis is used. This may be acceptable with off-line monitoring mechanisms in which monitoring events are written into files for postmortem consumption. For on-line monitors, however, this approach can produce unacceptable perturbation. Instead of performing monitoring activities in the user's code, Falcon uses concurrent monitoring, where most monitoring activities are on processors not running application code.

As depicted in Figure 1.5, local monitors perform trace data collection and processing, concurrently and asynchronously with the target application's execution. Local monitors and steering controllers typically execute on the target program's machine, but they may run concurrently on different processors, using a buffer-based mechanism for communication between the application and the monitoring mechanism. Therefore, the only direct program perturbation caused by Falcon is the execution of embedded sensors and the insertion of trace records into monitoring buffers. Such perturbation is generally predictable, and its effects on the correctness of timing information can be eliminated using straightforward techniques for perturbation analysis [19].

In order to control monitoring overheads and latency, Falcon's runtime system may itself be configured or steered in several ways, including changing the number of local monitors and communication buffers to configure the system for parallel programs and machines of different sizes. Such changes permit the selection of suitable monitoring performance for specific monitoring and steering tasks, and they may be used to adapt the monitoring system to dynamic changes in workload imposed by the target application. For example, when heavy monitoring is detected by a simple monitor-monitor mechanism, new local monitoring threads may be forked. Similarly, when bursty monitoring traffic is expected with moderate requirements on monitoring latency, then buffer sizes may be increased to accommodate the expected heavy monitoring load. Such parallelization and configuration of monitoring activities is achieved by partitioning user threads into groups, each of which is assigned to a specific local monitor. When a new application thread is forked, it can be added to the local monitor with the least amount of work.

The amount of trace data generated by inserted sensors and collected by the run-time monitoring mechanism is usually too large and the information too low-level to be directly useful to any human user. Trace data filtering and analysis must be performed to generate information that is interesting to end users. Related research concerning on-line trace analysis includes Snodgrass' work on *update networks* [29] and our own past work on real-time monitoring [24]. In [30], information to be monitored is modeled by temporal relations in a hierarchical structure with primitive relations at the bottom of the structure and composed relations at the top. The resulting hierarchy of relations is transformed into an update network – a directed acyclic graph, in which the tuples of the primitive relations enter the nodes at the bottom and the tuples of the composed relations flow out of the nodes at the top.

Falcon offers a flexible on-line trace analysis mechanism similar to update networks. However in Falcon's approach, trace data is processed in different physical components of the monitoring system. At the lowest level, simple trace data filtering and analysis can be performed by the extended sensors. For example, in the atmospheric modeling application, values of windfields may be filtered or eliminated since their complete visualization is expensive. At the local monitor level, trace data is further analyzed to produce higher level information. As in the steering of the atmospheric modeling code in Sec. 1.3.1, discrepancies between the computed values of an atmospheric species and the observed values can be detected by simple algorithms. Finally, trace data analysis can be performed by separate processes linked with the central monitor. An example of such an analysis process is presented next, and problems to be dealt with when performing on-line trace analysis will be discussed in more detail.

On-line Event Ordering

Displays like the thread life-time view of Figure 1.4 can provide users with insights into program progress and correctness. However, such displays generally have strict requirements in terms of the accuracy of the timestamps that they expect and the order in which events are presented to them. Misorderings can both confuse users and cause failures of the animation itself. For example, natural causal ordering would require that a thread_fork event precede any event executed by the newly created thread. A display that shows a child running before it has been forked by its parent does not make any sense. Furthermore, suppose that the first event for this child thread is a condition_wait event. In the thread life-time view of Figure 1.4, this event is represented by a change in the color and fill pattern of that thread's horizontal bar. However, if the thread_fork event has not been received by the display system, the horizontal bar does not yet exist. When the display system attempts to perform a color-change action on this non-existent object, it may crash.

The out-of-order events that cause problems for the display system cannot have occurred in the program's execution. Instead, misorderings existing in the event stream are due to the buffering and processing methods employed in the monitoring system. The diagnosis and correction of out-of-order events is a common problem in parallel and distributed monitoring systems. Existing systems (e.g., ParaGraph [12] and SIEVE [25]) rely on a sort by timestamp value to impose a total order on all events stored in event files. The on-line nature of the Falcon monitoring system precludes any use of such a solution, and sorting by timestamp order does not entirely eliminate the problem of out-of-order events [3]. In addition, coarse clock granularities and poor clock synchronization among different processors may lead to event timestamps that do not accurately reflect the actual order of program execution.

Falcon offers a general mechanism for approaching this problem. In particular, all events are processed by an *ordering filter* before they are sent to the display system. This filtering algorithm follows a "minimum-intervention policy." Specifically, it examines each event in the stream arriving from the monitoring system, checks the applicable ordering rules for this event type, and if no rules are violated, forwards the event to the display system. If a rule violation is indicated, the event is held back until the rules are satisfied. As an example, consider the ordering rule that the lifetime view of Figure 1.4 uses to enforce orderings for a mutex lock event. Actually, a mutex lock is recorded as two separate events: a mutex_begin_lock event indicating that a thread has attempted to obtain the lock and a mutex_end_lock event indicating that a thread has succeeded in obtaining the lock. The following ordering rule is observed by the filter for a mutex_end_lock:

```
mutex_end_lock t m n <- ((thread_init t || thread_fork pt t) &&
                        (mutex_init m || mutex_alloc m) &&
                        (mutex_unlock m n-1) )
```

The parameters associated with the event mutex_end_lock are t, the id of the thread attempting to obtain the lock, m, the id of the mutex variable, and n, the sequence number indicating the number of successful lock attempts on this particular mutex variable. This rule may then be translated as: "a mutex_end_lock event with parameters t, m, and n, may be passed on to the display system if thread t has been initialized or forked by a parent thread, mutex variable m has been initialized or allocated, and the mutex_unlock event for variable m, sequence number n - 1 has already been passed on to the display system." Armed with similar rules for other events, the ordering filter can enforce sufficient ordering to ensure proper functioning of the thread lifetime display. Note that at present, this system only addresses the issue of event ordering. This is adequate to compensate for minor clock variations, but perhaps insufficient when the clocks on different processors vary widely. However this system may provide the basis for more general approach to the timestamp problem as we extend Falcon to more distributed systems.

This section has examined the basic components of the on-line monitoring system of Falcon. The next section presents our approach to the other component of interactivity, on-line steering.

1.3.3 Interactive Steering

As high performance computing applications move away from the batch-oriented style of processing, making these applications interactive is a daunting task. The challenge exists not only in building new applications with interactivity, but also in reengineering existing applications to become interactive ones. A few programmers turn directly to integrated graphical user interfaces to build interactivity into their applications, but this approach is fraught with difficulties. First, most developers of the high performance computing applications are non-computer scientists, who may not have the background or the inclination to become GUI programmers. Second, most high performance computing systems are not known for high performance graphics support. Increasingly high performance front-end workstations tend to offer better graphics and visualization support, both in hardware and software, and are therefore a better place for running graphics-intensive code. However, the construction of such distributed computation and visualization systems is far from easy.

The interactive steering discussed in this paper offers an alternative way of providing interactivity to the high-performance applications. This approach separates the interactive activities from the computation-intensive part of the application and provides a dynamic link between these components. The responsibilities of such a steering component are to receive the application's run-time information from its coupled on-line monitoring system, display the information to the end user or submit it to a steering agent, accept steering commands, and enact changes that affect the application's execution. The application code is not directly exposed to the interaction with the user or other steering agents, but it needs to be instrumented with sensors that capture run-time information and provide entries for steering commands which may change the program's execution behavior. The basic requirement for steering is that the application code should behave correctly under any valid steering command. Other requirements can be derived by examining its use.

What is interactive steering?

Interactive steering can be defined as the interactive control and tuning of an application and its resources to improve application functionality and performance. This control and tuning is interactive in that an external entity interacts with the application to accomplish it. That outside entity may be a user sitting at a workstation, or it may be another program responding to application events and driven by a previously-encoded steering algorithm.

We call steering *human-interactive* if a human watching a display is the primary initiator of a steering action. If instead the initiator is an outside program we call the steering *algorithmic*. Algorithmic steering may not be commonly associated with interactive programs, but it is a natural extension of the facilities and requirements presented earlier in this paper. For example, to expect a human to watch an application and adjust it to compensate for load imbalances may be reasonable on an occasional basis, but no one is likely to babysit a 36-hour simulation that requires adjustments every five minutes. In this situation the solution is to feed the load information to an algorithm that is capable of balancing the load without human involvement. Using steering for this instead of embedding the load balancing algorithm into the application is still beneficial because it allows the algorithm to be expressed separately, where it is more easily understood, replaced and reused in other applications.

The different goals and types of steering exert different requirements on the steering system. For steering for performance, low overhead costs in monitoring and steering support are critical, simply because excessive overheads can easily offset performance gain obtained by on-line steering. Low steering latency may also be a critical requirement, particularly for algorithmic steering. Program events related to steering must be captured and processed, and the corresponding steering decision must be made while the decision is still relevant to the situation. Consider the on-line configuration of mutex locks presented in [20], where on-line algorithms change lock behavior from spin to blocking locks. Lock type is determined at runtime based on the time a lock call must wait before it obtains the lock. When the waiting time is above a certain threshold, the lock is a blocking lock. When the waiting time is relatively short, the lock is a spin lock. Since the reaction times required are on the order of a few tens of processor cycles, this application presents a formidable challenge for a steering system.

In the case of human-interactive steering, the demands on the steering system are not so extreme, as human response times will typically dwarf the latency times imposed by the system. However, if human interaction is to develop basic insight or to experiment with alternative solution methods and experimental parameters, more cooperation from the application may be necessary. To accomplish the parameter tuning described in Sec. 1.3.1 for example, it is necessary to synchronize the parameter modifications with the phases of the application to ensure that steering does not invalidate the computations. In some cases the design of the application makes this easy. The load balancing of the **MD** application described in [5] was facilitated because mechanisms were in place to handle molecules moving from domain to domain. These worked without modification when the domain boundaries themselves moved. In other cases it is clear that desired manipulations cannot be carried out without the direct cooperation of the application. A good example of this is the checkpointing and rollback facility discussed in Sec. 1.3.1. It is unlikely that such functionality could be provided without the knowledge of the application. A continuing challenge in a steering is to define the application interface to the steering system.

Falcon's Steering System

Falcon's on-line steering component is a natural extension of its monitoring facilities. Figure 1.6 depicts some internal features of steering as well as its relationship with other components of Falcon. Similar to local and central monitors, a *steering server* on the target machine performs steering, and a *steering client* provides the user interface and control facilities remotely. The steering server is typically created as a separate execution thread to which local monitors forward only those monitoring events that are of interest to steering activities. Such events tend to represent a small proportion of the total number of monitoring events, in part because simple event analysis and

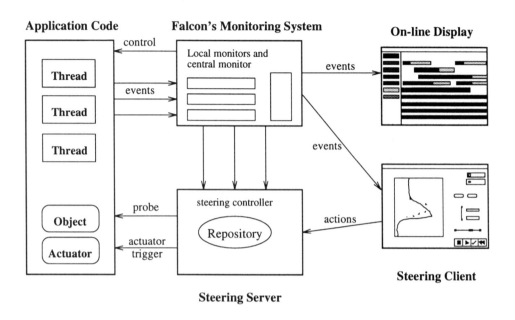

Figure 1.6: Overall structure of the steering system.

filtering is done by local monitors rather than by the steering server. Steering decisions are then made based on specific attributes of those events by human users or steering algorithms. Therefore, the primary task of each steering server is to read incoming monitoring events and to take the appropriate action in response. These responses are based on previously encoded decision routines and actions, which are encoded in steering event/action repository in the server. This repository contains entries for each type of steering event, specifying the appropriate action to take in response. The responses represented here may perform some actual steering action on the application, note the occurrence of some monitoring event for future reference, or simply forward the event to the client for display or further processing. The secondary task of each steering server is to interact with the remote steering client. The steering client is used to enable/disable particular steering actions, display and update the contents of the steering event repository, and input steering commands directly from end users to the server.

Falcon's steering library introduces several abstractions. The first of these is *program attributes*. Program attributes are defined by application developers and they represent values or characteristics in the application that can be modified by the steering system. They are defined in an object-based fashion, where developers may associate with each specific program abstraction one or multiple attributes and then export methods for operating on these attributes. This type of association is called a *steerable object* and it must be "registered" with the steering system. The steering repository in the steering server maintains a list of all registered steerable objects and their associated program attributes. In our initial implementation, we assume that all attributes correspond to specific variables in the application program.

Steering actions are composite operations to be performed by the steering system in response to monitoring events in the program. Steering actions may examine and modify program attributes, perform computation, and even initiate other actions. Falcon defines two mechanisms for modifying program attributes, *steering probes* and *actuators*. A steering probe is the simplest form of steering action. It is used in actions to query or update a specific program attribute asynchronously to the program's execution. However, if a program attribute can only be updated synchronously, it must be associated with an actuator.

An actuator is a portion of code that the developer inserts into his code at locations where it is "safe" for the steering system to take some action concerning the program attribute. Most of the time when the application executes the actuator code there are no pending actions and the actuator immediately returns control to the application. However, if the program attribute is to be synchronously modified by the steering system, the actuator becomes the instrument of that action. In particular, to update the program attribute synchronously, the steering system *asynchronously* sets the actuator so that the next time it is executed by the application code, it invokes a particular action *in the context of the application's thread of execution*. In this way, the responsibility for managing the synchronization of the steering system with the application rests with the application programmer and depends solely upon the placement of the actuators in the code. In simple situations, the action programmed into the actuator may just write a new value into the program attribute. For example, in the implementation of the steering of the atmospheric model as described in Sec. 1.3.1, the program variables corresponding to "Vertical Velocity" and "Vertical Eddy Diffusion Coefficient" would be identified by the application programmer as program attributes and be registered with the steering system. The programmer would place actuators at points in his code, perhaps between iterations, where those values could be changed without invalidating the calculations. When a human triggered a change at the user interface, an actuator action would be "programmed" or "armed" with an action which would write the changed value into the target program variable at the next opportunity. However, actuator actions are capable of encoding much more complex operations than this. For example, they should be capable of the operations necessary to ensure that modifications of program state do not violate program correctness criteria as in [2].

The discussion above presents a brief overview of the abstractions in the Falcon steering library and the manner in which they interact with the remainder of the Falcon system. The implementation and integration of the steering library and other steering facilities is not yet complete, though proof-of-concept demonstrations as in [5] have been quite successful. However, we believe that the steering system, together with Falcon's monitoring facilities represent a powerful and flexible basis upon which to build interactive computing and through which users can exploit the opportunities presented in this paper.

1.4   Conclusions and Future Research

We have discussed the utility and potential of interactive parallel programming in the context of two large-scale parallel application programs. We have also explained how an on-line program steering and monitoring system can assist in realizing this potential. At present, ambitious and determined applications programmers can create their own interactivity by building user interfaces for their applications. These are valid interactive programs, but they are point solutions. Scientists are interested in computing to the extent that it helps them do science. Accordingly, the goal of our work on Falcon and on monitoring and steering in general, is to make this functionality more easily available to non-expert users.

The **MD** and atmospheric modeling codes as well as the Falcon system are implemented on a 64-node KSR shared memory supercomputer. Falcon is also available on several other shared memory platforms, including SGI and SUN Sparc parallel workstations. A version of Falcon currently being completed also works with PVM across networked execution platforms. Similar portability is attained for the graphical displays used with Falcon. Notably, the Polka animation library can be executed on any Unix platform on which Motif is available [28]. Falcon's low-level monitoring mechanisms have been available via the Internet since early Summer, 1994. A version of Falcon offering on-line user interfaces for monitoring and monitor control will be released in 1995.

Current extensions of Falcon not only address additional platforms (e.g., an IBM SP machine now available at Georgia Tech and the monitoring of PVM programs running Cthreads, C, or Fortran programs), but also address several essential additions to its functionality. Currently users can insert into their code simple tracing or sampling sensors, where sensor outputs are forwarded to and then analyzed by the local and central monitors. We are now generalizing the notion of sensors to permit programmers to specify higher level 'views' of monitoring data like those described in [15, 24, 31]. Such views will be implemented with library support resident in both local and central monitors. We are also developing notions of composite and extended sensors that can perform moderate amounts of data filtering and combining before tracing or sampling information is actually forwarded to local and central monitors. Such filtering is particularly important in networked environments, where strong constraints exist on the available bandwidths and latencies connecting application programs to local and central monitors.

Our future work will address how such customized mechanisms may be used in conjunction with the remainder of the Falcon system. In addition, work in progress is addressing the monitoring of object-oriented, parallel programs, including the provision of default monitoring views and performance displays [21].

An important component of our future research is the use of Falcon with very large-scale parallel programs, either using thousands of execution threads or exhibiting high rates of monitoring traffic. For these applications it will be imperative that monitoring mechanisms are dynamically controllable and configurable. It must be possible for users to focus their monitoring on specific program components, to alter such monitoring dynamically, and to process monitoring data with dynamically enabled filtering or analysis algorithms. Moreover, such changes must be performed so that monitoring overheads are experienced primarily by the program components being inspected. Dynamic control of monitoring is also important for the efficient on-line steering of parallel programs of even moderate size. Specifically, program steering requires that monitoring overheads are controlled continuously so that end users or algorithms can perform steering actions in a timely fashion.

Longer term research with Falcon will address the integration of higher level support for program steering, including graphical steering interfaces, and the embedding of Falcon's functionality into a programming environment supporting the process of developing, tuning, and steering threads-based parallel programs, called LOOM. In addition, Falcon will be a basis for the development of distributed laboratories in which scientists can inspect, control, and interact on-line with virtual or physical instruments (typically represented by programs) spread across physically distributed machines. The specific example being constructed by our group is a laboratory for atmospheric modeling research, where multiple models use input data received from satellites, share and correlate their outputs, and generate inputs to on-line visualizations. Moreover, model outputs (e.g., data visualizations), on-line performance information, and model execution control may be performed by multiple scientists collaborating across physically distributed machines.

References

[1] BECKER. THOMAS, "Application-transparent Fault Tolerance in Distributed Systems," in *Proc. of the Second International Workshop in Configurable Distributed Systems*. IEEE Computer Society Press, May 1994.

[2] BIHARI, THOMAS E. AND SCHWAN, KARSTEN, "Dynamic Adaptation of Real-time Software," *ACM Transactions on Computer Systems*, May 1991, **9** No. 2, 143–174.

[3] BEGUELIN, ADAM AND SELIGMAN, ERIK, "Causality-preserving Timestamps in Distributed Programs," Technical Report CMU-CS-93-167, Carnegie Mellon University, Pittsburgh, PA, June 1993.

[4] COOPER, ERIC C. AND DRAVES, RICHARD P., "C threads," Technical report, Computer Science, Carnegie-Mellon University, CMU-CS-88-154, June 1988.

[5] EISENHAUER, GREG, GU, WEIMING, SCHWAN, KARSTEN, AND MALLAVARUPU,NIRU, "Falcon – Toward Interactive Parallel Programs: The On-line Steering of a Molecular Dynamics Application," in *Proceedings of The Third International Symposium on High-Performance Distributed Computing (HPDC-3)*, San Francisco, CA, Aug. 1994, 26–34.

[6] FOSTER, I. T. AND WORLEY, P. H., "Parallel Algorithms for the Spectral Transform Method," Technical Report ORNL/TM-12507, Oak Ridge National Laboratory, April 1994.

[7] GU, WEIMING, EISENHAUER, GREG, KRAEMER, EILEEN, SCHWAN, KARSTEN, STASKO, JOHN, VETTER, JEFFREY, AND MALLAVARUPU, NIRUPAMA, "Falcon: On-line Monitoring and Steering of Large-scale Parallel Programs," Technical Report GIT-CC-94-21, Georgia Institute of Technology, Atlanta, GA, April 1994.

[8] GOPINATH, PRABHA AND SCHWAN, KARSTEN, "Chaos: Why One Cannot Have Only an Operating System for Real-time Applications," *SIGOPS Notices*, July 1989, 106–125.

[9] GHEITH, AHMED AND SCHWAN, KARSTEN, "Chaos-arc – Kernel Support for Multi-weight Objects, Invocations, and Atomicity in Real-time Applications," *ACM Transactions on Computer Systems*, April 1993, **11** No. 1, 33–72.

[10] GU, WEIMING, VETTER, JEFFREY, AND SCHWAN, KARSTEN, "An Annotated Bibliography of Interactive Program Steering," *ACM SIGPLAN Notices*, Sept. 1994, **29** No. 9, 140–148.

[11] HAURWITZ, B., "The Motion of Atmospheric Disturbances on the Spherical Earth," *Journal of Mar. Res.*, 1940, **3**, 254–267.

[12] HEATH, MICHAEL T. AND ETHERIDGE, JENNIFER A., "Visualizing the Performance of Parallel Programs," *IEEE Software*, Sept. 1991, 29–39.

[13] HOLLINGSWORTH, JEFFREY K., MILLER, BARTON P., AND CARGILLE, JON, "Dynamic Program Instrumentation for Scalable Performance Tools," in *Proceedings of SHPCC'94*, 841–850, Knoxville, TN, May 1994.

[14] KUBOTA, S., HIROSE, M., KICHUCHI, Y., AND KURIHARA, Y., "Barotropic Forecasting with the Use of Surface Spherical Harmonic Representation," *Pap. Meteorol. Geophys.*, 1961, **12**, 199–215.

[15] KILPATRICK, CAROL E. AND SCHWAN, KARSTEN, "ChaosMON – Application-specific Monitoring and Display of Performance Information

for Parallel and Distributed Systems," in *Proceedings of the ACM/ONR Workshop on Parallel and Distributed Debugging*, Santa Cruz, CA, May 20-21, 1991, 57–67.

[16] KINDLER, T., SCHWAN, K., SILVA, D., TRAUNER, M., AND ALYEA, F., "A Parallel Spectral Model for Atmospheric Transport Processes," Technical report, Georgia Institute of Technology, Atlanta, GA, 1994.

[17] LEBLANC, THOMAS J. AND MELLOR-CRUMMEY, JOHN M., "Debugging Parallel Programs with Instant Replay," *IEEE Transactions on Computers*, April 1987, **C-36**, No. 4, 471–481.

[18] MASSALIN, HENRY AND PU, CALTON, "Threads and Input/Output in the Synthesis Kernel," in *Proceedings of the 12th Symposium on Operating Systems Principles*, SIGOPS, Assoc. Comput. Mach., Dec. 1989, 191–201.

[19] MALONY, ALLEN D., REED, DANIEL A., AND WIJSHOFF, HARRY A. G., " Performance Measurement Intrusion and Perturbation Analysis," *IEEE Transactions on Parallel and Distributed Systems*, July 1992, **3**, No. 4, 433–450.

[20] MUKHERJEE, BODHISATTWA AND SCHWAN, KARSTEN, "Experimentation with a Reconfigurable Micro-kernel," in *Proc. of the USENIX Symposium on Microkernels and Other Kernel Architectures*, Sept. 1993, 45–60.

[21] MUKHERJEE, BODHISATTWA, SILVA, DILMA, SCHWAN, KARSTEN, AND GHEITH, AHMED, "Ktk: Kernel Support for Configurable Objects and Invocations," *Distributed Systems Engineering Journal*, 1995. To Appear.

[22] MUKHERJEE, BODHISATTWA, "A Portable and Reconfigurable Threads Package," in *Proceedings of Sun User Group Technical Conference*, June 1991, 101–112.

[23] MARZULLO, KEITH AND WOOD, MARK, "Making Real-time Reactive Systems Reliable," *ACM Operating Systems Review*, January 1991, **25**, No. 1, 45–48.

[24] OGLE, D.M., SCHWAN, K., AND SNODGRASS, R., "Application-dependent Dynamic Monitoring of Distributed and Parallel Systems," *IEEE Transactions on Parallel and Distributed Systems*, July 1993, **4**, No. 7, 762–778.

[25] SARUKKAI, SEKHAR R. AND GANNON, DENNIS, "Parallel Program Visualization Using SIEVE.1," in *International Conference on Supercomputing*, ACM, July 1992.

[26] SCHWAN, KARSTEN, GOPINATH, PRABHA, AND BO, WIN, "CHAOS – Kernel Support for Objects in the Real-time Domain," *IEEE Transactions on Computers*, July 1987, **C-36**, No. 8, 904–916.

[27] SILBERMAN, I. S., "Planetary Waves in the Atmosphere," *J. Meteorol.*, 1954, **11**, 27–34.

[28] STASKO, JOHN T. AND KRAEMER, EILEEN, "A Methodology for Building Application-specific Visualizations of Parallel Programs," *Journal of Parallel and Distributed Computing*, June 1993, **18**, No. 2, 258–264.

[29] SNODGRASS, RICHARD, "Monitoring Distributed Systems: A Relational Approach," PhD thesis, Carnegie-Mellon University, Department of Computer Science, Carnegie-Mellon University, Pittsburgh, PA 15213, Dec. 1982.

[30] SNODGRASS, RICHARD, "The Temporal Query Language TQuel," *ACM Transactions on Database Systems*, June 1987, **12**, No. 2, 247–298.

[31] SNODGRASS, RICHARD, "A Relational Approach to Monitoring Complex Systems," *ACM Transactions on Computer Systems*, May 1988, **6**, No. 2, 157–196.

[32] SWINBANK, R. AND O'NEILL, A., "A Stratosphere - Troposphere Data Assimilation System," Climate Research Technical Note CRTN 35, Hadley Centre Meteorological Office, London Road Bracknell Berkshire RG12 2SY, March 1993.

[33] WASHINGTON, W. M. AND PARKINSON, C. L., *An Introduction to Three-dimensional Climate Modeling*, Oxford University Press, 1986.

[34] XIA, T. K., OUYANG, JIAN, RIBARSKY, M. W., AND LANDMAN, UZI, Interfacial alkane films. *Physical Review Letters*, September 28, 1992, **69**, No. 13, 1967–1970.

Methodologies for Developing Scientific Applications on the CRAY T3D

Nicholas A. Nystrom, William S. Young, and Frank C. Wimberly
Pittsburgh Supercomputing Center

Abstract

The Pittsburgh Supercomputing Center has successfully ported a number of significant scientific applications to the CRAY T3D. In this paper we will discuss techniques and tools found to be useful in developing and porting code for the T3D. Advantages of heterogeneous versus standalone implementations will be presented, and the current performance of several applications on the T3D will be compared to that observed on the CRAY C90.

1.1 Introduction

In 1992 the Pittsburgh Supercomputing Center (PSC) decided to acquire the first CRAY T3D scalable parallel computer to be delivered to a customer site. Shortly thereafter, the process began of choosing the initial set of third-party packages to be ported to the T3D with the goal of having them ready for production use by the time the hardware was made available to the PSC user community. Previous experience showed that a significant fraction (30-40%) of the Center's CRAY C90 (C916/512) cycles are delivered to a large set of users executing third-party applications packages, whereas MPP cycles tend to be consumed by a smaller group of users running their own codes. Emphasis was therefore placed on porting applications that would benefit a greater number of scientists, with each potential target considered on several criteria: demand of the package on the C90; availability of rights to the source and a distribution channel to users; and pre-existence of a parallel implementation which could be leveraged into a T3D version. The packages initially selected included (among others) GAMESS [6, 15], Amber 4 [13], CHARMM [2], and MaxSegs [21, 11]. Later in 1993 FIDAP and X-PLOR were evaluated as additional candidates for porting, and since then an ever-increasing number of third-party packages have been ported and set into production on the PSC's CRAY T3D.

Porting multiple third-party applications to the CRAY T3D has provided an abundance of experience and insights regarding programming methodologies, techniques, and tools leading to efficient parallel programs. Two principal approaches were taken in implementing packages on the T3D: *standalone*, in which the application executes wholly on the T3D, and *heterogeneous*, in which the application is distributed between the C90 and the T3D. Standalone ports were initiated for GAMESS and AMBER, while a heterogeneous approach was taken with MaxSegs and CHARMM. Successful heterogeneous versions of both packages [11, 4] were previously completed at the PSC using a CRAY Y-MP and TMC CM-2, paving the way for the C90-T3D version. As will be discussed, both standalone and heterogeneous approaches to porting packages to the T3D have certain strengths and can lead to cost-effective utilization of the machine.

Substantial experience was obtained by implementing communication strategies between processes residing on the T3D as well as between heterogeneous processes. Both are rich topics; when exploiting the T3D's high speed network [12] one must consider tradeoffs between various levels of portability and performance in the use of PVM and shared memory primitives, while a similarly robust array of choices exists for heterogeneous communications in the form of different message-passing frameworks, memory-resident file I/O, and named pipes.

Porting applications written in Fortran and C (and, more recently, C++) provides users with a critical view of programming tools and the overall software environment. The CRAY T3D Emulator, the TotalView debugger, and the Apprentice performance analyzer have been used extensively and productively.

This paper attempts to relate some of the salient features of porting scientific applications to the T3D. Its organization is as follows. Section 1.2 describes techniques, benefits, and drawbacks associated with distributing applications across the heterogeneous CRAY C90-T3D system, using the molecular simulation program CHARMM [2] as an example. Section 1.3 evaluates the alternative of executing computations wholly on the T3D, focusing on the *ab initio* quantum chemistry program GAMESS [6, 15]. Section 1.4 comments on tools and development approaches found to be useful at the PSC for T3D software development, and Section 1.5 summarizes key ideas.

1.2   Heterogeneous Computing

A computation is said to be *heterogeneous* if it is distributed across more than one type of host architecture. In this paper we shall restrict our attention to applications having components which execute concurrently on multiple architectures. Frequent communications increase the complexity of such applications beyond that associated with more simply segmented applications, in which phases executing on different hosts are temporally separated. A heterogeneous application may be distributed, for example, across a cluster of workstations, between a graphics workstation and a supercomputer, or between multiple supercomputers, each contributing its own strengths toward solving the problem at hand cost-effectively. The last case, as exemplified by the CRAY C90 and T3D, is the focus of this section.

The CRAY C90 and T3D are connected by up to four high speed (HISP) channels, each with a throughput of 200 megabytes per second. Data transfers across the high speed channels are mediated by I/O gateways. Each I/O gateway contains two CRAY T3D nodes in which some of the circuitry present in the processing nodes has been replaced by specialized components dedicated to interacting with the high speed and low speed channels (LOSP). The I/O gateways exist in addition to the T3D's processing nodes, and the number of I/O gateways may be tuned to the anticipated workload. For example, at the time of this writing the PSC's T3D consists of 256 processing nodes (512 processing elements) and eight I/O gateways. The I/O gateways negotiate control over the low and high speed channels, using the LOSP for control information in the form of requests and responses, and the HISP for data transfers. This arrangement provides an efficient mechanism for communication between the front-end C90 or Y-MP and the T3D which is transparent to user-level applications.

Communication between the C90 and T3D has been accomplished by a variety of mechanisms including message-passing, file I/O, and named pipes. Message passing using Distributed Heterogeneous SuperComputing (DHSC) [8] was the first such technique to be explored at the PSC. DHSC is a message-passing library written at the Pittsburgh Supercomputing Center to enable efficient communications between heterogeneous platforms. It was originally written for interfacing the CRAY Y-MP and the Connection Machines CM-2, and it has since been ported to the C90, T3D, workstations, and other systems. Several reasons for this include DHSC's early availability, familiarity with and confidence in DHSC due to previously successful heterogeneous computing projects (*e.g.* molecular dynamics distributed between the PSC's CRAY Y-MP and TMC CM-2 [4, 9]), and the convenience with which a message-passing approach could be incorporated into the programs being ported at the time. DHSC remains a method of choice for communicating small to medium size messages between the C90 and T3D, achieving an asymptotic bandwidth of approximately 20 MB/s. CRI's Network Parallel Virtual Machine (PVM) [14] is now available as an alternative message-passing interface between the T3D and its front end, offering increased portability and robustness at the expense of some loss of efficiency due to greater complexity of the PVM system. File I/O has been found to be especially effective when data transfers are infrequent and large. Data to be communicated between hosts is written to a memory-resident file (*i.e.* in /dev/mem, using the extended memory subsystem, the SSD), and tasks on the two hosts synchronize by locking and unlocking the file. Named pipes, implemented through special files via the mkfifo(2) system call, have also been profitably investigated as a communications mechanism, and in fact they are the construct upon which the T3D version of DHSC is built.

A consideration inherent in heterogeneous computing over and above simply communicating a stream of bits is the necessity of converting data formats when the native formats of hosts involved in the communication differ. In the case of the heterogeneous C90/T3D system, one commonly must address this issue when sending and receiving floating-point numbers (Cray arithmetic on the C90 vs. IEEE on the T3D) and integers (32-bit on the T3D vs. 64-bit on the C90). Message passing libraries typically offer the option of having the conversion done automatically. This is true for DHSC as well as for PVM, which uses XDR [18] conversion when the encoding is specified as PvmDataDefault. Alternatively, one may elect to do the conversion explicitly on one or another of the hosts, as is necessary when using memory-resident files or named pipes. The natural mechanism for such conversions is the pair of functions `cray2iec` and `iec2cray` provided in LibSci, CRI's scientific subroutine library.

A determining factor in heterogeneous communications performance is the latency. The performance of the methods listed above will vary from site to site depending on the computational power and system load of the front-end, the number of channels and I/O gateways, as well as other hardware and environmental characteristics.

The unique C90/T3D environment offers substantial advantages during the course of porting large, complex applications to the CRAY T3D. These benefits are first realizable when an application is just about to be ported to the T3D. The traditional approach to porting software proceeds in several stages: the entire program to be compiled for the target platform (which may be a substantial task when going to a different operating system or when nonportable code is involved), correct results for a suite of test problems are obtained, and finally the code is optimized and tuned. Reaching the optimization phase, which is where one would like to spend one's effort, can be a laborious and time-consuming task. This problem is exacerbated when porting production applications to most MPP's because limited memory on each processing element mandates distributing key data structures, even in inherently serial sections of code and in the initial port. Fortunately, the heterogeneous C90/T3D system presents a shortcut: the bulk of an application is compiled and executed on the C90, where it probably already runs, and only a small section is built to run on and be optimized for the T3D. Data is communicated between the two by one or more of the methods described above. The result is that parallelizable fragments of code can be developed in isolation, leading to the realization of an incremental parallelization process in which initial results are obtained very quickly. Optimal data distributions can be empirically determined for dominant aspects of the calculation while deferring their implementation in less sensitive parts of the program.

As a port progresses it often becomes apparent that certain sections of code take very little time, and the cost of porting them outweighs the benefits. Examples include the complex parsers and I/O systems found in many legacy codes. In these cases the final product may best be implemented as a heterogeneous program, leaving the inherently serial sections of code on the front-end. Of course the ideal solution would be to restructure the algorithms to eliminate nonparallel constructs; however, for a variety of reasons doing so is unfortunately rarely expedient.

Yet another advantage gleaned from coupling heterogeneous processors is the ability to exploit the strengths of each to perform a complex calculation while maximizing resource utilization. For example, scalable eigensolvers for large linear systems are still an active research topic, while vectorized solutions for platforms like the C90 are mature and efficient. In certain cases it may therefore require less real time to migrate data between hosts, manipulate it on the best-suited host, and transfer the data back.

Heterogeneous implementations of a number of production applications have been developed and are in use at the PSC by PSC and CRI staff, along with users of the center. These include (among others):

- CHARMM [2], a widely used molecular modeling program,

- Shake'n'Bake [10], which uses a direct method to glean phase data from X-ray crystallographic intensities,

- a Car-Parrinello program [5, 1] for incorporating quantum mechanics in molecular dynamics simulations, and

- MaxSegs [21, 11] and MultiSearch, protein and nucleic acid sequence comparison programs.

1.2.1   Example: "Hetero CHARMM"

CHARMM [2] employs molecular dynamics to address the behavior of solvated biological molecules, in particular the protein folding problem. The goal of using Newton's equations of motion to evolve collections of tens to hundreds of thousands of atoms for up to millions of timesteps mandates an aggressive pursuit of efficient computational approaches. To this end Charles L. Brooks III and William S. Young have developed heterogeneous versions of CHARMM using state of the art hardware available at the PSC. The project that began on the CRAY Y-MP/832 and TMC CM-2 [4, 9] has now been transferred to the CRAY C90 and T3D [19, 20].

Work is partitioned in this "Hetero CHARMM" as shown in Figure 1.1. Because computing interactions between pairs of water molecules accounts for more than 80% of the runtime in typical molecular dynamics simulations [9], those calculations constitute a natural target for parallelization. While comparatively cheap protein-protein and protein-water interactions are computed on the front-end vector processor, the demanding water-water interactions are distributed to the parallel computer.

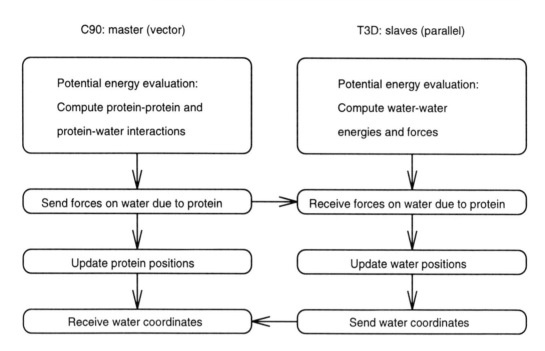

C90: master (vector)   T3D: slaves (parallel)

Potential energy evaluation:

Compute protein-protein and

protein-water interactions

Potential energy evaluation:

Compute water-water

energies and forces

Send forces on water due to protein

Receive forces on water due to protein

Update protein positions

Update water positions

Receive water coordinates

Send water coordinates

Figure 1.1: Data flow in "hetero CHARMM."

CHARMM consists of aproximately 200,000 lines of Flex (an augmented dialect of Fortran) source which is preprocessed into a smaller number of lines of Fortran77. Young wrote another 5,000 lines of Fortran which computes water-water interactions and propagates positions. While that functionality already exists in CHARMM, Young's contribution is specifically optimized for the T3D. Depending on the system under study, computations of the water-water interactions and coordinate propagation represent 50-99% of the runtime. For example, in a recent simulation of "native" apomyoglobin [3] the interactions between and propagation of the 4299 water molecules accounted for approximately 90% of the runtime.

Communications consist of regular packets of $3N$ floating-point numbers from the vector to the parallel processor (coordinates) and then back to the vector processor (forces). This implies a large number of relatively small messages. Because of the simplicity with which message-passing libraries can be interchanged, a fraction of the development of "Hetero CHARMM" was performed on the PSC's cluster of DEC Alpha workstations using PVM. The absence of PVM during the initial stages of access to T3D hardware fueled the development of DHSC and its subsequent use by CHARMM. Use of the DHSC message-passing library [8] is currently the method of choice for this communication in CHARMM, being somewhat more efficient than PVM. Interchange between IEEE and Cray floating point formats is accomplished using the vectorized CONVERT library [16].

"Hetero CHARMM" is currently in use by the Brooks group for research calculations. Using thirty-two CRAY T3D processors, the heterogeneous code completes a given problem two to three times faster than a single C90 processor, constituting an appreciable improvement in throughput.

1.3 Standalone Applications

The traditional approach to programming MPPs, namely to execute a given application entirely on the MPP in a SIMD or SPMD fashion, is of course also applicable to the CRAY T3D. In this case the focus shifts from communication between heterogeneous hosts to maximally exploiting the T3D's low-latency, high-bandwidth network [12] and optimizing single-PE performance.

The two optimizations most likely to increase the performance of standalone applications are maximizing single-PE performance and replacing key PVM calls with shared memory primitives. Increasing cache use is usually the best way to improve single-PE execution rates. That may involve restructuring loops, cache-aligning data, and inserting padding between arrays to avoid excessive hits on the same direct-mapped cache lines. The shared memory primitives `shmem_put` and `shmem_get` have very low latencies (on the order of one to two microseconds) and hence can be more than an order of magnitude faster than PVM sends and receives.

1.3.1 Standalone Example: GAMESS

GAMESS [6, 15], the General Atomic and Molecular Electronic Structure System, is a widely used, general-purpose, *ab initio* quantum chemistry program. GAMESS' prevalence in research, its readily available source, liberal distribution policy, and the pre-existence of a message-passing parallel implementation combine to recommend it as one of the first candidates for porting to the PSC's CRAY T3D. Theoretical methods parallelized in the August 18, 1994 release of GAMESS, which is currently available to end users at the PSC, are listed in Table 1.1.

Table 1.1 Parallel Functionality of GAMESS					
calculation	RHF	ROHF	UHF	GVB	MCSCF
energy	•	•	•	•	•
analytic gradient	•	•	•	•	•
num. Hessian	•	•	•	•	•
analytic Hessian	•	•		•	
MP2	•				
CI	•	•		•	•

GAMESS was first parallelized by Michael Schmidt and coworkers using the TCGMSG [7] message-passing library. Calls to one message-passing library's functions are often easily replaced with calls to analogous functions from a different message-passing library. The conversion from TCGMSG (for which no port was available for the T3D at the time of this project) to the T3D's flavor of PVM was facilitated by GAMESS' support for a file tcgstb.src containing wrappers matching TCGMSG's interface. The intention is that tcgstb.src should be ignored when compiling GAMESS for a parallel system using TCGMSG, compiled as a set of dummy routines when building a serial version of GAMESS, and supplemented with machine and environment-dependent code for use on other parallel platforms. Only the subset of TCGMSG described in Table 1.2 is used by GAMESS. Michael Lambert (PSC) wrote the initial implementation of TCGMSG functions in terms of PVM. Every TCGMSG function listed in Table 1.2 except for NXTVAL was written as a "wrapper" matching the expected TCGMSG calling sequence around PVM function calls. Implementation of NXTVAL was deferred because it implements a shared counter primarily used for load balancing a heterogeneous virtual machine, which would be of limited utility in the standalone T3D version of GAMESS. The initial PVM implementation of BRDCST is shown in Figure 1.2, with other TCGMSG functions written similarly.

The recent upgrade of the PSC's CRAY T3D from 16MB to 64MB of RAM per PE has facilitated significantly larger calculations using GAMESS. SCF gradient calculations, which were previously limited to about 200 basis functions (small by today's standards), can now be performed with over 950 basis functions (large for contemporary *ab initio* quantum chemistry). The memory upgrade also allows multi-configurational self-consistent field (MCSCF) calculations, for which GAMESS is best known and most widely

Table 1.2	
TCGMSG routines used by GAMESS	
name	description
PBEGINF	initialization
PEND	termination and cleanup
SYNCH	synchronize all processes
BRDCST	broadcast a message
DGOP	double global operations
IGOP	integer global operations
MDTOB	return number of bytes in n doubles
MITOB	return number of bytes in n integers
NXTVAL	simulate a shared counter
NICEFTN	Fortran wrapper for nice
NNODES	returns the number of processes
NODEID	returns logical node number
	of the current process

used, to be run in parallel. It is hoped that these capabilities will enable new research expanding the forefronts of science.

GAMESS Performance

Preliminary benchmarking for GAMESS on the T3D was done using the four test problems introduced by Schmidt, Baldridge, et al. [15]:

- puckered ADSbO ($C_4H_4O_2NSb$), C_s symmetry, RHF/3-21G*//RHF/3-21G*, 110 basis functions

- phosphinoaluminate ion ((CH_3)$_3$AlPH$_2^-$), C_s symmetry, RHF/6-31++G (d,p)//RHF/6-31G(d), 169 basis functions

- silicon cage (SiH[(CH_2)$_3$]$_3C_6H_3$), C_3 symmetry but run as C_1, RHF/6-31G(d), 288 basis functions

- cyclic AMP ($C_{10}H_{11}N_5O_6P^-$), C_1 symmetry, RHF/6-31G(d,p)//PM3, 389 basis functions.

These benchmarks represent a range of small to medium sized problems in computational chemistry. Additional RHF gradient calculations using up to

```fortran
      SUBROUTINE BRDCST(TYPE, BUF, LENBUF, FROM)
      INTEGER          TYPE, BUF, LENBUF, FROM
      INCLUDE 't3dtcg.inc'
      CALL PVMFBARRIER(PVMALL, 0, ISTAT)
      IF (FROM .EQ. MYPE) THEN
         IF (NPES() .GT. 1) THEN
            CALL PVMFINITSEND(PVMINPLACE, INFO)
            IF (IAND(TYPE, MSGDBL) .NE. 0) THEN
               CALL PVMFPACK(REAL8, BUF, LENBUF/8, 1, INFO)
            ELSE IF (IAND(TYPE, MSGINT) .NE. 0) THEN
               CALL PVMFPACK(INTEGER8, BUF, LENBUF/8, 1, INFO)
            ELSE IF (IAND(TYPE, MSGCHR) .NE. 0) THEN
               CALL PVMFPACK(BYTE1, BUF, LENBUF, 1, INFO)
            ELSE
               CALL PVMFPACK(INTEGER8, BUF, LENBUF/8, 1, INFO)
            END IF
            CALL PVMFBCAST(PVMALL, TYPE, INFO)
            IF (INFO .NE. 0) THEN
               WRITE(UNIT=*, FMT=*) 'Error doing a broadcast.'
               STOP
            END IF
         END IF
      ELSE
         CALL PVMFRECV(FROM, TYPE, INFO)
         IF (IAND(TYPE, MSGDBL) .NE. 0) THEN
            CALL PVMFUNPACK(REAL8, BUF, LENBUF/8, 1, INFO)
         ELSE IF (IAND(TYPE, MSGINT) .NE. 0) THEN
            CALL PVMFUNPACK(INTEGER8, BUF, LENBUF/8, 1, INFO)
         ELSE IF (IAND(TYPE, MSGCHR) .NE. 0) THEN
            CALL PVMFUNPACK(BYTE1, BUF, LENBUF, 1, INFO)
         ELSE
            CALL PVMFUNPACK(INTEGER8, BUF, LENBUF/8, 1, INFO)
         END IF
      END IF
      CALL PVMFBARRIER(PVMALL, 0, ISTAT)
      RETURN
      END
```

Figure 1.2: Implementation of the TCGMSG BRDCST function as a wrapper around CRAY T3D PVM calls.

950 basis functions and also MCSCF and CI calculations have been done on the T3D, the results of which will be published elsewhere.

Figure 1.3 is a standard portrayal of speedup versus number of processors. GAMESS scales moderately, running at roughly 50% efficiency on 128 PE's for the two largest benchmarks. Fewer T3D processors are used effectively for the smaller benchmarks: 32 PE's for phosphinoaluminate ion, and only 16 PE's for ADSbO. The ADSbO benchmark actually requires more time when run with 128 PE's than with 64 due to the problem simply being so small that communications dominate for large processor counts. The data appear to indicate saturation by approximately 400 basis functions, but further results are needed disambiguate effects possibly due to differences in the silicon cage and cyclic AMP datasets.

A more interesting comparison can be made using CRAY C90 single-processor GAMESS performance as a baseline. Figure 1.4 shows a log-log plot of single C90 CPU's required to complete identical calculations run on the T3D. In all cases, four T3D processors deliver greater throughput than one C90 CPU for identical calculations. Scalability increases dramatically with problem size; one can achieve the performance of a full 16-CPU C90 with only 64 T3D PE's for the cyclic AMP benchmark ($n_f = 389$), whereas 128 PE's are required for the phosphinoaluminate ion benchmark ($n_f = 169$). For the larger systems examined, 128 PE's deliver the equivalent performance of 23-24 C90 CPU's, indicating the T3D is cost-effective relative to the C90 for this type of calculation.

It must be noted that a conventional (*i.e.* I/O-based SCF) algorithm is preferred for problems of this size on the C90 using GAMESS; however, the cutoff (in terms of number of basis functions) at which direct SCF becomes more efficient than conventional SCF will decrease as GAMESS' two-electron integral evaluation algorithms become more efficient.

Communications account for approximately 10% of the total runtime for the larger datasets examined. Furthermore, the communication pattern consists of a large number of short messages, indicating that replacing the PVM implementation of TCGMSG with much lower latency shared-memory primitives will noticeably improve performance. Work toward this end is in progress.

The dominant components of SCF gradient calculations are moderately-to well-parallelized, with performance degradation resulting from load imbalance, communications delays, and suboptimal single-PE optimization. Two phases of the calculation, initial orbital selection and property evaluation,

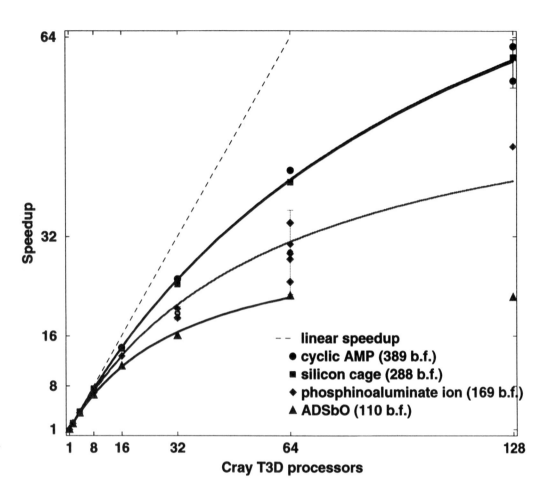

Figure 1.3: Scalability of GAMESS on the T3D. Error bars denote 95% confidence limits. See color plate XXIX.

consume an insignificant fraction of the runtime for single processor runs but constitute a clear bottleneck in large parallel runs; hence their parallelization is a prerequisite to good overall scalability on large processor counts.

GAMESS' performance on the CRAY T3D recommends the T3D as a cost-effective alternative to the C90 for carrying out certain large quantum chemical calculations. That assessment will be amplified as GAMESS' scalability is increased through replacing the PVM implementation of TCGMSG calls with one based on **shmem_get** and **shmem_put**, improving single-PE optimization, and parallelizing initial orbital selection and calculation of properties.

1.4   Software Tools

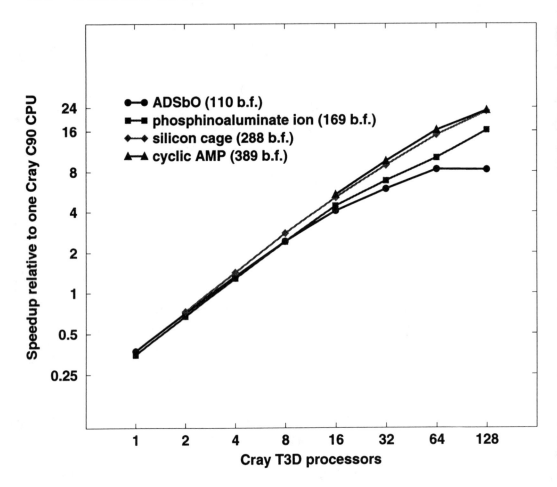

Figure 1.4: Scalability of GAMESS on the T3D. See color plate XXX.

Several tools developed or modified for the CRAY T3D have proven to be
extremely useful in creating new programs for and porting third-party applications to the T3D. Those tools include the CRAY T3D Emulator, the
TotalView debugger, the Apprentice performance tuner, the XBrowse source
code browser, and (to a limited extent) the CRAY T3D Simulator. The
interested reader is referred to results of the JNNIE collaboration [17] for
a broad view of tools for scalable parallel computers, and to the article by
Douglas Pase in this volume for further information on tools produced by
Cray Research, Inc.

The PSC's goal was to have key applications running immediately following shipment of its T3D. That ambitious goal was facilitated by the existence of the CRAY T3D Emulator, a product executable on a Cray Y-MP or C90 and designed to allow T3D code development in the absence of an actual T3D. The Emulator, used on Cray vector machines both at CRI and at PSC, was valuable for developing correct code with the new compilers and also for advancing the state of those compilers through extensive interaction with CRI. The Emulator provides extensive information on local vs. remote memory access patterns for optimizing CRAFT[1] programs, and it also provides estimates of message-passing times. Each program, excepting GAMESS, undertaken prior to shipment of the PSC's T3D was executing correctly under the Emulator before the hardware arrived, a result which greatly accelerated the development of applications on the actual machine. (With only minor modifications GAMESS ran correctly on the hardware, so no further attempt was made to execute it under the Emulator.)

The CRAY T3D Simulator was written at CRI to facilitate operating system development in advance of actual hardware. Hence it is a representation of the T3D, simulating the computer's behavior down to the level of instructions and registers. In the quest for code that would run as soon as hardware was available, the CRAY T3D Simulator was also tried by PSC staff, but it was quickly found that the level of detail accurately portrayed by the Simulator led to runtime expansion factors which prevented its use in developing large applications using realistic datasets. Hence it was found that the Simulator was best left to the purpose for which it was intended (i.e. OS development), and the computational scientists at the PSC turned their attention to T3D hardware that was becoming accessible first at CRI and later in Pittsburgh.

The TotalView debugger (licensed from BBN and modified by CRI for the T3D) and the Apprentice performance instrumentation tool were released soon after arrival of the PSC's CRAY T3D. Integration of both tools with XBrowse is invaluable for navigating unfamiliar code. The suite of software forms an intuitive system with a shallow learning curve.

TotalView does a very good job of allowing one to diagnose and resolve problems in complex code. Each process is handled by a separate window, and one may either examine core files or attach to existing processes. One

---

[1]CRAFT is a programming environment that includes extensions to Fortran to allow data distributions for parallel machines

has great control over the debugging session through the use of breakpoints, stepping through the code either by single steps or over function calls, editing variables and format strings, changing the value of the program counter, and evaluating code fragments. Support for message-passing on the level of XPVM would be helpful for correctness as well as performance debugging, although the existence of XPVM as a separate tool (albeit on workstation clusters) is a functional although inconvenient workaround.

The principal strength of the Apprentice is that, unlike many other performance tools, it is not trace-based. Hence one can analyze the results of full production runs rather than those of small prototypes. One can obtain detailed operation counts and performance statistics for any instrumented section of code, with immediate access to the associated source through an instance of XBrowse. Time spent performing various types of operations is readily obtained, as are overheads due to PVM communications and shared memory transfers. Direct identification of performance bottlenecks is seldom difficult. The primary shortcoming of the Apprentice (as is true of any intrusive, *i.e.* software-based, tool), is its interference with cache activity. The instruction and data caches on the EV-4 are each only 8 kilobytes (KB), so efficient cache usage is an important optimization concern. The effect of the extra instructions inserted for instrumentation by the Apprentice has been found to be noticeable but tolerable.

1.5   Conclusions

Both standalone and heterogeneous programming models have been employed on the CRAY T3D with favorable results. Standalone programs benefit from exceptionally low latency and high bandwidth communications, along with simplified scheduling and avoidance of contention with other C90 processes. Heterogeneous computing offers a number of advantages including incremental parallelization, concentration of development efforts on parallelizable sections of code, and exploitation of optimal hardware resources for each particular task.

The T3D tool suite has been extremely useful in developing correct and efficient programs. Early existence of the Emulator was clearly advantageous for developing applications that could be run very soon after hardware delivery, as were access to a cluster of workstations and tools for distributed software such as Xab. TotalView and the Apprentice continue to be mainstays, and while opinion naturally varies, many have found both tools to be intuitive and remarkably helpful.

Acknowledgements

Input data for the four GAMESS benchmarks was provided by Dr. Kim Baldridge, San Diego Supercomputer Center. Thanks also go to Dr. Michael Lambert, Pittsburgh Supercomputing Center, who wrote the initial implementation of TCGMSG using PVM and provided numerous insightful discussions.

References

[1] BOGUSLAWSKI, P., ZHANG, Q.-M., ZHANG, Z., AND BERNHOLC, J., "Structure of Monatomic Steps on the si(001) Surface," *Phys. Rev. Lett.*, 1994, **72** No. 23, 3694–3697.

[2] BROOKS, B. R., BRUCCOLERI, R. E., OLAFSON, B. D., STATES, D. J., SWAMINATHEN, S., AND KARPLUS, M., "CHARMM: A Program for Macromolecular Energy, Minimization, and Dynamics Calculations," *J. Comp. Chem.*, 1983, **4**, 187–217.

[3] BROOKS, CHARLES L. III, "Characterization of "Native" Apomyoglobin by Molecular Dynamics Simulation," *J. Mol. Biol.*, 1992, **227**, 375–380.

[4] BROOKS, CHARLES L. III, YOUNG, WILLIAM S., AND TOBIAS, DOUGLAS J., "Molecular Simulations on Supercomputers," *Intl. J. Supercomputer App.*, 1991, **5**, 98–112.

[5] CAR, R. AND PARRINELLO, M., *Phys. Rev. Lett.*, 1985, **55**, 2471.

[6] DUPUIS, M., SPANGLER, D., AND WENDOLOSKI, J. J., *National Resource for Computations in Chemistry Software Catalog, Program QG01*. University of California, Berkeley, 1980.

[7] HARRISON, R. J., now at Pacific Northwest Laboratory, v. 4.03, available by anonymous `ftp` in directory `pub/tcgmsg` from host `ftp.tcg.anl.gov`.

[8] MAHDAVI, J., HUNTOON, G. L., AND MATHIS, M. B., "Deployment of a HiPPI-based Distributed Supercomputing Environment at the Pittsburgh Supercomputing Center," in *Proceedings of the Workshop on Heterogeneous Processing*, 1992, 93–96.

[9] MERTZ, J. E., TOBIAS, D. J., BROOKS, C. L. III, AND SINGH, U. C., "Vector and Parallel Algorithms for the Molecular Dynamics Simulation of Macromolecules on Shared Memory Computers," *J. Comp. Chem.*, 1991, **12**, 1270–1277.

[10] MILLER, R., DETITTA, G. T., JONES, R., LANGS, D. A., WEEKS, C. M., AND HAUPTMAN, H. A., "On the Application of the Minimal Principle to Solve Unknown Structures," *Science*, 1993, 259:1430.

[11] NICHOLAS, H., GIRAS, G., HARTONAS-GARMHAUSEN, V., KOPKO, M., MAHER, C., AND ROPELEWSKI, A., "Distributing the Comparison of DNA and Protein Sequences Across Heterogeneous Supercomputers," in *Supercomputing '91 Proceedings*, 1991, 139–146.

[12] NUMRICH, ROBERT W., SPRINGER, PAUL L., AND PETERSON, JOHN C., "Measurement of Communication Rates on the Cray T3D Interprocessor Network," in *High-Performance Computing and Networking, International Conference and Exhibition*, W. Gentzsch and U. Harms, Eds., Munich, Germany, April 18-20, 1994. *Proceedings, Volume 2: Networking and Tools*, Springer-Verlag, 1994, 150–157.

[13] PEARLMAN, DAVID A., CASE, DAVID A., CALDWELL, JAMES C., SEIBEL, GEORGE L., SINGH, U. CHANDRA, WEINER, PAUL, AND KOLLMAN, PETER A., *AMBER 4.0*. University of California, San Francisco, 1991.

[14] *PVM and HeNCE Programmer's Manual, SR-2501 3.0*, 1994.

[15] SCHMIDT, MICHAEL W., BALDRIDGE, KIM K., BOATZ, JERRY A., ELBERT, STEVEN T., GORDON, MARK S., JENSEN, JAN H., KOSEKI, SHIRO, MATSUNAGA, NIKITA, NGUYEN, KIET A., SU, SHUJUN, WINDUS, THERESA L., DUPUIS, MICHEL, AND MONTGOMERY, JOHN A., JR., "General Atomic and Molecular Electronic Structure System," *J. Comp. Chem.*, 1993, **14** No. 11, 1347–1363.

[16] Supplied by Wayne Schroeder, San Diego Supercomputer Center.

[17] The Joint NSF-NASA Initiative on Evaluation is a collaborative project to evaluate the effectiveness of scalable parallel computing systems (SPC's) under credible scientific workloads and on a variety of SPC's. Further information is available on the World Wide Web at URL http://www.tc.cornell.edu/JNNIE/jnnietop.html.

[18] XDR: External Data Representation Standard. Technical Report Request for Comments 1014, Network Working Group, 1987.

[19] YOUNG, WILLIAM S. AND BROOKS, CHARLES L. III, "Dynamic Load Balancing Algorithms for Replicated Data Molecular Dynamics," April 1995.

[20] YOUNG, WILLIAM S. AND BROOKS, CHARLES L. III, "Optimization of Replicated Data Method for Molecular Dynamics," *J. Comp. Chem.*, in preparation.

[21] WATERMAN, M. S. AND EGGERT, M., "A New Algorithm for Best Subsequence Alignment with Application to tRNA-rRNA Comparisons," *J. Mol. Biol.*, 1987, **197**, 723–728.

Tuning I/O Performance on the Paragon: Fun with Pablo and Norma

Carl Winstead, Howard P. Pritchard, and Vincent McKoy
A. A. Noyes Laboratory of Chemical Physics
California Institute of Technology
Pasadena, California 91125

Abstract

We describe our experiences using the Pablo performance analysis system to characterize I/O performance on the Intel Paragon. This work is part of a collaborative effort that brings together developers of I/O performance-analysis tools and computational scientists with I/O-intensive parallel applications. The purpose of this collaboration is to allow testing and refinement of tools on "real" applications at production scale, and to explore I/O strategies that may lead to improved application performance. We discuss our application's I/O requirements, our strategy for improving its I/O performance on the Paragon, and the use of Pablo to characterize performance. We note aspects of the Paragon's system software that affected both our application and Pablo, and we describe certain subtleties of I/O measurement that suggested improvements in the way statistics are presented.

1.1 Introduction

Massively parallel processors (MPPs) continue to advance rapidly in raw computational power as measured by theoretical peak speed or performance on simple benchmarks [1]. Projected improvements in microprocessors will support this trend for some time to come [3]. Interprocessor communication bandwidth and latency also have improved dramatically in recent generations of MPPs and seem likely to improve further. However, it is becoming increasingly evident that delivering high performance to actual applications depends as much on the performance of the storage hierarchy—including cache, main memory, disk, and possibly external connections—as on the nominal processor speed or the speed of the interconnection network.

Most issues that arise in dealing with cache and main memory on a distributed-memory MPP are identical to those that arise on a single-processor machine; consequently, both compiler developers and applications programmers can bring the benefit of many years' experience to bear in addressing these issues. Disk I/O on a multiprocessor machine is a different case altogether: there is no common wisdom for how such I/O should be performed under various circumstances. Indeed, at the moment there are no standards for parallel I/O; the design of the file system, the calls through which the application accesses it, and the optimal strategies for reading and writing data are all generally vendor-specific. In this period of experimentation on the part of vendors, equally vigorous experimentation on the part of users is called for, both to bring out the strengths and weaknesses of various I/O architectures and to develop, if possible, some general strategies and rules of thumb that may be widely useful. There is a need, also, for the development of performance-analysis tools to support I/O characterization on MPPs.

Interaction among vendors, tool developers, and end users interested in parallel I/O clearly provides an opportunity for synergism. However, such interactions do not come naturally; applications programmers, for instance, do not generally cross paths with tool developers, nor do they tend to report back to vendors systematically on their experiences with I/O hardware and software. The NSF Grand Challenge project on *Parallel Methodologies for I/O Intensive Grand Challenge Applications* was organized precisely to provide a framework that brings together vendors, computer scientists interested in I/O system software, performance-analysis tool developers, and the developers and users of large-scale, I/O-intensive parallel applications. Within this framework, computer scientists have the opportunity to test their software on a variety of "real" applications—meaning not only actual user programs, but such programs run for production-scale problems on large machines. Applications programmers have both opportunity and added incentive to experiment with I/O hardware, software, and tools, while vendors obtain rapid and extensive feedback that may be of use in designing next-generation parallel I/O systems.

We are involved in this initiative as the developers and users of a scientific application with large I/O requirements. This program, whose purpose is to calculate low-energy electron-molecule collision cross sections accurately from first principles, is now in production use on a number of machines, including the Intel Touchstone DELTA, Intel Paragon, and CRAY T3D. We describe here recent work to characterize and optimize its I/O performance on the Paragon. This work was done in collaboration with Daniel Reed's group at the University of Illinois, who are the developers of Pablo, a performance-analysis package for parallel programs [5]. Pablo was initially oriented toward analysis of computational and communication performance but is currently being extended to support I/O analysis as well. Both sides of the collaboration hope to gain insight from this early experiment in the use of Pablo to characterize I/O performance on an MPP.

In the following sections, we first briefly outline our application in order to explain how our I/O requirements arise. We describe the I/O approach initially taken on the Paragon and the reasons for that approach; we then describe our strategy for optimizing I/O performance on the Paragon's Parallel File System (PFS). Pre- and post-optimization performance will be illustrated for a modest-sized problem using Pablo trace data. We will discuss in some detail how Pablo was used in our case, with an emphasis on lessons learned in applying it to production-scale runs on a large Paragon. We conclude with some remarks on the subtleties and ambiguities that can arise in measuring I/O rates.

1.2 The Application

Low-energy electron-molecule collisions are a feature of many natural and manmade physical systems. Examples include the upper atmosphere, interstellar clouds, and gas lasers. Perhaps the most important technology in which such collisions play a role is the processing of materials by low-temperature plasmas. Plasma processing is used extensively in the semiconductor industry, where etching, doping, cleaning, and other steps in microelectronics fabrication are carried out using plasma reactors. Continued progress in reactor design and process optimization will, it is widely believed, require the development of robust three-dimensional plasma models[4]. However, the development of such models cannot take place without a considerable improvement in the data base of fundamental collision information. Because electron-molecule collisions are largely responsible for the generation of reactive species in the plasma, a knowledge of electron-molecule collision probabilities, or cross sections, is especially important. These cross sections can be rather difficult to measure, however, and the cross section data base is, in fact, fragmentary for molecules of practical interest.

An alternative to experimental measurement is direct calculation of electron-molecule collision data. All physical information, including the collision cross sections, can be obtained from the solution of Schrödinger's equation for the electron-molecule system. However, a typical molecule has many electrons of its own, and at low collision energies these must be treated on an equal footing with the impinging electron. We thus are faced with a problem in many-particle quantum mechanics, governed by a Schrödinger equation (a second-order partial differential equation) of very high dimension. Direct solution is out of the question, and approximation methods must be devised.

We employ a variational principle known as the Schwinger multichannel (SMC) principle to arrive at an accurate but tractable expression for the cross section [6]. Using the SMC principle, we reduce the problem to that of solving a system of linear equations of fairly modest dimension. Solution of this system is quite easy; however, construction of the coefficient and right-hand-side matrices defining the linear system is very numerically intensive. Fortunately, the necessary steps in this construction are well suited to implementation on distributed-memory MPPs.

To be more specific, our variational principle for the scattering amplitude f, a complex number whose square modulus yields the cross section, takes the form

$$
\begin{aligned}
-2\pi f_{mn}(\vec{k}_{\text{in}}, \vec{k}_{\text{out})} &= \langle \Psi_n^{(-)}(\{\vec{r}_i\}; \vec{k}_{\text{out}}) | V | S_m(\{\vec{r}_i\}; \vec{k}_{\text{in}}) \rangle \\
&+ \langle S_n(\{\vec{r}_i\}; \vec{k}_{\text{out}}) | V | \Psi_m^{(+)}(\{\vec{r}_i\}; \vec{k}_{\text{in}}) \rangle \\
&- \langle \Psi_n^{(-)}(\{\vec{r}_i\}; \vec{k}_{\text{out}}) | A^{(+)} | \Psi_m^{(+)}(\{\vec{r}_i\}; \vec{k}_{\text{in}}) \rangle. \quad (1.1)
\end{aligned}
$$

Here the $\langle \cdot | \cdot | \cdot \rangle$ notation indicates complex conjugation on the left and integration over the variables $\{\vec{r}_i, i = 1, \ldots, N+1\}$, which are the coordinates of the N molecular electrons plus an additional scattering electron. $\Psi_m^{(+)}$ and $\Psi_n^{(-)}$ are $(N+1)$-electron wavefunctions; m and n are labels for the internal state of the molecule before and after the collision, while the $(\pm)$ superscripts refer to boundary conditions. $\Psi_{m,n}^{(\pm)}$ are functions of the electron coordinates $\{\vec{r}_i\}$ and depend also on the vectors $\vec{k}_{\text{in}}$ and $\vec{k}_{\text{out}}$ defining the velocity of the scattered electron at long times before and after the collision. V is the potential of interaction between the $(N+1)$th electron and the molecule; the $(N+1)$-particle wavefunctions $S_{m,n}$ are the interaction-free wavefunctions, i.e., those that are obtained by setting $V = 0$. The remaining quantity, $A^{(+)}$, is a rather complicated operator:

$$A^{(+)} = \left(\frac{1}{N+1} - P\right)(E - H) + VP - VG_P^{(+)}V. \tag{1.2}$$

In Eq. (1.2), E is the system energy, H is the Hamiltonian (energy) operator for the system (containing differential and multiplicative terms), P is a projector that selects "open channels"—i.e., energetically accessible states—and $G_P^{(+)}$, the projected version of the interaction-free Green's function, may be written formally as

$$G_P^{(+)}(E) = \lim_{\varepsilon \to 0^+} P\left[E - (H - V) + i\varepsilon\right]^{-1}. \tag{1.3}$$

Equation (1.1) is variationally stable: first-order errors in $\Psi_{m,n}^{(\pm)}$ produce second-order errors in the scattering amplitude f_{mn} calculated from Eq. (1.1). To obtain a computational method from this fact, we introduce in the usual way a linear expansion of $\Psi_{m,n}^{(\pm)}$:

$$\Psi_m^{(+)}(\{\vec{r}_i\}, \vec{k}_{\text{in}}) = \sum_{I=1}^{M} x_I(\vec{k}_{\text{in}})\chi_I(\{\vec{r}_i\})$$

$$\Psi_n^{(-)}(\{\vec{r}_i\}, \vec{k}_{\text{out}}) = \sum_{I=1}^{M} y_I(\vec{k}_{\text{out}})\chi_I(\{\vec{r}_i\}). \tag{1.4}$$

That is, we express $\Psi_{m,n}^{(\pm)}$ as sums of known functions $\chi_I(\{\vec{r}_i\})$ with unknown coefficients x_I and y_I. To determine these coefficients, we insert Eq. (1.4) in Eq. (1.1) and impose variational stability as a requirement:

$$\frac{\partial f_{mn}}{\partial x_I} = \frac{\partial f_{mn}}{\partial y_J} = 0, \quad \forall I, J. \tag{1.5}$$

This procedure leads to matrix equations of the form

$$
\begin{aligned}
Ax &= b, \\
y^\dagger A &= c^\dagger,
\end{aligned}
\tag{1.6}
$$

where the superscript $\dagger$ signifies the Hermitian conjugate, i.e, the complex conjugate of the transpose. The scattering amplitude can be expressed in terms of the solution to either of Eqs. (1.6), e.g., as

$$
-2\pi f_{mn} = c^\dagger x
\tag{1.7}
$$

In Eqs. (1.6) and (1.7), the matrix elements are defined by

$$
\begin{aligned}
A_{IJ} &= \langle \chi_I | A^{(+)} | \chi_J \rangle, \\
b_I &= \langle \chi_I | V | S_m(\vec{k}_{\text{in}}) \rangle, \\
c_I &= \langle \chi_I | V | S_n(\vec{k}_{\text{out}}) \rangle.
\end{aligned}
\tag{1.8}
$$

As mentioned earlier, evaluation of the matrix elements, Eq. (1.8), is computationally much more demanding than solving the linear system, Eq. (1.6). The reason this is so is that both $A^{(+)}$ and V include two-electron operators. Even when we represent $\{\chi_i\}$ and $S_{m,n}$ as (antisymmetrized) products of one-electron functions, these two-electron terms give rise to integrals involving four such one-electron functions and the coordinates of two electrons. The most numerous class of two-electron integrals has the form

$$
\int d^3 r_1 \int d^3 r_2 \, F_a(\vec{r}_1) F_b(\vec{r}_1) |\vec{r}_1 - \vec{r}_2|^{-1} F_c(\vec{r}_2) \exp(i\vec{k} \cdot \vec{r}_2).
\tag{1.9}
$$

Though, with proper choice of the functions $\{F_a(\vec{r}), a = 1, \ldots, N_F\}$ these integrals can be performed analytically, there are approximately $\frac{1}{2} N_F^3 N_{\vec{k}}$ different integrals to evaluate, where $N_{\vec{k}}$ is the number of $\vec{k}$ vectors required. It is fairly typical in our work to compute 10^{10} to 10^{11} such integrals in constructing the matrix elements of Eq. (1.8). Both the evaluation of these integrals and the arithmetic manipulations necessary to construct from them the matrix elements of Eq. (1.8) are formidable tasks.

Fortunately, both of these tasks are ideally suited to an MPP implementation. These steps are illustrated schematically in Figure 1.1. The evaluation of any given two-electron integral, Eq. (1.9), can be done independently by a

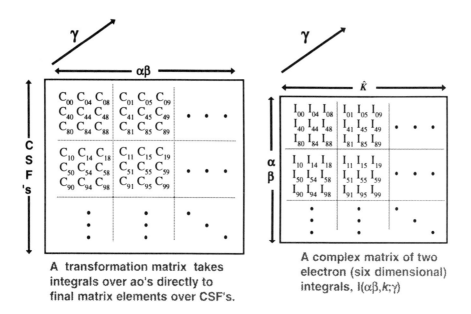

A transformation matrix takes integrals over ao's directly to final matrix elements over CSF's.

A complex matrix of two electron (six dimensional) integrals, $I(\alpha\beta,k;\gamma)$

Figure 1.1: Distribution of the two-electron integral computation. By encoding the rules for combining integrals into a distributed transformation matrix, the transformation procedure is cast in the form of a matrix multiplication.

self-contained collection of subroutines. Each processor in an MPP thus can be assigned to compute a different subset of these integrals. The transformation of these integrals into the matrix elements of Eq. (1.8) is so organized that the principal computational step is multiplication of large, dense, distributed matrices [2].

It is useful at this point to distinguish between the construction of the elements of b and c, on the one hand, and the construction of the elements of A. In the former case, the vector $\vec{k}$ in Eq. (1.9) depends on the energy E; thus, these elements must be computed "from scratch" at each of the (typically many) energies where we wish to determine cross sections. On the other hand, in the evaluation of A, $\vec{k}$ appears as an integration variable when we employ a spectral representation of the Green's function of Eq. (3). This integration is accomplished by means of a numerical quadrature that is formulated to be independent of E. After the transformation step illustrated in Figure 1.1, the angular portion of this quadrature is performed, and sets of quadrature data labeled by the magnitude $|\vec{k}|$ are stored to disk; see Figure 1.2. These data are then read back as often as desired to complete the Green's-function quadrature and construct A at specific energies. The storage and retrieval

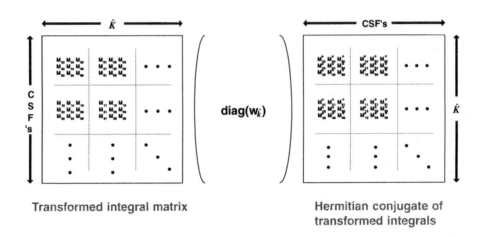

Figure 1.2: Quadrature over the direction of $\vec{k}$ can be done by a variant of distributed-matrix multiplication. The distributed product matrix is stored to disk, to be retrieved when the quadrature over $|\vec{k}|$ is performed.

of this quadrature dataset, whose size can range, depending on problem parameters, from tens of megabytes to gigabytes, is our principal I/O task.

1.3 I/O on the Paragon

The 512-processor Intel Paragon delivered to the Concurrent Supercomputing Consortium (CSCC) in December of 1993 was one of the first large Paragons in the field, and we ported our production program from the CSCC's 512-processor Touchstone DELTA to the Paragon early in its friendly-user phase. Consequently, we encountered early and imperfect versions of the hardware and software, a circumstance that affected our initial approach to I/O.

The most natural means of reading and writing the Green's function quadrature dataset, which has the form of a series of distributed matrices, is to use Intel's `cread()` and `cwrite()` calls and the I/O mode known on the Paragon as M_SYNC and on the DELTA simply as I/O mode 2. In this mode, all processors write or read "simultaneously," contiguous blocks of data belonging to given processors are stored in processor-number order, and the I/O requests may vary in size from processor to processor. The last feature accommodates datasets that do not map evenly onto the processor mesh. Unfortunately, this natural approach crashed the Paragon with some regularity. The source of the problem lay in the combination of a relatively small ratio of I/O to compute nodes and a bug in the OSF/1 operating system that has since become rather widely known as the NORMA bug. The Paragon's Parallel File System (PFS) is striped across a number of RAID disk arrays, which are managed by I/O processors connected to the main communications network. In essence, caching of the I/O requests raining in from the 512 compute processors upon the small number of I/O processors could exhaust free memory on the I/O nodes, leading to an unrecoverable situation that necessitated a reboot of the system.

In order to obtain a working program that would enable us to make use of the Paragon, we adopted an extremely conservative approach to I/O: access to the quadrature dataset was mediated through node 0. All nodes except 0 replaced writes with messages sent to node 0 and reads with messages received from node 0. Only node 0 opened, read, or wrote the quadrature files. This approach requires ancillary message traffic (principally to inform node 0 of request lengths), but its most significant drawback is of course that I/O is serialized. Still, for datasets smaller than 100 Mbyte or so, the resulting overhead was not intolerable, and NORMA-related crashes were avoided.

Some months later, when we began doing calculations on the Paragon that required Gbyte and larger datasets, I/O performance again became a pressing issue. Though the NORMA bug in OSF was still present, other aspects of the system had in the meantime become more stable; moreover, additional I/O nodes had been added to the CSCC Paragon, and the memory per I/O node increased to 32 Mbyte from 16 Mbyte. As a consequence of these improvements, global I/O from a 512-processor partition had become a possible, and indeed recommended, option. However, the natural M_SYNC mode was still unattractive for performance reasons: as implemented, it obtained the file pointer information necessary to accommodate variable-length per-processor requests by serializing the I/O. The recommended high-performance I/O mode was "M_RECORD," which has the characteristics of M_SYNC except that requests must have a fixed size across all processors. Intel further recommended that this request size be the size of a disk block or a multiple thereof, and be in addition an integral multiple of the PFS stripe size. This last step ensures that requests will be scattered uniformly across I/O nodes (as PFS is configured on the CSCC Paragon, each successive stripe is managed by a different I/O node) and that each request can be filled by a single I/O node. Together, these measures both improve performance and decrease the likelihood of NORMA-related problems.

Implementing M_RECORD I/O efficiently required some rethinking on our part, as well as consultation with CSCC and Intel staff. The quadrature data are expensive to compute and are typically produced in per-processor increments much smaller than the block and stripe sizes of the CSCC Paragon's PFS (both 64 Kbyte); several distributed matrices would usually have to be combined to make up a single 64 Kbyte processor record. However, accumulating the data in memory over long periods risks the loss of several hours' work in the event that the job's time limit expires or a system failure occurs. The approach we have chosen assembles the processor records directly on disk (Figure 1.3). This requires that each processor explicitly maintain its own file pointer ("M_UNIX" mode), since corresponding writes by different processors will not be contiguous. (However, if the distributed matrix is large enough that only one request would fit in the stated record size, we of course use M_RECORD mode.)

When the quadrature data are required by the program, the reading subroutine fills a 64 Kbyte buffer on each processor by reading the appropriate file in M_RECORD mode. Data requests from the calling program are satisfied out of that buffer, with actual cread()'s being done only as needed to refill the buffer. This phase of I/O is also illustrated in Figure 1.3.

Writing the dataset in M_UNIX mode is extremely inefficient. However, the dataset is written only once, and that is in the course of the program's most computationally intensive phase. On the other hand, the dataset is typically read dozens of times in a less computationally intensive phase. Thus it is far more important to achieve efficient reading than efficient writing, and the approach described here accomplishes that end. Actual I/O performance will be discussed further in Sec. 1.5.

1.4   Pablo

During the period in which we were tuning our I/O performance, we were also, as part of the I/O Grand Challenge project, working with the developers of the Pablo performance-analysis system to instrument our program as a test case for recent extensions to Pablo that support I/O characterization. This collaboration provided us an opportunity to gain experience with a modern performance-analysis tool and to assess its usefulness, while providing the developers with an opportunity to "field-test" Pablo on a large-scale MPP and a production application.

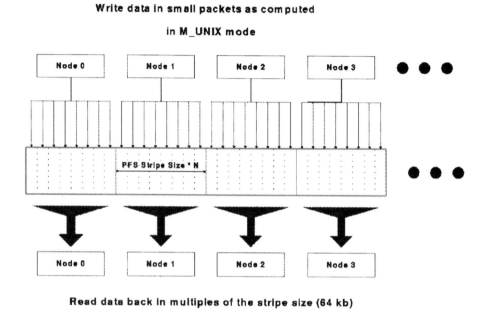

Figure 1.3: Our strategy for efficient I/O on the Paragon's Parallel File System involves reorganization of the dataset as it is written so that large blocks may subsequently be read in M_RECORD mode.

Pablo is described extensively elsewhere [5]. Here we provide only a brief summary of key features. Instrumenting a program requires source-code modifications; these can be done semi-automatically for C code, but FORTRAN code must be hand edited. (Our application uses a mixture of C and FORTRAN.) The Paragon version of Pablo has been configured to trace not only the standard file access calls of C and FORTRAN but also the Intel-specific calls (gopen(), cread(), etc.) that are critical to obtaining high performance for parallel I/O.

Pablo is trace-based; events selected for tracing are logged, together with appropriate descriptive information and a timestamp, on each processor. After a run is completed, the individual processors' trace files are typically transferred to a workstation, where they can be merged and analyzed in a variety of ways, using either an X-Windows graphical interface or command-line tools. Statistics can be presented as tables, two- or three-dimensional graphs, or even as animations or sonifications.

We first verified the correct functioning of the instrumented code on a small Paragon, using input sets for test cases that ran quickly and generated very small files. When satisfied that everything was working correctly, we then tried larger runs on the 512-processor Paragon. Certain points were immediately apparent. For instance, nonselective tracing on a large number of processors quickly generated huge amounts of trace data. Aside from the unwieldiness of the trace files, this implied both significant I/O overhead due to tracing and the potential for serious perturbation of the program, as the uncoordinated pausing of the various processors to flush their trace buffers to disk disrupted the loosely-synchronous character of the computation. More seriously still, the flood of trace data was itself capable of overwhelming the I/O nodes and causing a NORMA-related system crash.

These observations suggested that tracing be restricted—for instance, by instrumenting only I/O and not communication. Moreover, improvements were made in Pablo's management of trace buffers and in the coordination of trace-buffer flushing among processors. Provision was also made for generating on-the-fly summaries to reduce trace volume. With these changes, tracing extended runs became possible.

1.5   Performance Characterization

We have done a number of instrumented runs of our application, using various approaches to I/O. In this section, we use Pablo-generated statistics to characterize a medium-sized run employing the two approaches to I/O described in Sec. 1.3: the "naive" approach, in which node 0 does all I/O on the quadrature dataset, and the "sophisticated" approach, in which large records are assembled in M_UNIX mode, to be retrieved in M_RECORD mode. These results illustrate the usefulness of Pablo for analyzing the I/O behavior of the program, as well as some subtleties that can arise when dealing with parallel I/O.

The test case considered here generates 20.8 Mbytes of quadrature data, contained in two files of equal size. This dataset comprises a series of 172×172 double-precision matrices, or about 231 Kbytes per matrix. To provide a better comparison with larger problems that would be run on 512 processors, we ran this test case on 128 processors. The "natural" I/O request size under these circumstances, i.e., one processor's share of one matrix, is thus approximately 1,850 bytes. In considering these test results, it should be borne in mind that an actual cross section study would repeat the final phase of the computation, in which the entire dataset is read, many times.

We look first at the behavior while writing the quadrature data. Figure 1.4 shows the write durations vs. elapsed time for the original, naive approach. Each group of near-simultaneous writes arises as node 0 stores the various processors' sections of a finished pair of matrices to the two files composing the dataset. (The last write is an exception: there, final results are being saved.) In Figure 1.5, the corresponding information is shown for the sophisticated approach. The same data are being written, but now each processor is managing its own file pointers and doing its own writes. We see that the time required for the average write is considerably increased from that required under the naive approach, Figure 1.4. This is in part an expected consequence of switching to M_UNIX mode. As described earlier, the purpose of using this inefficient mode of writing is to assemble data blocks that may be read with maximal efficiency. On the other hand, a closer inspection of Figure 1.5 shows that the elapsed time for writing a pair of matrices in M_UNIX mode—the width of one of the stacks of points in the figure—is not nearly as large as a simple multiplication (2 files × 128 processors × ~2.5 seconds per average write) would suggest. Clearly, parallelism in the writes is largely compensating for the long write durations.

Figures 1.6 and 1.7 show read performance using the naive and sophisticated approaches, respectively. The relevant reads are the last two, occurring between six and seven thousand seconds of elapsed time; the reads occurring early in the run are of input data. We have obviously done some tuning of the input data reads between the two versions of the program, though we have not discussed those optimizations here. With respect to the reading of the quadrature dataset, it may appear that the vertical scale in Figure 1.6 is too distorted by the initial reads to make a meaningful comparison between Figures 1.6 and 1.7 possible. However, as we just saw for the writes, the duration of the individual reads turns out not to be the most important quantity in a parallel read request: it is the *width*, rather than the height, of the final two clumps of points that contains the most relevant information, and there has been a decrease in that width from Figure 1.6 to Figure 1.7.

These observations are reinforced by summary statistics generated from merged trace data using some of Pablo's command-line tools. The statistics indicate that, with the naive approach, reading the dataset required 211 processor-seconds, vs. 55 processor-seconds with the sophisticated approach. Moreover, the factor of four improvement implied by these two numbers

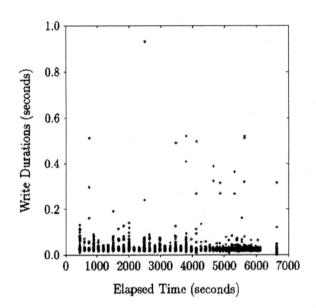

Figure 1.4: Write durations vs. elapsed time for the naive version of the program.

underestimates the improvement in time to completion. Again the reason is parallelism. Though the 211-second figure is a fair measure of elapsed time for the naive approach, the 55-second figure for the sophisticated approach is generated by summing the processor-seconds spent in *concurrent* reads. This sum is almost certainly far larger than the actual elapsed time, which could be as low as 0.43 seconds ($55 \div 128$) in the ideal case where all processors' reads were perfectly synchronized and identical in duration. (Rough timings indicate that the actual elapsed time is a few seconds.)

USimilar considerations affect the I/O rates computed and reported in the summary data. For example, the reported aggregate throughput for reading one of the files in the quadrature dataset is 515 Kbyte/second. However, this number is obtained as the quotient of bytes read and processor-seconds spent reading, and thus once more does not take into account concurrency. In this case, there is an additional clue that something is amiss: the mean read throughput to an individual node, 457 Kbyte/second, is almost the same as the "aggregate" throughput.

We do not view the difficulty of interpreting these statistics primarily as a weakness in Pablo, although improvements in Pablo's presentation of data

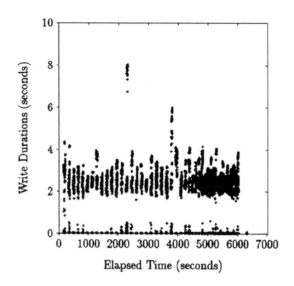

Figure 1.5: Write durations vs. elapsed time for the sophisticated version of the program.

suggested by this work have already been implemented. Rather, there is an inherent ambiguity in the definition of I/O times and rates on concurrent processors. No single definition will fit all circumstances; in fact, the most appropriate measure may depend not only on the degree of parallelism in the I/O but also on what is being written or read. For example, in reading the quadrature dataset, the processors request disjoint subsets of a shared data object. Under these conditions, it is natural to think of the I/O rate as the aggregate amount of data that the processors receive divided by the wall-clock time required to retrieve the data object from the file system. For other types of reads, different rate computations would be more meaningful. For instance, the rate for reading input needed on all processors is best defined in terms of the actual file size rather than the aggregate bytes transferred, since the distribution of multiple copies is a form of parallel overhead, while the best rate measure for applications in which I/O operations are not coordinated among processors might be that used by Pablo in the statistics reported above, i.e., bytes received divided by processor-seconds.

nfortunately, the syntax of parallel I/O, at least on MPPs with which we are familiar, does not provide a performance-analysis tool such as Pablo with much help in making these somewhat subtle distinctions. For example, on the Paragon, the I/O mode is specified at the time the file is opened with

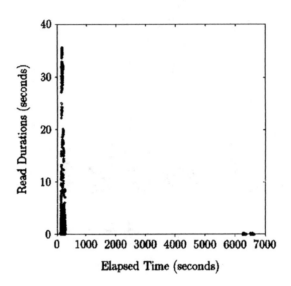

Figure 1.6: Read durations vs. elapsed time for the naive version of the program.

gopen() and may be changed with a setiomode() call, but the mode is not referred to in the read and write calls that actually transfer the data. Since the gopen() or setiomode() may occur in an entirely different part of the program than the actual read or write, the source code in the vicinity of an I/O operation may give no hint whatsoever about the degree of parallelism.

These ambiguities may prove difficult to resolve without explicitly introducing the concept of global, or multiprocessor I/O operations into the performance analysis. On the Paragon, one step in this direction might be to inquire about the I/O mode in force at the time a read or write is encountered (using the iomode() system call) and include that information in the trace data, where it could be used, together with timestamps, to provide guidance in the presentation of statistics. However, it would still be possible to overlook parallelism in many cases—for example, where an application manages distributed data by having each processor maintain its own file pointer and/or files. Ultimately, it may be necessary to obtain a picture of the I/O from the point of view of the file system rather than that of the computational processes. However, doing so would probably require modification of the operating system to add some tracing capability on the I/O processors, whereas the Pablo runtime system at present consists of libraries linked to the user's application. We hope that, as this Grand Challenge

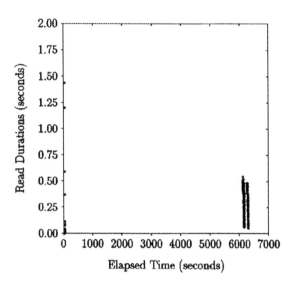

Figure 1.7: Read durations vs. elapsed time for the sophisticated version of the program.

project continues, it will be possible to explore developments of this nature.

1.6   Conclusions

We have described the use of the Pablo performance-analysis tool to characterize I/O in our parallel electron-molecule scattering application. As an early test of Pablo's I/O-analysis features in production-scale runs, this work revealed areas where improvement was needed in stability, scalability, and data presentation. We have illustrated how Pablo trace data are useful in understanding the relative performance of different I/O strategies for our application. Since I/O syntax on current MPPs makes it difficult for tools such as Pablo to identify the presence and the extent of parallelism in I/O, some care may be needed in deriving overall performance from per-processor trace statistics.

Acknowledgements

We would like to thank Dan Reed, Ruth Aydt, and the other members of the Pablo group for extensive assistance and advice on Pablo, and Al Bessey and Mahesh Rajan of Intel for insight into I/O on the Paragon's PFS and aid in benchmarking. The CSCC is supported in part by the National Science Foundation. We gratefully acknowledge support of our research by the National Science Foundation through the Grand Challenge project Parallel I/O Methodologies for I/O Intensive Grand Challenge Applicationsthe, Air Force Office of Scientific Research, and SEMATECH, Inc.

References

[1] DONGARRA, J. J., " Performance of Various Computers Using Standard Linear Equations Software," ORNL Tech. Rep. CS-89-85, available from `netlib.ornl.gov`.

[2] HIPES, P., WINSTEAD, C., LIMA, M., AND McKOY, V., "Studies of Electron-Molecule Collisions on the Mark IIIfp Hypercube," *Proceedings of the Fifth Distributed Memory Computing Conference, Volume I: Applications,* D. W. Walker and Q. F. Stout, Eds., IEEE Computer Society, Los Alamitos, CA, 1990, 498.

[3] HOLLINGSWORTH, R. J., quoted in Port, O., "Wonder Chips," *Business Week,* July 4, 1994, 86.

[4] NATIONAL RESEARCH COUNCIL, *Plasma Processing of Materials: Scientific Opportunities and Technological Challenges,* National Academy, Washington, D. C., 1991.

[5] REED, D. A., AYDT, R. A., MADHYASTHA, T. M., NOE, R. J., SHIELDS, K. A., AND SCHWARTZ, B. W., "An Overview of the Pablo Performance Analysis Environment," Tech. Rep., Univ. of Illinois at Urbana-Champaign, Dept. of Computer Science, 1992.

[6] TAKATSUKA, K. AND McKOY, V., "Extension of the Schwinger Variational Principle beyond the Static-Exchange Approximation," *Phys. Rev. A,* 1981, **24,** 2473.

Prospects of Solving Grand Challenge Problems

Rajan Gupta
Los Alamos National Laboratory
Los Alamos, New Mexico 87545

Abstract

The recent woes of the supercomputer industry and changes in federal funding have caused some scientists to re-evaluate the means by which they hope to solve Grand Challenge problems. In this paper, I evaluate the potential of Massively Parallel Processors (MPPs) within this context and the state of today's MPPs. I stress that for solving large-scale problems MPPs are crucial and that it is essential to seek a balance between CPU performance, memory access time, inter-node communications, and I/O. To achieve this it is important to preserve certain characteristics of the hardware while selecting the "hottest" processor to design the machine around. I emphasize that for long-term stability and growth of parallel computing, priority should be given to standardizing software so that the same code can run on different platforms and on machines ranging from clusters of workstations to MPPs.

1.1 Introduction

The premise that millions of simple off-the-shelf computers working together can provide a many-fold increase in computational power over conventional supercomputers and be more cost-effective has been the cornerstone of parallel computing since its inception. This maxim is as true today as it was in the early eighties. The challenges of MPPs have been in the development of efficient inter-node communication networks, fast memory access, and the software paradigms needed to program these machines efficiently. While the industry has made tremendous strides in both hardware and software, massively parallel machines are still not the obvious choice for large-scale applications. As a scientist who is interested in solving problems using MPPs and needs a factor of a thousand to a million times the computer power available today, I present my views on what it would take to get there.

There are five points to make. In Sec. 1.2, I present, as an example of successful code optimization, a strategy for lattice Quantum Chromodynamics (LQCD) calculations on the CM-5. The existing MPPs, CM-5, Cray T3D, and Intel Paragon, are compared in Sec. 1.3. I show that the performance of all current MPPs is limited by memory access time. In order to overcome this bottleneck in future MPPs, the CPU and memory design should support pipelined memory access and have register files of a minimum size, which my experience suggests should be at least 64 words long. The sociological reasons why MPPs have not been a resounding success are given in Sec. 1.4. The advantages and disadvantages of MPPs versus clusters of workstations are discussed in Sec. 1.5. I argue that large-scale fine-grained problems require the resources of an MPP, while clusters of workstations are best suited for coarse-grained problems, and I make a case for the dire need for common software that will allow problems to run on a variety of platforms, and on environments ranging from clusters of workstations to MPPs. In Sec. 1.6, I describe some of the ongoing LQCD-motivated projects to construct specialized MPPs in the teraflop (TFLOP) class. These special purpose computers (defined to be those built specifically to solve a limited class of problems) can have a significant impact on Grand Challenge problems and help in the development of MPP technology over the next few years. Finally, the conclusions are presented in Sec. 1.7.

1.2 Road Map to Optimization on the CM-5

I will give only a simplified view of LQCD calculations since this is a diverse audience. The core operation that constitutes the bulk ($> 90\%$) of computer time is a matrix multiply that can be done in parallel at each site (or at least on every red or black site) of the lattice

$$A = B + C * D$$

where A, B, C, D are 3×3 complex matrices. The matrix D has to be communicated from a nearest neighbor in every $1/4 - 3/4$ of the operations. The geometry of the lattice is a 4-dimensional hypercube with periodic boundary conditions. Today we can simulate $32^3 \times 64$ lattices. However, looking into the future, the systems we would like to simulate contain $100^3 \times 200$, i.e., $\approx 10^8 - 10^9$ points. The number of variables needed per point are approximately $100 - 200$. At each point the basic matrix operation has to be repeated $10^8 - 10^9$ times when working with what is called the quenched approximation, and $10^{12} - 10^{13}$ times with the full theory. This makes LQCD an extremely large data- and memory-intensive problem that will require (short of miraculous improvements in algorithms) petaflop-years of computational power to solve completely. Even with these conservative estimates I believe that LQCD will be within the scope of MPPs built using mass-produced hardware that will be available in the next decade or two.

LQCD is an extremely simple problem to parallelize. It requires only nearest-neighbor communications along the grid axes and the computation to communication ratio is relatively high. For every 24 bytes communicated, one typically performs 66 floating-point operations. In addition, all the code is user-developed. Past experience shows that it takes on the order of ten to twelve man-months to develop highly tuned codes for a new architecture. For these reasons LQCD calculations are always among the earliest users of an MPP and have provided significant guidance in developing and debugging both the hardware and the software.

Given the characteristics of LQCD, we chose to use the data parallel programming model on the CM-5, as it is simpler and therefore faster to implement than message-passing. Data parallel programming has the potential drawback that the user makes no distinction between points in the interior and those on the boundary of the sublattice stored in each processor. Thus, there are unnecessary memory moves when the nearest-neighbors of interior points are addressed. In a message-passing program one can circumvent this by having separate loops over interior and boundary points, but with some overhead due to the specialized array layouts. On the CM-5 it turns out that there is no difference in efficiency between data parallel versus message-passing versions of LQCD codes. The advantage of message-passing programs, as demonstrated by the MILC collaboration [3], is portability. Their code, initially developed for the Intel Paragon, ported successfully to the CM-5 and the Cray T3D with a few day's work.

Our program is written in CM Fortran (CMF) with all the computationally-intensive portions isolated into short subroutines. We choose CMF because (a) on the CM-5 it was the least "buggy" and most optimized compiler, (b) it was the most convenient language for the collaboration, and (c) it is adequate for our purposes, as we aimed to get performance by replacing the compute-intensive subroutines with CDPEAC (assembly language) versions. Keeping the overall control in CMF has allowed us to develop codes for new physics quickly and to incorporate algorithm changes with very little effort.

The routines that we converted to CDPEAC are short, typically 10 to 100 lines of code. We maintain both the CMF and CDPEAC versions of these modules and are thus able to make performance and integrity checks at any given time. The CDPEAC routines allow us to choose the vector length appropriate to each case, optimize loads and stores, and merge loads with flops efficiently. We find it efficient to load vectors as needed and do not pay any penalty compared to an optimization strategy in which a given vector is loaded only once and preserved in the registers until all the operations involving it are complete. The advantage of our approach is that the code and array layouts are much simpler and therefore easier to debug and modify.

As a result of CDPEAC optimization, the compute-intensive modules achieved $40 - 50$ Mflops/node on single adds or multiplies and $90 - 100$ Mflops/node on chained multiply-adds. The 25% loss in single node performance is due to the memory structure on the CM-5, i.e., DRAM page faults reduce the peak performance from 128 to 100 Mflops. Internode communications were implemented through CSHIFT as we were unable to improve upon this TMC-supplied communications routine. Communications reduced the overall sustained performance of our codes to between 25 and 35 Mflops/node. Another place where we were not able to come up with a reasonable optimization strategy is the case of masked operations. Masked operations in CMF are implemented only at the time of the final store, thus a red-black masking reduces the performance by a factor of roughly two.

The entire process of code development (50,000 lines of CMF) and CD-PEAC optimization took us ten man-months. We developed and optimized the code during the acceptance test period and were in full production mode by June, 1993, when the CM-5 at Los Alamos National Laboratory (LANL) was first made available for long runs. At that point our code was ≈ 4.5

times faster than the CM Fortran version. Significant compiler improve-ments brought this factor down to ≈ 2 by December, 1993, and there have not been any appreciable changes since.

To summarize, our optimization strategy on the CM-5 allowed us to get the best possible performance from day one and decoupled us from the day-to-day changes of the CMF compiler. We had the freedom to stay with a given working version of the compiler as we did not rely on it for performance. In addition to floating-point performance, the CM-5 has fast disk access to the shared-disk array (SDA) and a reasonable I/O bandwidth that allows us to write data to an Exabyte tape unit. This entire package (floating-point performance, SDA, and tape storage) is necessary in order to suc-cessfully undertake our Grand Challenge calculations. Looking beyond our interests alone, we feel that Thinking Machines Corporation has developed a high performance MPP that provides a stable production environment for a large class of Grand Challenge problems. Their departure from the hardware arena, therefore, is a tragedy for the nation as they were both the pioneers and leaders in MPP technology.

Since the general subject here is debugging and performance tools, it is perhaps mandatory that the question, "What tools would have made our task easier?" be addressed. There are two things we would have liked: first, that PRISM (the X-window based debugger) be available during the code development stage (Jan-May, 1993), and second, a better array of hardware diagnostic routines to identify chips that fail intermittently or under certain circumstances only. Other than CDPEAC optimization, we do not use any fancy constructs or try to push the limits of the CMF compiler. As a result we have needed the minimum in terms of debugging and performance analysis tools. PRISM is a remarkable debugging tool and, in the last year, we have often wondered why it is not available for UNIX workstations such as SUNs.

1.3 Comparison of Existing MPPs and the Lessons Learned

The three MPPs with which I am familiar are the CM-5, Intel Paragon, and the Cray T3D. Each of these uses a different custom-designed network and a different topology of interconnections between the nodes. In order to compare them, I give a brief description of their main features.

The CM-5 uses a custom-designed floating point accelerator (DASH chip) that also serves as the memory controller. Each node is controlled by a SPARC chip and the network is a fat tree. The communication bandwidth is realistically 10 Mbytes (MB)/sec and is the major bottleneck in the CM-5. The network interface (NI) and the network are proprietary while the memory and disks in the SDA are commercial commodities. The peak I/O bandwidth to the SDA is about 100 MB/sec and our codes sustain a significant fraction of it unless there is competition from other jobs. The peak speed per node is 128 Mflops while the LQCD codes sustain $\approx$ 30, the main limitation being internode communications.

The T3D is connected as a 3-dimensional toroidal grid with a data bandwidth of 300 MB/sec in each direction. Each node is controlled by a Digital Equipment Company (DEC) Alpha chip with a peak speed of 150 Mflops. The host processor is a YMP or a C-90; the attached disks are Cray DD301s which can sustain a transfer rate of 50-100 MB/sec depending on the configuration. The LQCD kernel sustains $\approx$ 60 Mflops on a single node with data restricted to fit in the cache, but only $\approx$ 25 Mflops when arrays were scaled up to realistic sizes. There is no chaining of adds and multiplies on the Alpha and for performance one needs to unroll the matrix multiply loops and separate multiply and add operations into two separate loops. Since the processor pipeline is six deep (it takes six cycles to get back the result), it is therefore difficult to optimize computations with only a 32-word register file. A positive feature is that the fast communications network makes the latency of on-node versus off-node memory access virtually identical. The bottom line is that, for large-scale problems, the potential of the Floating-Point Unit (FPU) is not realized due to the slow memory access.

The T3D is built out of mostly custom designed chips. The DEC Alpha is expensive and its power consumption is too high for large-scale packaging. Given that the performance of the T3D is limited by memory access time, I believe that it may serve CRI the interim purpose of getting a share of the market (largely based on the past reputation of their X-MP, Y-MP, and C-90 line) while developing the first round of parallel software, but eventually they will need to move to mass-produced technology if they hope to provide a cost-effective product in the teraflop range.

The Intel Paragon is arranged as a 2-dimensional mesh with a data bandwidth of 200 MB/sec/channel using a custom designed NI chip. The processor is the i860XP with a peak speed of 100 Mflops in single precision mode. The memory access is slow if data are not in cache or lie outside the 512-word page limit as there is a DRAM latency of 7-8 cycles for page faults. LQCD codes sustain ≈ 27 Mflops on a single node MILC. Internode communications are fast, and the performance stabilizes at ≈ 23 Mflops for 16 or more processors. The positive feature of the Intel i860 line has been that the codes are compatible between the older Intel machines, such as the Hypercube and Delta, and the Paragon. The critical drawback, so far, for large-scale calculations is that the I/O bandwidth to the outside world is very low.

Thus one finds that despite their completely different hardware and peak performance of the FPU, all three MPPs give roughly the same per node performance. The reason for this is that they are all limited by memory access or inter-node communications. The floating point unit can, in each case, process data much faster than the network can supply it. Looking at the last 10 years, it is clear that the increase in performance of the FPU has outstripped that of memory access and I/O, and this trend will continue. Thus, the emphasis for future hardware development should be on getting data to the registers efficiently rather than just on the peak rate of the FPU.

There are three features of the hardware that I believe are essential for getting performance. First, memory access needs a pipelined architecture. In most large-scale applications the efficiency of an intermediate-cache-based architecture is very low and requires significant hand tuning of code. Therefore, our preference is for pipelined access of main memory rather than through a cache. Second, the length of the pipeline required to hide the memory latency should dictate the length of the register file. Our present experience suggests that this length is eight, in which case the register file should be at least 64 words long. Lastly, data from neighboring elements are needed only as part of some calculation. The data should, therefore, go directly from the NI to the register file rather than through the processor's memory. I believe that imposing some standards with respect to these features would make the development of optimizing compilers possible and provide compatibility of software across platforms.

Another drawback is that each of these machines has a very large number of custom-designed and proprietary chips. As a result they are neither very cost-effective nor massively scalable machines.

Finally, the most critical point is that each of the three has its own proprietary software. The cost of developing the software is very high and the lag-time between the delivery of the hardware and efficient implementation of user codes is very large. The typical lag-time has been two years, while the lifetime of a given technology is roughly 3-4 years. On the Connection Machines, codes written in CMF port between the CM-200 and the CM-5 but the compilers are very different and routines optimized in the respective assembly languages are totally unportable. Intel has maintained the same software through their i860, Delta, and Paragon line, nevertheless they are still not able to deliver more than 25% efficiency for simple codes like LQCD. The delivery of the T3D started in late 1993 and its software environment is still evolving.

1.4 Why Have the MPPs Not "Succeeded?"

Why have the MPPs not had as much commercial success as some of us had expected? The demands on MPP vendors have been formidable. They have had to develop all the hardware and software in-house, and in addition teach potential customers how to use the machines. This has required a large investment in money and talent. They have also had to deliver a much more powerful machine than the best supercomputers in order to make it worthwhile for users to switch. Lastly, since the MPPs are supposed to be made of mass-produced chips, people expect performance to keep pace with the latest developments in technology. These demands would not be fatal if the revenue base for large-scale computing had grown.

To understand why this revenue base did not grow as expected, we need to understand the sociology of industrial, research, and commercial applications that "need" many orders of magnitude more computer power than that provided by workstations. The developers of these applications have been slow to adapt to MPPs, or worse still, have ignored them altogether. To present my perspective I would like to partition the use of computers for such large-scale projects into three categories—evolutionary, revolutionary, and research.

Evolutionary projects are those for which computations have been done for the last forty years on whatever machine was affordable. The problem has been incrementally scaled up in size as the computers became more powerful. The software base is, therefore, very large as it has been developed over a very long period of time and, unfortunately, all of it is for serial or, at best, for vector machines. The human investment needed to port these hundreds of millions of lines of code to MPPs is very large and, given the mode in which this type of computing has functioned, there is very little intellectual or financial pressure to migrate to MPPs. A very large proportion of industrial applications fall into this category.

Revolutionary projects require that the old way of doing business be discarded, as for example when a completely new product or process is needed. Also, the simulations needed to design this product may require many orders of magnitude more computer power than was previously available to the R&D group, necessitating new ideas and algorithms.

A prime example of the revolutionary use of computing is computer-assisted animations by the entertainment industry. The hardware best suited for this application seems to be a cluster of multi-processor Silicon Graphics machines. Since computer-assisted animations became fashionable almost at the same time as parallel computing, the software development effort has been, to a large extent, for parallel processing. More examples of industrial problems that require large-scale computing are given in Sec. 1.5 where clusters of workstations and MPPs are compared.

Research projects are, loosely speaking, those being addressed by scientists at universities and national labs and involve new algorithms and their implementation on emerging computer technologies. One would expect MPPs to have their initial impact here and that has indeed been true. These projects are largely funded by federal or state grants and the current climate of funding uncertainty has had a very negative impact. It is essential for the success of this technology, including its timely transfer to industry, that a sufficiently large pool of the state-of-the-art high performance machines be available to researchers for the development of the new generation of applications.

It is clear that the active participation of industry is needed, as universities and national labs do not provide a sufficiently large revenue base for three or even two MPP vendors to thrive. Unfortunately, the industrial world is, by and large, not revolutionary. For example, automobile manufacturers continue to produce essentially the same car year after year making only cosmetic changes. The managers and most of the scientists predate the MPP and are understandably not overly anxious to switch. Their reluctance to embrace a new technology is strengthened by the fact that all of the MPPs are significantly different, that there is a very large installation cost, and that there is no guarantee that a particular vendor will be around in a few years time. Also, the transfer of technology from academia to industry is proceeding at a rate that is very slow compared to the mean lifetime of an MPP. This is largely due to the long time required for the development, incorporating the latest algorithms, of a new generation of parallel codes for industrial applications. The situation should change significantly when the parallel codes being developed start producing significantly better data. Then the potential for revolutionary changes in design through simulations should become obvious. At that time industry will have no choice but to embrace and support this technology.

To summarize, a number of factors, including increased performance of workstations, lack of an easy migration path from existing serial code to MPPs, a large financial overhead in the development of system software, lack of stability amongst the MPP vendors, and a climate of uncertain funding situations, have contributed to a slow acceptance of MPPs as a vital technology. I feel that in the long run MPPs, and more generally, parallel computing, will dominate industrial design and production. It is therefore essential that MPP technology be adequately funded through the current development stage.

1.5 Closely Coupled MPP Versus Large Clusters of Workstations

There is widespread belief that MPP technology has yet to prove itself and that it is very expensive to convert codes that have been developed incrementally over the last 40 years to MPPs and, at the same time, there is a growing recognition that parallel computing is the way of the future. In the face of these conflicting beliefs, there has grown tremendous enthusiasm about the potential of large clusters of workstations. There are four reasons for this, (a) the power of individual workstations has grown by a factor of 100 in the last ten years, (b) there is a very large user base and a large number of third party software vendors, (c) there is no large setup cost to adding more nodes, and (d) workstations connected via the internet (or LANs) are idle for a very large fraction of the time and can be tapped into "for free" during that time. So let me discuss this resource from the perspective of solving LQCD and other fine-grained Grand Challenge problems.

Fundamentally, there is no conceptual difference between closely coupled MPPs and a very large cluster of workstations with regard to parallel computing. I will assume the ideal situation that both types of systems are made up of similar mass-produced chips and that communications are through message-passing. It is then clear that any code that can run on a cluster can run efficiently on an MPP, while the converse in not true for all problems, especially Grand Challenges. The question of efficiency includes cost, communication latency, and turnaround-time between the formulation of the problem and getting the final results. When evaluating the two, the focus should be on the ability to sustain the production environment appropriate for solving real problems and not just in a proof of principle.

The technical problem in parallel computing common to both platforms is in developing the software (operating system and compiler) that allows (a) efficient implementation of codes that are intrinsically parallel, (b) a production environment for problems that require many months equivalent of computing resources and have a significant amount of I/O to and from external storage devices, and (c) the most transparent migration path for existing serial codes to these environments. It is important to accept the underlying similarity of the two platforms and develop software that is common to both. I stress in the strongest possible terms that this should be the national goal. Once we can run the same problem on either platform, then the question of efficiency of a given platform can easily be decided by trial on a case by case basis.

My contention is that the problems best suited to run on a cluster of workstations are the very coarse-grained. I define these problems as ones that can run on a single (or few) workstations and produce the desired result in a reasonable amount of time, but have to be run thousands of times in order to gather statistics or explore a multi-dimensional parameter space. Each sub-problem is essentially independent of the other and generates only a small amount of information that needs to be saved at the end or communicated to the other processes. Examples are database searches, exploration of parameter space, statistical analysis of systems with a few tens of thousands of points or particles such as in biological molecules. It may well be that such problems constitute the bulk of society's computational needs today. I am therefore very optimistic that there exists a large commercial base to fund the development of software for clusters of workstations. So if we firmly commit to ensuring that this development effort is common to both clusters of workstations and MPPs, we have a cost-effective path to teraflop and petaflop computing.

Let me now present the characteristic of a number of problems that definitely need closely-coupled MPPs. First I will make the point using LQCD and then move on to problems of interest to industry.

LQCD: This is a statistical Monte Carlo problem. At present we are doing simulations using $32^3 \times 64$ lattices. For each data point we first generate 25 GB of data. The code for doing this requires 3 GB of memory and 100 GFLOP hours. This data set is then analyzed by ten different programs each using between 1-10 GB of memory and 10-25 Gflop hours. With 15% of the resources of a 1024 node CM-5 we can process 100 data points in a year. I am willing to make a wager that, in the next five years, a problem with similar characteristics, if simulated on a cluster of 256 workstations, will not yield 500 data points in one year. The only conditions on the wager are that the cluster is not used as a dedicated resource (otherwise an MPP is clearly more cost effective) and that the performance of each node is similar to what we see on the MPP today, i.e., less than or equal to 50 Mflops.

Comprehensive Hydrocode for Automotive Design (CHAD) [5]: The goals of this project are to simulate combustion inside cylinders, underhood cooling, external aerodynamics, and air conditioning. The code uses a fully unstructured 3D grid with $10^5 - 10^8$ elements and roughly 500 words of memory per element. The algorithm is based on full implicit integration. To simulate combustion inside the cylinders, each run requires $\sim 10^5$ flops per cycle and per element, where a run consists of about 500 cycles. Global communication is needed roughly 100 times in each cycle, i.e., it is a fine grained problem. A single run, corresponding to a fixed cylinder geometry and air/fuel ratio, with 10^5 elements would take roughly 300 hours on a workstation with a sustained performance of 20 Mflops. At present a sample of, say, 100 runs is used to answer a specific question about the working of a given cylinder. To design a new cylinder would take many orders of magnitude more computing power. The CHAD code is being designed and written for parallel machines. Thus it can be used for evolutionary (on a small cluster of workstations) or revolutionary (MPP) design development. Only time will tell how aggressively the auto industry will use such tools.

Casting of Large and Complex parts [4]: In many industrial processes it is necessary to model casting processes with geometries as large as a cubic meter while at the same time resolve structures on the scale of millimeters or less. The parallel algorithms being developed at LANL use a finite volume, semi-implicit computational fluid dynamics approach. The basic scheme requires the implicit solution of several parabolic and elliptic partial differential equations per computational cycle. For stability these computations need to be done in double precision. The lattice is a 3-D unstructured grid with $10^6 - 10^7$ cells. The number of words of data per cell are $200 - 300$. Data communications are global because of the unstructured grid and the implicit scheme. Typical CPU requirements are $50 - 100$ microseconds (MS) per cell per cycle on the CM-5, and a given run simulates flow for a duration of many seconds, i.e., many thousands of timesteps.

Another example of a fine grained problem that uses computational fluid dynamics methods is Process Chemistry. To simulate processes like metal and oil refining and aluminum smelting requires resources very similar to those described in the previous two examples.

Global Ocean Modeling [9] This code uses a 3D grid with roughly $1280 \times 1000 \times 20$ cells requiring 4.5 GB of memory. Each time step covers 30 minutes of ocean dynamics. A run evolves the state of the ocean over one month and requires roughly 8000 MFLOP hours. The communication of data between cells during a run is fine-grained. The data archived is ~ 50 GB per simulated year, and so far 30 years of ocean dynamics have been simulated. The spatial resolution is currently 31 kilometers (km) at the equator and they hope to reduce this to a few km. To get to this characteristic scale of ocean dynamics requires a thousandfold increase in computing power over what is currently available.

Lastly, let me describe the study of the large-scale structure of the universe as an example of an N-body problem [6]. A typical large gravitational N-body simulation contains 20 million mutually interacting particles. Through the use of "fast" approximate methods called treecodes, a simulation of about 1000 timesteps can be completed in around 30 hours on a 512-node Intel Paragon. The memory required is around 100-300 bytes per particle, which translates to six GB for a 20 million particle simulation. Since the force law is long-range, global communication is required among the processors. By careful coding of the algorithm, the non-local data can be reduced to as little as 10%. This still requires communication of roughly 1 MB of data per timestep (in several thousand messages of ~ 100 bytes) to each processor, giving a required bisection bandwidth of several hundred MB/sec.

To summarize, I believe that for the foreseeable future clusters of workstations will be the medium of choice for coarse-grained problems while MPPs will remain the more effective platform for very large, fine-grained problems such as the ones just described that need a dedicated production environment. This debate should in fact be irrelevant in the long run if we invest in system software, compilers, and computing paradigms that apply to both MPPs and clusters of workstations. In that case we will be ready to exploit the resources of both types of hardware and determine from experience which is more practical. Unfortunately, in the short term we are faced with a widespread belief that industry is not going to deliver the next generation MPP (teraflop capability) in the next few years or, if it does, it will be prohibitively expensive and not very reliable. Under these grim prospects for the availability of a large cost-effective MPP, what is the future for solving such Grand Challenge problems? The answer, in some cases, seems to be specialized research projects. In the next section I will briefly describe the on-going efforts to develop special-purpose machines to solve LQCD.

1.6   Special Purpose MPP for LQCD

Lattice QCD simulations have historically played a major role in the development of parallel computing. So it is no surprise that there are three major ongoing projects to deliver teraflop-scale computing capability. In each case the principle motivation for these projects is still LQCD. The software effort is minimal; it essentially stops at whatever is needed to run LQCD problems. The fact that a number of other Grand Challenge problems can be solved on these machines is an added bonus. Below, I give a brief description of each.

The CP-PACS project is based at Tsukuba University, Japan [7]. This is a joint undertaking between computer scientists and physicists at Tsukuba University and Hitachi Ltd. The processor is custom-designed, based on the super-scalar Hewlett Packard PA-RISC 1.1 chip, but with enhancements. They have introduced slide window registers and preload and poststore instructions in order to overcome memory latency. The memory (DRAM) is pipelined by multi-interleaved banks and a storage controller. The communication is via a 3D hyper-crossbar — x-direction, y-direction, and z-direction crossbars — so that a maximum of three switches are needed for any transfer. The message-passing is through wormhole routing and there is an option for global synchronization. The full machine will consist of 1024 nodes (they may increase the number of nodes depending on funding) with a peak speed of 300 GFLOPS, 500 GB of RAID5 disks, and an expected availability by mid-1996.

The APEmille project is based at Rome University, Italy [1]. This is a follow up on the Ape 100 project which is currently being marketed by Alenia Spatzio. The topology of the APEmille is a 3D torus. The programming paradigm is SIMD complemented with a local addressing feature. Each processing board consists of 8 nodes arranged in a $2 \times 2 \times 2$ topology. By having 2 multipliers and 2 adders per node they hope to achieve 200 MFLOP performance with a 50 MHz clock. Each node will have 2-8 megawords (MW) of memory and can directly address the memory of its 6 neighbors through a communication device. To achieve a high I/O bandwidth each set of 128 nodes is connected to disks and peripherals through a host workstation with a 100 MB/s transfer rate. The time frame for completion of this machine is 1998.

I would like to dwell on the lone U.S. entry, the 0.5 teraflop project [2]. This project is based at Columbia University and is the most cost-effective. It uses a really mass produced chip, the Texas Instruments digital signal processor (DSP) TMS320C31, for 32 bit floating point operations with a per-unit price of $\sim$ \$50. The DSP comes with a C compiler, consumes only one Watt of power, and has peak performance of 50 Mflops. The big drawback is that the DSP does not have an operating system; however one expects to see 64-bit DSPs with more functionality in the near future. Each node is laid out on a $2.7'' \times 1.7''$ card mounted on a mother board through standard SIMM connectors. It consists of three elements, the DSP, a node gate array, and 2 MB of DRAM as shown in Figure 1.1. The only custom chip is the node gate array which serves as the memory controller and the network switch, and has a specialized cache for pre-loads. The DSP has some direct memory access (DMA) capability. The total power consumption of the node is about two Watts. To get to teraflop scale requires 16K processors which are mounted on 256 boards, each with 64 processors. Thus, by my criteria, this machine is pretty close to an ideal MPP in terms of its simplicity, mass-produced components, and packaging. The machine can be ready by 1996 for a projected \$3 million in development cost and hardware. The extreme simplicity of this design is made possible because this machine is expected to solve only one problem; nevertheless, if funded and successful, this project will demonstrate that a system with 16K processors can provide a reliable production environment with current technology.

In addition to these three ongoing projects there is a proposal for a Multidisciplinary Teraflops project centered at M.I.T. [8]. This is an outgrowth of an earlier LQCD project and a collaboration with Thinking Machines Corporation. The goal of the scientists was to concentrate on the design of a single element −− the embedded accelerator. The accelerator design would use commodity products and be more general purpose, i.e., be efficient for a number of large-scale problems. Sixteen of these accelerators (each capa-

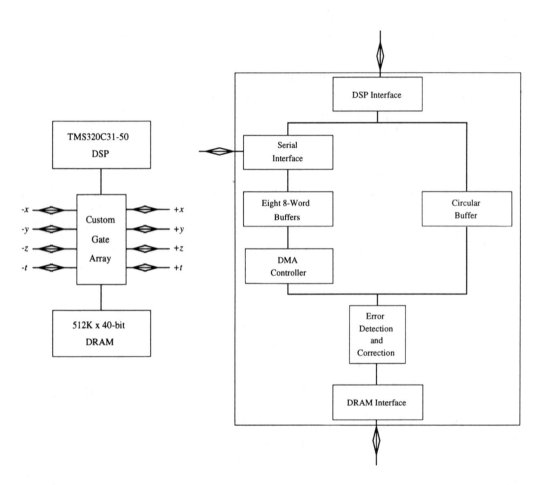

Figure 1.1: Schematic of *a* the node and *b* the custom gate array of the 0.5 Teraflop project.

ble of sustaining 200 Mflops) would be attached to a node on the follow-up machine to the CM-5 and piggy-back on TMC's message-passing software. The project would use the next generation Connection Machine network for communications, which was supposed to sustain 500 MB/sec transfer rate per node. Since there is not going to be a follow-on machine to the CM-5, this project is stalled until an alternate network can be found that suits the purpose.

I believe that the characterization "special purpose" or "general purpose" and the debate surrounding it should not be made a central issue in the development of large-scale computing. In a sense all machines are special-purpose in that they do some problems much better than others. In serial machines one does not complain about this because the software is common and issue is only of efficiency. In the field of MPPs, the industry is still searching for solutions to problems of hardware reliability, software paradigms, communications, and I/O speed in addition to those of efficiency. In this semi-research environment we should learn what works from every successful project and move on.

If any or all of the above projects deliver close to projected performance, then they will have set new standards which the commercial vendors will find hard to ignore. However, to convert this success into a general-purpose commercial product will depend on developments in software. It is therefore essential that the software development effort is not platform-specific, and is common to clusters of workstations and MPPs. If this goal is achieved then it will be simpler to harness the ever-growing hardware capability, and allow an enterprising company to develop a cost-effective teraflop scale MPP by the end of this decade. Otherwise, the investment for developing the software and for educating the user community will remain too high for a startup company.

1.7 Speculations and Conclusions

Let me conclude with a few remarks concerning first software and then hardware. It is absolutely essential to push for common software for both MPPs and clusters of workstations. It is in the long-term interest of all vendors to make a joint effort to provide mutually compatible software. In fact this should be a national strategy and given the highest priority by MPP vendors.

The most cost-effective migration path for existing serial codes to a parallel environment is via a small cluster of workstations as it avoids the initial expense of buying an MPP. If the software is common to both platforms. then the problems best suited for MPPs can exploit that technology cost-effectively and without interruption at the appropriate stage in code development.

Since this workshop is taking place so soon after the upheaval at Thinking Machines, it is difficult to avoid speculating on what the future of MPPs would have been with them around. For those of us who have known many of the people involved in developing the Connection Machines and have worked closely with them, the breaking up of the company has been very disheartening. On a more impersonal level, it is a national tragedy that will set back parallel computing for some time to come. The biggest legacy of the pre-1994 Thinking Machines is the software. In my opinion, their CMF compiler is the best implementation of data parallel computing while the CMMD library is the cleanest and has the largest functionality for message-passing codes. Even more importantly, they were close to having a synthesis of the two, i.e., global array declarations with facility for doing either message-passing or data parallel computing. The efforts towards this synthesis should be pursued vigorously as it fits into the long term goal of a common software. In terms of TMC's contribution to tools for program development, PRISM is by far the best debugger I have used. To summarize, I believe that, if TMC closes shop completely, then it is vital that every effort be made to preserve their software investment and to work towards making it available on a variety of platforms.

Concerning hardware there are two issues that I would like to stress. First, in all problems that I am familiar with, the data to be communicated are needed immediately afterwards for computations and do not need to be stored in memory first. It is therefore important that we figure out efficient ways of removing the unnecessary stores and loads. Second, the biggest bottleneck in obtaining high performance on today's MPP is moving data between memory (local or off-node) and the register files. It would therefore help tremendously in the design and long term stability of optimizing compilers if memory access were pipelined and the size and characteristic of register files were standardized. Today's technology shows that high efficiency in loads and stores can be achieved with a pipe of length eight. In that case a register file that is at least 64 words long would be needed to implement a complex $A + B \times C$ efficiently. Another very useful way to hide the communication without latency would be to allow for pre-fetches and stores in memory via DMA so that it could be done without interrupting computations.

It is common knowledge among those who have simulated very large systems that it is very easy to compute for long periods of time but extremely difficult to store, restore, or frequently access large data files. I/O to disks and storage media is a major limiting factor today and will continue to be the Achilles heel as the disparity between FPU speed and data bandwidth to various peripherals grows. It seems like it will take a miracle to get these two aspects of computing balanced without developing equally efficient parallel I/O to disk and peripherals.

What can we look forward to? Pundits who study the computer market forecast that the entertainment industry will drive I/O capability, PC's and simple control processors will drive improvements in speed and packaging of components like memory and CPU, and signal processing will provide ways of increasing communication bandwidth. I would like to add that Grand Challenge problems should be used as the motivation for the design of the glue, i.e., the software paradigms and fast inter-node communications strategies to produce cost-effective MPPs with teraflop and petaflop capabilities. I am totally convinced that parallel computing will be the platform on which all large-scale computations are done in the future. It is therefore my wish and sincere hope that commercial vendors will accept some common standards and strive towards a common software.

Acknowledgements

I thank Ann Hayes and Margaret Simmons for inviting me to participate in this workshop, and Andy White for prodding the large-scale users at LANL to think about the future of high performance computing. I also thank Rich Brower, Doug Kothe, Bob Malone, Bob Mawhinney, Manjit Sahota, Doug Toussaint, A. Ukawa and Mike Warren for providing information about their projects, and Tanmoy Bhattacharya, Ralph Brickner and Wendy Schaffer for discussions. I gratefully acknowledge the tremendous support provided by the Advanced Computing Lab at Los Alamos. The simulations of QCD described here would not have been possible without the resources of the CM-5 at LANL and I thank DOE for a Grand Challenges allocation. The CD-PEAC optimizations of LQCD were carried out by my collaborator Tanmoy Bhattacharya.

References

[1] APEMILLE, information is available on WWW from `http://chimera.roma1.infn.it` by following the topic "Ape Preprints."

[2] ARSENIN, I., et al., *Nucl. Phys. B* (Proc. Suppl.), **34**, 1994, 820.

[3] BERNARD, C., OGILVIE, M. C., DEGRAND, T. A., DETAR, C., GOTTLIEB, S., KRANSITZ, A., SUGAR, R. L., AND TOUSSAINT, D., MILC collaboration. For details please contact Doug Toussaint at doug@klingon.physics.arizona.edu.

[4] For further details please contact Doug Kothe at dbk@lanl.gov.

[5] For further details please contact Manjit Sahota at sahota@lanl.gov.

[6] For further details please contact Mike Warren at msw@qso.lanl.gov.

[7] IWASAKI, Y., *Nucl. Phys. B* (Proc. Suppl.), **34**, 1994, 78; UKAWA, A., *Nucl. Phys. B* (Proc. Suppl.), **42**, 1995, 194.

[8] *Multidisciplinary Teraflop Project*, a copy of the proposal can be obtained from Prof. John Negele (negele@mitlns.mit.edu), Physics Department 6-308, M.I.T., Cambridge, MA 02139.

[9] SMITH, R., DUKOWICZ, J., AND MALONE, R., *Physica D*, **60**, 1992, 38. For more information contact Rick Smith at rds@lanl.gov

A Practical Approach to Portability and Performance Problems on Massively Parallel Supercomputers

David M. Beazley
Department of Computer Science
University of Utah
Salt Lake City, Utah 84112

Peter S. Lomdahl
Theoretical Division
Los Alamos National Laboratory
Los Alamos, New Mexico 87545

Abstract

We present an overview of the tactics we have used to achieve a high-level of performance while improving portability for a large-scale molecular dynamics code, SPaSM. SPaSM was originally implemented in ANSI C with message-passing for the Connection Machine 5 (CM-5). In 1993, SPaSM was selected as one of the winners in the IEEE Gordon Bell Prize competition for sustaining 50 Gflops on the 1024-node CM-5 at Los Alamos National Laboratory [8]. Achieving this performance on the CM-5 required rewriting critical sections of code in CDPEAC assembler language. In addition, the code made extensive use of CM-5 parallel I/O and the CMMD message-passing library. Given this highly specialized implementation, we describe how we have ported the code to the CRAY T3D and high performance workstations. In addition we will describe how it has been possible to do this using a single version of source code that runs on all three platforms without sacrificing any performance. Sound too good to be true? We hope to demonstrate that one can realize both code performance and portability without relying on the latest and greatest prepackaged tool or parallelizing compiler.

1.1   Introduction

One of the promises of massively parallel supercomputing has been its ability to open up whole new areas of exciting computational challenges for scientists in a wide range of fields from physics to medicine. However, as research in the last decade has shown, tackling new problems on parallel machines also requires one to rethink old algorithms and learn new programming techniques to make use of the parallel programming environment. While parallel machines have been promoted as having very high performance, more often than not getting high performance on a particular machine is much more difficult than most vendors would like one to believe. For this reason, many researchers have sounded the call to develop a standardized set of parallel programming tools and languages to make parallel programming easier [5].

Unfortunately it seems that many of the efforts to develop tools and languages have sacrificed code performance in favor of portability or ease of use. Often times, solutions are overengineered or not realistically applicable to the problem at hand. Given the fact that the main motivation for using a parallel machine in the first place is to get high performance for solving a large-scale problem, compromising performance in favor of using a completely overengineered tool or language claiming to do everything seems unacceptable.

In this paper we present an overview of our real-life experiences developing an application code for the CM-5 and later porting it to the CRAY T3D and workstations. During our code development, we found the state of parallel programming tools/language development to be disappointing at best and of little consequence whatsoever to the final outcome of our project. Rather than relying on others to make the latest and greatest parallelizing compiler or tool, we adopted an aggressive approach of doing everything ourselves using whatever means available on any given machine. As we will show, this approach has not only greatly simplified code development, but it has allowed us to achieve a high degree of code portability without sacrificing performance. It has also allowed us to keep up with the extremely rapid pace of computing technology since we have not had to rely on specialized tools to be developed for every machine we decide to use. While tool developers have the best of intentions, it is our belief that high code performance does not come for free. It never has in the past and it will not in the future (if you do not believe this, consider the difficulty of getting 30% of the peak performance solving a real problem on your desktop workstation). Furthermore, we contend that no compiler or tool is going to understand your problem as well as you do. With all of the disclaimers now out of the way, we hope that our approach will provide an alternative to application programmers who are disappointed with the current state of parallel programming tools or languages.

1.2 Molecular Dynamics and the Need for Speed

Our research interests have been in the area of large-scale molecular dynamics in order to study the dynamical properties of materials such as fracture, dislocation dynamics, and ductile-brittle transition. The idea behind an MD simulation is really quite simple: one solves Newton's equations of motion $F = ma$ directly for a large collection of N atoms [1]. To simplify this general N-body problem for materials simulations, we assume each atom only interacts with other atoms that are nearby. Thus, a cutoff distance r_{max} is specified and any atoms that are further away from each other than r_{max} do not interact (this is valid in many materials due to screening effects). While a short-range molecular dynamics simulation greatly simplifies the problem, we are still faced with a considerable computational challenge due to relatively short length and time scales accessible. Realistic simulations must often involve a very large number of atoms and be run for a large number of timesteps. Atoms may also interact according to complicated many-body potentials. The details of our algorithm are not discussed here, but they can be found in [3, 4, 8].

One of the goals of our work has been to model macroscopic properties in materials. This problem is especially difficult considering the fact that a speck of dust can contain considerably more than a billion (10^9) atoms.

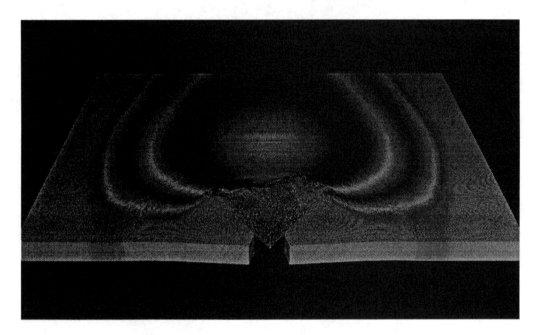

Figure 1.1: Fracture experiment with 104,031,072 atoms. See color plate XXXI.

Simulations with more than a billion atoms are still out of reach today, but there has been considerable interest in developing codes capable of simulating more than 100 million atoms on parallel machines [7, 9, 4, 8, 6]. To date, the largest test simulation, which we recently performed on a 1024-node CM-500, involved million atoms.

Figure 1.1 shows a snapshot from a recent fracture experiment involving a plate of 104,031,072 atoms (roughly $1620 \times 1620 \times 40$ atoms) While this may seem like a lot of atoms, this plate would only be about 0.3 microns wide with a thickness of 0.008 microns (as a sidenote, it is interesting to point out that it is now possible to produce integrated circuits with these length scales so such simulations are nearly large enough to provide direct comparison with experiment). In the experiment, a notch is placed in the side of the plate and the plate pulled apart under a constant strain rate of 0.002. This is done by introducing an initial velocity profile and slowly expanding the boundaries in the x-direction. There are periodic boundary conditions in the x and z directions. The atoms interact according to a tabulated short-range pair-potential. As the simulation progresses, the plate fractures when the overall strain reaches approximately 4%.

This simulation required more than 150 hours of CPU time on a 512 processor CM-5 and used 11.6 Gbytes of RAM. A total of 8550 timesteps were performed with each timestep requiring approximately 58.7 seconds. Of that time, 21.3 seconds were spent handling the 14473 message-passing operations performed by each node in a single step. In addition, the code performed 906 gigabytes of file I/O and presented massive visualization problems as each output file was more than 1.6 Gbytes in size. Visualization was performed by Mike Krogh of the Advanced Computing Laboratory using a 256-node CM-5.

Hopefully, by now we have convinced the reader that simulations with more than 100 million atoms present a formidable computational problem involving a significant number of computation, communication, I/O, and visualization complications. Even more sobering is physical reality. A 100 million atom simulation is still a pretty small simulation when compared to real materials. Furthermore, 8550 timesteps only corresponds to approximately 85 picoseconds of real time. Lastly, this simulation used a relatively simple inter-atomic interaction. Simulating materials such as metals or silicon will require many-body potentials. We have implemented several of these potentials and to provide a point of comparison, performing a similar experiment with silicon would have required more than 1100 hours of CPU time on a 512 node CM-5. Considering the fact that we would like to perform billion-atom simulations over several nanoseconds, we will clearly need a rather substantial improvement in computing power. Of course it is becoming increasingly clear that we are not going to be able to perform an MD simulation of the 10^{25} atoms in a glass of beer anytime in the foreseeable future [11].

1.3 Portability Issues

In developing our CM-5 code, code portability was a non-issue. We used any means possible to get high performance on the CM-5 including optimizations to improve communications overhead and CDPEAC assembler to use the vector units [4]. This was certainly justified considering the 30 million dollar cost of the CM-5 and our desire to see what kinds of problems could be performed on such a machine. Recently, we were faced with porting this code from the CM-5 to the T3D. This section describes our approach which focuses on three main areas: eliminating CPDEAC, fixing the message-passing, and solving the I/O headache.

1.3.1 Eliminating CDPEAC

Ironically, our choice to use CDPEAC on the CM-5 made our code more portable than if we had used CMF or C*. The approximately 1000 lines of CDPEAC assembler code were isolated to only a few code modules and the original C code was still available. Thus, removing the CDPEAC simply required adding a few conditional compilation directives and making a few small code modifications. This required less than an hour of effort and resulted in a code that was entirely written in ANSI C. ANSI C is supported on virtually every machine we are aware of, so it is easily portable.

1.3.2 Fixing the Message-Passing

In order to run on the T3D we needed to change all of our message-passing from CMMD to a combination of PVM and Cray shared-memory. Since CMMD has substantially more functionality than PVM, it was going to be moderately difficult to change all of the code to use a new library. Rather than taking this approach, we decided it would be easier to implement our own message-passing wrapper library for the CMMD functions we used. The idea here is very simple: rename each CMMD call in the code (we replaced "CMMD" by the word "SPaSM" in the function names). The new "functions" are then implented using a combination of macros and C code. Thus on the T3D, we simply implemented the functionality of the CMMD functions listed in Table 1.1 using a combination of PVM and shared memory. On the CM-5, this wrapper library is a set of macros.

This approach simplified the porting process considerably. The wrapper library could be developed and tested independently of the production code. When the library was complete, it was linked with the production code and we were able to run SPaSM on the T3D within a few minutes. The I/O capabilities were still horribly broken (see next section), but we were able to verify the correct operation of the code and run a few simple test cases. While writing our own message-passing library may seem complicated, bringing the code up on the T3D required the effort of one person working for 3 days. This effort included the time to learn how to use PVM and the CRAY T3D C compiler.

1.3.3 The I/O Headache

Our CM-5 code made extensive use of the parallel I/O capabilities provided by the CMMD library. In CMMD, four basic I/O modes are possible. In CMMD_local mode, each node can manipulate files independently of the other nodes. In CMMD_independent mode each node opens the same file, but the nodes can read or write the file independently although some care must usually be made when writing. CMMD_sync_bc (synchronous broadcast) mode allows all nodes to manipulate files as if a single process were running. For example, if all nodes execute an `fprintf` statement in this mode, only one copy of the output will appear (as if printed by a single process). This mode is particularly useful for reading input parameters from files or standard input, as the data read are automatically broadcast to all of the nodes. Finally, CMMD_sync_seq (synchronous sequential) mode allows the nodes to write large amounts of data in parallel to devices such as the scalable disk array (SDA). In this mode, each node will write the contents of a local buffer to a single file in node order. Node 0 will write data, followed by node 1, node 2, etc... This is particularly useful for saving results and later restarting as this mode provides the highest possible bandwidth to parallel I/O devices.

Unfortunately, the T3D supports none of these modes. This leads to all sorts of bizarre I/O behavior unless one makes some rather substantial code modifications. Early versions of our T3D code provided little or no I/O support (many features were simply removed to get the code to compile at all). Any I/O that was provided was patched together using numerous conditional compilation directives and other hacks. Finding this situation unacceptable, we eventually decided to write our own I/O library much in the same spirit as our message-passing wrapper library. Our I/O library copied the functionality of the CM-5 code. In order to provide support for different I/O modes, we had to implement wrappers around the UNIX file

Table 1.1		
Required CMMD Functions		
CMMD_send_block	CMMD_receive_block	CMMD_send_noblock
CMMD_send_and_receive	CMMD_reduce_int	CMMD_reduce_double
CMMD_sync_with_nodes	CMMD_set_global_or	CMMD_get_global_or
CMMD_msg_pending	CMMD_all_msgs_done	

operations and CMMD extensions shown in Table 1.2.

Providing fully functional I/O support required a somewhat more complicated programming effort than before. The final library consisted of more than 1000 lines of ANSI C code. In order to mimic CMMD parallel I/O operations, the library maintains a list of open files and the I/O "mode" of each file. According to the file mode, nodes may coordinate in message-passing operations in order to properly read or write files. For example, file pointers and other information will be passed around to ensure that files are written properly. Similarly, when reading from standard input, node 0 will actually perform the read but will broadcast the data to all of the other nodes, mimicking the behavior of the CM-5. This all occurs behind the scenes so the actual source code does not have to worry about the details of how each I/O mode is implemented on a particular machine. While the I/O library is fairly complex, the entire library was implemented in less than week and provided a working solution to one of the major obstacles preventing real production work on the T3D.

1.3.4 General Comments and Results

This approach of writing our own message-passing and I/O wrappers has dramatically improved code portability across many different platforms. Shortly after porting the code to the T3D, we were able to bring the code up on a single processor workstation in a simulated message-passing environment (the code thinks it is doing message-passing, but the wrapper library simply copies buffers around). In addition, we were able to run the code on a multiprocessor SPARCcenter 2000 running Solaris using a shared-memory multithreaded approach.

It is extremely important to emphasize that we use only one version of source code that compiles on all platforms. The only difference between machines is the wrapper library used. When running on the CM-5, we use the CM-5 wrapper library. On the T3D we use the T3D wrapper. This has greatly simplified code maintenance and debugging since new code modules

Table 1.2		
UNIX and CMMD File Operations in I/O Library		
fprintf	fscanf	read
write	fopen	open
fgets	CMMD_set_open_mode	CMMD_set_io_mode
CMMD_fset_io_mode		

can be developed on a single processor workstation and later run on the CM-5/T3D without modification. This has proved to be especially useful considering the reliability and uptime of most massively parallel machines. As further proof of the effectiveness of this approach, a new code module for modeling silicon was developed entirely on a CM-5E over a period of several months. This code compiled and produced the correct results on the T3D without a single code modification.

Lastly, we should point out that this approach has resulted in no performance penalty. In fact, CM-5 performance improved slightly due to better code organization. The CDPEAC kernels are also still available due to the modular design. On other machines, by writing our own wrapper libraries we are able to optimize communications and I/O without affecting the main source code. Recently, our original PVM based message-passing library was replaced by a new library that used the Cray shared-memory library entirely. This resulted in a factor of four performance increase in communication speed.

1.4 Performance Issues

While portability is nice, we have not lost sight of our real goal of getting the highest performance possible. We have taken a rather aggressive approach to performance optimization on most machines. We are skeptical that any compiler is going to magically be able to map our problem onto the machine in such a way that we get high performance. Furthermore, we do not want to always be waiting for better tools or compilers in order to run fast. While it may seem crazy to some people, we argue that the best way to get high performance is to understand the underlying architecture of the machine. In particular, an understanding of superscalar RISC microprocessors will be extremely useful as this type of processor is used in most parallel machines today.

1.4.1 A Self-Evaluation

Prior to the installation of the T3D at Los Alamos, we knew that getting high performance would depend on how effectively we could use the DEC Alpha in the T3D processing nodes. With this in mind, we set out on a mission to answer the question "How well does our C code use the SPARC processor on the CM-5?" We assumed if we could not use the SPARC very

Table 1.3		
Dynamic distribution of instructions executed.		
Instruction type	Cycles	%
LOAD	33703588	32.0%
FP (floating point)	27908776	26.5%
ALU (integer)	18874774	17.9%
STORE	14585631	13.8%
CONTROL (branches)	7079666	6.7%
NOP (no operation)	3234324	3.1%
Total	105386759	100.0%

well we probably would not be able to do very well on the Alpha either. To our knowledge, this question had never be addressed in any great detail on the CM-5 since most efforts were focused on using the vector units. Our goal was to see if we could understand our code's behavior before running on the T3D. Most of this work has been described in [2] so many of the details will be omitted here.

Since our application was dominated by the force computation, we extracted this part of the code so we could analyze it in detail. To analyze the code, we dumped the assembler output from the compiler and studied it with a SPARC achitecture manual in hand [10]. By running a small test problem, we were able to determine a dynamic instruction profile as shown in Table 1.3 and the timing breakdown in Table 1.4. In addition, we developed a simple cache simulator of the 64K direct-mapped cache that produced the results in Table 1.5 for the same test problem.

By performing this analysis we find that our C code is spending nearly 65% of its time stalling the processor. Most of these stalls are created by memory accesses which result in particularly bad performance on the SPARC since every memory access stalls the pipeline by 1-2 cycles (regardless of whether it is a cache miss or hit). Fortunately our cache simulator indicates a low cache miss rate. This is also suggested by Table 1.4 as nearly 90% of the time can be accounted for (executing instructions, known memory stalls and stalls on the floating point unit).

Table 1.4 Time Distribution of Code Activity			
	Num cycles	Time (sec)	%
Executing useful instructions	105386759	3.19	36%
Memory access stalls	109000000	3.30	37%
Floating point stalls	47000000	1.42	16%
Unknown stalls	33000000	1.00	11%
Total		8.91	100.0%

1.4.2 Performance Strategies

The fact that our code stalls the processor 65% of the time on the SPARC suggests several serious performance problems. The most significant of these problems is the fact that every double-precision load causes a 2 cycle stall on the pipeline [10]. This suggests that one should try to reduce memory operations as much as possible. While this may sound obvious, it is surprising to learn how many unnecessary memory operations are performed in a code. For example, in one section of code, a feature to improve modularity resulted in a series of unncessary floating point and memory operations that were executed in about 80% of the iterations in a particular loop. Working around this problem resulted in a 58% overall code speedup. Furthermore, any variables referenced by pointers in C will never be stored into registers and reused. Thus, speedups can be obtained by copying commonly used variables into local variables first (which will place values into registers). The performance strategies we have used are listed below :

- Reduce memory operations.

- Reorder floating point.

- Inlining.

- Increased use of local variables.

- Loop unrolling.

These optimizations are widely known and are probably familiar to most users. One could argue that these optimizations should be performed by the compiler. Yet, by applying these tactics directly to the code, we get huge speedups even when compiling with full compiler optimization. It seems clear that one will almost always be able to beat the compiler at these things if one is clever. It is important to note that all of these optimizations can be made to the C code (no assembler code required).

1.4.3 Performance Results

By applying the above strategies to our CM-5 code, we achieve a 119% speedup. Even more remarkable is the fact that the C code now only runs 2.2 times slower than the CDPEAC code even though the peak performance of the VUs is more than 20 times higher than that of the SPARC. When the same code is run on the CM-5E which uses a 40 Mhz SuperSPARC, we get a 95% speedup and the C code actually runs 5% faster than the CDPEAC code. This rather startling fact certainly leads us to wonder whether using the VUs was really worth the effort required. One of the difficulties in using the VUs is that vectorizing an inherently unstructured calculation is always going to result in extra work being performed. Clearly the difficulty in effectively using the VUs cannot be understated.

On the T3D, the same performance strategies result in a 183% speedup. As a result, the code sustains calculation rates between 27-41 Mflops/node which represents 18-27% of the peak performance. This is better performance than most other T3D applications that we are currently aware of.

As proof that the same optimizations can result in speedups on other RISC machines, Table 1.6 shows the performance speedups on a variety of platforms. In all cases, code was compiled with full compiler optimization. We see large speedups in all cases.

Table 1.5					
Simulated Cache Performance					
	Total	Hits	%	Miss	%
Instruction Fetch	104907504	104851000	(99.9%)	56504	(0.1%)
Data Fetch	33280936	33123800	(99.5%)	157136	(0.5%)
Stores	14552064	14536988	(99.9%)	15076	(0.1%)

1.5 Conclusions

While tool and language developers have the the best of intentions, we hope we have demonstrated that both portability and performance are possible by simply taking a direct approach to the problem. Probably the best approach is to keep program development simple and straightforward. By programming in ANSI C, we have been able to focus our entire effort on effectively using the machine rather than always trying to figure out how to use a new set of compiler directives or tools for every new machine that comes along. By using wrapper libraries, we have been able to eliminate hardware dependencies from the main source code resulting in simplified code maintenance and debugging since only one version of source code is used for all machines. This simplified approach actually makes performance tuning easier because we do not need to worry about the extra layers of abstraction that a parallelizing compiler or tool would add. Instead, we have one simple task—making the RISC processor run as fast as possible. As it turns out, tactics for making code run fast on one RISC architecture seem to be quite effective at producing speedups on other RISC architectures so this effort is not wasted.

Lastly, we would like to close with a philosophical note. As scientists working on a problem, our approach has given us almost complete control over all aspects of our problem. With the complexity of modern machines, this is extremely important because we are able to understand virtually all aspects of our code from the algorithms used to their mapping onto the underlying hardware. Without this knowledge, we do not see how we could believe any answers generated (it is not clear whether anyone should believe any results generated on a parallel machine in the first place considering their "proven" reliability). How could an experimental chemist or physicist believe the outcome of an experiment if they did not understand all aspects of the laboratory techniques used to generate the data? Why should computational science be any different? We firmly believe that this is important and hope that users and software developers realize that a "black-box" approach is not necessarily the best or only way to use a parallel machine.

Acknowledgements

We would like to acknowledge the many people who have provided assistance with this work. Adam Greenberg, Mark Bromley, Mike Drumheller, Denny

Table 1.6 Performance of Production Code on a Test Problem (time in seconds)				
System	N	Unmodified	Optimized	Speedup
32 Node CM-5 (33 Mhz SPARC)	1024000	42.63	19.54	119%
32 Node CM-5 (CDPEAC)	1024000		8.87	
32 Node CM-5E (40 Mhz SuperSPARC)	1024000	11.37	5.83	95%
32 Node CM-5E (CDPEAC)	1024000		6.11	
32 Node T3D (150 Mhz DEC Alpha)	1024000	8.57	3.03	183%
HP-735 (99 Mhz HP-PA 7100a)	32000	4.62	1.61	187%
IBM Power2 (66 Mhz Rios 2)	32000	4.98	1.9	155%

Dahl, and Burl Hall of Thinking Machines Corporation provided major assistance with our questions about the CM-5 architecture and making performance measurements on the CM-5E. Wayne Vieira of Cray Research has provided valuable assistance with the T3D. We would also like to acknowledge the Advanced Computing Laboratory for its generous support and Dave Rich for his ongoing assistance. We acknowledge Mike Krogh for his visualization work and our collaborators in molecular dynamics research, Niels Grønbech-Jensen, Pablo Tamayo, Brad Holian, and Timothy Germann. This work was performed under the auspices of the U.S. Department of Energy.

References

[1] ALLEN, M. P.AND TILDESLEY, D. J., *Computer Simulations of Liquids*, Clarendon Press, Oxford, 1987.

[2] BEAZLEY, D. M. AND LOMDAHL, P. S., "A Practical Analysis of Code Performance on High Performance Computing Architectures," Los

Alamos National Laboratory Report (preprint), 1994.

[3] BEAZLEY, D. M. AND LOMDAHL, P. S., "Message-Passing Multi-Cell Molecular Dynamics on the Connection Machine 5," *Parall. Comp.*, **20**, 1994, 173-195.

[4] BEAZLEY, D. M., LOMDAHL, P. S., TAMAYO, P. AND GRØNBECH-JENSEN, N., "A High Performance Communications and Memory Caching Scheme for Molecular Dynamics on the CM-5." *Proc. of the 8th International Parallel Processing Symposium (IPPS'94)*, IEEE Computer Society, 1994, 800-809.

[5] COOK, C. R., PANCAKE, C. M., AND WALPOLE, R., *Proc. of Supercomputing '94*, IEEE Computer Society, 1994, 126-133.

[6] DENG, Y., McCOY, R., MARR, R., AND PEIERLS, R., "Molecular Dynamics on Distributed-memory MIMD Computers with Load-balancing," *Applied Math Letters* (to appear).

[7] GILES, R. C. AND TAMAYO, P., "A Parallel Scalable Approach to Short-Range Molecular Dynamics on the CM-5," *Proc. of SHPCC'92*, IEEE Computer Society, 1992, 240.

[8] LOMDAHL, P. S., TAMAYO, P.,GRØNBECH-JENSEN, N., AND BEAZLEY, D. M., *Proc. of Supercomputing '93*, IEEE Computer Society, 1993, 520-527.

[9] PLIMPTON, S., "Fast Parallel Algorithms for Short-Range Molecular Dynamics," Sandia National Laboratory Report, SAND91-1144, UC-705, 1993.

[10] *SPARC RISC User's Guide*, Cypress Semiconductor, San Jose, 1990.

[11] Special thanks to Dietrich Stauffer for putting things into perspective.

Chapter 5

Updates and Working-Group Summaries

There are currently efforts to establish projects that address some of the problems faced by applications developers working on parallel systems. Two of these projects are the High-Performance Fortran Forum (HPFF) and Ptools. Each of these was covered at the workshop, and summaries of their goals and progress are included in this section. The Ptools effort, a direct outgrowth of our fourth workshop in Keystone, Colorado, 1993, is directed toward establishing communication among the three primary groups (users, developers and vendors) who are the focus of this workshop series. Cherri Pancake, the Chair of Ptools, summarizes the organization in her paper "Collaborative Efforts to Develop User-Oriented Parallel Tools." HPFF, organized by Prof. Ken Kennedy of Rice University, has as its focus the definition of parallel constructs that extend and enhance the Fortran language. Mary Zosel, the Executive Director of HPFF, updates the latest version of High-Performance Fortran (HPF) as put forward by the Forum. Her talk is summarized in this chapter by Weiming Gu, a student attendee who acted as "scribe" during her talk.

Previous workshops (1988, 1989, 1991) had diVided participants into Working Groups for the purpose of considering in detail problems and solutions relevant to the theme of the workshop. In 1993, the organizers, feeling that working groups had outlived their usefulness, abandoned the formula. However, based on responses to the workshop evaluation, it was decided that perhaps this was too hasty, and the working groups were reinstated for 1994. There were four such groups at Cape Cod, who were each asked to consider problems and solutions relevant to their group. Position papers were required and presentation of these position papers on the last day of the workshop was part of the closing session. Three of those position papers are included in this section. The first, based on working group number one, addressed the issues of Integrated Environments vs. Toolkits, and their conclusions and position is given in the summary by Diane Rover, et al. The second working group was asked to consider whether commodity software should or could be leveraged for MPP systems. Their summary is given by James McGraw. Finally, working group number three took on the problems of Tools for Workstation Clusters, and the paper by Bob Dilly puts forth their ideas.

Collaborative Efforts to Develop User-Oriented Parallel Tools

Cherri M. Pancake

Department of Computer Science Oregon State
University Corvallis, Oregon 97330

Abstract

There is growing evidence that software tools are under-appreciated
and under-utilized by the parallel programming community. Moreover, it has become clear that usability issues are more important
than technological capabilities in determining a tool's success. If
a tool is difficult to learn or does not directly respond to user
requirements, it will not be adopted by users. The Parallel Tools
Consortium is a direct response to criticisms that parallel tool
developers are working in isolation from the user community. It
provides a forum where tool researchers, implementors, and users
can work together to identify tool requirements and evolve tools
that are both useful and usable. This paper establishes why collaboration is required if parallel tools are to become responsive
to user needs.

1.1 Introduction

The need for useful and machine-independent – or at least portable – tools
to facilitate high-performance computing (HPC) has become critical. In discussing the barriers to future progress in HPC, a recent report from the
National Science Foundation stated that:

> The most important impediment to the use of new highly parallel systems has been the difficulty of programming these machines and the wide variation that exists ... across generations of machines as well as the machines in a given generation. Application software developers are understandably reluctant to re-implement their large-scale production codes on multi-computers when significant effort is required to port the codes across parallel systems as they evolve [7].

An increased level of effort in parallel tools research, however, is not sufficient to guarantee progress. Significant effort and expense have been devoted to the development of tools to support parallel programming, and a growing number of tools are available commercially or in the public domain. But those tools have not been successful among application programmers, who criticize them for being hard to use and for failing to provide the types of information really needed. There is a general perception that tools are conceived and developed without user input, then "thrown over the wall" to the user community in the expectation that they will be adopted and valued [14]. A new organization was formed in November of 1993 to address this problem. The goal of the Parallel Tools Consortium (Ptools) is to provide a forum where tool researchers, tool implementors, and tool users collaborate to identify user needs for tool support. This paper reviews some of the evidence on why current tools are unpopular. It then describes the motivation for establishing Ptools and its strategy for improving tool usability through close collaboration with the user community.

1.2   Evidence of Tool (Dis)Use

The final session of the 1993 Keystone Workshop on Parallel Computing Systems, which brought together tool developers and users, articulated the problem: A lot of smart people are developing parallel tools that smart users just won't use [17]. Surveys and interviews have found that most users prefer hand-coded instrumentation over current parallel tool offerings. Kuehn [6] estimated that some 99% of the technical programmers at his institution rely on PRINT statements in spite of the availability of debuggers and performance tools. Our studies have revealed rates almost as high in a variety of research and industrial settings [16]. Even within so-called "tool-disposed" groups, some 40% avoid parallel tools [15]. Among people who do use tools, a surprisingly large number develop in-house or personal tools rather than use those that are available commercially or in the public domain [15,16]. Parallel tools have the potential for greatly assisting the application development process, and may well be more important to parallel than to serial programmers [14,9,16]. Hand-coded instrumentation is a reliable (albeit tedious) method for gathering the information needed to debug or tune serial programs, but I/O in the parallel environment can seriously perturb timing relationships, masking errors and performance bottlenecks or provoking new ones. Technological factors, such as the time delay involved in offloading the contents of I/O buffers and problems in obtaining reliable global timestamps, can result in improperly ordered or lossy information. The complexity of parallel computers and their susceptibility to small variations in the run-time environment also suggest that mechanisms for gathering information need to be of an accuracy and efficiency beyond the scope of most application programmers. Why, then, are parallel tools so under-utilized? It can be argued that there is some tradition of antipathy to tools, and that these are unpopular among serial programmers, too. However, a recent survey contrasted tool use among comparable populations of parallel and serial users. Serial programmers are significantly more likely to employ tools than are parallel programmers, and almost 80% of those with vector programming experience report tool use [2]. Studies of parallel users indicate that:

- Tool information often is presented in a fashion that reflects the tool's organization, rather than the logical patterns employed by users.

- The information sought by the user may be available only indirectly, via multiple operations or through assimilation from multiple sources.

- At best, the tool is considered clumsy and hard to learn; at worst, the user assumes it cannot provide the desired information.... [T]he audience for parallel tools is made up of scientists, engineers, and other technical programmers.

- They do not approach programming in the same way as their computer science counterparts, nor are they tolerant of tools that are complicated or non-intuitive [15].

In a number of recent workshops sponsored by such diverse groups as ARPA, NSF, ONR, NASA, ACM, and HPCCI, users have complained that tool developers are more concerned with conducting interesting research or adding "bells-and-whistles" than with creating tools that will actually be used. Although this attitude is unnecessarily cynical, it does reflect the current perception that parallel tools are developed under supply-push rather than demand-pull economics [13]. That is, tools are not being designed to match user requirements and user strategies for developing parallel applications.

Tool developers do not ask users the "right" questions. If a tool designed for a particular programming task is not applied to that activity, the developer asks the user why it is not being used. What needs to be asked instead is how the user does go about the task, why it is performed in that way, and what he/she does to simplify or streamline the effort.

The dominant motivation for current tool design appears to be the exposing of available technology, whose intrinsic value is obvious to tool researchers and implementors. Unfortunately, it is not clear to the user community that such technology can be applied easily or effectively to typical program development strategies. Today's tools may be technologically sophisticated, but they lack the critical ingredient: usability.

1.3   The Basis for Tool Usability

The concept that usability should be the driving factor in software design and implementation is not particularly new; it has appeared in the literature under the guises of usability engineering, user-centered design, and iterative design [11,8,12,1]. There is no firm consensus on what methodology is most appropriate, nor on the frequency with which users should be involved in design decisions (cf. [4,5]). What is clear is that usability can only be accomplished with the active participation of actual users. It is instructive to apply the lessons from experimental usability engineering to the subject of parallel tools. First and foremost is the notion that meaningful, useful software is driven by concrete needs. Such requirements can be identified only by soliciting input directly from the user community. Specifically, a tool will not be useful unless it facilitates tasks that the user already does, and that are time-consuming, tedious, or error-prone when performed manually. If, instead, a tool's design is driven by the kinds of support that tool developers are ready or able to provide, it will miss the mark. A corollary to this is the fact that usefulness and ease-of-use, two key components of usability, can be ensured only if users are actively incorporated into the software design cycle.

Tool users are the only ones who will have the insight needed to accurately identify features which represent potential sources of confusion.

The tradition of soliciting user feedback only during the very early and very late stages of development is not adequate. During early stages, the design is too amorphous for a user to grasp completely, while during late phases such as alpha testing, the software structure has already been solidified in ways that may impede usability. Ease-of-learning is another key factor for attracting users. The time a user invests to learn a tool will not be warranted unless it can be amortized across many applications of the tool. In addition, lack of regular use may force the user to re-learn a tool many times over. Tool complexity is therefore a dis-incentive, not just for new users, but also for those who have not used the tool for a period of time. The short lifespan of most parallel computers exacerbates this problem. Like it or not, most parallel programmers will end up migrating their applications across several machine platforms over the course of time. The investment in learning a tool will probably not be warranted unless the tool is supported on more than one platform, and behaves in a consistent way across platforms. As illustrated in Figure 1.1, the central tenet of usability engineering can be summarized as "know and involve the users." The most accepted way of doing this is through a process of iterative refinement [3,10]. Representative groups of users are exposed to the software at various stages in development, in a variety of testing and interviewing situations. The user feedback obtained is then used to refine the design, with the result serving as input to the next iteration of the design process. This allows the developer to tune and tailor the tool in response to user reactions. The point of iterative design is that tool usability depends on how well and how easily a tool responds to user needs—so it can only be ensured through collaboration with actual users.

1.4   Ptools' Collaborative Strategy

The Parallel Tools Consortium brings together representatives from the federal, industrial, and academic sectors to address the issues of what parallel users need in tool support and how user feedback can be incorporated effectively into the tool development cycle. The last few years have yielded considerable progress in tool technology and in efforts to define standards for parallel languages and operating environments. At the same time, the user community has accumulated a considerable experience base in parallel

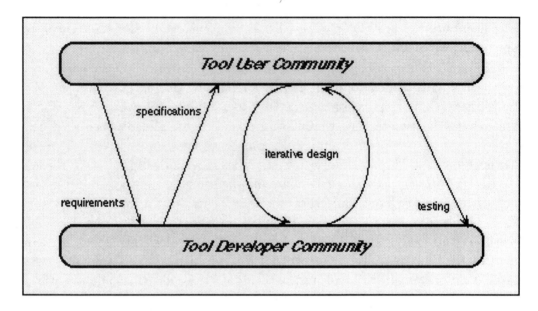

Figure 1.1: Usability engineering applied to tool design.

programming. If tool developers and users collaborate, it should be possible to leverage these results in order to arrive at tools that not only do things users want to do, but also are implementable across a range of parallel and clustered systems.

The parallel tools community is a varied one [13]. The largest concentration of tool researchers is currently at academic institutions, although some will be found in federally funded and industry research centers. Implementors of tool products typically work in the industrial sector. Users, on the other hand, tend to be clustered in the national laboratories, with increasing numbers in technical areas of industry, such as seismic imaging, pharmaceutical engineering, and aerospace or automotive engineering. Forging a collaboration between such diverse and professionally segregated groups is not a simple task. Yet each group brings expertise that is not duplicated in the others. Historically, tool researchers have provided the impetus for technological advances, yielding new theories, paradigms, techniques, and representational models. The implementor group is the repository of most expertise in developing robust, efficient implementations for specific real-world parallel computers. The third group, users, forms the customer base for parallel tools and thereby establishes the basic requirements. They also embody more than a decade's experience in developing applications for those machines, including practical strategies that have been proven effective by trial-and-error. As portrayed in Figure 1.2, it is the combination of these strengths which forms the foundation for Ptools efforts.

The primary activity of the Consortium is to sponsor tool development projects, in which all three groups are active. Each project focuses on a tool component responding to a specific, demonstrable need arising from the user group. The research community participates by identifying or inventing technological capabilities that answer the user need. Implementors from at least two organizations work with the others to provide development support, and to ensure that the component will work effectively and efficiently in production-level environments. Together, the participants arrive at a standard definition for the tool component, a specification of its user interface, and a public implementation, intended to be a model for future, proprietary implementations. This development strategy is illustrated in Figure 1.3. The goal of Ptools is to evolve a series of practical, user-oriented tools that are portable across a full range of parallel computers and workstation clusters. The emphasis on public implementations of tool components, rather than productized, stand-alone tools, is intended to address three problems that would impede that goal:

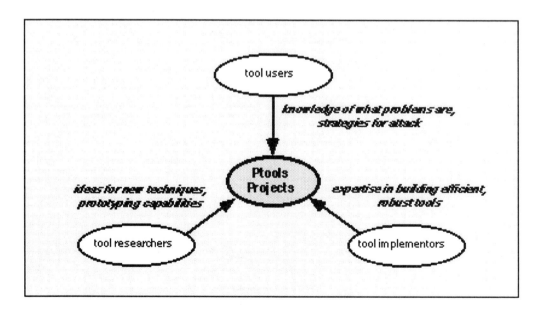

Figure 1.2: Input for Ptools collaborations.

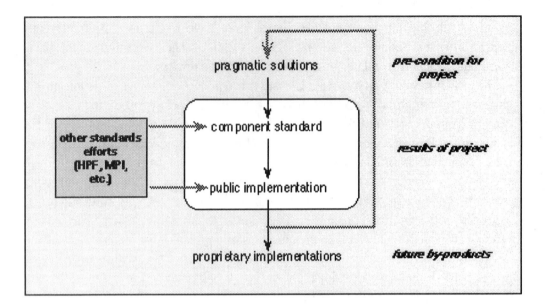

Figure 1.3: Ptools' project-oriented strategy.

1. It is difficult to attract new users to an "unknown" tool, particularly if the tool involves a dollar investment. The availability of a public domain version that works on at least a few common platforms, even if the efficiency is sub-optimal, will allow prospective users to try it out before investing.

2. The public availability of a tool is not enough to encourage widespread use, unless efficient, productized implementations are also forthcoming across a range of machine platforms. Formulating Ptools projects as small components that can be integrated into a variety of larger tools encourages vendors to develop proprietary implementations. Because a component can be integrated into an existing tool, added to a toolkit base, or implemented as a stand-alone tool, each organization can leverage the substantial investment it has already made in platform-specific tool infrastructures.

3. There is a particular need for short-term projects whose results can be released quickly. If users can see evidence that their active collaboration leads to improved tool usability, they may be encouraged to interact in other ways with the tool development community, as well as to participate in future Ptools projects.

To expedite the development process, Ptools projects also attempt to leverage off existing standards work as much as possible. Liaisons are maintained with standards groups such as MPI (Message-Passing Interface), HPFF (High Performance Fortran Forum), SIO (Scalable I/O Initiative), POSIX, and PVM (Parallel Virtual Machine, the de facto leader in message-passing systems). Where appropriate, those groups are asked to add hooks or other means of facilitating tool support; they also review Ptools project plans for compliance with current standards and compatibility with anticipated future directions. Moreover, the reference implementation is intended not as a rigid standard, but as a starting point for future cycles of refinement. It is to be hoped that the availability of each user-oriented component will lead to the identification of new needs and strategies that can be instrumental in improving tool support for parallel programming. To this end, components are developed incrementally and a special attempt is made to keep all interfaces — with the user or with the underlying language or run-time system — clearly defined and as flexible as possible. This aspect should also be instrumental in attracting vendors to develop proprietary versions of tool components.

1.5   Conclusions

A build-it-and-they-will-come mentality has dominated the design of parallel tools for some time. It is increasingly clear, however, that creating an elegant, powerful tool employing the latest technology is not enough. Usability is the key to success; users simply do not adopt tools that fail to respond to their needs. Research in the area of usability engineering indicates that five design principles can have significant impact on usability:

- tools must be based on demonstrable user requirements

- actively involve users throughout tool design

- minimize tool complexity to reduce the learning curve

- support the tool across multiple machine platforms to amortize the user's investment

- employ iterative refinement techniques to improve tool usability

These principles form the basis of the Parallel Tools Consortium collaborative strategy to improve tool support for high-performance computing. Ptools serves as a forum where tool researchers, implementors, and users collaborate in identifying user needs and how tools might support those needs. Sponsored projects focus on a particular user requirement and evolve a tool component that can be implemented in a relatively short period and then integrated into a variety of existing toolkits or infrastructures. The outcome of each project is a public definition of the requirement and its solution, plus a public implementation; the intention is that industry will develop proprietary products based on the reference implementation. The consortium, then, offers an infrastructure for collaboration, bringing together participants who have distinct contributions to offer, but who would be unlikely to work together under normal circumstances. It facilitates the process of iterative design, whereby users participate actively in the development effort so that tool products can become truly responsive to their needs.

References

1. CARROLL, J. M. AND ROSSON, M. B., "Human-Computer Interaction Scenarios as a Design Representation," *Proc. HICSS-23*, 1990, 555-561.

2. COOK, C. R., PANCAKE, C. M., AND WALPOLE, R., "Are Expectations for Parallelism Too High? A Survey of Potential Parallel Users," *Proc. Supercomputing '94*, 1994, 126-133.

3. HAYES, A. H., SIMMONS, M. L., REED, D., "Summary of the 1993 Workshop Report: Instrumentation for Parallel Computing Systems: A Dialogue Between Users and Developers," Los Alamos National Laboratory Technical Report, 1993.

4. HOLTZBLATT, K. AND BEYER, H., "Making Customer Centered Design Work for Teams," Communications of the ACM, **36**, No. 10, Oct. 1993, 93-103.

5. JEFFRIES, R., MILLER, J. R., WHARTON, C., AND UYEDA, K. M., "User Interface Evaluation in the Real World: A Comparison of Four Techniques," PROC. CHI'91, 1991, 119-124.

6. KARAT, C-M., CAMPBELL, R., AND FIEGEL, T., "Comparison of Empirical Testing and Walkthrough Methods in User Interface Evaluation," *Proc. CHI'92*, 1992, 397-404.

7. KUEHN, J., "NCAR User Perspective," *Proc. 1992 Supercomputer Debugging Workshop*, Jan. 1993.

8. MARCUS, A., "Human Communications Issues in advanced UIs," Communications of the ACM, **36**, No. 4, April 1993, 101-109.

9. MCGRAW, J. R. AND AXELROD, T. S., "Exploiting Multiprocessors: Issues and Options," in *Programming Parallel Processors*, R. G. Babb, ed., Addison-Wesley Publishing Company, 1988, 7-26.

10. NEILSEN, J., "Iterative User-Interface Design," *Computer*, Nov. 1993, 32-40.

11. NEILSEN, J., "The Usability Engineering Life Cycle," *Computer*, March 1992, 12-22.

12. NORMAN, D. A. "Cognitive Engineering," in *User Centered System Design*, D. A. Norman and S. W. Draper, Eds., Erlbaum Associates, 1986, 31-62.

13. NSF Blue Ribbon Panel on High Performance Computing: From Desktop to Teraflop: Exploiting the U. S. Lead in High Performance Computing, National Science Foundation, 1993.

14. PANCAKE, C. M., "A Collaborative Effort in Parallel Tool Design," in *Environments and Tools for Parallel Scientific Computing*, J. Dongarra and B. Tourancheau, Eds., *SIAM*, 1994, 112-118.

15. PANCAKE, C. M., "Software Support for Parallel Computing: Where Are We Headed?" *Communications of the ACM*, **34**, No. 11, Nov. 1991, 5264.

16. PANCAKE, C. M., AND COOK, C., "What Users Need in Parallel Tool Support: Survey Results and Analysis," *Proc. Scalable High Performance Computing Conference*, 1994, 40-47.

17. PANCAKE, C. M., et al., results of user surveys conducted on behalf of Intel Supercomputer Systems Division, IBM Corporation, and CONVEX Computer Corporation, 1989-1993.

High-Performance Fortran Forum Status Report

Mary Zosel[1]
Lawrence Livermore National Laboratory

1.1 Introduction

An overview of the High-Performance Fortran Forum, 1994 (HPFF94) was given to the participants by Mary Zosel of Lawrence Livermore National Laboratory, who is currently the Executive Director of HPFF94. A summary of her remarks is presented here, thanks to the efforts of Weiming Gu, a student attendee.

1.2 Where We Are

The current status of the High-Performance Fortran (HPF) Survey, which lists announced products related to HPF, companies who have formally announced efforts to support HPF, and companies who have expressed interests in HPF was presented first.

One of the positive results of the HPF discussion is that, according to the survey, it has had an influence on regular Fortran's standards. The International Standards Office (ISO) plans to release a new Fortran standard – Fortran95 – during 1996, which may contain something similar to HPF's FORALL statement and HPF's PURE functions. Inclusion of these concepts into sequential codes will certainly make parallelization much easier. HPFF94

---

[1]Summary prepared by Weiming Gu, Georgia Institute of Technology

has also recommended inclusion of user-defined elemental functions and small changes to the I/O statements to facilitate parallel I/O.

1.3 Where We Are Going

HPFF94 had planned four meetings in 1994; the charter of the Forum was developed at the first meeting in January 1994. The Charter put forth four goals: (1) to issue HPF 1.0 Clarifications, Corrections, Interpretations (CCI), (2) to gather user requirements for HPF extensions, (3) to encourage implementation, and (4) to discuss possible simple additions to the HPF 1.0.

There are many complex issues raised by HPF and by the CCI for HPF 1.0; some of the following examples illustrate these issues. Intrinsic functions that inquire about data mapping may be useful to programmers who want to know how data are exactly mapped; while HPF supports intrinsic functions, this set has not yet been defined. Additionally, HPF 1.0 supports the notion of "extrinsic" functions, which turn out to be a very useful concept; however, users would like to extend "extrinsic" to modules and block data, as well as routines. The definition of what the mix and match of data and functions between different types of extrinsic kinds is also under study. A new extrinsic type (without a name right now), which instructs the compiler that the called routine is to be run on only one processor, is also under definition. There is a case where INHERIT should be removed; when a portion of an array is passed to a subroutine, INHERIT does not make sense. New HPF/HPF_LOCAL library routines should be defined, to

LOCAL_BLKCNT(ARRAY,DIM,PROC),
LOCAL_LINDEX(LOCAL_LINDEX(ARRAY, BLK,DIM,PROC),
LOCAL_UINDEX(ARRAY,BLK,DIM,PROC),
MY_PROCESSOR(), etc.

In the requirements activity, three subjects have been identified: parallel I/O support, tasking control support, and irregular data support. There is a consensus that asynchronous I/O is necessary. The primary issues of facilitating tasking are to support load balancing and assist in breaking algorithms into tasks that do completely different jobs. Irregular data support is crucial for certain applications, but associated issues such as index lists and rugged arrays are very difficult to support at the compiler level.

On the implementation side, some benchmark collections give the only results so far. There are some benchmarks for HPF codes by John Levesque of Applied Parallel Research (APR), and some benchmarks to challenge HPF by Joel Saltz of the University of Maryland.

An interesting proposal that has come out of HPFF94 is one to define an HPF kernel. This kernel should contain a subset of the language that performs well across many hardware platforms. There are other proposals from HPFF that have not been discussed yet, such as the elimination of BLOCK(n), direct alignment only with no offsets, strides, etc.

1.4   Conclusions

The above results of these discussions will appear in an updated language document of HPF 1.1. A requirements document and a benchmark suite will be available in the public domain, and the CCI documentation which contains many questions and answers will also be available. Given these accomplishments, it is clear that we are making steady progress toward a standard for parallel Fortran.

Summary of Working Group on Integrated Environments Vs. Toolkits

Diane T. Rover
Michigan State University

Allen D. Malony
University of Oregon

and
Gary J. Nutt
University of Colorado

Many hands make light work. Too many cooks spoil the broth.

1.1 Introduction

The nature of high performance computing and communication (HPCC) environments implies that a programmer normally requires a comprehensive set of debugging and performance tools to create, validate, and tune the software. The toolmaking community has responded with a broad range of debugging and performance tools (see [6,13]). However, tool builders have been notably *unsuccessful* at creating tools that the user community will use; Pancake states that "... only one in fifty research tools are usable or useful ...," that "... one in twenty parallel tools from the industry succeed ...," and that even for the widely-acclaimed ParaGraph performance tool [7]: "I know of only a handful of people around the country who use it." At the same time, some users faced with programming immensely complex parallel and distributed applications have found tools to be absolutely essential, albeit imperfect.

Thus, we have a problematic situation in which an apparent abundance of tools are being avoided by most users. So, there are two issues here: (1) the abundance of tools, and (2) their lack of widespread use. A variety of factors may contribute to the situation. Several are not unique to HPCC systems. For example, in commercial systems, end users are often reluctant to use new software, particularly in the business market, because they are not convinced that the software will actually make their work easier and because of the learning curve. A similar barrier exists in HPCC systems. The primary group using HPCC facilities to address significant application problems consists of *domain-oriented programmers*. A domain-oriented programmer is an expert in the application domain (e.g., a physicist, a doctor, a mechanical engineer, etc.) who has learned programming as a tool to aid in problem solving. Domain-oriented programmers are focused on solving their problem, not on learning more about software tools, architectures, etc. Time spent on debugging and tuning is *overhead* for the programmer; therefore, any additional time for learning or using tools is perceived as a risky investment.

There is a significant conflict that must be resolved by a domain-oriented programmer before committing to a tool: when is the investment in knowledge of tools and execution architectures likely to pay off in more effective application software? What is the likelihood that the investment can be amortized across other projects? How difficult will it be to learn the tools? Will the tool really be useful? Will the knowledge about using the tools be reusable? Does the schedule for the current application merit introducing the overhead of learning to use the tools? There is no simple answer to these questions—the decision to invest in a tool can only be made by the end user, either because there are no other alternatives, or because the user is willing to speculate that the return on the invested time will be worthwhile in the long run [14].

In commercial systems, an approach to resolving the user's dilemma is application integration. It is explicitly intended to enable and encourage end users to use application software. Integration technology may be the kind of technology that needs to be applied to HPCC tool environments to address the domain-oriented programmer's dilemma. If the technology can assist by making tools easy to learn, easy to use, consistent, and with clear added value, then integration is a means to address the usage issue. Coincidentally, integration is also a means to address the abundance issue. With many tools, often it is not clear how one tool relates to the others and how it could be used in combination with others. For example, design tools abound in both the electronic design automation (EDA) and computer-aided software engineering (CASE) markets. Vendors of these tools increasingly support some *framework* that defines the relationships among tools, whereby tools from different vendors can be intermingled by a user in the design process in a plug-and-play manner on a platform [3]. Moreover, the application of tools within a framework often embodies a *methodology* that facilitates the design process [9]. Networked systems, in general, are addressing users' needs for application interoperability. For example, products such as SunSoft's ToolTalk^{TM} are becoming available; this service enables independent applications to communicate via messages with other applications without having direct knowledge of each other. The real benefit of incorporating diverse tools into a single environment is that it may enhance their usefulness and usability, bringing greater productivity to the end user and possibly broadening the user base.

Nonetheless, integration is not without its naysayers and caveats. A point of immediate debate for debugging and performance tools involves the maturity of tool building technology: should the focus shift from making sure each tool works to making sure tools can work together? In short, two wrongs do not make a right. Even if we can assume that individual tools are well-built, there seems to be a fine line between synergy and complexity as tools are added to a user's repertoire. Some tools will be better integrated than others, and the quality of integration is a subjective issue resolvable only by the user. Additionally, integration often implies some type of standard interface between tools. There have been several efforts in this direction, such as for trace data formats, profiling interfaces, and portable software (e.g., communication and math libraries). However, by and large, there is significant resistance to any extensive standardization effort.

The topic of integration of debugging and performance tools has surfaced recently not only in this working group but also in panels, both at this workshop [17] and at the Supercomputing '94 Conference [20]. The participants represent all sectors (industry, academic research, and government labs) and present a diversity of views. One thing that was clear from these meetings is that integration means different things to different people. By definition, integration means that components function as members of a unified, coherent whole. Minimally, this may imply that a tool can be used along side other tools in a single environment toward a common purpose. More comprehensively, it may reflect extensive tool interrelationships. Furthermore, there are (possibly subtle) differences in what is implied by an *integrated environment* versus a *toolkit*. In the former, a set of tightly-coupled tools exhibit a particular functionality. In the latter, loosely-coupled tools may exhibit some level of interoperability. Furthermore, an environment may be closed or open, indicating whether external tools (developed by other tool builders) can be incorporated into the environment. An *extensible* tool that can add new features may or may not use this capability to interface with other tools in an environment. Finally, while portability of an environment would seem desirable, in practice, an environment may be specific to an application domain, a system, a language, etc. The working group's perspective on an integrated environment should become clear to the reader in subsequent sections.

The motivation for this and other forums is to gain a more thorough understanding of integration—the technology itself and its potential impact on tool users and developers. In the following sections, we summarize the discussions of the working group, which focus on the properties of integration and examples of its adding or subtracting value. Section 1.2 presents properties of an integrated environment. In Sec. 1.3, we consider several models for integrated environments based on existing tools to illustrate the state of the art. Section 1.4 presents a collection of instances that demonstrate how integration either assists or hinders the domain-oriented programmer. Section 1.5 concludes with an overall assessment of the challenges posed by integration to users and developers.

1.2 Properties of Integration

Integration is defined by various levels, dimensions, characteristics, and properties. The working group discussed the different aspects of integration prior to evaluating it with respect to debugging and performance tools. First, take a moment to consider how integration applies to generic applications. A set of integrated applications can be characterized as follows:

P resentation Integration. All applications have a common view and control behavior (similar user interaction). This is typically accomplished via a graphical user interface (GUI). For example, the interface employs a verb-object, point-and-select paradigm.

B ehavioral (Control) Integration. All applications have similar commands with similar semantics, enabling users to extrapolate control behavior across applications. For example, deleting an object is always accomplished with the same set of detailed actions. An application programming interface (API) facilitates this level of integration, since control aspects are typically defined internal to an application. This also extends to communication and synchronization between applications.

D ata Integration. Tools can exchange or share structured data via several mechanisms. For example, a calendar application can use the same data as an application that does time reporting.

I nterlocking Functions. The functions of the tools are complementary, enabling the user to compose them to achieve more sophisticated processing.

An integrated tool environment may address similar issues depending on the scope of integration:

P resentation Integration. Tools should provide debugging and performance reports using consistent views, command names, etc. Use of window toolkits, e.g., X Motif or Tcl/Tk, encourage a certain amount of presentation integration. However, integrating views from different tools is problematic. For example, even the mapping of colors to data attributes may be significant, where the same color should have the same interpretation in related views.

B ehavioral (Control) Integration. Once a programmer has learned to use one tool in the environment, it should be easy to extrapolate the knowledge to use other tools, i.e., the programmer applies a familiar logical model of behavior to new tools. For example, consistent semantics in user-tool and tool-tool interaction (i.e., messaging between tools) may be supported by a tool API available to tool builders who want to build fully-integrated tools. Technically, this may be the most difficult level of integration to achieve. Moreover, this level can be related (ultimately) to the user's problem-solving process or work model that is supported by the use of computers and these tools.

D ata Integration. Tools should use a common event format and be able to pass intermediate results among themselves. Data integration can take advantage of a common underlying trace format, e.g., PICL [7] or SDDF [18]. The self-defining data format of SDDF has addressed some of the issues of dealing with a semantically-rich set of debugging and performance data. Data integration also involves the processing and synchronizing of the event data by multiple tools, using either real-time or post mortem presentation.

I nterlocking Functions. The tools must collectively support the user's requirements for functionality. The tool set should provide functions to accomplish most analyses, and the tools should be combinable (composable or integrable) to realize new functions. In addition to *function composition*, however, *separation of function* should be maintained so that a programmer can invoke only what's needed. The basic facilities provided as part of the environment and as "seed tools" in the environment should encourage interlocking functions.

Thus, in summary, an *idealized* integrated environment would enable a programmer—whom we assume is an expert developing applications in some domain—to combine a heterogeneous set of debugging and performance tools to be used to study a specific program from unique perspectives. Ideally, the tools in the environment would: have a consistent presentation/interaction model, exhibit consistent behavior, functionally complement one another, and be interconnectable to define composite tools. We assume that the domain-oriented programmer is not willing to invest in a large learning curve; that any investment, however small, will be weighed against its pay-back; and that the programmer typically is not willing to take on the tool builder's role by personally customizing or extending tools. Moreover, because of the state of evolution of tool technology and the state of acceptance of various tools in specific domains, the environment must be able to incorporate various stand-alone tools developed by a diverse set of tool builders. A programmer needs to be able to access from within the environment a tool that's already being used regularly. While an idealized environment would completely integrate the tools with respect to presentation/interaction, behavior, interoperation, etc., the pragmatics of the situation imply that the environment accomplish as much integration as possible given the inevitable conflicts that will exist across a set of tools. Ultimately, the programmer may find compromises acceptable, e.g., it may be sufficient that the tools can operate on the same data although they have distinctly different user interfaces.

1.3 An Overview of Current Work in Integrated Environments

Several integrated parallel tool environments have been proposed and/or developed by tool researchers and builders. We introduce some of them briefly in this section, leaving details to the cited literature. However, we present additional aspects and architectural details of two environments from the authors' own work to provide the reader with a context for solidifying the integration concepts in Secs. 1.1 and 1.2 and critiquing the issues in Secs. 1.4 and 1.5. This section is intended to reflect the various tools and features that were referred to during the working group discussion.

The following integrated parallel tool environments support the use of multiple, possibly heterogeneous, tools that cooperate for carrying out one or more analyses of the same parallel program. Stand-alone tools built by different developers are referred to as heterogeneous tools by Hao et al. [5]. An integrated environment may support off-line tool usage, such as ParaVision [15]; homogeneous on-line tool usage, such as Paradyn [8]; or a combination of the two, such as TAU [2], SPI [1], VIZIR [5], and Intel's ParAide [19]. Off-line tool usage refers to post-mortem presentation of data, or post-processing of data after program execution; and on-line tool usage refers to real-time processing of data during program execution. Integrated parallel tool environments rely on particular mechanisms to capture, process, and consume debugging and performance data. Figure 1.1 shows some of the basic technologies in use for tool integration [22].

Tools are integrated with the support of debuggers, operating systems, languages and compilers, and runtime libraries to capture execution and program information from the application processes. Operating system interprocess communication abstractions, such as remote procedure call (RPC), socket, and pipe, are commonly used for transferring debugging and performance data; for example, sockets are used in Pablo [18] and Issos [16], pipes in Paradyn [8], and remote procedure calls in ParAide's TAM [19]). Some tools, such as Hewlett Packard's VIZIR [5], implement customized high-level

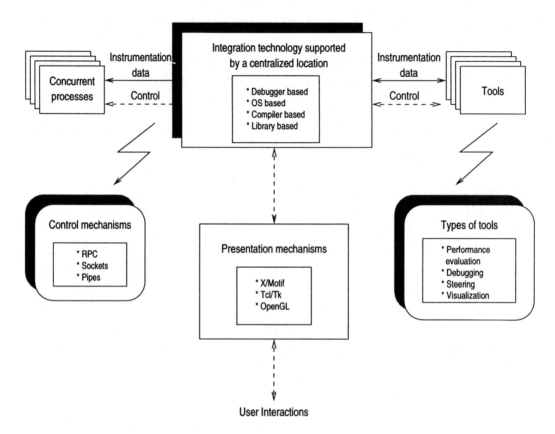

Figure 1.1: Basic components and technologies for a typical integrated parallel tool environment.

protocols, developed on top of operating system functions. Graphics libraries and graphical user interfaces, such as OpenGL, Tcl/Tk, and X/Motif, provide the user with a consistent view and control of the environment. With these technologies in mind, we next take a closer look at the architectures of the ParaVision and TAU environments.

ParaVision [15] is based upon a general model of an integrated environment shown in Figure 1.2, which depicts some important relationships among components in a multiple tool environment. In this model, an integrated environment contains facilities to *instrument* programs to observe their execution, to analyze behavior as recorded by the instrumentation, and to *present* behavior using a spectrum of views (ranging from tabular to visual, real-time to post-mortem, static to animated, and qualitative to quantitative); debuggers, program data visualizers, and performance tuning tools

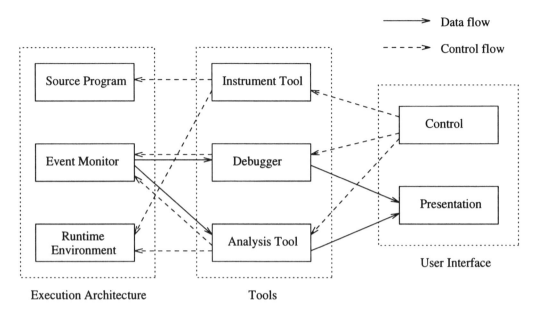

Figure 1.2: An integrated tool environment (ParaVision).

share these facilities. A goal of this environment is to enable domain-oriented programmers to configure the instrumentation, analysis, and reporting tools from a perspective that they choose rather than from any *a priori* view, thus meeting the needs of the programmer in different situations. This so-called *observation perspective*, which is a set of views of program behavior that provides complementary presentations of specific aspects of behavior, has its origins in the *multiple views* specified by LeBlanc, Mellor-Crummey, and Fowler [10]. The multiple views concept has been a guiding principle in visualization tool design. For example, IPS-2 provides an instance of a hierarchically related set of observation perspectives and indicates that an arbitrary hierarchy can be implemented (by the tool builder) as required [12]. Pablo employs a mechanism for interconnecting fixed atomic modules to process events from user-defined instrumentation to provide different observation perspectives [18]. VISTA specifies an integrated tool environment that supports multiple display and analysis strategies via diverse tools [21].

More specifically, ParaVision represents a prototypical integrated tool environment derived from the architecture shown in Figure 1.3. An observation perspective is realized through a set of tools and views, including, for example, ParaGraph and its Space-time Diagram [7]. The perspective manager registers and launches tools that are to be added to an observation perspective.

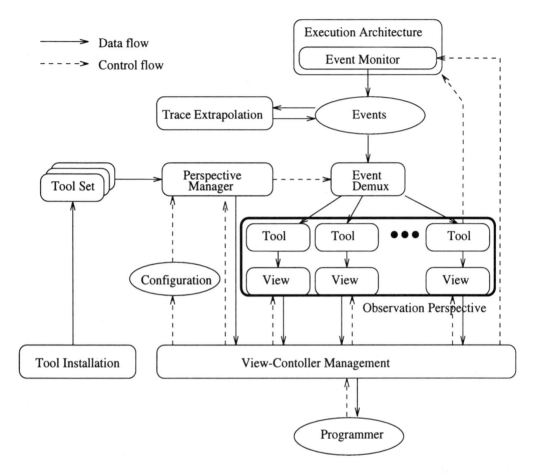

Figure 1.3: The prototype environment architecture (ParaVision).

TAU (Tuning and Analysis Utilities) is a visual programming and performance analysis environment for pC++ [2,11]. Figure 1.4 shows the pC++ programming environment and the associated TAU tools architecture. Elements of the TAU graphical interface represent objects of the pC++ programming paradigm: collections, classes, methods, and functions. These language-level objects appear in all TAU utilities. TAU uses the Sage++ toolkit as an interface to the pC++ compiler for instrumentation and accessing properties of program objects. TAU is also integrated with the pC++ runtime system for profiling and tracing support. It uses Tcl/Tk for graphics.

The TAU tools are implemented as graphical hypertools. While they are distinct tools, they act in concert as if they were a single application. Each tool implements some well-defined tasks. If one tool needs a feature of

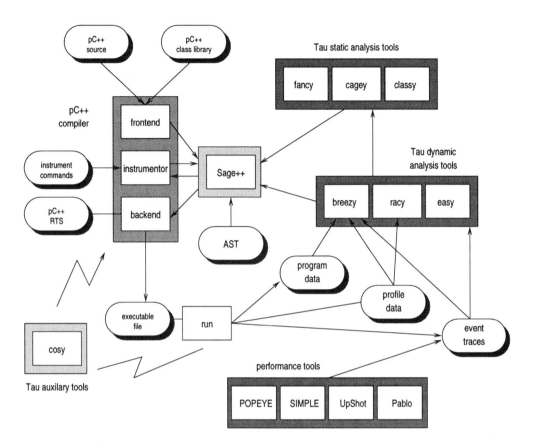

Figure 1.4: Programming and performance analysis environment and toolset architecture (TAU).

another one, it sends a message to the other tool requesting it (e.g., display the source code for a specific function). This design allows easy extensions. The TAU tools also support global features. If a global feature is invoked in any of the tools, it is automatically executed in all currently running TAU tools. Examples of global features include select-function, select-class, and switch- application.

The user can choose to compile a program for profiling, tracing, and breakpoint debugging. In these cases, the instrumentor is invoked to do the necessary instrumentation in the abstract syntax tree (AST). The compilation and execution of pC++ programs can be controlled by COSY. This tool provides a high-level graphical interface for setting compilation and execution parameters and selecting the parallel machine where a program will run. The program and performance analysis environment, shown on the right side of the figure, includes the integrated TAU tools, profiling and tracing support, and interfaces to stand-alone performance analysis tools developed partly by other groups. The TAU toolset provides support for accessing static information about the program and for querying and analyzing dynamic data obtained from program execution.

These examples demonstrate that developers are looking toward integration and that various implementation strategies are possible. The next two sections return to the heart of the working group discussion-users' needs and the integration debate.

1.4   Potential Value of Integration

The working group's attention turned to the issue of user requirements for tools: do requirements imply the need for integration, and if so, what features of integration may benefit the user? Both developers and users acknowledge that there are instances in which an integrated tool environment may either *add value to* or *detract value from* the users' program or performance analysis tasks. The group identified examples of each.

E xamples of Value Added. Examples of situations in which integration provides a clear benefit include:

- Hooking together a source code-level debugger with a visualizer. These tools can complement one another: a visualizer can expose problems, while the debugger provides traceability to the code; alternatively, the debugger can dynamically control the monitoring and, hence, the scope (time-scale, resources, variables, etc.) of the visualizer.

- Inserting additional instrumentation at runtime, e.g., via a debugger or other dynamic mechanism. When monitoring a program, a user does not necessarily know prior to execution what program or performance data will be of most interest, especially in the case of unexpected problems.

- Combining a scientific visualization system with performance tools. For a domain-oriented programmer, program output from a scientific visualization system provides a visual means to assess program correctness and to identify program state. These can then be viewed simultaneously with performance information. Additionally, scientific visualization systems have some inherent advantages for displaying performance data, such as ability to handle large data files.

- Including steering technology, to support program steering, or real time control of program execution (e.g., [4]). Based on debugger or visualizer output, a programmer could alter some aspect of the program (or the program itself) while it is executing, providing a dynamic stimulus/response capability.

- Synchronizing trace-driven displays from multiple tools. Time-correlated views are essential to the multiple views (observation perspective) concept, even when applied across heterogeneous tools.

- Incorporating memory usage information and memory system performance with other tools. That is, the programmer recognizes the impact of memory accesses on system performance and wants better facilities to analyze the causes and effects.

- Integrating the compiler with performance tools. The compiler has program information useful to performance tools; and, conversely, a performance tool has performance information of potential use to the compiler.

- Supporting "what if" scenarios. This may involve similar capability as program steering, although it may include prediction technology. A programmer is interested in tool support to predict and compare behavior of application "alternatives."

- Integrating performance prediction models with performance tools. Predicted performance can be compared with actual performance for validation and benchmarking purposes; and actual performance parameters and workload characteristics can be extracted for use with models.

- Providing a programmatic interface (API) to tools. This facilitates application use of tool functions as well as extension of tool functionality.

E xamples of Value Detracted. Examples of potential pitfalls of integration include:

- Increased costs. The nature of the costs of integration varies, including startup costs, or the time and perturbation of invoking the integrated environment compared to an individual tool; tool interface complexity, which relates to development overhead, reliability, and maintainability; and tool performance problems, e.g., due to additional overheads in handling compatible data formats.

- Constrained usability or applicability of stand-alone tools. Conformance with an integrated environment may constrain an existing tool. For example, data integration may constrain what a user can observe (i.e., which data are available to a tool); and control integration may constrain how a tool can be used.

- Inconsistency with a tool user's present base of knowledge. Issues to be addressed include ease of learning, ease of retention, and other human-computer interaction (HCI) factors.

- Greater disparity among novice versus expert users. Dealing with different types of users (e.g., different frequencies of using tools, different backgrounds in computing experience) is an unresolved problem for stand-alone tools. Integration compounds the problem. An integrated environment may be too complex for the novice or infrequent user and yet too cumbersome and slow for the expert user.

- Tool selection problems. What functions are supported by various tools, and how can a user's problem-solving needs be met? Is the choice of a tool clear?

- Tool navigation problems. What are the appropriate paradigms and technologies for accessing and using multiple tools in a coordinated fashion?

- Response time of environment. Increased data management and transfer overhead can cause unacceptable delays in any individual tool's typical response time to service user requests. A user needs feedback on whether some request is likely to incur excessive overhead.

- Insufficient expertise to build an integrated environment. Effective integration requires expertise from multiple disciplines, and generally speaking, such expertise has not been cultivated within the tool building community. Additionally, integration technology is not yet well defined and continues to mature with advances in other areas.

- User dissatisfaction. If a user is dissatisfied with one component of an integrated environment, he/she may never use the environment again, despite the merits of individual tools.

- Testing. Testing of integrated tools is orders of magnitude more difficult than testing of individual tools.

1.5   Challenges to Users and Developers

Clearly, the fate of integrated tool environments depends upon their value to the user. The examples of Sec. 1.4 represent the challenges to users and developers: maximizing the benefits and avoiding the pitfalls so as to attain the greatest possible value. Two of the major obstacles in this effort are:

1. For users—being motivated to use an environment having more than one tool when individual tools have not seemed to meet their requirements; and

2. For developers—building an environment that is adaptable/portable/customizable to moving targets (e.g., parallel/distributed computing platforms and user requirements) when stand-alone tools cannot seem to keep pace.

These dilemmas will not be resolved easily.

The working group summarized its discussions with the following conclusions and recommendations.

- Source code information (from compilers) is critical to virtually all tools in order to make them useful.

- Integrated environments (but not necessarily the application) must be able to run on a workstation.

- At least some of the environment's functionality must be accessible via a command line interface (versus graphical user interface).

- Functionality should be decoupled enough so that full overhead is not incurred when only a limited subset of the environment is used.

- Creation of an integrated environment requires interdisciplinary collaboration, for example, with HCI, software engineering, artificial intelligence (AI), and users' application domains.

- Intra-disciplinary collaboration is also required, that is, between designers at all levels (hardware, operating system, compiler, and so on).

- The tool integration substrate that enables integration must be multilayered (e.g., data, control, and presentation), but it may not be desirable to establish a single, common substrate.

- Extensibility is a critical characteristic of the substrate.

- The principal advantage of integration to the user is that tools can potentially be easier to use.

- The principal disadvantage is that the user's task may actually be harder to accomplish.

- Finally, despite increasing dialogue between tool users and developers, the users' "wish list" is still probably very different from what environment developers think it is.

Acknowledgements

On behalf of the entire group, the authors thank Cherri Pancake for guiding and moderating the working group discussion. We also thank all the participants who contributed their experiences and insights, with special thanks to the tool users for giving their perspectives. We also thank Aleksandar Bakic at Michigan State University for assistance with the final figures.

References

1. BHATT, DEVESH, JHA, RAKESH, STEEVES, TODD, BHATT, RASHMI, AND WILLS, DAVID, "SPI: An Instrumentation Development Environment for Parallel/Distributed Systems," Proc. of Int. Parallel Processing Symposium, April 1995.

2. BROWN D., HACKSTADT, S., MALONY, A., MOHR, B., "Program Analysis Environments for Parallel Language Systems: The TAU Environment," Proc. of the Second Workshop on Environments and Tools For Parallel Scientific Computing, Townsend, Tennessee, May 1994, pp. 162-171.

3. FUGGETTA, A., "A Classification of CASE Technology," IEEE Computer, 26 (12), December 1993, pp. 25-38.

4. GU, WEIMING, EISENHAUER, GREG, KRAMER, EILEEN, SCHWAN, KARSTEN, STASKO, JOHN, AND VETTER, JEFFREY, "Falcon: On-line Monitoring and Steering of Large-Scale Parallel Programs," Technical Report GIT-CC-94-21, 1994.

5. HAO, MING C., KARP, ALAN H., WAHEED, ABDUL, AND JAZAYERI, MEHDI, "VIZIR: An Integrated Environment for Distributed Program Visualization," Proc. of Int. Workshop on Modeling, Analysis and Simulation of Computer and Telecommunication Systems (MASCOTS '95) Tools Fair, Durham, North Carolina, Jan. 1995.

6. HAYES, ANN, SIMMONS, MARGARET, AND REED, DANIEL, "Workshop Report: Instrumentation for Parallel Computer Systems: A Dialogue Between Users and Developers," Keystone, Colorado, April 1993.

7. HEATH, MICHAEL T. AND ETHERIDGE, JENNIFER A., "Visualizing the Performance of Parallel Programs," IEEE Software, 8(5), September 1991, pp. 29-39.

8. HOLLINGSWORTH, J. K. AND MILLER, B. P., "Dynamic Control of Performance Monitoring on Large Scale Parallel Systems," Proc. of Int. Con. on Supercomputing, Tokyo, Japan, July 19-23, 1993.

9. KLEINFELDT, S. ET AL., "Design Methodology Management," Proc. IEEE, 82(2), 1994, pp. 231-250.

10. LeBlanc, T., Mellor-Crummey, J., and Fowler, R., "Analyzing Parallel Program Executions Using Multiple Views," Journal of Parallel and Distributed Computing, 9, 2, June, 1990, pp. 203-217.

11. Malony, A., Mohr, B., Beckman, P., Gannon, D., Yang, S., Bodin, F., and Kesavan, S., "Implementing a Parallel C++ Runtime System for Scalable Parallel Systems," Proceedings of Supercomputing '93, Portland, Oregon, November 15-19, 1993.

12. Miller, B. P., et al., "IPS-2: The Second Generation of a Parallel Program Measurement System," IEEE Transactions on Parallel and Distributed Systems, 1(2), April 1990, pp. 206-217.

13. Miller, Bart and McDowell, Charlie, editors, Proceedings of 3rd ACM/ONR Workshop on Parallel and Distributed Debugging, San Diego, California, May 1993.

14. Nutt, Gary J. and Baillie, Clive F., "Integrated Debugging and Tuning Environments," University of Colorado, October 1994.

15. Nutt, Gary J. and Griff, Adam J., "Extensible Parallel Program Performance Visualization," Proc. of Int. Workshop on Modeling, Analysis and Simulation of Computer and Telecommunication Systems (MASCOTS '95), Durham, North Carolina, Jan. 1995.

16. Ogle, David M., Schwan, Karsten, and Snodgrass, Richard, "Application-Dependent Dynamic Monitoring of Distributed and Parallel Systems," IEEE Transactions on Parallel and Distributed Systems, 4(7), July 1993, pp. 762- 778.

17. Pancake, Cherri, moderator, "Panel: Integrated Environments: Should We Work Toward This End?," Workshop on Debugging and Performance Tuning for Parallel Computing Systems, Chatham, Massachusetts, October 1994.

18. Reed, Daniel A., Aydt, Ruth A., Madhyastha, Tara M., Noe, Roger J., Shields, Keith A., Schwartz, Bradley W., "The Pablo Performance Analysis Environment," Dept. of Comp. Sci., Univ. of Ill., 1992.

19. RIES, BERNHARD, ANDERSON, R., BREAZEAL, D., CALLAGHAN, K., RICHARDS, E., AND SMITH, W., "The Paragon Performance Monitoring Environment," Proceedings of Supercomputing '93, Portland, Oregon, Nov. 15-19, 1993.

20. ROVER, DIANE T., "Performance Evaluation: Integrating Techniques and Tools into Environments and Frameworks," Roundtable, Supercomputing '94, Washington DC, November 1994.

21. WAHEED, A., KRONMULLER, B., SINHA, ROOMI, AND ROVER, D. T., "A Toolkit for Advanced Performance Analysis," Proc. of Int. Workshop on Modeling, Analysis and Simulation of Computer and Telecommunication Systems (MASCOTS '94) Tools Fair, Durham, North Carolina, Jan. 31- Feb. 2, 1994, pp. 376-380.

22. WAHEED, A., AND ROVER, DIANE T., "A Structured Approach to Instrumentation System Development and Evaluation," to appear in Proceedings of Supercomputing '95, San Diego, California, December 1995.

Leveraging Commodity Software for MPPs

James McGraw
Lawrence Livermore National Laboratory

1.1 Executive Summary

This Working Group was directed to consider the following question:

How do we leverage commodity software for MPP systems? Do we even want to? Or, is NT on 500 nodes with the Borland C++ toolset the future? Or, if you can spell Fourier, are you part of the solution or part of the problem?

The group met for three sessions. The final result was a list of five recommendations:

1. Fund a parallel tool laboratory to identify and evaluate tools, and make them ready for heavy-duty use.

2. Create a working group of tool builders from vendors and research institutions to define an interface for the extraction of debugging and performance information.

3. This workshop should encourage participation by developers of lower-level software (PC, Mac, and workstation) to help identify opportunities for leverage.

4. Create a working group of vendors, researchers and users to adapt lower-level style guides for specific platforms, and develop a higher-level guide defining basic functionality for specific tools.

5. Tool builders from industry, academia, and national labs should form a Special Interest Group (SIG)in one of the Computing Societies to define interoperable modules of software development tools for high performance computers.

1.2   Motivation

High-performance computing has been distinguished by a number of individual companies and national laboratories, each pursuing solutions essentially independent of others. Our premise is that there are insufficient resources to maintain the current path. This is especially evident in the recent demise of traditional funding sources, as evidenced perhaps, by the reorganization of Thinking Machines and Kendall Square.

There are a number of possible solutions to this lack of resources:

1. Increase resources. This can be done through increased government support, or increased commercial support.

2. Increase efficiency through cooperation. Agencies can encourage cooperation between companies. Consortia like PTOOLS can assist here. Finally, industry can initiate cooperation.

3. Alter direction. This may result in the death of the industry, or in attrition to a sustainable effort.

1.3   History

To some extent, the industry has been moving toward commodity software for some time. For example, Los Alamos National Laboratory (LANL) decided in the early 80's to cease development on CTSS (their in-house OS) in favor of Unicos, the Cray version of the Unix Operating System. There were a number of advantages to this, but the third party software that was expected to appear never did. It is likely that market forces played a role.

Perhaps the most visible example of successfully leveraged commodity software is Unix. One reason may be due to its inculcation into the student population. Also, the rise of the workstation market made it important to sites like the Los Alamos National Laboratory. C and Fortran may not be the

best choices for parallel systems, languages, nor may Unix be the best choice
of OS on parallel machines, but they are familiar and relatively portable.

Another example of successfully leveraged software is third party application codes such as Gaussian. Even though they may not provide the greatest
performance, they do provide a consistent user interface in a validated code
across multiple platforms.

It seems the biggest lesson to be learned here is that consistency and
reliability will prove, in the long run, more important than absolute performance. There will always be those users who require ultimate performance;
however, the majority of users, as in the PC and workstation market, just
need to get their jobs done with the least amount of effort.

1.4   Discussion of Posed Questions

What are the software resources or building blocks that we are trying to
leverage? Do we just want standard formats for various pieces (e.g., every
accounting package can read a Quicken data file)? How about standard icons,
user interfaces (like the Mac)? Standard formats are clearly necessary but
not sufficient. Libraries/code bases/tools are needed. We currently spend
too much time dealing with the low level details (such as decoding symbol
table information from an object file) which could be better spent on higher-
level work. But these kinds of software components do not really exist. For
example, one company spent eight person-years modifying the debugger tool
gdb to work with their environment – the internal hooks just weren't there.

Will we run into similar problems trying to leverage PC software? Is
workstation software a better base? Answer: unknown. Given the proliferation of software for PC's and Macs, the interfaces appear to be effective
as building blocks for higher-level tools and interoperability. However, the
kinds of tool platforms may not be effective for large scientific applications.

What needs to be done to leverage low-end software? Two different types
of interfaces need to be considered: interfaces between tools and interfaces to
users. If the interfaces between the front and back ends are properly designed,
then we should be able to leverage either or both components. This should
apply at least to compilers and debuggers. User interfaces are expensive to
develop but are insufficiently funded. Are the benefits of good user interfaces
and tools sufficient to fund the cost? Customers seem unwilling to pay for

software, and the market is not big enough. The hidden costs and lost opportunities due to lack of good tools are real, but often ignored.

If the market is not big enough, perhaps we should just use lower-end software on parallel systems, despite its shortcomings, and leave the support of "extreme" computing to whatever the government is willing to pay for. One advantage to using, for example, NT as the operating system, is that third-party developers may be more willing to parallelize and tune for an operating system that will be around for a while, even if a particular machine goes away. On the other hand, the performance inefficiencies of using low-end software can be excessive (consider for example the size and speed of most word processors on PCs).

Vendors need interfaces that can be plugged into, so they do not have to write everything themselves. Users need interfaces that are stable and sufficiently fast, so that they do not have to rewrite their software every year. How can we phrase this so that it gets across to the funding agencies? How can we get industry to work more closely together so that these interfaces exist (perhaps we cannot because where is the advantage, especially for bigger companies)?

1.5   Commentary on Recommendations

The recommendations of this group came out of a process geared toward making constructive recommendations for change. While not directed at specific agencies or groups, there was a clear effort to identify who should have the "action item" for the recommendation. The process began by having participants generate a list of candidate recommendations. Options were then studied for clarity, commonality, and merit. The following five were deemed by consensus to be the most important messages to convey.

Recommendation 1: Fund a parallel tool laboratory to identify and evaluate tools, and make them ready for heavy-duty use.

This recommendation comes out of a fundamental recognition that current tools developed for HPC systems are not in heavy use by the intended audience. A critical part of the problem is maturing good research software into robust software for reliable and inter-operable multi-platform use. At present, it appears that funding agencies have a higher priority and spend much more on developing research tools than in making them interoperable and robust. Collaborations among researchers, national labs, and vendors could make valuable progress toward getting these tools into high use. Such collaborations would bring together the tools, tool builders, and tool users in one place.

The "action item" for this recommendation belongs to two groups. Funding agencies need to indicate a serious interest in supporting this line of effort. It will be expensive and less glamorous than the research side. Parties interested in carrying out the work need to identify appropriate sets of collaborators. Given the nature of the software problem, it may make sense to have a small number of centers, each one developing tools for a specific type of programming model (e.g., message-passing vs. shared memory) as opposed to many small efforts to move a specific tool into production use.

Recommendation 2: Create a working group of tool builders from vendors and research institutions to define an interface for the extraction of debugging and performance information.

This recommendation is based on the recognition that debugging and performance tools need to be built using information gathered from a wide variety of sources and presently there are no standard interfaces for passing on this information. This recommendation requires (at a minimum) the cooperation of hardware specialists that can generate performance data, OS developers, and compiler writers. With greater commonality across hardware platforms, operating systems, and compilers, debugging and performance tools can be built much more reliably and move more readily to new platforms.

The "action item" for this recommendation clearly belongs with the tool builder community. By recognizing the need for this type of interaction and sharing, they can offer substantial leverage to interested hardware and OS-types to make their participation mutually beneficial. However, it should also be recognized that this recommendation may be the hardest one to make a reality.

Recommendation 3: This workshop should encourage participation by developers of lower-level software (PC, Mac, and workstation) to help identify opportunities for leverage.

The final wording of this recommendation is actually much more general than the 2-3 options from which it was derived. The original options were along the lines of funding efforts by software companies to build component-based tools and to identify PC applications and technology that we want to have in "Apex" machines. The group recognized that we really didn't know what was relevant inside these PC applications and software companies.

Therefore, a more modest and specific proposal was accepted to encourage the workshop to help us open a dialog of discussion to learn and pursue opportunities. Clearly the hard part is determining what incentive can be offered for the PC companies to participate.

Recommendation 4: Create a working group of vendors, researchers and users to adapt lower-level style guides for specific platforms, and develop a higher-level guide defining basic functionality for specific tools.

Recommendation 5: As an enhancement to both recommendation 1 and 2, tool builders from industry, academia, and national labs should form a SIG to define interoperable modules of software development tools for high performance computers.

This recommendation addresses our view that the problem of adequate software tools is long-term and requires continuous close communication among those that will shape the future of the field. Interoperability is the key to the successful incorporation of new tools into any environment. The choice of a SIG vehicle indicates our support for strong but informal standards, as opposed to the more rigid structure of a "standards committee." As key representatives of software tool development come to agreement on the nature and types of interfaces, new tool building efforts will have better guidance on how their interfaces can be constructed to work well. At the present time, most of the interfaces to the critical tools are ill-defined, unpublished, and changing. Developing some common ground rules should act to give these interfaces more stability.

Working Group: Tools for Workstation Clusters

Robert Dilly
International Business Machines
Kingston, New York, 12401

At the outset, I must apologize for any inaccuracies in representing the discussion in our working group. We got off to a very slow start and I volunteered to moderate so that our time might be spent productively.

1.1 A Cluster is Not an MPP

Our working group initially spent a fairly substantive amount of time discussing the differences and similarities between clusters and MPPs. Most folks engaged in parallel computing have an intuitive grasp of the distinction so this might be viewed as superfluous. Through this discussion, however, we concluded that the differentiating factors are less than one might expect. The trend, given faster networks and decreasing price/performance of workstations, would seem to be toward increasing usage of clusters to tackle problems formerly targeted only for MPPs.

Some of the differentiating factors are as follows:

Factors	Clusters	MPP
Latency	milliseconds	microseconds
Network Interfaces	commodity	proprietary
Autonomy (refers to the freedom of individual nodes)	yes	no
Homogeneity	varies	yes
Global Time	lower consistency/resolution	yes
Resource Management	shared	dedicated
Traffic	"free for all"	controlled
File Systems, Accounting	NFS, AFS, NIS	parallel file system
Topology	varies	fixed
Security	tough issue	manageable
Granularity	high	medium to low

We discussed several examples to "test" these guidelines. Given that the product I am most familiar with, the IBM SP Parallel Environment, runs on clusters as well as the IBM SP, I pointed out that it has some attributes that we attributed to clusters. We concluded after a brief discussion that the majority of factors fell in the MPP category so the SP would be considered an MPP. An ATM-connected cluster was also cited as an example of a system with very good performance. It was decided that since it was built of "off-the-self" components, this system would fall into the cluster category.

The issue of homogeneous versus heterogeneous clusters was also touched upon. While the group felt that heterogeneous configurations were interesting, we concluded that for the most part they were not very practical by today's standards. For the most part, subsequently, the focus was on homogeneous workstation clusters. Certainly tools that operate on heterogeneous clusters will be significantly more complex and time-consuming to develop.

We considered expressing various machine models along a continuum:

- Heterogeneous Computing

- Homogeneous Clusters

- Dedicated Clusters

- Message Passing Machines

- Shared Memory Machines

This approach was abandoned after attempting to work with it for a while. We agreed the simpler model was adequate for our purposes.

1.2 Programming Paradigm Versus Machine Configuration

Having discussed taxonomy at length and finding numerous examples for which classification remains a judgement call, we considered whether the programming model might be a more important factor in considering what tools are necessary. A number of specific experiences were shared highlighting some tools unique to one environment or the other, but the general conclusion was that many tools, especially for code development, could and should function similarly independent of platform. Both PVM and MPI were considered as programming models suitable for both environments. It was observed that there were implementations of these standards for MPPs and clusters.

The group concluded that a large portion of the tools we were thinking about should behave the same regardless of platform, like PVM and MPI. Implementations would naturally vary, but the focus should be on easing the user's transition from platform to platform. User's will understand that cluster performance will not equal that of the MPP and may use the cheaper cluster resource to develop and test codes. It is important as codes are moved between platforms that similar tools are available.

1.3 Debuggers

Working from the "state-of-the-art" tools, the group noted that debuggers seemed to be the most straightforward tools to design for both MPP and cluster use. Thinking Machines' *mptrace* was cited as an example of an API that encourages the creation of other tools. The group felt that if standard interfaces to ptrace functionality were available on workstations, it would improve the ability to build debuggers and other tools for clusters. [ed. note: there is some encouraging work at NASA-Ames on a debugger called p2d2 which considers these issues to a certain extent.]

As is obviously the case with many of these tools, implementation will vary from system to system let alone from MPPs to clusters. The opportunity to preserve the interface is much greater when considering the more portable programming paradigms, such as MPI and PVM as stated above. HPF (and other languages providing a more abstract view of parallel) would seem to require a different view of the system, hopefully one that maps more closely to the level of abstraction at which the programmer specified a solution. The most obvious difference is the need for a global view of data objects which are in fact distributed. The programmer should expect one view of the data by default since this was the way it was specified in the HPF source.

So we conclude dthat the differences may be more a function of the programming paradigm than of platform when one focuses on the user interface. The cluster versus MPP differences should be handled in the implementation layer

1.4 Parallelizers

A. K. Pretrenko warns about potential confusion between the terms "parallelized" and "paralyzed" with respect to code. In spite of the warning, we will use the common term, parallelizer.

The group felt that of all the tools discussed, this was the one in which the most work had yet to be done and in which perhaps the greatest opportunity exists. HPF was discussed as a practical foray into this realm. Again, the notion that the programming paradigm drives more of the tool to be unique than the underlying platform was woven into the conversation.

Of the five issues considered, some are not new to those working with MPPs and certainly not for message-passing environments. The ability to adjust granularity to optimize performance for a particular virtual machine is a fundamental requirement. Avoiding synchronization is more critical than it tends to be with MPPs and we cited load balancing communication operations as an important element. We also recognized that as workstations themselves offer the ability to run shared memory codes, two levels of parallelism are possible if suitable cluster codes can be developed.

The fifth issue stems from a recurring concern that completely homogeneous clusters are too restrictive a target for practical work. Even within some machines we defined as MPPs, there are differences between node resources that make it important to be able to utilize them properly. Obvious examples are for I/O and other non-cpu resources, but extends to, as we mentioned above, the possibility that some nodes may support local shared memory programming. Actually, many of the preceding issues demand a method of specifying a number of parameters describing the target machine. Well-understood examples are latency, bandwidth, memory size and hierarchy and raw processor speed. We agreed that other metrics would be needed to adequately tune codes through automatic parallelization for clusters and the variability of performance still could be very high.

1.5 Performance Tools

The number one issue here was easy: clocks. The efforts of Ptools and other groups in this area underscore its importance. Work is ongoing in spite of how fundamental the function is. Perhaps the reason this is difficult to solve simply is because the requirements may conflict:

- Should be cheap to read.

- Should be synchronized (without undue overhead).

- Must have "sufficient" resolution.

We felt that I/O performance was important but difficult given that typical Unix tools do not differentiate well between local disk operations and those that access the network. As mentioned above, memory hierarchy usage is important, in particular that of application-specific cache and paging performance. Getting this for an entire node is generally much simpler than getting it just for a specific application.

Finally, since clusters are so dependent on the network, we felt that gathering detailed network interface information was key. We discussed security at length, recognizing that balancing the need for this data against security concerns would not be trivial. This seemed like an area where the tools should be implementable but were currently lacking.

1.6 Scheduling

Although we started this discussion chronologically earlier, we came back to it a number of times during our sessions. In some ways, it links to almost everything else we discussed. It has significant interactions with performance and although we didn't focus on heterogeneous clusters, we recognized that scheduling for them presented some very complex interactions.

We discussed gang scheduling and checkpointing at some length concluding that the area was ripe with opportunities for research and development.

We also discussed fault-tolerance in this context but dismissed it as a near-term priority based on the practical experience that it cost too much in performance. The current solution to this seems to be user-written checkpoint handling built into each application. Process migration was also considered an aspect of this item.

We developed 3 criteria for partitioning systems:

- Time/Space

- Static/Dynamic

- Dedicated/Shared Environment

To support various combinations of these user requirements, we recognized that tools would have to evolve well beyond anything typically used in Unix today. NQS and DQS were discussed as examples of "system wide" schedulers and Condor was cited as one providing a very low-level view. Of particular concern was accounting for the influence of network topology when allocating resources; this would seem to require detailed (and probably dynamic) knowledge of the network and the ability to allocate small jobs within a single subnet.

We discussed sociological issues that emerge when desk-top machines are included in a cluster and the importance of an integrated reservation function. It is clear that users may want access to the cluster on demand, but in the case on non-dedicated clusters, this can cause unpredictable performance for individual users. This demands more flexibility in the scheduling system, and makes the need to reserve time, especially off-shift, critically important.

1.7 System Management Tools

We acknowledged that some work was being done in this area, citing the schedulers as concrete examples. Still, managing a cluster-based virtual machine is a very difficult and time-consuming task. It seems that the state-of-the-art in this area is largely a matter of writing complicated scripts. What we would like to have that does not lend itself to this is the ability to measure the state of the machine as a whole. Single system image was a term bandied about in the past.

One of the three key areas discussed was configuration management of both hardware and software. A second, bridging these, is file name-space management to improve on the current usage of NFS or AFS. The third interlocks with parallelization and scheduling: that of allocating and characterizing node resources. All of these become particularly difficult for heterogeneous clusters, but cohesive system management tools are barely addressed for the simpler case today.

1.8 Pearls of Wisdom

Pankaj Mehra, who summarized our discussion for presentation, collected a number of observations that we considered thought-provoking but did not particularly fit elsewhere. By way of conclusion, they are enumerated here:

- A cluster is not an MPP; tools may make it feel like one but they may not make it run like one.

- Both Virtual Machine (VM) state and configuration are complex entities; tools are needed for monitoring and control.

- Performance numbers obtained from clusters can be trusted but variability could be high.

- Variance in performance of parallel jobs is inversely proportional to the strictness with which the VM software imposes itself on the underlying cluster.

- Sociological issues necessitate development of tools to facilitate reservation, scheduling and configuration of resources, especially in the desktop environment.

- Fault tolerance is a critical component of scheduling and systems management.

- Because of network scaling problems, cluster performance does not degrade gracefully.

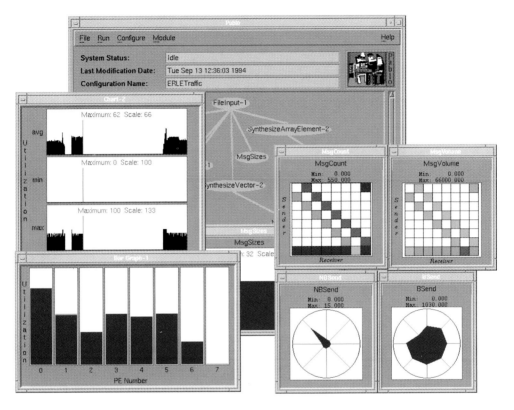

Plate I (Fig. 1.4 on page 34): Erlebacher Dynamic Behavior (Pablo Performance Environment).

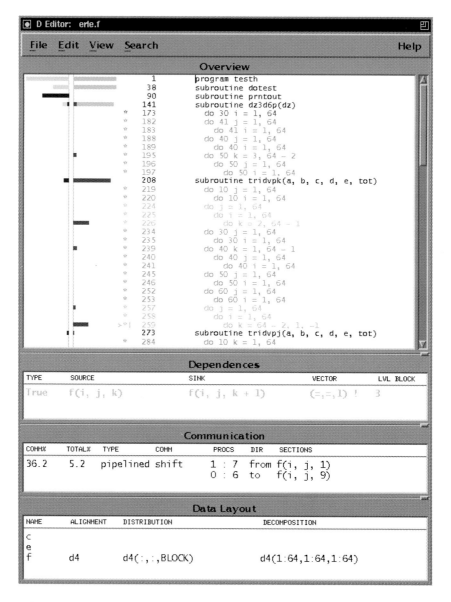

Plate II (Fig. 1.6 on page 39): D Editor performance overview.

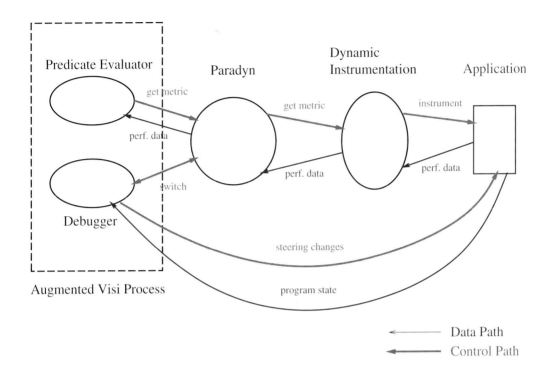

Plate III (Fig. 1.2 on page 61): The steering configuration.

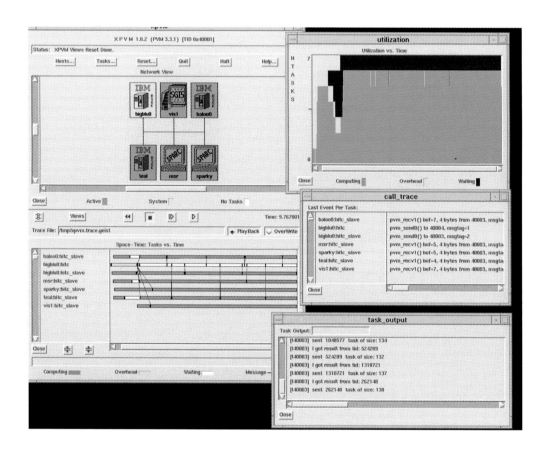

Plate IV (Fig. 1.1 on page 68): Snapshot of the XPVM interface being used for real-time monitoring of a distributed PVM application.

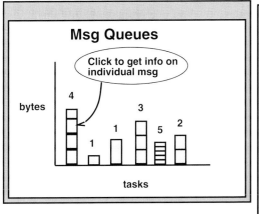

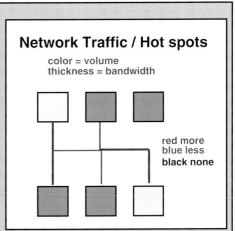

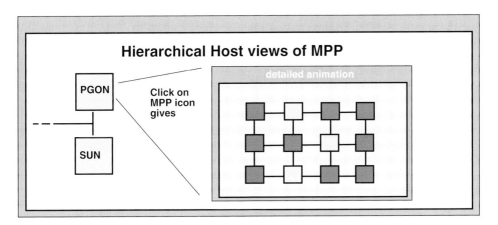

Plate V (Fig. 1.2 on page 71): Sketch of future views being added to XPVM. Shown are message queue sizes and content, network traffic and hot spots, and hierarchical host views for multiprocessor hosts.

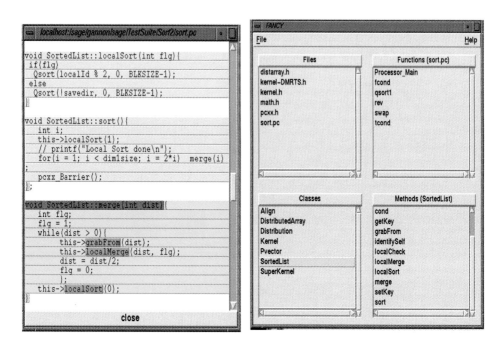

Plate VI (Fig. 1.4 on page 91): Class browser and code view tool.

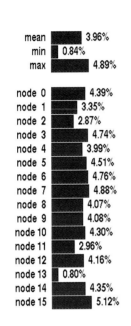

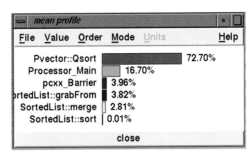

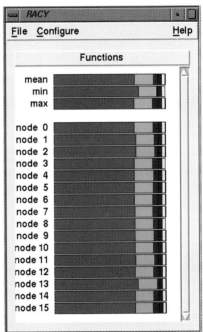

Plate VII (Fig. 1.6 on page 93): Performance profiles from racy on 16 node SGI challenge.

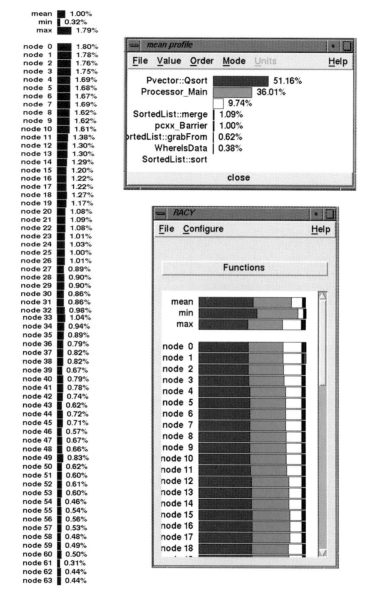

Plate VIII (Fig. 1.7 on page 94): Performance profiles from racy on 64 node Paragon.

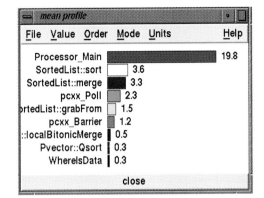 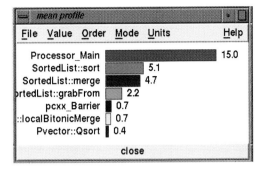

Plate IX (Fig. 1.8 on page 96): The modified algorithm. On the left, the mean profile showing total time spent in each function including the functions it calls for 64 nodes on the Intel Paragon. On the right, the same graph but for 16 nodes of the SGI Challenge.

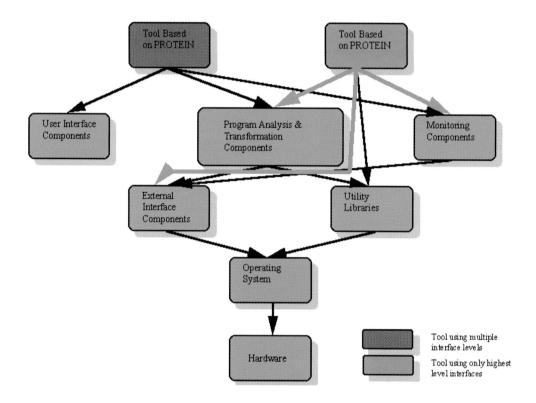

Plate X (Fig. 1.1 on page 169): Categories of tool infrastructure components, showing dependency hierarchy.

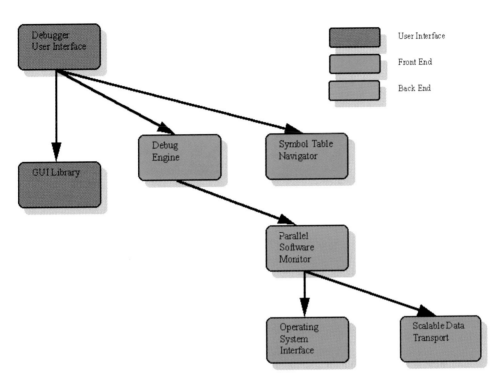

Plate XI (Fig. 1.2 on page 173): A parallel debugger built from infrastructure components.

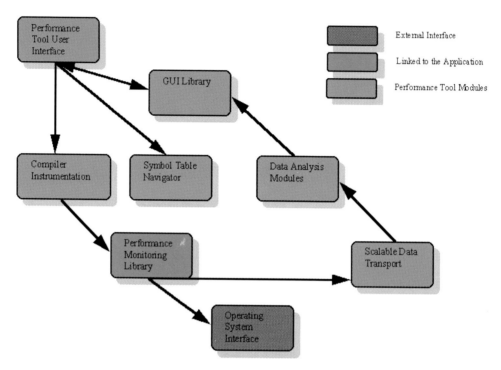

Plate XII (Fig. 1.3 on page 174): A parallel performance tool built from infra-structure components.

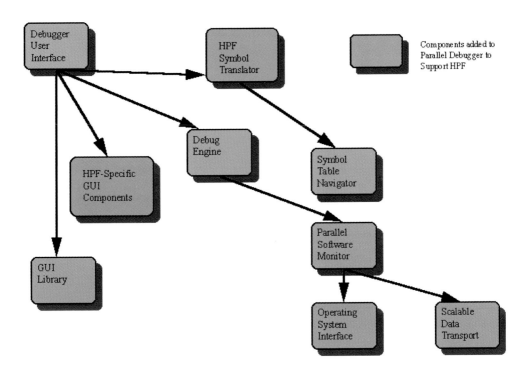

Plate XIII (Fig. 1.4 on page 176): An HPF debugger built from infrastructure components.

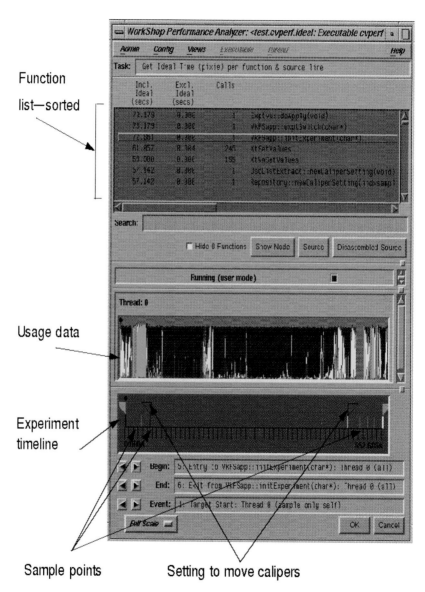

Function list—sorted

Usage data

Experiment timeline

Sample points   Setting to move calipers

Plate XIV (Fig. 1.1 on page 185): Performance Analyzer Main Window Display.

Time

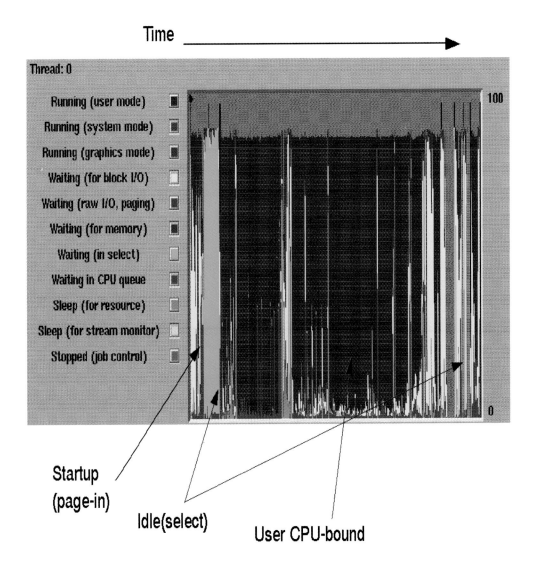

Plate XV (Fig. 1.2 on page 186): Usage Stripchart for a single thread.

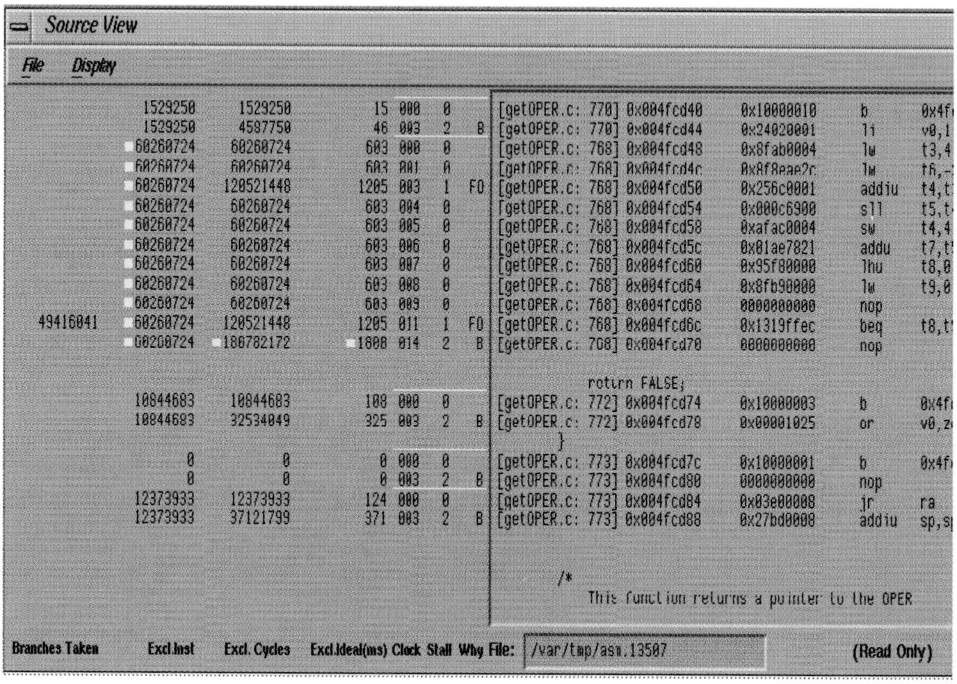

Plate XVI (Fig. 1.4 on page 190): Annotated disassembly view.

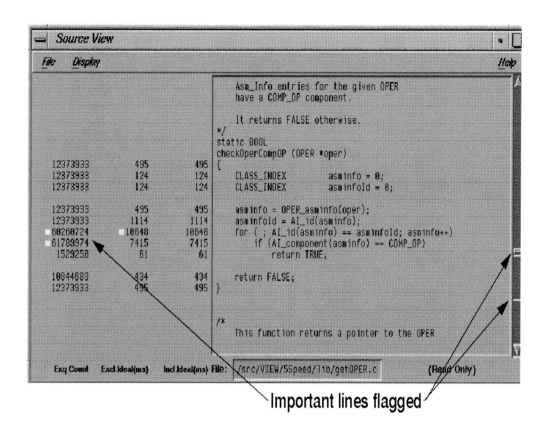

```
                                     Asm_Info entries for the given OPER
                                     have a COMP_OP component.

                                     It returns FALSE otherwise.
                                  */
                                  static BOOL
                                  checkOperCompOP (OPER *oper)
   12373933        495       495   {
   12373933        124       124       CLASS_INDEX        asminfo = 0;
   12373933        124       124       CLASS_INDEX        asminfold = 0;

   12373933        495       495       asminfo = OPER_asminfo(oper);
   12373933       1114      1114       asminfold = AI_id(asminfo);
   60260724      10648     10648       for ( ; AI_id(asminfo) == asminfold; asminfo++)
   61789974       7415      7415           if (AI_component(asminfo) == COMP_OP)
    1529258         61        61               return TRUE;

   10844689        434       434       return FALSE;
   12373933        495       495   }


                                  /*
                                     This function returns a pointer to the OPER

 Exq Count   Excl.Ideal(ms)   Incl.Ideal(ms) File:  /src/VIEW/SSpeed/lib/getOPER.c        (Read Only)
```

Important lines flagged

Plate XVII (Fig. 1.5 on page 191): Annotated source view.

List of DSOs

Working Set View: <test.cvperf.Ideal: Executable cvperf Thread 0>

Admin Config   Help

Text or DSO Region Name	Ideal Time	Counts of: Instrs.	Funcs.	Pages	% Coverage of: Instrs.	Funcs.	Pages	Avg. Covg. of Touched: Pages	Funcs.
libSgm.so.1	0.0%	117248	1028	129	6.6%	7.4%	28.2%	28.8%	74.6%
libXm.so.1	0.6%	374218	3328	410	29.7%	41.2%	67.1%	39.3%	78.1%
libXt.so	0.5%	65868	738	72	50.7%	61.9%	76.4%	58.8%	81.7%
libXmu.so	0.0%	17468	169	21	*NONE*	*NONE*	*NONE*	0.0%	0.0%
libXpm.so	0.0%	13636	93	15	12.0%	26.9%	66.7%	15.7%	58.6%
libX11.so.1	1.8%	139988	1194	149	19.5%	29.3%	43.6%	41.0%	60.7%
libgen.so	0.0%	6856	45	9	*NONE*	*NONE*	*NONE*	0.0%	0.0%
libw.so	0.0%	8476	115	10	*NONE*	*NONE*	*NONE*	0.0%	0.0%
libC.so	0.5%	15816	292	21	5.2%	8.6%	14.3%	26.8%	80.7%
libc.so.1	23.4%	130920	1717	161	10.5%	15.8%	35.4%	23.0%	71.3%
libXext.so	0.0%	14492	171	17	*NONE*	*NONE*	*NONE*	0.0%	0.0%

Search: [   ]   ∧ ∨

Selected DSO: libc.so.1, link time address: 0x0faa0000, size 521312
  Total pages = 161 (page size 4096), working set = 57, cord'd working set = 23, cord2'd working set = 14, tables = 34
Selected page: <none>

Untouched Page ▣   Unused Functions ▣   Executed Insts. ▣   Unused Insts. ☐   Table Data ☐

Map of DSO pages

0x0faa0000
0x0fab0000
0x0fac0000
0x0fad0000
0x0fae0000
0x0faf0000
0x0fb00000
0x0fb10000

Page map of selected DSO

Plate XVIII (Fig. 1.6 on page 192): Working Set View.

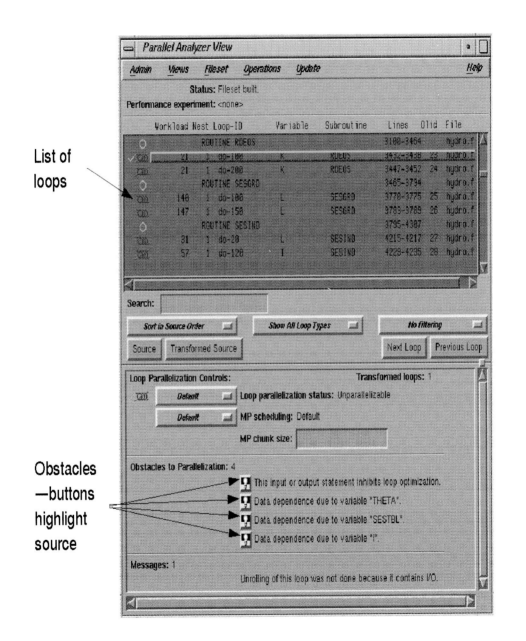

Plate XIX (Fig. 1.7 on page 194): Parallel Analyzer view.

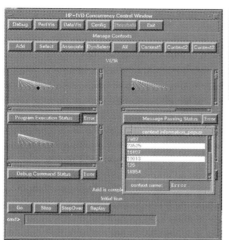

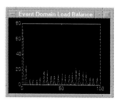

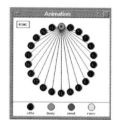

Event domain views using Matlab as an analytic and visualization engine, integrated with VIZIR.

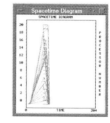

VIZIR provides control and synchronization of the environment.

Typical application visualization displays from ParaGraph, synchronized and integrated with VIZIR.

Plate XX (Fig. 1.2 on page 204): Multiple views from multiple domains and tools to visualize and analyze on-the-fly execution behavior of a distributed program.

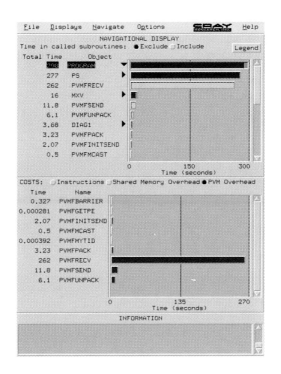

Plate XXI (Fig. 1.4 on page 223): Main window of Version 1.

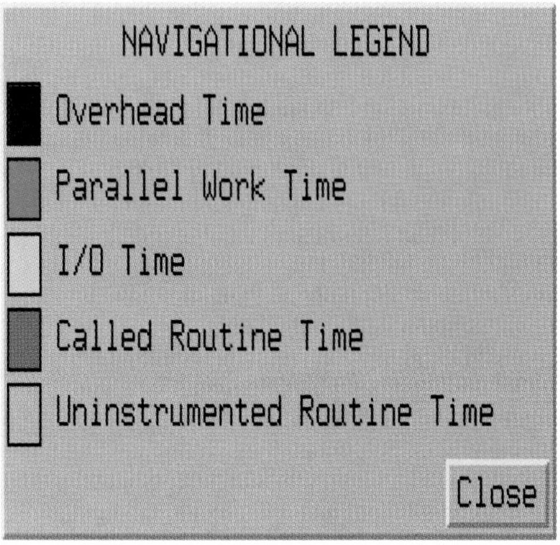

Plate XXII (Fig. 1.5 on page 224): Apprentice legend.

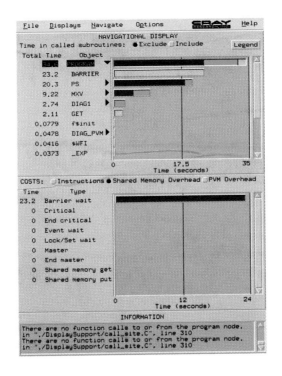

Plate XXIII (Fig. 1.6 on page 225): Main window of Version 2.

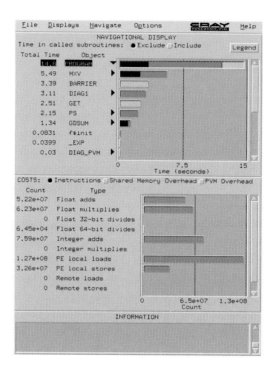

Plate XXIV (Fig. 1.8 on page 227): Main window of Version 3.

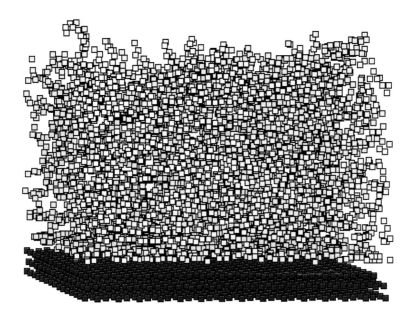

Plate XXV (Fig. 1.1 on page 249): A visual representation of a sample system for the molecular dynamics simulation. The white-yellow particles are the pseudoatoms of the alkane chains. The red particles represent the gold substrate.

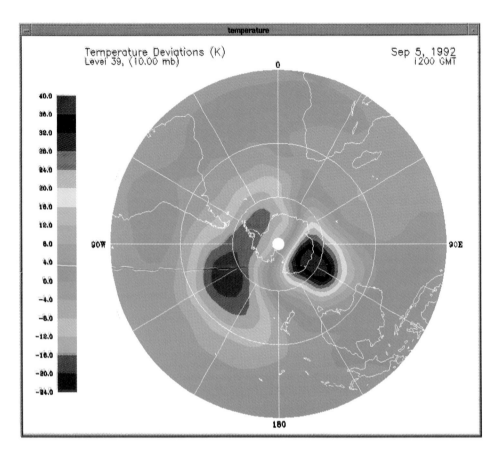

Plate XXVI (Fig. 1.2 on page 251): A sample plot of southern hemisphere temperature distribution as used by the global climate transport model.

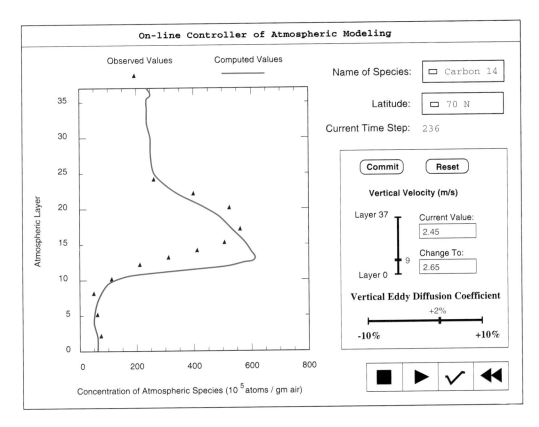

Plate XXVII (Fig. 1.3 on page 254): An application specific display for on-line control of the atmospheric modeling code.

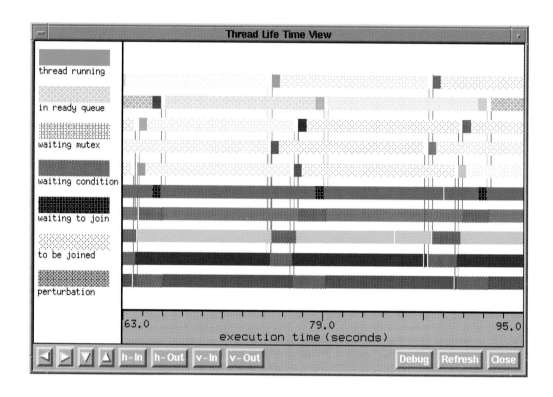

Plate XXVIII (Fig. 1.4 on page 256): A thread life-time display derived from traces of MD program behavior.

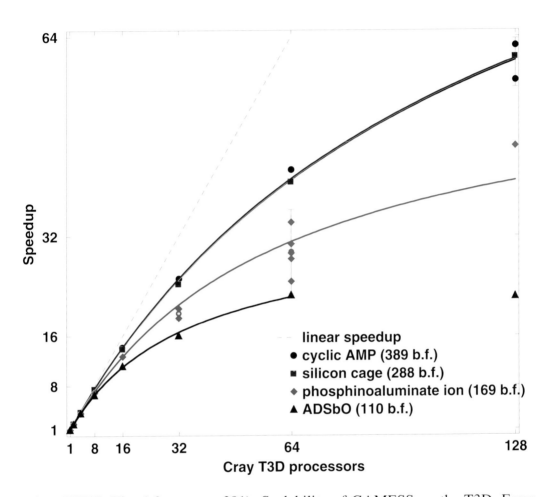

Plate XXIX (Fig. 1.3 on page 291): Scalability of GAMESS on the T3D. Error bars denote 95% confidence limits.

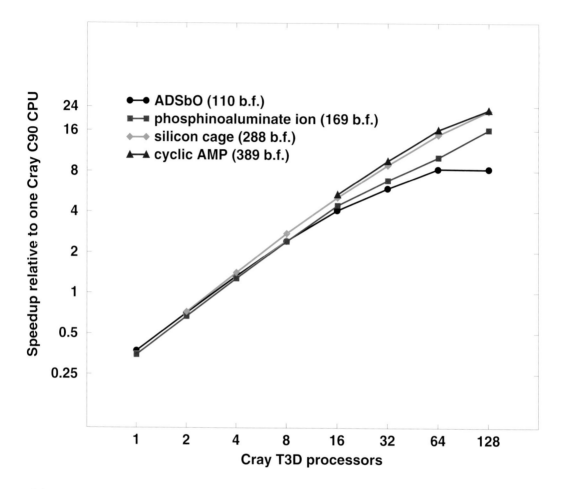

Plate XXX (Fig. 1.4 on page 292): Scalability of GAMESS on T3D.

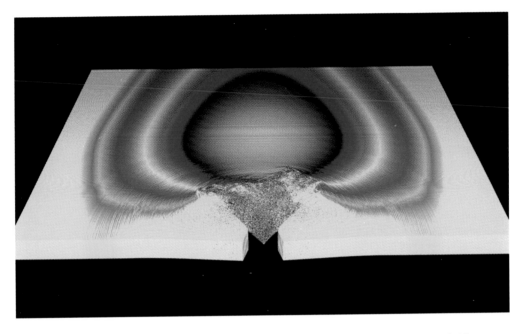

Plate XXXI (Fig. 1.1 on page 340): Fracture experiment with 104,031,072 atoms.

IEEE Computer Society Press Publications

The world-renowned Computer Society Press publishes, promotes, and distributes a wide variety of authoritative computer science and engineering texts. These books are available in two formats: 100 percent original material by authors preeminent in their field who focus on relevant topics and cutting-edge research, and reprint collections consisting of carefully selected groups of previously published papers with accompanying original introductory and explanatory text.

Submission of proposals: For guidelines and information on CS Press books, send e-mail to csbooks@computer.org or write to the Acquisitions Editor, IEEE Computer Society Press, P.O. Box 3014, 10662 Los Vaqueros Circle, Los Alamitos, CA 90720-1264. Telephone +1 714-821-8380. FAX +1 714-761-1784.

IEEE Computer Society Press Proceedings

The Computer Society Press also produces and actively promotes the proceedings of more than 130 acclaimed international conferences each year in multimedia formats that include hard and softcover books, CD-ROMs, videos, and on-line publications.

For information on CS Press proceedings, send e-mail to csbooks@computer.org or write to Proceedings, IEEE Computer Society Press, P.O. Box 3014, 10662 Los Vaqueros Circle, Los Alamitos, CA 90720-1264. Telephone +1 714-821-8380. FAX +1 714-761-1784.

Additional information regarding the Computer Society, conferences and proceedings, CD-ROMs, videos, and books can also be accessed from our web site at www.computer.org.